Mathematics
Today

SECOND EDITION

Curriculum and Instruction

Janet S. Abbott
Coordinator of Mathematics
Chula Vista City School District
Chula Vista, California

David W. Wells
Formerly Director of Instruction
and Mathematics Education
Oakland Schools
Pontiac, Michigan

Consulting Educators

Barbara A. Jacobs
Teacher
Jefferson County Public Schools
Louisville, Kentucky

Sandra Joyner
Elementary Resource Teacher
Dothan City School System
Dothan, Alabama

Sharon Owens
Teacher
Metropolitan-Nashville Public
Schools
Nashville, Tennessee

Fred Rectanus
Mathematics Resource Teacher
Portland Public Schools
Portland, Oregon

Charlotte Remaley
Mathematics Curriculum
Specialist
Hampton City Schools
Hampton, Virginia

Mary Ann Shields
Teacher
Tecumseh Middle School
Tecumseh, Oklahoma

Sally Syren
Basic Education Coordinator
Elementary Mathematics
San Diego Unified School District
San Diego, California

Mathematics
Today

SECOND EDITION

 Harcourt Brace Jovanovich, Publishers

Orlando   San Diego   Chicago   Dallas

PICTURE CREDITS

Key: (t) top, (b) bottom, (l) left, (r) right.

Cover: HBJ Photo/John Petrey
Pages 1(b), HBJ Photo/Alec Duncan; 13(b), Michal Heron; 16 (both), HBJ Photo/Alec Duncan; 17 (l), Peter Arnold, Inc.; 23(t), Blaise Zito Associates, Inc.; 23(tc), HBJ Photo/Beverly Brosius; 23(bc), Chuck O'Rear/West Light; 23(b), Blaise Zito Associates, Inc.; 24, HBJ Photo/Richard Eskite; 25, Halley Ganges; 28, Halley Ganges; 37, HBJ Photo/ Alec Duncan; 41, George Hall/Woodfin Camp & Associates; 44,45,47,49,50,51, HBJ Photo/Richard Eskite; 55(l), HBJ Photo/Rodney Jones; 62, HBJ Photo/Rodney Jones; 64(1), Nawrocki Stock Photo; 64(r), HBJ Photo/Rodney Jones; 69, HBJ Photo/Sam Joosten; 72, HBJ Photo/Rodney Jones; 74, HBJ Photo/Rodney Jones; 76, KDKA Radio; 78, G.E. Research & Development Center; 86 (all), HBJ Photo/Beverly Brosius; 95(t), D & L Heaton/Uniphoto; 95(b), Kent & Donna Danner; 98, Ford Motor Co.; 104, E.R. Degginger; 110, Kent & Donna Danner; 112, D & L Heaton/ Uniphoto; 114, Frank Wing/Stock Boston; 119, NASA; 124(t), Richard Laird/Leo de Wys, Inc.; 126(t), Joseph DiChello; 126(b), R. Krubner/H. Armstrong Roberts, Inc.; 130(bl), E.R. Degginger; 130(br), Les Moore/Uniphoto; 137(r), Nawrocki Stock Photo; 137(l), Brent Jones; 155(l), Peter Menzel/Stock, Boston; 155(r), Steve Solum/Bruce Coleman, Inc.; 156, Rhoda Sidney/Leo de Wys, Inc.; 157(l), Steve Solum/Bruce Coleman, Inc.; 157(r), Donald G. Dietz/Stock, Boston; 162, Great America; 175, Peter Menzel/Stock, Boston; 183(t), Photri; 186(tr), Uniphoto; 190, HBJ Photo/ Rodney Jones; 191, Tracy E. Eiler/Stock, Boston; 193, HBJ Photo/b.b. Steel; 198, Photri; 202, Halley Ganges; 203, Halley Ganges; 215(t), Marsha Perry/Photo Options; 215(b), Fred Maroon/Photo Researchers; 216, Tom Bean/Tom Stack & Associates; Pages 218, Michal Heron; 220, Nicolas Sapieha/Stock, Boston; 224, Chuck O'Rear/Woodfin Camp & Associates; 228, Grant Heilman/Grant Heilman Photography; 230, David Aronson/Stock, Boston; 232(l), Steve Price/Photo Options; 232(r), George Harrison/Grant Heilman Photography; 234(t), Al Satterwhite/The Image Bank; 234(b), Robert Lee II; 238, Arps/Photri; 239, Halley Ganges; 240(t), Brown Brothers; 240(b), HBJ Photo/b.b. Steel; 241, HBJ Photo/b.b. Steel; 242(t), Eric Kroll/Taurus Photos; 242(b), HBJ Photo/b.b. Steel; 243, HBJ Photo/b.b. Steel; 245, Fred Maroon /Photo Researchers; 246(t), Leo de Wys, Inc.; 246(b), Bruce Roberts/Photo Researchers; 248, Steve Vidler/Leo de Wys, Inc.; 256, HBJ Photo/Rodney Jones; 258, J. Messerschmidt/Leo de Wys, Inc.; 261(t), Marsha Perry/Photo Options; 261(b), Nicholas Sapieha/Stock, Boston; 269(l), B. Mamba/H. Armstrong Roberts, Inc.; 276(l), Roy Roper/H. Armstrong Roberts, Inc.; 276(c), Dave Logen/H. Armstrong Roberts, Inc.; 276(r), Wendell Metzen/H. Armstrong Roberts, Inc.; 282, Roy Roper/H. Armstrong Roberts, Inc.; 290, Eric Carle/Shostal Associates; 292, Peter Beney/FPG International; 294, Wendell Metzen/H. Armstrong Roberts, Inc.; 304(t), B. Mamba/H. Armstrong Roberts, Inc.; 315(b), HBJ Photo/Beverly Brosius; 317, Fred Mayer/Woodfin Camp & Associates; 318(b), HBJ Photo/Beverly Brosius; 320, HBJ Photo/Rodney Jones; 339(b), HBJ Photo/Earl Kogler; 346, HBJ Photo/David Powers; 357, HBJ Photo/David Powers; 363, HBJ Photo; 369(l), Focus on Sports, Inc.; 369(r), Ann Chwatsky/Leo de Wys, Inc.; 374(t), Long Photography/FPG International; 374(b), Focus on Sports, Inc.; 376, Focus on Sports, Inc.; 380, Mark Kauffmann/Sports Illustrated; 382(t), Manny Millan/Sports Illustrated; 382(b), Long Photography/FPG International; 386, Ann Chwatsky/Leo de Wys, Inc.; 387(1), Norman Tomalin/Bruce Coleman, Inc.; 387(r), Ozzie Sweet/Shostal Associates; 395(l), Owen Franken/Stock, Boston; 395(t), Richard Weiss/Peter Arnold, Inc.; Pages 395(r), Michos Trovaras/Art Resource; 396, Jean Claude Lejeune/Stock Boston; 398, Owen Franken/Stock, Boston; 400, Summer Productions/Taurus Photos; 402(t), Richard Weiss/Peter Arnold, Inc.; 402(b), Michos Trovaras/Art Resource; 408, Van Bucher/Photo Researchers, Inc.; 410, Mitchel Funk/The Image Bank; 412(l), Steve Vidler/Leo de Wys, Inc.· 412(r), Van Phillips/Leo de Wys, Inc.

Art Credits

Breuel, Shirley Cribb 76, 86, 87, 362, 414; Clay, Jesse B. 120, 178, 212, 250 (top); Cole, Olivia 237; Dubin, Jill 247; Galkin, Simon 21, 131; Henderson, Meryl 13; Intergraphics, Tucson, Arizona 1, 2, 6, 8, 9, 14, 17, 20, 25 (bottom), 29, 30, 32, 34, 35, 42, 44, 46, 56, 60, 65, 70, 75, 78, 79, 80, 81, 82, 84, 86, 91, 96, 98, 100, 101, 102, 104, 109, 110, 111, 112, 113, 114, 116, 117, 121, 122, 124, 129, 144, 152, 158, 159, 160, 161, 164, 166, 169, 170, 172, 173, 174, 175, 183, 184, 185, 186, 188, 192, 193, 194, 195, 197, 204, 207, 220, 235, 243, 244, 254 (top), 257, 260, 264, 269, 270, 272, 273, 278, 280, 284, 286, 287, 289, 292, 294, 295, 296, 298, 300, 302, 304, 305, 307, 315, 316, 318, 319, 322, 326, 327, 328, 329, 331, 332, 333, 339, 340, 341, 342, 343, 344, 347, 350, 351, 352, 354, 356, 358, 359, 363, 372, 373, 376, 377, 379, 380, 386, 391, 415; Leigh, Grant 230; Lipstein, Morissa 2, 58; Murdocca, Sal 36, 231, 254 (center), 255, 256, 257; Noble, Jim 326, 330; Snyder, Joel 200, 384; Stewart, Pat 232, 233 (top); Sup, Clare 233 (bottom); Tien 5, 91, 272, 273.

Production and Layout

Dimensions and Directions, Ltd.

CONTENTS

UNIT I: Chapters 1–4

Chapter 1   Addition and Subtraction Facts — 1

Addition Facts	2
Addition Facts	4
Grouping Addends	6
Subtraction Facts	8
Subtraction Facts	10
Problem Solving • Choosing the Operation	12
Families of Facts	14
Problem Solving • One- and Two-Step Problems	16

FEATURES

Thinker's Corner	7, 15
Calculator	11
Enrichment: Probability	21
Computer Applications	23

REVIEW AND TESTING

Chapter Review	18
Chapter Test	20
Additional Practice	22
Maintenance • Mixed Practice	24

Chapter 2   Numeration — 25

Hundreds, Tens, and Ones	26
Thousands	28
Rounding To Tens, Hundreds	30
Rounding To Thousands	32
Problem Solving • Drawing a Picture	34
Comparing and Ordering Numbers	38
Ten Thousands and Hundred Thousands	40
Millions	42
Money	44
Problem Solving • Working Backwards to Count Change	46

FEATURES

Thinker's Corner	27, 29, 31, 43, 45
Career: Poll Taker	37
Calculator	39
Enrichment: Roman Numerals	51
Computer Applications	53

REVIEW AND TESTING

Mid-Chapter Review	36
Chapter Review	48
Chapter Test	50
Additional Practice	52
Maintenance • Mixed Practice	36, 54

v

Chapter **3** Addition and Subtraction 55

Adding Two-Digit Numbers	56
Adding Three-Digit Numbers	58
Adding: More Than One Regrouping	60
Estimating Sums	62
Adding Greater Numbers	64
More Than Two Addends	66
Subtracting Two-Digit Numbers	70
Subtracting Three-Digit Numbers	72
Problem Solving • Choosing the Operation	74
Estimating Differences	76
Subtracting: More Than One Regrouping	78
Zeros in Subtraction	80
Subtracting Greater Numbers	82
Adding and Subtracting Money	84
Non-Routine Problem Solving	86

FEATURES

Thinker's Corner	57, 59, 61, 67, 71
Calculator	63, 77
Career: Store Clerk	69
Enrichment: Palindromes	91

REVIEW AND TESTING

Mid-Chapter Review	68
Chapter Review	88
Chapter Test	90
Additional Practice	92
Problem Solving Maintenance	93
Maintenance • Mixed Practice	68, 94

Chapter **4** Multiplication and Division Facts 95

2 and 3 as Factors	96
4 and 5 as Factors	98
6 and 7 as Factors	100
8 and 9 as Factors	102
Properties of Multiplication	104
Multiplication Facts	106
Missing Factors	110
Dividing by 2 and 3	112
Dividing by 4 and 5	114
Problem Solving • Understanding the Operation/Two Uses of Division	116
Dividing by 6 and 7	118
Dividing by 8 and 9	120
Properties of Division	122
Division Facts	123
Quotients and Remainders	124
Problem Solving • Choosing the Operation	126

FEATURES

Thinker's Corner	97, 101, 111
Calculator	107, 115
Consumer: Telephone	109
Enrichment: Prime Numbers	131

REVIEW AND TESTING

Mid-Chapter Review	108
Chapter Review	128
Chapter Test	130
Additional Practice	132
Common Errors	133
Cumulative Review	134
Maintenance • Mixed Practice	108, 136

UNIT II: **Chapters 5–7**

Chapter **5** Graphing 137

Bar Graphs	138
Pictographs	140
Problem Solving • Collecting Data to Make Graphs	142

FEATURES

Enrichment: Graphing Ordered Pairs	151
Computer Applications	153

Line Graphs   **144**
Locating Points on a Grid   **146**

REVIEW AND TESTING
Chapter Review   **148**
Chapter Test   **150**
Additional Practice   **152**
Maintenance • Mixed Practice   **154**

Chapter **6** Multiplying by One-Digit Numbers   155

Multiplying Two-Digit Numbers   **156**
Regrouping Ones   **158**
Regrouping Ones and Tens   **160**
Multiplying Three-Digit Numbers   **162**
Greater Products   **164**
Problem Solving • Using Tables   **166**
Multiplying Four-Digit Numbers   **170**
Multiplying Money   **172**
Problem Solving • Too Much
  Information   **174**

FEATURES
Thinker's Corner   **159, 163, 171**
Calculator   **165**
Career: Chefs   **169**
Enrichment: Even and Odd
  Products   **179**

REVIEW AND TESTING
Mid-Chapter Review   **168**
Chapter Review   **176**
Chapter Test   **178**
Additional Practice   **180**
Problem Solving Maintenance   **181**
Maintenance • Mixed Practice **168, 182**

Chapter **7** Dividing by One-Digit Numbers   183

Two-Digit Quotients   **184**
More 2-Digit Quotients   **186**
Three-Digit Quotients   **188**
Placing the First Digit   **190**
Finding Averages   **192**
Non-Routine Problem Solving   **194**
Zero in the Quotient   **198**
Four-Digit Quotients   **200**
Dividing Money   **202**
Problem Solving • Using Estimation **204**

FEATURES
Thinker's Corner   **191, 199, 201, 203**
Calculator   **189**
Career: Food Services   **197**
Enrichment: Divisibility Rules for
  2, 3, and 5   **209**

REVIEW AND TESTING
Mid-Chapter Review   **196**
Chapter Review   **206**
Chapter Test   **208**
Additional Practice   **210**
Common Errors   **211**
Cumulative Review   **212**
Maintenance • Mixed Practice **196, 214**

Chapter **8** Measurement 215

Centimeter	216	Cup, Pint, Quart, and Gallon	254
Meter and Kilometer	218	Ounce, Pound, and Ton	256
Perimeter	220	Degrees Fahrenheit	258
Area	222	Problem Solving • More Than One	
Multiplying to Find Area	224	Step	260
Volume	226		
Multiplying to Find Volume	228	**FEATURES**	
Milliliter and Liter	230	Thinker's Corner	**221, 225**
Gram and Kilogram	232	Consumer: Reading Maps	237
Problem Solving • Missing		Enrichment: Fractional Areas	265
Information	234	Computer Applications	267
Degrees Celsius	238		
Time	240	**REVIEW AND TESTING**	
Time Intervals	242	Mid-Chapter Review	236
Problem Solving • Using a Schedule	244	Chapter Review	262
Inch	246	Chapter Test	264
Foot, Yard, and Mile	248	Additional Practice	266
Perimeter and Area	250	Maintenance • Mixed Practice	236, 268
Volume	252		

Chapter **9** Fractions and Mixed Numbers 269

Fractions	270	Problem Solving • Using Estimation	
Fractions and Groups	272	with Mixed Numbers	304
Finding Parts of a Group	274		
Equivalent Fractions	276		
Finding Equivalent Fractions by		**FEATURES**	
Multiplying	278	Thinker's Corner	**273, 281, 283, 299**
Comparing Fractions	280	Calculator	**275**
Finding Equivalent Fractions by		Consumer: Changing Units of	
Dividing	282	Measure	289
Mixed Numbers	284	Enrichment: Probability as a	
Non-Routine Problem Solving	286	Fraction	309
Fractions and Mixed Numbers	290		
Adding Fractions	292	**REVIEW AND TESTING**	
Sums of 1 and Greater Than 1	294	Mid-Chapter Review	288
Subtracting Fractions	296	Chapter Review	306
Adding and Subtracting Mixed		Chapter Test	308
Numbers	298	Additional Practice	310
Adding Fractions with Unlike		Common Errors	311
Denominators	300	Cumulative Review	312
Subtracting Fractions with Unlike		Maintenance • Mixed Practice	288, 314
Denominators	302		

UNIT IV: **Chapters 10–11**

Chapter **10**   Multiplying by Two-Digit Numbers   315

Multiplying by 10 • Mental Math   **316**
Multiplying by Tens   **318**
Multiplying Two-Digit Numbers   **320**
Problem Solving • Guess and
   Check   **322**
Multiplying Three-Digit Numbers   **326**
Multiplying Money   **328**
Problem Solving • More Than One
   Step   **330**

FEATURES
Thinker's Corner   **319, 327**
Calculator   **321**

Consumer: Mail-Order Buying   **325**
Enrichment: The Lattice Method of
   Multiplying   **335**

REVIEW AND TESTING
Mid-Chapter Review   **324**
Chapter Review   **332**
Chapter Test   **334**
Additional Practice   **336**
Problem Solving Maintenance   **337**
Maintenance • Mixed Practice   **324, 338**

Chapter **11**   Dividing by Two-Digit Numbers   339

Dividing by Tens   **340**
Rounding Divisors Down   **342**
Correcting Overestimates   **344**
Problem Solving • Interpreting the
   Remainder   **346**
Rounding Divisors Up   **350**
Correcting Underestimates   **352**
Two-Digit Quotients   **354**
Dividing Money   **356**
Problem Solving • Choosing the
   Operation/Using Number
   Sentences   **358**

FEATURES
Thinker's Corner   **343, 345, 355**
Calculator   **349, 353**
Career: Carpet Installers   **349**
Enrichment: Prime Number Sieves **363**

REVIEW AND TESTING
Mid-Chapter Review   **348**
Chapter Review   **360**
Chapter Test   **362**
Additional Practice   **364**
Common Errors   **365**
Cumulative Review   **366**
Maintenance • Mixed Practice   **348, 368**

UNIT V: **Chapters 12–13**

Chapter **12**   Decimals   369

Tenths   **370**
Hundredths   **372**
Comparing Decimals   **374**
Problem Solving • Working
   Backwards   **376**
Adding Decimals   **380**
Subtracting Decimals   **382**
Zeros in Addition and Subtraction   **384**
Problem Solving • Using Estimation
   with Decimals   **386**

FEATURES
Thinker's Corner   **373, 381**

Calculator   **375**
Consumer: Choosing the Better Buy **379**
Enrichment: Decimal Measures   **391**

REVIEW AND TESTING
Mid-Chapter Review   **378**
Chapter Review   **388**
Chapter Test   **390**
Additional Practice   **392**
Problem Solving Maintenance   **393**
Maintenance • Mixed Practice   **378, 394**

Points, Lines, and Line Segments 396
Rays and Angles 398
Polygons 400
Congruent Line Segments and
    Polygons 402
Problem Solving • Using Geometric
    Patterns 404
Circles 408
Lines of Symmetry 410
Solid Geometric Figures 412
Non-Routine Problem Solving 414

FEATURES
Thinker's Corner 397
Calculator 409
Career: Landscape Architect 407
Enrichment: Drawing Similar
    Figures 419

REVIEW AND TESTING
Mid-Chapter Review 406
Chapter Review 416
Chapter Test 418
Additional Practice 420
Common Errors 421
Cumulative Review 422
Maintenance • Mixed Practice 406

TABLE OF MEASURES 424
TABLE OF SYMBOLS 425
GLOSSARY 426
INDEX 434

Addition and Subtraction Facts

Ramona listed 11 possible names for her baby guinea pigs. She crossed off 5 names.

- Which number sentence could you use to find how many are left?

  6 + 5 = 11   or
  11 - 5 = 6

Sarah buys 7 bags of wood-chips for her hamster cage. She uses 3 bags.

- How many bags are left?

1

Addition Facts

Did you know that some parrots can talk? Martin is raising 4 parrots that can talk. He buys 3 more talking parrots.

● How many parrots does he have in all?

Think   You need to know how many talking parrots **in all**. So add.

$$4 + 3 = 7$$

Martin has **7 parrots** in all.

● Here are two ways to show addition.

```
                  addend →   4
                  addend →  +3
  4 + 3 = 7 ←  sum      →   7
```
The answer is the sum.

● These properties will help you to add.

Order Property of Addition You can add two addends in either order. The sum is always the same.	$\begin{array}{c} 3 \\ +2 \\ \hline 5 \end{array}$ $\begin{array}{c} 2 \\ +3 \\ \hline 5 \end{array}$	$4 + 5 = 9$ $5 + 4 = 9$
Zero Property of Addition When one of two addends is 0, the sum equals the other addend.	$\begin{array}{c} 3 \\ +0 \\ \hline 3 \end{array}$ $\begin{array}{c} 0 \\ +1 \\ \hline 1 \end{array}$	$6 + 0 = 6$ $0 + 8 = 8$

PRACTICE • Add.

1. $9 + 7 = \underline{\ ?\ }$ **2.** $6 + 7 = \underline{\ ?\ }$ **3.** $0 + 4 = \underline{\ ?\ }$ **4.** $8 + 6 = \underline{\ ?\ }$

5. $3 + 8 = \underline{\ ?\ }$ **6.** $5 + 0 = \underline{\ ?\ }$ **7.** $6 + 9 = \underline{\ ?\ }$ **8.** $9 + 3 = \underline{\ ?\ }$

9. $\begin{array}{c} 7 \\ +4 \\ \hline \end{array}$ **10.** $\begin{array}{c} 3 \\ +6 \\ \hline \end{array}$ **11.** $\begin{array}{c} 8 \\ +5 \\ \hline \end{array}$ **12.** $\begin{array}{c} 2 \\ +9 \\ \hline \end{array}$ **13.** $\begin{array}{c} 0 \\ +6 \\ \hline \end{array}$ **14.** $\begin{array}{c} 1 \\ +5 \\ \hline \end{array}$ **15.** $\begin{array}{c} 4 \\ +5 \\ \hline \end{array}$

EXERCISES • Add.

16. $5 + 7 = \underline{\ ?\ }$ **17.** $6 + 6 = \underline{\ ?\ }$ **18.** $9 + 8 = \underline{\ ?\ }$ **19.** $6 + 4 = \underline{\ ?\ }$

20. $4 + 9 = \underline{\ ?\ }$ **21.** $8 + 4 = \underline{\ ?\ }$ **22.** $0 + 9 = \underline{\ ?\ }$ **23.** $8 + 8 = \underline{\ ?\ }$

24. $7 + 3 =$ _?_   **25.** $6 + 1 =$ _?_   **26.** $2 + 7 =$ _?_   **27.** $7 + 5 =$ _?_

28. $9 + 9 =$ _?_   **29.** $3 + 3 =$ _?_   **30.** $0 + 5 =$ _?_   **31.** $7 + 8 =$ _?_

32. $\begin{array}{r}9\\+6\\\hline\end{array}$	**33.** $\begin{array}{r}4\\+7\\\hline\end{array}$	**34.** $\begin{array}{r}9\\+5\\\hline\end{array}$	**35.** $\begin{array}{r}6\\+8\\\hline\end{array}$	**36.** $\begin{array}{r}1\\+0\\\hline\end{array}$	**37.** $\begin{array}{r}7\\+2\\\hline\end{array}$	**38.** $\begin{array}{r}3\\+5\\\hline\end{array}$
39. $\begin{array}{r}5\\+8\\\hline\end{array}$	**40.** $\begin{array}{r}7\\+9\\\hline\end{array}$	**41.** $\begin{array}{r}3\\+9\\\hline\end{array}$	**42.** $\begin{array}{r}6\\+5\\\hline\end{array}$	**43.** $\begin{array}{r}4\\+6\\\hline\end{array}$	**44.** $\begin{array}{r}8\\+1\\\hline\end{array}$	**45.** $\begin{array}{r}9\\+4\\\hline\end{array}$
46. $\begin{array}{r}7\\+7\\\hline\end{array}$	**47.** $\begin{array}{r}4\\+8\\\hline\end{array}$	**48.** $\begin{array}{r}8\\+9\\\hline\end{array}$	**49.** $\begin{array}{r}9\\+2\\\hline\end{array}$	**50.** $\begin{array}{r}0\\+2\\\hline\end{array}$	**51.** $\begin{array}{r}5\\+9\\\hline\end{array}$	**52.** $\begin{array}{r}7\\+6\\\hline\end{array}$
53. $\begin{array}{r}8\\+3\\\hline\end{array}$	**54.** $\begin{array}{r}8\\+7\\\hline\end{array}$	**55.** $\begin{array}{r}6\\+6\\\hline\end{array}$	**56.** $\begin{array}{r}8\\+4\\\hline\end{array}$	**57.** $\begin{array}{r}9\\+9\\\hline\end{array}$	**58.** $\begin{array}{r}4\\+9\\\hline\end{array}$	**59.** $\begin{array}{r}8\\+8\\\hline\end{array}$

Mental Math   Addends that are the same are called doubles.
Use the doubles as addends to give each sum.

60. _?_ + _?_ = 6   **61.** _?_ + _?_ = 14   **62.** _?_ + _?_ = 8

63. _?_ + _?_ = 18   **64.** _?_ + _?_ = 12   **65.** _?_ + _?_ = 16

Mental Math   Use the order property of addition to find the missing addends.

66. $4 + 5 =$ _?_ $+ 4$ **67.** $3 + 8 = 8 +$ _?_   **68.** _?_ $+ 5 = 5 + 9$

69. $6 +$ _?_ $= 7 + 6$ **70.** $7 + 5 =$ _?_ $+ 7$ **71.** $6 + 9 = 9 +$ _?_

PROBLEM SOLVING • APPLICATIONS

Copy and complete the chart. Show how many in all.

Robin's Pet Shop								
72. Brown dogs	7	**73.** Red parrots	8	**74.** White cats	5
Black dogs	5	Blue parrots	6	Gray cats	6
Dogs in all	?	Parrots in all	?	Cats in all	?
75. Green turtles	8	**76.** Brown hamsters	4	**77.** Gray rabbits	9
Brown turtles	7	White hamsters	9	Black rabbits	7
Turtles in all	?	Hamsters in all	?	Rabbits in all	?

Addition Facts

Find each sum.

1. $\begin{array}{r} 7 \\ +1 \\ \hline \end{array}$	**2.** $\begin{array}{r} 2 \\ +9 \\ \hline \end{array}$	**3.** $\begin{array}{r} 2 \\ +5 \\ \hline \end{array}$	**4.** $\begin{array}{r} 2 \\ +8 \\ \hline \end{array}$	**5.** $\begin{array}{r} 4 \\ +4 \\ \hline \end{array}$	**6.** $\begin{array}{r} 4 \\ +1 \\ \hline \end{array}$
7. $\begin{array}{r} 3 \\ +1 \\ \hline \end{array}$	**8.** $\begin{array}{r} 7 \\ +7 \\ \hline \end{array}$	**9.** $\begin{array}{r} 6 \\ +2 \\ \hline \end{array}$	**10.** $\begin{array}{r} 5 \\ +4 \\ \hline \end{array}$	**11.** $\begin{array}{r} 3 \\ +0 \\ \hline \end{array}$	**12.** $\begin{array}{r} 1 \\ +1 \\ \hline \end{array}$
13. $\begin{array}{r} 9 \\ +2 \\ \hline \end{array}$	**14.** $\begin{array}{r} 6 \\ +4 \\ \hline \end{array}$	**15.** $\begin{array}{r} 2 \\ +1 \\ \hline \end{array}$	**16.** $\begin{array}{r} 5 \\ +0 \\ \hline \end{array}$	**17.** $\begin{array}{r} 2 \\ +2 \\ \hline \end{array}$	**18.** $\begin{array}{r} 7 \\ +2 \\ \hline \end{array}$
19. $\begin{array}{r} 6 \\ +1 \\ \hline \end{array}$	**20.** $\begin{array}{r} 3 \\ +6 \\ \hline \end{array}$	**21.** $\begin{array}{r} 8 \\ +2 \\ \hline \end{array}$	**22.** $\begin{array}{r} 4 \\ +5 \\ \hline \end{array}$	**23.** $\begin{array}{r} 2 \\ +4 \\ \hline \end{array}$	**24.** $\begin{array}{r} 1 \\ +7 \\ \hline \end{array}$
25. $\begin{array}{r} 9 \\ +1 \\ \hline \end{array}$	**26.** $\begin{array}{r} 8 \\ +0 \\ \hline \end{array}$	**27.** $\begin{array}{r} 8 \\ +4 \\ \hline \end{array}$	**28.** $\begin{array}{r} 2 \\ +0 \\ \hline \end{array}$	**29.** $\begin{array}{r} 5 \\ +1 \\ \hline \end{array}$	**30.** $\begin{array}{r} 6 \\ +5 \\ \hline \end{array}$
31. $\begin{array}{r} 3 \\ +8 \\ \hline \end{array}$	**32.** $\begin{array}{r} 3 \\ +4 \\ \hline \end{array}$	**33.** $\begin{array}{r} 9 \\ +3 \\ \hline \end{array}$	**34.** $\begin{array}{r} 7 \\ +3 \\ \hline \end{array}$	**35.** $\begin{array}{r} 8 \\ +7 \\ \hline \end{array}$	**36.** $\begin{array}{r} 4 \\ +8 \\ \hline \end{array}$
37. $\begin{array}{r} 3 \\ +2 \\ \hline \end{array}$	**38.** $\begin{array}{r} 5 \\ +2 \\ \hline \end{array}$	**39.** $\begin{array}{r} 3 \\ +9 \\ \hline \end{array}$	**40.** $\begin{array}{r} 0 \\ +8 \\ \hline \end{array}$	**41.** $\begin{array}{r} 7 \\ +0 \\ \hline \end{array}$	**42.** $\begin{array}{r} 8 \\ +5 \\ \hline \end{array}$
43. $\begin{array}{r} 5 \\ +7 \\ \hline \end{array}$	**44.** $\begin{array}{r} 7 \\ +8 \\ \hline \end{array}$	**45.** $\begin{array}{r} 0 \\ +7 \\ \hline \end{array}$	**46.** $\begin{array}{r} 9 \\ +6 \\ \hline \end{array}$	**47.** $\begin{array}{r} 0 \\ +9 \\ \hline \end{array}$	**48.** $\begin{array}{r} 8 \\ +9 \\ \hline \end{array}$
49. $\begin{array}{r} 8 \\ +6 \\ \hline \end{array}$	**50.** $\begin{array}{r} 9 \\ +5 \\ \hline \end{array}$	**51.** $\begin{array}{r} 0 \\ +2 \\ \hline \end{array}$	**52.** $\begin{array}{r} 6 \\ +7 \\ \hline \end{array}$	**53.** $\begin{array}{r} 0 \\ +3 \\ \hline \end{array}$	**54.** $\begin{array}{r} 4 \\ +6 \\ \hline \end{array}$
55. $\begin{array}{r} 7 \\ +6 \\ \hline \end{array}$	**56.** $\begin{array}{r} 1 \\ +8 \\ \hline \end{array}$	**57.** $\begin{array}{r} 9 \\ +0 \\ \hline \end{array}$	**58.** $\begin{array}{r} 1 \\ +2 \\ \hline \end{array}$	**59.** $\begin{array}{r} 5 \\ +3 \\ \hline \end{array}$	**60.** $\begin{array}{r} 1 \\ +5 \\ \hline \end{array}$
61. $\begin{array}{r} 8 \\ +8 \\ \hline \end{array}$	**62.** $\begin{array}{r} 0 \\ +5 \\ \hline \end{array}$	**63.** $\begin{array}{r} 5 \\ +6 \\ \hline \end{array}$	**64.** $\begin{array}{r} 6 \\ +8 \\ \hline \end{array}$	**65.** $\begin{array}{r} 6 \\ +9 \\ \hline \end{array}$	**66.** $\begin{array}{r} 4 \\ +9 \\ \hline \end{array}$

67. 6 +3	68. 9 +8	69. 1 +0	70. 1 +9	71. 3 +7	72. 4 +0
73. 4 +2	74. 8 +3	75. 7 +5	76. 3 +5	77. 7 +4	78. 9 +7
79. 4 +3	80. 1 +6	81. 0 +4	82. 2 +7	83. 3 +3	84. 5 +9
85. 6 +0	86. 6 +6	87. 9 +4	88. 0 +1	89. 4 +7	90. 1 +3
91. 1 +7	92. 2 +6	93. 5 +5	94. 7 +9	95. 2 +3	96. 5 +8
97. 9 +9	98. 0 +6	99. 1 +4	100. 8 +1		

PROBLEM SOLVING • APPLICATIONS

Climb the mountain 9 times.
The first time add 1 to each number.
The second time add 2.
The third time add 3, and so on.
The last time you will add 9.
How fast can you climb?

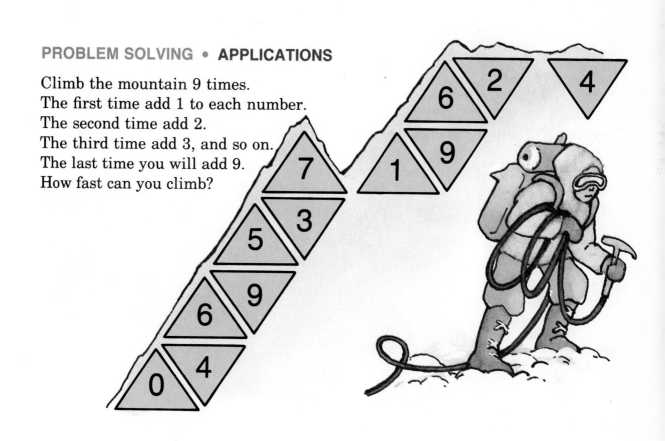

Grouping Addends

A *veterinarian* is a doctor who treats animals. There are 3 cats, 4 dogs, and 2 rabbits waiting to see Dr. Hill.

● How many animals are waiting to see Dr. Hill?

Think   You need to know how many animals **in all.** So add.

3 + 4 + 2 = ?

The *grouping property of addition* will help you find the answer.

Grouping Property
You can group addends differently.
The sum is always the same.
Do the work in the parentheses, (   ), first.

(3 + 4) + 2 = ?   3 + (4 + 2) = ?
   7   + 2 = 9   3 +   6   = 9

There are **9 animals** waiting to see Dr. Hill.

● Here is another way to add three numbers.

You can add down.   You can add up.

$$\begin{matrix} 5 \\ 2 \\ +4 \end{matrix} \Big\} \to \begin{matrix} 7 \\ +4 \\ \hline 11 \end{matrix}$$

$$\begin{matrix} 5 \\ 2 \\ +4 \end{matrix} \Big\} \begin{matrix} 5 \\ +6 \\ \hline 11 \end{matrix}$$

● Sometimes you can group to make 10.

$$\left.\begin{matrix} 3 \\ 7 \end{matrix}\right] \quad 7 + 4 + 6 = 17$$
$$\begin{matrix} +5 \\ \hline 15 \end{matrix}$$

$$\left.\begin{matrix} 5 \\ 6 \\ +5 \end{matrix}\right]$$
$$\begin{matrix} \hline 16 \end{matrix}$$

PRACTICE • Add.

1.	2.	3.	4.	5.	6.	7.
6	7	6	3	9	4	0
3	3	1	0	1	3	9
+2	+4	+8	+7	+7	+6	+5

EXERCISES • Add.

8.	9.	10.	11.	12.	13.	14.
2	2	8	6	4	6	5
3	5	2	2	3	4	2
+7	+4	+3	+5	+5	+2	+9

15.	16.	17.	18.	19.	20.	21.
4	7	2	9	3	1	2
1	2	2	1	0	3	5
2	0	1	6	4	2	0
+6	+5	+6	+0	+5	+4	+4

Mental Math • Give the sum.

22. $(8 + 1) + 7 = $ ___?___

23. $8 + (1 + 7) = $ ___?___

24. $(1 + 7) + 8 = $ ___?___

25. $2 + (3 + 6) = $ ___?___

26. $(2 + 3) + 6 = $ ___?___

27. $(3 + 6) + 2 = $ ___?___

Find the missing addend.

★ **28.** $3 + 5 + $ ___?___ $ = 17$

★ **29.** $6 + $ ___?___ $ + 2 = 16$

★ **30.** $5 + $ ___?___ $ + 4 = 15$

★ **31.** ___?___ $ + 3 + 4 = 13$

★ **32.** ___?___ $ + 3 + 6 = 17$

★ **33.** $3 + 7 + $ ___?___ $ = 11$

PROBLEM SOLVING • APPLICATIONS

34. Dr. Hill treats 4 toy poodles, 2 Irish setters, and 5 collies. How many dogs does he treat in all?

35. Dr. Cortez treats only farm animals. She treats 8 cows, 6 pigs, and 3 horses at one farm. How many farm animals does Dr. Cortez treat?

★ **36.** Dr. Lusing treats different kinds of animals at the zoo. In one cage, there are 4 tigers. There are 3 more lions than tigers. There are 2 more leopards than tigers. How many animals does he treat?

THINKER'S CORNER

___?___ $ + $ ___?___ $ = 13$

What are the addends if:
- their difference is 1?
- their difference is 3?
- their difference is 5?

Subtraction Facts

Ty's cat had 6 kittens. He gave 4 kittens to his friends.

● How many kittens did Ty have left?

Think You want to find how many kittens **are left.** So subtract 4 from 6.

$$6 - 4 = 2$$

Ty had **2 kittens** left.

● Here are two ways to show subtraction.

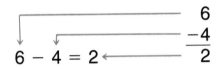

◀ The answer in subtraction is the **difference.**

Subtract   **Check**

● You can use addition to check subtraction.

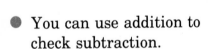

These should be the same.

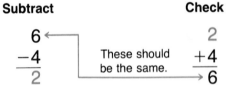

PRACTICE • Subtract. Check your answers.

1. $13 - 5 = \underline{\quad?\quad}$ **2.** $11 - 2 = \underline{\quad?\quad}$ **3.** $8 - 6 = \underline{\quad?\quad}$ **4.** $12 - 3 = \underline{\quad?\quad}$

5. $15 - 6 = \underline{\quad?\quad}$ **6.** $13 - 4 = \underline{\quad?\quad}$ **7.** $9 - 2 = \underline{\quad?\quad}$ **8.** $10 - 6 = \underline{\quad?\quad}$

9. $\begin{array}{r} 14 \\ -\ 7 \\ \hline \end{array}$ **10.** $\begin{array}{r} 7 \\ -5 \\ \hline \end{array}$ **11.** $\begin{array}{r} 3 \\ -0 \\ \hline \end{array}$ **12.** $\begin{array}{r} 11 \\ -\ 6 \\ \hline \end{array}$ **13.** $\begin{array}{r} 15 \\ -\ 7 \\ \hline \end{array}$ **14.** $\begin{array}{r} 17 \\ -\ 8 \\ \hline \end{array}$ **15.** $\begin{array}{r} 10 \\ -\ 6 \\ \hline \end{array}$

EXERCISES • Subtract. Check your answers.

16. $17 - 9 = \underline{\quad?\quad}$ **17.** $14 - 6 = \underline{\quad?\quad}$ **18.** $13 - 9 = \underline{\quad?\quad}$ **19.** $12 - 7 = \underline{\quad?\quad}$

20. $18 - 9 = \underline{\quad?\quad}$ **21.** $7 - 7 = \underline{\quad?\quad}$ **22.** $13 - 6 = \underline{\quad?\quad}$ **23.** $9 - 5 = \underline{\quad?\quad}$

24. $12 - 9 = \underline{\quad?\quad}$ **25.** $10 - 8 = \underline{\quad?\quad}$ **26.** $8 - 0 = \underline{\quad?\quad}$ **27.** $14 - 8 = \underline{\quad?\quad}$

28. 16 − 7	29. 14 − 5	30. 11 − 7	31. 15 − 8	32. 12 − 6	33. 6 −1	34. 10 − 4
35. 11 − 8	**36.** 16 − 9	**37.** 12 − 8	**38.** 4 −0	**39.** 13 − 7	**40.** 16 − 8	**41.** 15 − 8
42. 9 −9	**43.** 15 − 9	**44.** 13 − 8	**45.** 10 − 3	**46.** 12 − 4	**47.** 11 − 9	**48.** 14 − 9

Follow the rules to find the **OUTPUT**.
Then find the missing **INPUT**.

★ **49. Rule:** Subtract 8 from the **INPUT**.

INPUT	OUTPUT
17	9
14	?
16	?
13	?
?	7

★ **50. Rule:** Subtract 7 from the **INPUT**.

INPUT	OUTPUT
16	?
14	?
12	?
15	?
?	6

PROBLEM SOLVING • APPLICATIONS

51. The Love Pet Store has 13 kittens. They sell 7 kittens. How many kittens are left?

★ **53.** Ty is doing an experiment for 12 days to find his cat's favorite foods. The first 3 days he tried Brand A with the cat. The next 3 days he tried Brand B. How many days are left for the experiment?

★ **54.** Cage B has 5 black cats. Cage C has 4 cats. Cage D has 6 white cats. Cage E has 2 more cats than cage C. How many more cats are there in Cage E than in Cage B?

52. Rosie is reading a book about the care of kittens. She reads 4 pages. There are 12 pages in the chapter. How many pages are left for her to read in the chapter?

Subtraction Facts

Find each difference.

1. 9
  −8

2. 4
  −4

3. 9
  −1

4. 9
  −0

5. 5
  −3

6. 5
  −4

7. 1
  −0

8. 3
  −1

9. 7
  −1

10. 4
  −3

11. 3
  −3

12. 5
  −1

13. 9
  −3

14. 3
  −2

15. 7
  −2

16. 1
  −1

17. 6
  −4

18. 7
  −0

19. 4
  −2

20. 8
  −4

21. 13
  − 7

22. 8
  −8

23. 12
  − 9

24. 9
  −9

25. 10
  − 6

26. 17
  − 9

27. 13
  − 8

28. 14
  − 6

29. 16
  − 8

30. 11
  − 9

31. 4
  −1

32. 7
  −7

33. 8
  −0

34. 7
  −5

35. 8
  −1

36. 6
  −0

37. 6
  −5

38. 10
  − 5

39. 5
  −2

40. 7
  −3

41. 6
  −3

42. 2
  −1

43. 4
  −0

44. 10
  − 7

45. 6
  −1

46. 5
  −5

47. 9
  −6

48. 10
  −4

49. 8
  −2

50. 2
  −0

51. 18
  − 9

52. 11
  − 8

53. 14
  − 9

54. 13
  − 4

55. 15
  − 9

56. 17
  − 8

57. 15
  − 7

58. 13
  − 9

59. 13
  − 5

60. 16
  − 7

61. 11
  − 3

62. 12
  − 6

63. 10
  − 8

64. 11
  − 5

65. 11
  − 7

66. 13
  − 6

67. 15
  − 8

68. 12
  − 4

69. 12
  − 8

70. 10
  − 9

71. 8
  −6

72. 11
  − 2

73. 9 −4	74. 10 − 1	75. 3 −0	76. 6 −2	77. 10 − 2	78. 7 −6
79. 8 −7	80. 9 −2	81. 8 −3	82. 8 −5	83. 9 −7	84. 14 − 7
85. 7 −4	86. 6 −6	87. 9 −5	88. 5 −0	89. 10 − 3	90. 2 −2
91. 0 −0	92. 12 − 3	93. 15 − 6	94. 14 − 8	95. 12 − 5	96. 12 − 7
97. 11 − 4	98. 11 − 6	99. 14 − 5	100. 16 − 9		

CALCULATOR • Missing Signs

You can play this game with pencil and paper or with a calculator. The ● is either a + or − sign. Find the missing sign and the missing number.

Example $4 + 3 + 6 + 8$ ● $\underline{\quad ? \quad} = 15$

1. Add the given numbers.

$$\boxed{4} \; \boxed{+} \; \boxed{3} \; \boxed{+} \; \boxed{6} \; \boxed{+} \; \boxed{8} \; \boxed{=} \quad \boxed{21.}$$

2. Compare 21 and 15 by subtraction. $21 − 15 = 6$

3. This tells you to subtract 6.

$$\boxed{4} \; \boxed{+} \; \boxed{3} \; \boxed{+} \; \boxed{6} \; \boxed{+} \; \boxed{8} \; \boxed{-} \; \boxed{6} \; \boxed{=} \quad \boxed{15.}$$

EXERCISES • Find the missing sign and the missing number.

1. $5 + 6 + 3 + 4$ ● $\underline{\quad ? \quad} = 12$

2. $7 + 3 + 2 + 5$ ● $\underline{\quad ? \quad} = 11$

3. $8 + 3 + 7 + 2$ ● $\underline{\quad ? \quad} = 6$

4. $9 + 8 + 9 + 2$ ● $\underline{\quad ? \quad} = 2$

5. $7 + 6 + 2 + 5$ ● $\underline{\quad ? \quad} = 9$

6. $8 + 6 + 5 + 7$ ● $\underline{\quad ? \quad} = 18$

7. $1 + 8 + 3 + 9$ ● $\underline{\quad ? \quad} = 25$

8. $6 + 2 + 5 + 4$ ● $\underline{\quad ? \quad} = 22$

PROBLEM SOLVING · STRATEGIES

Choosing the Operation

1 QUESTION	2 PLAN	3 ANSWER	4 CHECK

Example 1

Robert and Dana each have a fish tank. Robert has 9 guppies in his tank. Dana has 7 mollies in her tank. How many fish do they have in all?

Step 1   Read the problem.
What is the question?

Think   How many fish **in all**?

Step 2   Make a plan.
What do you do?

Think   The key facts are 9 guppies and 7 mollies. You add 9 and 7 to find how many **in all.**

Step 3   Find the answer.

$$\begin{array}{r} 9 \\ +7 \\ \hline 16 \end{array}$$

Step 4   Check your answer.
Add the other way to check.

$$\begin{array}{r} 7 \\ +9 \\ \hline 16 \end{array} \checkmark$$

Robert and Dana have **16 fish** in all.

Example 2

Cobb buys 7 cans of fish food. He uses 4 of the cans. How many cans of fish food does he have left?

Step 1   Read the problem.
What is the question?

Think   How many cans **are left?**

Step 2   Make a plan.
What do you do?

Think   The key facts are 7 cans and 4 cans. You subtract to find how many cans **are left**.

Step 3   Find the answer.

$$\begin{array}{r} 7 \\ -4 \\ \hline 3 \end{array}$$

Step 4   Check your answer.
Use addition to check subtraction.

$$\begin{array}{r} 3 \\ +4 \\ \hline 7 \end{array} \checkmark$$

Cobb has **3 cans** of fish food left.

PROBLEMS •

Write ADD or SUBTRACT to show which operation you would use to find the answer. Then solve the problem.

1. Cobb has 3 snails in a tank. Lyn has 2 snails in a tank. How many snails do they have in all?

2. Sue has 8 angelfish. She gives two of them to Aux. How many angelfish are left?

3. The Ocean Pet Shop sells 3 kinds of goldfish food and 5 kinds of tropical fish food. How many kinds of fish food does the shop sell in all?

4. Steve has 6 fish in his tank. Then he buys 2 fish with his allowance. A friend gives him 4 more. How many fish does he have in all?

5. John buys 9 bags of gravel to put in his fish bowl. He uses 5 bags to cover the bottom of the bowl. How many bags does he have left?

6. Regina has 11 books about pets. She gives 7 to a friend. How many books does she have left?

7. In Su Tien's fishbowl, there are 2 adult fish, 9 baby fish, and 2 goldfish. How many fish does she have in all?

Write Your Own Problem

You have a fish bowl with 3 fish in it. Your friend has a fish tank with 9 fish in it.

a. Write a story problem about the fish. Have the problem use addition.

b. Write a story problem about the fish. Have the problem use subtraction.

Families of Facts

Ramona has a family of guinea pigs that belong to the breed called Teddies. There are 3 babies and 2 parents. Ramona has 5 Teddies in all.

● Write four number sentences using 3, 2, and 5.

You can make

two addition sentences	and	two subtraction sentences.
3 + 2 = 5		5 − 2 = 3
2 + 3 = 5		5 − 3 = 2

These four number sentences are related. They make up a **family of facts.**

● Look what happens when two numbers are the same.

6 + 6 = 12   12 − 6 = 6

There are only two number sentences in this family because the addends are **doubles.**

PRACTICE • Complete the sentences.

1. 6 + 5 = __?__

5 + 6 = __?__

11 − 5 = __?__

11 − 6 = __?__

2. 7 + 6 = __?__

6 + __?__ = 13

13 − __?__ = 7

__?__ − 7 = 6

3. 14 − __?__ = 9

14 − 9 = __?__

9 + __?__ = 14

__?__ + 9 = 14

EXERCISES • Complete the sentences.

4. $7 + \underline{?} = 10$

  $3 + \underline{?} = 10$

  $10 - 3 = \underline{?}$

  $\underline{?} - 7 = 3$

5. $17 - \underline{?} = 9$

  $\underline{?} - 9 = 8$

  $\underline{?} + 8 = 17$

  $8 + \underline{?} = 17$

6. $16 - \underline{?} = 7$

  $9 + 7 = \underline{?}$

  $16 - 7 = \underline{?}$

  $7 + \underline{?} = 16$

Complete the family of facts.

7. $4 + 5 = 9$

  $9 - 4 = 5$

8. $9 + 6 = 15$

  $6 + 9 = 15$

9. $8 + 7 = 15$

  $15 - 7 = 8$

Use the three numbers. Write two addition sentences and two subtraction sentences.

★ **10.** 8, 5, 13

★ **11.** 6, 8, 14

★ **12.** 5, 7, 12

★ **13.** 3, 9, 12

★ **14.** 8, 9, 17

★ **15.** 5, 9, 14

PROBLEM SOLVING • APPLICATIONS

For each exercise, choose the number sentence that shows the answer.

16. Ramona listed 11 possible names for her baby guinea pigs. She crossed off 5 names. How many names are left on the list?

  a. $6 + 5 = 11$

  b. $5 + 6 = 11$

  c. $11 - 5 = 6$

  d. $11 - 6 = 5$

17. Ramona has 4 daily chores to complete for her guinea pigs. She has done 3 of them. How many more must she do?

  a. $3 + 1 = 4$

  b. $1 + 3 = 4$

  c. $4 - 1 = 3$

  d. $4 - 3 = 1$

THINKER'S CORNER

For each group of numbers, write as many addition sentences and subtraction sentences as you can. You can use a number more than one time.

a. 4   9
    8
  13   5

b. 9   8
    17
  6   2

c. 7   2
    3
  5   10

PROBLEM SOLVING • STRATEGIES

One- and Two-Step Problems

You can use subtraction to find:

- How many **are left**.
- How many **more than**.
- How many **more** are needed.

Example 1

Sarah buys 7 bags of woodchips for her hamster cage. She uses 3 bags. How many bags **are left**?

Think Subtract to find how many **are left**.

How many in all	—	How many are used	=	How many are left
7	—	3	=	4

There are **4 bags** left.

Example 3

Barney's family is taking their dog with them on vacation. Barney will have to pack 16 cans of food for the dog. Barney packed 5 cans and then found 3 more cans in the pantry. How many more cans does he need?

Think There is a **hidden question**.

[1] How many cans does he have?

$5 + 3 = 8$

[2] To find how many more he needs, subtract.

$16 - 8 = 8$

Barney needs **8 more cans** of food.

Example 2

Linda has 5 guppies in her fish tank. Tommy has 3 guppies. How **many more** guppies does Linda have **than** Tommy?

Think Subtract to **compare**.

How many Linda has	—	How many Tommy has	=	How many more than
5	—	3	=	2

Linda has **2 more guppies** than Tommy.

PROBLEMS • Solve each problem.

1. George has 12 pictures of his cat. He puts 8 of the pictures in his photo album. How many pictures are left?

2. Anne has 5 white kittens and 2 black kittens. She gave 3 kittens to her sister. How many kittens does Anne have left?

3. Betty needs 8 mollies. She has 3 mollies. Jamie gives her 2 more. How many more does she need?

4. Yolando bought 10 cans of cat food. The cat has eaten 4 cans of food. How many cans of cat food are left?

5. Joanne has 13 cans of dog food and 6 cans of cat food. How many more cans of dog food than cat food does she have?

6. The Pampered Pet Store has 8 black guinea pigs and 3 brown ones. How many more black guinea pigs than brown pigs are there?

7. Carla's brother has 17 guppies. Carla has 8 guppies. How many more guppies does Carla's brother have than Carla?

8. Joe's dog won 14 ribbons at dog shows. Joe gives his younger sister 6 of the ribbons. How many ribbons does Joe have left?

9. Paula needs 16 plants for her fish tank. She could only buy 6 plants at the fish store and 2 plants at the pet store. How many more plants does Paula need?

★ 10. Velma's cat has won 7 blue ribbons and 8 red ribbons in pet shows. Leroy's cat has won 6 blue ribbons and 3 red ribbons. How many more ribbons does Velma's cat have than Leroy's cat?

CHAPTER REVIEW

Part 1: VOCABULARY

For Exercises 1–8, choose from the box at the right the word that completes each statement.

1. To find how many in all, you __?__. (Page 2)

2. The numbers to be added are called the __?__. (Page 2)

3. The answer in addition is called the __?__. (Page 2)

4. $2 + 3 = 3 + 2$ is an example of the __?__ property of addition. (Page 2)

5. $(2 + 2) + 5 = 2 + (2 + 5)$ is an example of the __?__ property of addition. (Page 6)

6. To find how many are left, you __?__. (Page 8)

7. The answer in subtraction is called the __?__. (Page 8)

8. Four related number sentences make a __?__. (Page 14)

add
addends
addition
difference
family of facts
grouping
order
related facts
subtract
subtraction
sum

Part 2: SKILLS

Add. (Pages 2–3)

9. $7 + 5 = $ __?__   10. $6 + 6 = $ __?__   11. $8 + 9 = $ __?__   12. $4 + 6 = $ __?__

13. $9 + 4 = $ __?__   14. $1 + 6 = $ __?__   15. $5 + 0 = $ __?__   16. $3 + 9 = $ __?__

17.	18.	19.	20.	21.	22.	23.
0	8	3	1	3	3	9
+6	+5	+3	+0	+7	+1	+9

24.	25.	26.	27.	28.	29.	30.
8	4	9	6	7	8	6
+7	+3	+8	+9	+6	+8	+8

Add down. Check by adding up. (Pages 6–7)

31.	32.	33.	34.	35.	36.	37.
3	2	8	3	5	6	5
5	6	7	7	2	4	2
+4	+3	+2	+2	+9	+2	+7

Subtract. Check your answers. (Pages 8–9)

38. $11 - 2 = \underline{\ ?\ }$ **39.** $10 - 6 = \underline{\ ?\ }$ **40.** $15 - 6 = \underline{\ ?\ }$ **41.** $17 - 8 = \underline{\ ?\ }$

42. $\begin{array}{r} 12 \\ -\ 8 \\ \hline \end{array}$	**43.** $\begin{array}{r} 14 \\ -\ 6 \\ \hline \end{array}$	**44.** $\begin{array}{r} 17 \\ -\ 9 \\ \hline \end{array}$	**45.** $\begin{array}{r} 13 \\ -\ 6 \\ \hline \end{array}$	**46.** $\begin{array}{r} 9 \\ -5 \\ \hline \end{array}$	**47.** $\begin{array}{r} 12 \\ -\ 7 \\ \hline \end{array}$	**48.** $\begin{array}{r} 7 \\ -7 \\ \hline \end{array}$

49. $\begin{array}{r} 15 \\ -\ 9 \\ \hline \end{array}$	**50.** $\begin{array}{r} 14 \\ -\ 7 \\ \hline \end{array}$	**51.** $\begin{array}{r} 11 \\ -\ 4 \\ \hline \end{array}$	**52.** $\begin{array}{r} 15 \\ -\ 8 \\ \hline \end{array}$	**53.** $\begin{array}{r} 13 \\ -\ 7 \\ \hline \end{array}$	**54.** $\begin{array}{r} 18 \\ -\ 9 \\ \hline \end{array}$	**55.** $\begin{array}{r} 13 \\ -\ 8 \\ \hline \end{array}$

Complete the number sentences to make a family of facts. (Pages 14–15)

56. $7 + \underline{\ ?\ } = 12$ **57.** $14 - 8 = \underline{\ ?\ }$ **58.** $10 - 4 = \underline{\ ?\ }$ **59.** $8 + \underline{\ ?\ } = 11$

$\quad\ \ 5 + \underline{\ ?\ } = 12$ $\quad\ \ 6 + 8 = \underline{\ ?\ }$ $\quad\ \ 10 - 6 = \underline{\ ?\ }$ $\quad\ \ 3 + \underline{\ ?\ } = 11$

$\quad\ 12 - 5 = \underline{\ ?\ }$ $\quad\ 14 - \underline{\ ?\ } = 8$ $\quad\ \ 6 + \underline{\ ?\ } = 10$ $\quad\ 11 - 3 = \underline{\ ?\ }$

$\quad\ \underline{\ ?\ } - 7 = 5$ $\quad\ \ 8 + 6 = \underline{\ ?\ }$ $\quad\ \ 4 + \underline{\ ?\ } = 10$ $\quad\ 11 - 8 = \underline{\ ?\ }$

Part 3: PROBLEM SOLVING • APPLICATIONS

60. There are 5 parrots in a cage. Tom puts in 9 more parrots. How many parrots are there in all? (Pages 12–13)

61. A pet store has 12 guppies in the fish tank. Jim buys 3 guppies at the store. How many guppies are left in the fish tank? (Pages 12–13)

62. Robert has 6 gerbils. He gave 4 to Sally. How many gerbils does he have left? (Pages 12–13)

63. Carol bought 6 cans of dog food on Monday. Her brother bought 7 cans on Wednesday. How many cans of dog food did they buy in all? (Pages 12–13)

64. Melinda's cats need 14 cans of cat food for one week. She has 6 cans. How many more cans of cat food does she need? (Pages 16–17)

65. Kristen has 1 hamster. Matt has 4 hamsters. How many more hamsters does Matt have than Kristen? (Pages 16–17)

66. Anthony had 3 mollies. He bought 2 more. Then he gave 1 mollie to his sister. How many mollies did he have left? (Pages 16–17)

67. Jan needs 12 packages of fish food. She has 2 packages at home and 3 packages at school. How many more does she need? (Pages 16–17)

CHAPTER TEST

Add.

1. 2 +6	**2.** 9 +9	**3.** 6 +4	**4.** 5 +8	**5.** 4 +7	**6.** 8 +9

Subtract.

7. 17 − 9	**8.** 12 − 3	**9.** 13 − 6	**10.** 16 − 9	**11.** 14 − 8	**12.** 15 − 8

13. $2 + 5 + 4 = $ __?__

14. $1 + 3 + 7 = $ __?__

15. $3 + 5 + 2 = $ __?__

16. $4 + (1 + 9) = $ __?__

17. $(6 + 2) + 6 = $ __?__

18. $8 + (3 + 4) = $ __?__

Write the number sentence to complete each family of facts.

19. $6 + 2 = 8$

$2 + 6 = 8$

$8 − 2 = 6$

20. $15 − 7 = 8$

$8 + 7 = 15$

$7 + 8 = 15$

21. $6 + 8 = 14$

$14 − 6 = 8$

$8 + 6 = 14$

Solve.

22. Latonya has 8 turtles. She gives away 5 of them. How many turtles are left?

23. Carol has 2 parakeets. She buys 4 more parakeets. How many parakeets does she have in all?

24. Christopher has 5 packages of wood chips. Doug has 8 packages. How many more packages does Doug have than Christopher?

25. Jeremy has 9 turtles. He gives 2 turtles to Joan and 4 turtles to Jackie. How many does he have left?

ENRICHMENT

Probability

● Copy this table.

Roll a number cube 30 times.
Record a check(√) in the tally
column for each roll.
Put the check next to the number
that lands face up.
Count the checks. Complete the
total column.

Number	Tally	Total
1		
2		
3		
4		
5		
6		

Which number had the greatest total?

Are the numbers in the total column close to one another?

● Copy this table.

Now use two number cubes. Roll
them 30 times.
For each roll put the check (√) next
to the sum of the numbers that
land face up.
Count the checks. Complete the
total column.

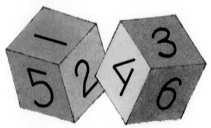

Which three numbers had
the greatest totals?

Which three numbers had
the least totals?

Number	Tally	Total
1		
2		
3		
4		
5		
6		
7		
8		
9		
10		
11		
12		

ADDITIONAL PRACTICE

SKILLS

Add. (Pages 2–7)

1. 4 +4	**2.** 5 +4	**3.** 3 +0	**4.** 1 +3	**5.** 4 +3	**6.** 2 +6
7. 8 +7	**8.** 9 +6	**9.** 6 +7	**10.** 5 +6	**11.** 8 +3	**12.** 7 +9
13. 4 6 +8	**14.** 4 6 +4	**15.** 7 3 +5	**16.** 3 4 +3	**17.** 9 0 +1	**18.** 7 5 +2

19. $(8 + 2) + 6 = $?   **20.** $6 + (6 + 4) = $?   **21.** $9 + (8 + 2) = $?

Subtract. (Pages 8–11)

22. $14 - 8 = $?   **23.** $15 - 7 = $?   **24.** $11 - 9 = $?   **25.** $14 - 5 = $?

26. 9 −9	**27.** 11 − 8	**28.** 17 − 8	**29.** 3 −0	**30.** 14 − 7	**31.** 12 − 4

Complete the number sentences to make a family of facts. (Pages 14–15)

32. $7 + 2 = $?   **33.** $15 - 6 = $?   **34.** $8 + $? $= 12$ **35.** $3 + $? $= 5$

$2 + 7 = $? $15 - 9 = $? $12 - 4 = $? $2 + 3 = $?

$9 - 2 = $? $9 + 6 = $? $4 + $? $= 12$ $5 - 3 = $?

$9 - 7 = $? $6 + 9 = $? $12 - 8 = $? $5 - $? $= 3$

PROBLEM SOLVING • APPLICATIONS

36. Susan has 4 cans of cat food. She buys 3 more. How many cans does she have in all? (Pages 12–13)

37. Tim bought 8 dog bones for his dog. The dog ate 4 of the bones. How many bones are left? (Pages 12–13)

38. Gomez wants 14 plants. He has 6 plants. Maria gives him 2 plants. How many more plants does he need? (Pages 16–17)

39. Jesse has 5 books about animals. Linda has 9 animal books. How many more books does Linda have than Jesse? (Pages 16–17)

COMPUTER APPLICATIONS
Computer Basics

Suppose you want to find 9 + 7. Your ears <u>hear</u> the problem or your eyes <u>see</u> it. This is the **input**. Your brain <u>remembers</u> the problem. This is **storage**. Another part of your brain <u>adds</u> the numbers. This is **processing**. Your mouth <u>speaks</u> the answer or your hand <u>writes</u> it down. This is the **output**.

Now compare this with a computer.

1. INPUT The **keyboard** is used to **input** information.

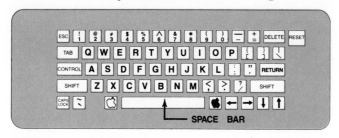

On video games, a joy stick or paddle is used for the input.

2. STORAGE The computer stores the input in its **memory**. It can also be stored on tapes or diskettes.

3. PROCESSING Once the input is in the memory, the computer's "brain" (**central processing unit**) does the work. Its brain is a tiny "chip" that can fit on your thumb.

4. OUTPUT The **output** (answer) is shown on a television screen or the output can be printed.

EXERCISES • Answer these questions about a computer.

1. What is used to input information?

2. How big is the computer's brain?

3. Where does a computer store the input?

4. What part of a computer does the work?

5. What two ways are used to show output?

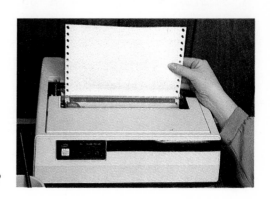

MAINTENANCE

Chapter 1

Mixed Practice • Choose the correct answers.

1. 300
   70
 + 8

A. 378   **B.** 415
C. 108   **D.** not here

2. 200 + 40 + 7 = ?

A. 607   **B.** 247
C. 267   **D.** not here

3. Which sign means "less than?"

A. >   **B.** <
C. =   **D.** not here

---

4. Which sign means "greater than?"

A. =
B. <
C. >
D. not here

5. Which group of numbers is in order from least to greatest?

A. 101, 110, 111
B. 111, 110, 101
C. 110, 101, 111
D. not here

6. Which amount is seventy-eight cents?

A. 780¢
B. $.078
C. $0.78
D. not here

---

7. Which amount is four dollars and twenty-seven cents?

8. How much is the amount?

9. How much is the amount?

A. $4.270   **B.** 427¢
C. $4.27   **D.** not here

A. $0.56   **B.** $5.60
C. $0.51   **D.** not here

A. $1.87   **B.** $1.77
C. $1.82   **D.** not here

---

10. Robert has 5 pairs of slacks. His brother, Andy, has 3 pairs of slacks. How many pairs of slacks do they have together?

A. 8   **B.** 9
C. 53   **D.** not here

11. Maria has 6 sweaters, 4 skirts and 5 blouses. How many pieces of clothing does she have?

A. 15   **B.** 9
C. 11   **D.** not here

Numeration

For a social studies project, Howard wrote to a pen pal about his stamp collection. Howard wrote that he has two thousand, three hundred fifty-six stamps.

● Write the number in standard form.

The teachers at Pinelock Elementary school send the lunch count to the cafeteria manager every morning. On Tuesday, the lunch count for the fourth grade is 86.

● Round 86 to the nearest ten.

Hundreds, Tens, and Ones

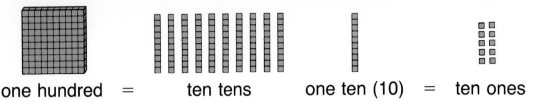

one hundred = ten tens   one ten (10) = ten ones

Every day, the secretary for Pinelock Elementary
School finds how many students are present.
Today, there are **four hundred eighteen** students.

418 ◀ There are three digits:
4, 1, and 8

Our number system uses ten digits to name numbers.

● The **place** of the **digit** in a number tells you its **value.**

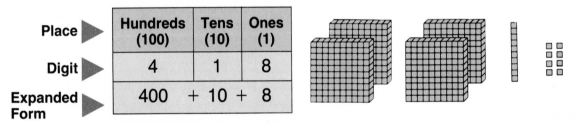

Place ▶	Hundreds (100)	Tens (10)	Ones (1)
Digit ▶	4	1	8
Expanded Form ▶	400	+ 10 +	8

Read: **four hundred eighteen**   Write the **standard** form: **418**

● Sometimes a number has a zero in one of the places.

hundreds	tens	ones
2	0	6

Read: **two hundred six**
Write in standard form: **206**

PRACTICE • Write the numbers in standard form.

1.

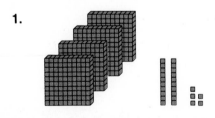

2.

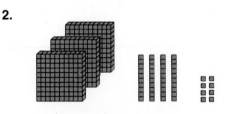

3.

hundreds	tens	ones
3	9	4

4.

hundreds	tens	ones
2	3	0

5. 9 hundreds 5 tens 2 ones

6. 4 hundreds 8 tens 7 ones

7. six hundred four

8. five hundred twenty-one

EXERCISES • Write the numbers in standard form.

9.

hundreds	tens	ones
2	5	4

10.

hundreds	tens	ones
2	4	5

11.

hundreds	tens	ones
6	1	0

12.

hundreds	tens	ones
9	0	3

13. 8 hundreds 2 tens 6 ones

14. 7 hundreds

15. nine hundred sixteen

16. two hundred five

17. 200 + 70 + 8

18. 300 + 90 + 4

19. 700 + 20

20. 600 + 2

21. 3 hundreds
    5 tens
    7 ones

22. 7 hundreds
    3 tens
    2 ones

23. 5 hundreds
    4 tens
    8 ones

★ 24. 5 tens
    9 hundreds
    6 ones

★ 25. 6 ones
    0 tens
    7 hundreds

★ 26. 3 hundreds
    2 ones
    4 tens

Write the numbers in expanded form. Then write the numbers in words.

27. 962   28. 403   29. 526   30. 971   31. 683

Mental Math   Name 100 more.

32. 417   33. 201   34. 27   35. 743   ★ 36. 999

PROBLEM SOLVING • APPLICATIONS

Write the numbers in Exercises 37 and 38 in standard form.

37. On Friday, there were four hundred fifty-eight students present.

38. In one week, there were one hundred sixty-three students absent.

39. On Monday, four hundred twenty-three students were present. On Tuesday, four hundred sixteen students were present. Would you **ADD** or **SUBTRACT** to find how many more students were present on Monday than on Tuesday?

THINKER'S CORNER

My ones digit is 3. My hundreds digit is 1 less than my ones digit. My tens digit is 7 more than my hundreds digit. What number am I?

Thousands

One thousand (1,000) =   ten hundreds

The social studies teacher, Mr. White, assigns each student a pen pal to learn more about people in other lands.

Howard is writing to his pen pal to tell him about his stamp collection. Howard has **two thousand, three hundred fifty-six stamps.**

● What number should he write to tell his friend this?

Place ▶	Thousands (1,000)	Hundreds (100)	Tens (10)	Ones (1)
Digit ▶	2	3	5	6
Expanded Form ▶	2,000 +	300 +	50 +	6

Read: **two thousand, three hundred fifty-six**

Write the standard form: **2,356** ◀ A comma separates the thousands and hundreds.

● The **2** in 2,356 is in the **thousands place.**
Its **value** is **2,000.**

- In what place is the 3?   What is its value?
- In what place is the 5?   What is its value?
- In what place is the 6?   What is its value?

PRACTICE • Write the numbers in standard form.

1.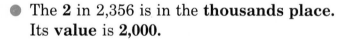

2.

thousands	hundreds	tens	ones
4	0	2	3

3. 6 thousands
   4 hundreds
   8 ones

4. two thousand,
   seven hundred
   eighty

5. 2,000 + 800 + 9

EXERCISES • Write the numbers in standard form.

6.	thousands	hundreds	tens	ones
	2	6	4	8

7.	thousands	hundreds	tens	ones
	8	9	0	4

8. 9 thousands 4 hundreds 6 tens 2 ones

9. 3 thousands 5 hundreds 9 ones

10. six thousand, four hundred ninety-six

11. 2,000 + 80 + 4

12. 3,000 + 400 + 70 + 2

Write the number in words.

13. 1,704   14. 4,023   15. 9,008   16. 3,987

Write the digit that is in the thousands place and its value.

17. 8,436   18. 1,742   19. 4,705   20. 1,395

21. 7,642   22. 9,013   23. 8,540   24. 4,317

Write the numbers in expanded form.

25. 3,694   26. 4,520   27. 5,400   28. 4,861

29. 6,792   30. 7,432   31. 1,804   32. 2,813

Mental Math   Name 1,000 more.

33. 8,530   34. 6,432   35. 3,742   36. 7,894

PROBLEM SOLVING • **APPLICATIONS**

Write the numbers in standard form.

37. Binh's friend has a stamp collection with five thousand, six hundred four stamps.

38. Rosa's uncle sent her some new stamps. She now has two thousand, three hundred sixty-six stamps.

Solve.

39. Jimmy is starting a stamp collection. He has 8 stamps. He buys 7 more. How many stamps does Jimmy have in all?

THINKER'S CORNER

My ones digit is 3. My tens digit is 6. My hundreds digit is one more than my tens digit. My thousands digit is the same as my ones digit. What number am I?

Rounding To Tens, Hundreds

Every day the school lunchroom manager, Mrs. Campbell, needs to know how many students are eating lunch. The teachers send their lunch count to the cafeteria early each morning. Today, there are 86 fourth-grade students eating lunch. Mrs. Campbell rounds 86 to the nearest ten.

● Round 86 to the *nearest ten*.

Think 86 is between 80 and 90.

86 is closer to 90.
86 rounded to the *nearest ten* is **90**.

● Round 150 to the *nearest hundred*.

Think 150 is between 100 and 200.

When a number is halfway between, round up.

150 is halfway between 100 and 200.

150 rounded to the *nearest hundred* is **200.**

● Round 322 to the *nearest hundred*.

Think 322 is between 300 and 400.

322 is closer to 300.
322 rounded to the *nearest hundred* is **300**.

● Rounding to the *nearest dollar* is like rounding to the nearest hundred.

$1.42 rounds to $1.00.

$1.75 rounds to $2.00.

$1.50 rounds to $2.00.

PRACTICE • Round to the nearest ten.

1.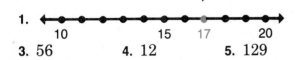

3. 56   4. 12   5. 129

2.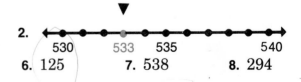

6. 125   7. 538   8. 294

Round to the nearest hundred.

9.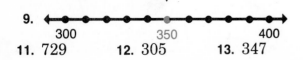

11. 729   12. 305   13. 347

10.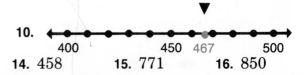

14. 458   15. 771   16. 850

EXERCISES • Round to the nearest ten.

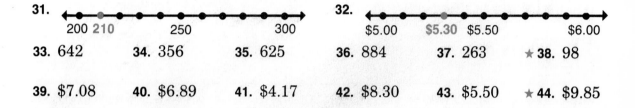

17. 40 45 **48** 50

18. 20 **25** 30

19. 74   **20.** 532   **21.** 45   **22.** 352   **23.** 121   **24.** 29

25. 53   **26.** 19   **27.** 77   ★**28.** 299   ★**29.** 296   ★**30.** 97

Round to the nearest hundred or to the nearest dollar.

31. 200 **210** 250 300

32. $5.00 **$5.30** $5.50 $6.00

33. 642   **34.** 356   **35.** 625   **36.** 884   **37.** 263   ★**38.** 98

39. $7.08   **40.** $6.89   **41.** $4.17   **42.** $8.30   **43.** $5.50   ★**44.** $9.85

PROBLEM SOLVING • APPLICATIONS

Round each number to tell how many. Round to the *nearest hundred*.

45. This week, 597 first graders ate lunch in the cafeteria.

46. Last week, 482 first graders ate lunch in the school cafeteria.

Solve.

47. Mr. Peck is the kindergarten teacher. He has 9 students who buy lunch and 6 students who bring their lunch. How many of his students eat lunch at school?

★**48.** Ann, Bill, and Carla each guessed the number of students in the cafeteria. Ann's number, rounded to the nearest ten, is 80. What is the greatest number Ann could have guessed?

THINKER'S CORNER

Use these digits to answer the riddle. 1 2 3 4 5 6 7 8 9

I am the smallest 4-digit number with all digits greater than 5 and with all my digits different.
What number am I?

Rounding To Thousands

The school newspaper often uses rounded numbers in stories. Suppose there are actually 2,174 people at a school art fair.

● About how many people would the paper report attended the art fair?

Round 2,174 to the *nearest thousand*.

Think 2,174 is between 2,000 and 3,000.

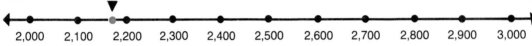

| 2,000 | 2,100 | 2,200 | 2,300 | 2,400 | 2,500 | 2,600 | 2,700 | 2,800 | 2,900 | 3,000 |

The newspaper reported that **about 2,000 people** attended the art fair. You can round numbers without using the number line.

● Round 4,216 to the *nearest thousand*.

● Round 2,739 to the *nearest thousand*.

● Round 8,568 to the *nearest thousand*.

Think 4,216 is between 4,000 and 5,000.

4,216 ◀ The hundreds digit is less than 5.

4,000 ◀ The thousands digit stays the same.

So 4,216 rounded to the nearest thousand is 4,000.

Think 2,739 is between 2,000 and 3,000.

2,739 ◀ The hundreds digit is greater than 5.

3,000 ◀ Add 1 to the thousands digit.

So 2,739 rounded to the nearest thousand is 3,000.

Think 8,568 is between 8,000 and 9,000.

8,568 ◀ The hundreds digit is 5.

9,000 ◀ Add 1 to the thousands digit.

So 8,568 rounded to the nearest thousand is 9,000.

PRACTICE • Round to the nearest ten.

1. 39   2. 65   3. 53   4. 17   5. 726   6. 634

Round to the nearest hundred.

7. 870   8. 754   9. 342   10. 519   11. 2,561   12. 1,880

Round to the nearest thousand.

13. 5,208   14. 6,496   15. 2,531   16. 8,964   17. 6,038   18. 5,756

EXERCISES • Round to the nearest ten.

19. 15   **20.** 72   **21.** 58   **22.** 84   **23.** 62   ★**24.** 97

25. 232   **26.** 674   **27.** 888   **28.** 659   **29.** 384   ★**30.** 796

Round to the nearest hundred.

31. 356   **32.** 625   **33.** 884   **34.** 242   **35.** 439   ★**36.** 985

37. 7,628   **38.** 8,317   **39.** 2,574   **40.** 6,428   **41.** 5,793   ★**42.** 1,958

Round to the nearest thousand.

43. 3,264   **44.** 2,342   **45.** 9,347   **46.** 6,768   **47.** 7,384   **48.** 5,056

49. 21,851 **50.** 34,036 **51.** 68,675 **52.** 54,909 **53.** 75,513 ★**54.** 49,578

Round 87,615 to the nearest

★**55.** ten.   ★**56.** hundred.   ★**57.** thousand.

Round 597,024 to the nearest

★**58.** ten.   ★**59.** hundred.   ★**60.** thousand.

PROBLEM SOLVING • APPLICATIONS

61. Mr. Brown needs 2,650 multicolored felt markers for art supplies. He orders 2,650 rounded to the nearest thousand. How many does he order?

62. There are 2,488 people attending the art fair. The newspaper reporter rounds 2,488 to the nearest thousand. What number does he write?

63. Lawanda buys 8 small pictures at the art fair. Greg buys 5 large pictures. How many more pictures does Lawanda buy than Greg?

★**64.** Carla chose a number at the art fair raffle. Her number, rounded to the nearest hundred, is 300. What is the smallest number Carla could have chosen?

Numeration • **33**

PROBLEM SOLVING • STRATEGIES

Drawing a Picture

Example

On the first day of school, Marcus, Amiko, Heidi, and Miguel found their names written on cards on their desk. Their desks were in four rows across the front of the room.

Heidi sits in the fourth seat. Marcus sits next to Heidi. Miguel sits between Amiko and Marcus.

● Show where Marcus, Amiko, Heidi, and Miguel sit across the front.

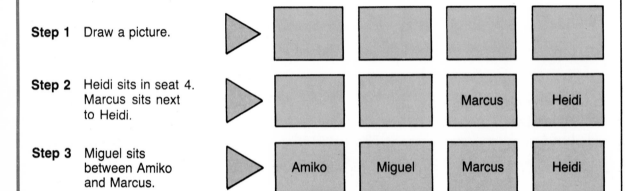

Step 1 Draw a picture.

Step 2 Heidi sits in seat 4. Marcus sits next to Heidi.

		Marcus	Heidi

Step 3 Miguel sits between Amiko and Marcus.

Amiko	Miguel	Marcus	Heidi

PROBLEMS • Solve each problem.

1. In science class, Anna, Pablo, Dirk and Heather sit across the front of the room. Anna sits in the third seat. Anna sits between Pablo and Heather. Dirk sits next to Pablo. In what seat does Dirk sit?

Seat 1	Seat 2	Seat 3	Seat 4
		Anna	

2. Henry, Eric, Mary Jo, and Sue Ellen are standing in line for lunch. Henry is just behind Eric. Mary Jo is between Henry and Sue Ellen. Who is first in line?

Front
of
Line ●————●————●————●
                         Mary Jo

3. The students in Room 13 follow this schedule on Tuesday mornings. Reading class comes after science class. Math class comes before science class. Gym class comes between math and science. Which class comes first?

First

4. Four students have birthdays in October. Jason's birthday comes before Rodney's. Kristin's birthday comes between Rodney's and Jason's. Melinda's birthday comes after Rodney's. Whose birthday comes first?

5. The fourth grade at Walker School has four soccer teams. The Blue team has won more games than the Yellow team. The Green team has won more games than the Red team. The Green team has won 2 <u>less</u> than the Yellow team. Which team has won the most games?

winner

6. Four students from Room C ride Bus 194 home from school. Derrick's stop comes before Regina's. Regina's stop comes before Missy's. Jim's stop comes between Derrick's and Regina's. Whose stop comes second?

   **last stop**

7. Four students are growing plants for a science project. Miranda's plant is shorter than Tina's. Karl's plant is taller than Tina's and shorter than Anthony's. Whose plant is the shortest?

8. There are 4 fourth grade classrooms in Walker School. Room A has more students than Room C. Room C has more students than Room D. Room B has 1 *less* student than Room D. Which room has the most students?

Greatest Number

9. Four students from Westridge Elementary live on the same street and walk to school. Pedro's house is farther from school than Tiffany's. Jim's house is between Pedro's and Tiffany's. Tiffany's house is farther from school then Ny's. Whose house is farthest?

MID-CHAPTER REVIEW

Write the numbers in standard form. (Pages 26–29)

1.	hundreds	tens	ones
	3	6	8

2.	thousands	hundreds	tens	ones
	3	9	4	5

3. 6 hundreds 2 tens

4. 8 thousands 1 hundred 7 ones

5. nine hundred eighteen

6. five thousand, two hundred nine

In the number 3,942 what digit is in the (Pages 26–29)

7. tens place?

8. thousands place?

9. hundreds place?

Round to the nearest ten. (Pages 30–31)

10. 45

11. 34

12. 382

Round to the nearest hundred. (Pages 30–31)

13. 739

14. 650

15. 3,501

Round to the nearest thousand. (Pages 32–33)

16. 7,499

17. 2,500

18. 34,687

Solve.

19. Jane, Sue, Mary, and Ann are in line. Jane is behind Sue and in front of Mary. Mary is between Jane and Ann. Who is first in line? (Pages 34–35)

20. Ken runs slower than John. David runs faster than John and slower than Mel. Who is the fastest runner? (Pages 34–35)

MAINTENANCE • MIXED PRACTICE

Add or subtract.

1.
$$\begin{array}{r} 3 \\ +6 \\ \hline \end{array}$$

2.
$$\begin{array}{r} 18 \\ -9 \\ \hline \end{array}$$

3.
$$\begin{array}{r} 12 \\ -8 \\ \hline \end{array}$$

4.
$$\begin{array}{r} 5 \\ +9 \\ \hline \end{array}$$

5.
$$\begin{array}{r} 4 \\ +5 \\ \hline \end{array}$$

6.
$$\begin{array}{r} 9 \\ -7 \\ \hline \end{array}$$

7.
$$\begin{array}{r} 15 \\ -8 \\ \hline \end{array}$$

8.
$$\begin{array}{r} 9 \\ +4 \\ \hline \end{array}$$

9.
$$\begin{array}{r} 7 \\ +7 \\ \hline \end{array}$$

10.
$$\begin{array}{r} 9 \\ +8 \\ \hline \end{array}$$

11.
$$\begin{array}{r} 16 \\ -9 \\ \hline \end{array}$$

12.
$$\begin{array}{r} 14 \\ -6 \\ \hline \end{array}$$

13. John had 8 pencils. He gave away 7. How many pencils did he have left?

14. Ellen had 8 pencils. She bought 3 more. How many does she now have?

CAREER APPLICATIONS

Poll Taker

Maria Gomez takes opinion polls. The Parkview school board hired her to find out how teachers, students, and parents felt about changing the length of the school year.

Maria made a table to show the data she collected.

Opinion Poll	Prefer 12-month school year	Prefer 10-month school year
Teachers	18	12
Students	216	459
Parents	714	326

EXERCISES • Use the table to help you answer the school board's questions.

1. How many teachers prefer a 12-month school year? a 10-month school year? Round both numbers to the nearest ten.

2. How many students prefer a 12-month school year? A 10-month school year? Round both numbers to the nearest hundred.

3. How many parents prefer a 12-month school year? A 10-month school year? Round both numbers to the nearest hundred.

4. Which plan is preferred by more teachers? By more students? By more parents?

PROJECT Take a similar opinion poll in your school. Record your results in a table. What recommendations would you make to your teacher?

Comparing and Ordering Numbers

Daryl helps the librarian put the books back on the shelves.
He puts 64 books on the top shelf and 25 books on the second shelf.

● Daryl compares the number of books on each shelf.

64 **is greater than** 25.   25 **is less than** 64.

64 > 25   **25 < 64**

The library has 473 science books.
It has 471 picture books.

● Use > or < to compare the numbers.

473 ● 471

Think	Same number of hundreds: 4

Same number of tens   7
Compare the ones: 3 > 1

So **473 > 471.**

NOTE: The tip of the symbol, > or <,
always points to the smaller
number.

● Write in order from least to greatest.

8,789   8,625   8,756

Think	8,625 < 8,756 and 8,756 < 8,789

So **8,625   8,756   8,789** shows
the order from least to greatest.

PRACTICE • Use > or < to compare the numbers.

1. 14 ● 34   2. 78 ● 179   3. 92 ● 218

4. 215 ● 205   5. 3,102 ● 854   6. 1,552 ● 1,523

EXERCISES • Use > or < to compare the numbers.

7. 65 ● 56   8. 37 ● 33   9. 54 ● 152

10. 514 ● 541   11. 612 ● 3,512   12. 798 ● 789

13. 3,416 ● 3,742   **14.** 7,894 ● 5,894   **15.** 9,002 ● 9,007

Write in order from least to greatest.

16. 635; 630; 640

17. 289; 265; 286; 270

18. 3,706; 3,760; 3,710; 3,701

19. 8,418; 9,460; 1,664; 759

★ **20.** 52,094; 57,321; 48,923; 60,092

★ **21.** 805,302; 890,001; 482,976; 600,731

PROBLEM SOLVING • APPLICATIONS

22. Write the prices in order from least to greatest. Which store has the lowest price?

Bookstore	Price for Book Collection
Albert Books	$224.00
Corner Bookstore	$219.00
The Bookworm	$197.00

23. Write the number of books in order from least to greatest.

Library	Number of Books
Fourth Street	3,694
Eighth Street	2,985
Main Street	748
Webster	3,148
Adams	1,790

CALCULATOR • Numeration

Enter and add each set of numbers on your calculator. If you enter all numbers correctly, your sum will match the **Check Sum.** Then compare the sums. Which is greater?

Set A

- Forty-six thousand, eight hundred
- Fifty thousand, six hundred eleven
- Two hundred fourteen thousand, nine hundred five
- Three hundred thousand
- Ten thousand, seven hundred two

Check Sum: 623,018

Set B

- Thirty-eight thousand, five hundred nine
- One hundred seventy thousand, one hundred seventy
- Forty thousand, thirty-two
- Eight million

Check Sum: 8,248,711

Ten Thousands and Hundred Thousands

Tyrone's math teacher, Mr. Tai, told the class to look in the local newspaper to find large numbers. Tyrone saw a table showing the number of seats in six football stadiums.

TODAY'S SPORTS

Stadium	Number of Seats
Texas	65,101
Rose Bowl	106,721
Superdome	71,330
Astrodome	50,496
JFK	105,000
Orange Bowl	75,459

● Tyrone wanted to compare the number of seats in the Rose Bowl and the John F. Kennedy (JFK) Stadium.

To compare the numbers, he must be able to read the numbers in the table.

	Thousands Period			Ones Period		
	hundred thousands	ten thousands	one thousands	hundreds	tens	ones
Rose Bowl	1	0	6	7	2	1
JFK	1	0	5	0	0	0

Each group is called a **period**.

Each period has three **digits**.

A comma separates each period.

Rose Bowl: **106,721**

Read: **one hundred six thousand, seven hundred twenty-one**

JFK Stadium: **105,000**

Read: **one hundred five thousand**

This is how he compared the number of seats.

Compare the thousands period.

Rose Bowl: 106,721   JFK Stadium: 105,000

106 thousand *is greater than* 105 thousand.

So **106,721**   >   **105,000**

◀ The Rose Bowl has more seats.

PRACTICE • Copy each number. Write the comma in the correct place. Then read the number.

1. 345280   2. 24332   3. 45024   4. 2483   5. 801004

6. Write in standard form: eight hundred sixty thousand, two hundred forty-five.

Use > or < to compare the numbers.

7. 60,372 ● 65,101   8. 110,532 ● 87,432   9. 432,504 ● 423,145

EXERCISES • Match.

Column I	Column II
10. three hundred twenty-four thousand, eight hundred five	A. 324,865
11. thirty-four thousand, sixty-five	B. 32,465
12. 300,000 + 20,000 + 4,000 + 800 + 50	C. 304,065
13. thirty-two thousand, four hundred sixty-five	D. 34,065
14. thirty-four thousand, six hundred fifty	E. 324,805
15. 300,000 + 20,000 + 4,000 + 800 + 60 + 5	F. 34,650
16. three hundred four thousand, sixty-five	G. 324,850

Write the numbers in standard form.

17. five thousand, eight hundred sixty-four

18. twenty-four thousand, one hundred twenty-three

19. three hundred seventy-six thousand, four hundred

20. six hundred seven thousand, two hundred fifty-two

21. five hundred thirty thousand, six hundred twenty

PROBLEM SOLVING • APPLICATIONS

Use the table at the top of page 40 to answer the questions.

22. Write in words the number of seats in Texas Stadium.

23. Which stadium has fifty thousand, four hundred ninety-six seats?

24. Compare the Orange Bowl and the Superdome. Which stadium has more seats? Use > or < to compare the numbers.

25. Which stadiums have fewer seats than the Orange Bowl? Use > and < to compare the numbers.

26. Which stadiums have more seats than the Texas Stadium? Use > or < to compare the numbers.

27. List the stadiums in order from the greatest number of seats to the least number of seats.

Millions

Tony is studying about space in science. Mrs. Sibert, his science teacher, tells the class to imagine driving a spaceship through space. The planet Mars is the first destination.

● Tony must find the number of miles from earth to Mars and report the number to the class.

Tony finds the number 48,571,200. To report the number, Tony must be able to read millions.

Millions Period			Thousands Period			Ones Period			
hundred million	ten million	one million	hundred thousand	ten thousand	one thousand	hundred	tens	ones	
	4	8 ,	5	7	1 ,	2	0	0	

Each group is called a **period**.

Each **period** has **three digits**.

A comma separates each period.

Read **forty-eight million, five hundred seventy-one thousand, two hundred.**

Write the standard form: **48,571,200**

● **The 4 in 48,571,200 is in the ten millions place. Its value is 40,000,000.**

- In what place is the 8?   What is its value?
- In what place is the 7?   What is its value?
- In what place is the 5?   What is its value?
- In what place is the 2?   What is its value?

PRACTICE • Write the numbers in standard form.

1. 1 million, 437 thousand, 800

2. 17 million, 860 thousand, 245

3. 9 million, 54 thousand, 388

4. 256 million, 3 thousand, 600

Write the digit that is in the millions place.

5. 8,425,062

6. 14,071,539

7. 643,578,410

EXERCISES • Write the numbers in standard form.

8. 2 million, 475 thousand, 389

9. 8 million, 204 thousand, 87

10. 1 million, 742 thousand, 897

11. 13 million, 386 thousand, 920

12. 53 million, 80 thousand, 200

13. 5 million, 26 thousand, 516

14. 725 million, 8 thousand, 121

15. 7 million, 700 thousand

16. 164 million, 252

17. 39 million, 4

Write the digit that is in the ten-millions place.

18. 13,068,475

19. 154,702,811

20. 261,250,786

21. 590,126,240

22. 42,005,326

23. 634,289,750

Mental Math   Name 100,000 more.

24. 9,535,480

25. 49,497,224

26. 2,180,925

PROBLEM SOLVING • APPLICATIONS

Distance in miles from the sun.	
Mercury	36,000,000
Venus	67,230,000
Earth	92,960,000
Mars	141,700,000
Jupiter	483,700,000
Saturn	885,200,000

27. Which planet in this table is between thirty-six million miles and seventy-three million miles from the sun?

28. Which planets in the table are more than 70,000,000 miles from the sun?

29. Uranus is closer to the sun than Neptune. Uranus is farther from the sun than Saturn. Pluto is farther than Neptune. Which planet is closest to the sun?

THINKER'S CORNER

Read this cartoon.

● How many days will it take to spend $1,000,000?

● About how many years is this?

Money

Angela works in the school store.

On Monday morning, Luis bought a notebook and 2 pencils. He gave Angela 1 dollar, 1 half dollar, 1 quarter, 1 dime, 1 nickel, and 2 pennies.

● How much did he give Angela?

Think To solve the problem, Angela must count the money.

Angela counts nickels by 5's.

| 5 | 10 | 15 | 20 | 25 | 30 | 35 |

35¢
$0.35
35 cents

She counts dimes by 10's.

| 10 | 20 | 30 | 40 | 50 | 60 | 70 |

70¢
$0.70
70 cents

This is how Angela counted the money.

$1.00 → $1.50 → $1.75 → $1.85 → $1.90 → $1.91 → $1.92

Luis gave Angela **$1.92.**

PRACTICE • How much money is there?

1.

2.

3.

4.

EXERCISES • How much money is there?

5.

6.

Find the totals.

									Total
7.					1	2		3	?
8.			1	1		1	2		?
9.			2		3			4	?
10.	1	1	3		2		3	4	?
11.	2		4		5		3	6	?

Write the amounts in words.

12. $0.37

13. $1.70

★ **14.** $3.28

★ **15.** $80.59

PROBLEM SOLVING • APPLICATIONS

CHOOSE • mental math • pencil and paper • calculator SOLVE

16. Carl went to the school store to buy pencils and erasers. He gave the clerk 3 dimes, 2 nickels, and 4 pennies. How much money did he give the clerk?

17. Latonya bought a notebook, a ruler, and pencils from the school store. She gave the clerk 1 dollar, 2 quarters, 2 dimes, and 4 pennies. How much money did she give the clerk?

18. Tu bought paper, pencils, and erasers for $0.78. He gave the clerk 1 quarter, 3 dimes, 3 nickels, and 3 pennies. Did he give the clerk enough money? If not, how much more did he need?

THINKER'S CORNER

Martha Sue had $1.00 in coins. She had 12 coins in all. What combination of coins did she have?

Numeration • **45**

PROBLEM SOLVING • STRATEGIES

Working Backwards to Count Change

Example

When Angela counts change, she starts
to count with the cost of the item.
Then she counts by 25's (quarters),
or by 10's (dimes), or by 5's (nickels),
or by 1's (pennies or dollars).
On Tuesday, Kaley buys a T-shirt for
$3.79. She gives Angela $5.00.

● How much change does Angela give Kaley?

Cost		1 penny		2 dimes		1 dollar
$3.79	→	$3.80	→	$4.00	→	$5.00

◀ End with the amount given.

Angela gives Kaley **1 dollar + 2 dimes + 1 penny**, or **$1.21.**

PROBLEMS • Complete. Find the amount of change.

1. **Cost:** $2.25   **Amount Given:** $5.00

   Cost + __?__ quarters + __?__ dollars

   $2.25 ⟶ $3.00 ⟶ $5.00   **Change:** __?__

2. **Cost:** $3.82   **Amount Given:** $5.00

   Cost + __?__ pennies + __?__ nickel + __?__ dime + __?__ dollar

   $3.82 ⟶ $3.85 ⟶ $3.90 ⟶ $4.00 ⟶ $5.00   **Change:** __?__

3. **Cost:** $7.44   **Amount Given:** $10.00

   Cost + __?__ penny + __?__ nickel + __?__ quarters + __?__ dollars

   $7.44 ⟶ $7.45 ⟶ $7.50 ⟶ $8.00 ⟶ $10.00   **Change:** __?__

4. Cost: $8.47　　　**Amount Given:** $10.00

Cost + ___?___ pennies + ___?___ quarters + ___?___ dollars

$8.47 ⟶ $8.50 ⟶ $9.00 ⟶ $10.00　**Change:** ___?___

Find the amount of change. Choose A, B, C, D, or E.

Cost	Amount Given		

5. $0.28　　___?___　　A.　

6. $1.45　　___?___　　B.　

7. $0.34　　___?___　　C.　

8. $0.52　　___?___　　D.　

9. $1.98　　___?___　　E.　

10. José buys a pad of paper and a box of crayons for $0.68. He gives Angela $1.00. How much change does he receive?

11. Rita spent $0.42 at the store. She gave the clerk $0.65. Her change was 3 pennies and some dimes. How many dimes did she receive?

12. Rosa gave the clerk $1.00 for $0.59 worth of supplies. The clerk gave Rosa a quarter, a penny and some nickels. How many nickels did she have?

★ **13.** Leo bought a sweatshirt and gym shorts for $14.00. He gave Angela a $20 bill. He received two bills as change. What were the bills?

CHAPTER REVIEW

Part 1: VOCABULARY

For Exercises 1–7, choose from the box at the right the word that completes the sentence.

1. The place of the digit in a number tells you its __?__. (Page 26)

2. One hundred is equal to ten __?__. (Page 26)

3. Digits are grouped by 3's. Each group is called a __?__. (Page 40)

4. In the number 37,168, the 3 is in the __?__ place. (Page 40)

5. To find which number is greater or smaller, we __?__ numbers. (Page 38)

6. The symbol < means __?__. (Page 38)

7. The number 4,688 __?__ to the nearest thousand is 5,000. (Page 32)

```
compare
hundreds
hundred thousands
greater than
group
less than
millions
numeration
period
rounded
tens
ten thousands
value
```

Part 2: SKILLS

Write the numbers in standard form. (Pages 26–29, 40–43)

8.
hundreds	tens	ones
4	1	8

9.
thousands	hundreds	tens	ones
7	0	3	2

10. 3 hundreds 4 tens

11. 2 thousands 7 hundreds 5 tens 8 ones

12. 7 hundreds 5 tens 3 ones

13. 9 thousands 4 tens 6 ones

14. 800 + 30 + 7

15. 6,000 + 300 + 8

16. eighty-nine million, fifty-five thousand, one hundred seven

17. six million, two hundred twelve thousand, five hundred ten

In the number **714,635,280** what digit is in the (Pages 26–29, 40–43)

18. tens place?

19. hundred-thousands place?

20. millions place?

21. thousands place?

22. ten-millions place?

23. hundred-millions place?

Use > or < to compare the numbers. (Pages 38–39)

24. 76 ⬤ 70 **25.** 581 ⬤ 582 **26.** 6,401 ⬤ 6,301 **27.** 26,421 ⬤ 24,592

Round to the nearest ten. (Pages 30–31)

28. 62 **29.** 45 **30.** 27 **31.** 74

Round to the nearest hundred or to the nearest dollar. (Pages 30–31)

32. 212 **33.** 135 **34.** $5.52 **35.** $3.78

Round to the nearest thousand. (Pages 32–33)

36. 6,837 **37.** 8,418 **38.** 4,029 **39.** 3,545

Count the money. Write the total. (Pages 44–45)

40.    **41.**

42.   **43.**

Write the amounts in words. (Pages 44–45)

44. $0.75 **45.** $0.90 **46.** $1.38 **47.** $10.62

Part 3: *PROBLEM SOLVING • APPLICATIONS*

48. A T-shirt costs $4.29. You give the clerk $5.00. What is your change? (Pages 46–47)

49. Pencils cost $0.10 each. Amy buys 3 pencils. She gives the clerk $0.50. What is her change? (Pages 46–47)

50. Matt spent $0.67 at the store. He gave the clerk $0.75. His change was 3 pennies and one other coin. What was the other coin? (Pages 46–47)

51. Wang-Tu gave the clerk $1.00 for $0.73 worth of supplies. The clerk gave Wang-Tu 2 pennies, 1 nickel, and some dimes. How many dimes did he receive? (Pages 46–47)

52. Marcus, Sue, Dirk, and Pablo are in line to have their pictures taken. Marcus is behind Sue and in front of Dirk. Dirk is between Marcus and Pablo. Who is first in line? (Pages 34–35)

53. Jason, Karl, Lisa, and Latonya ride their bikes to school. Lisa arrives before Jason. Jason arrives before Karl. Latonya arrives between Lisa and Jason. Who arrived last? (Pages 34–35)

CHAPTER TEST

Write the numbers in standard form.

1.

hundreds	tens	ones
6	2	7

2.

thousands	hundreds	tens	ones
9	3	1	4

3. 5 hundreds 8 ones

4. 2 thousands 3 tens 9 ones

5. forty-eight thousand, three hundred sixty-seven

6. 3 million, 295 thousand, 843

Round to the nearest ten.

7. 67

8. 34

9. 185

10. 372

Round to the nearest hundred or nearest dollar.

11. 752

12. 401

13. $6.43

14. $7.65

Round to the nearest thousand.

15. 4,593

16. 6,051

17. 7,824

18. 68,649

Use < or > to compare the numbers.

19. 22 60

20. 348 ● 351

21. 2,831 ● 978

22. 171 ● 97

Count the money. Write the total.

23.

Solve.

24. Joan, Mary, Lil, and Alice are in line. Joan is just behind Mary. Lil is between Alice and Mary. Who is last in line?

25. Chris spent $0.58 at the store. He gave the clerk $0.75. His change was 2 pennies and some nickels. How many nickels did he receive?

ENRICHMENT

Roman Numerals

The ancient Romans used these symbols to name numbers.

| 1 | 5 | 10 | 50 | 100 | 500 | 1,000 |

To find the value of a Roman numeral you can add or subtract.

Rule 1. Add when the values are the same.

III	XX	CCC	MM
1 + 1 + 1	10 + 10	100 + 100 + 100	1,000 + 1,000
3	20	300	2,000

Rule 2. Add when the symbol for a greater value comes first.

VII	XV	LXII	CXI	MD
5 + 1 + 1	10 + 5	50 + 10 + 1 + 1	100 + 10 + 1	1,000 + 500
7	15	62	111	1,500

Rule 3. Subtract when the symbol for a smaller value comes first.

IV	IX	XL	CXIV	CM
5 − 1	10 − 1	50 − 10	100 + 10 + (5 − 1)	1,000 − 100
4	9	40	114	900

EXERCISES • What number is named?

1. LXV
2. XLVI
3. XXIX
4. CXXIV

5. CCCXXXIII
6. LXXIX
7. DXC
8. MDLX

Write the Roman numeral.

9. 2
10. 6
11. 13
12. 19
13. 25
14. 34

15. 63
16. 118
17. 345
18. 870
19. 955
20. 1,492

ADDITIONAL PRACTICE

SKILLS

Write the numbers in standard form. (Pages 26–29)

1. 7 hundreds 8 tens 5 ones

2. 2 thousands 5 hundreds 9 ones

3. one hundred thirty-two

4. six thousand, one hundred twelve

Write the digit in the hundreds place. (Pages 26–29)

5. 4,689   **6.** 3,794   **7.** 1,423   **8.** 8,179

Write the digit in the thousands place. (Pages 26–29)

9. 4,812   **10.** 9,634   **11.** 7,583   **12.** 5,049

Round each number. (Pages 30–33)

Nearest ten: **13.** 47   **14.** 84   **15.** 362

Nearest hundred: **16.** 340   **17.** 680   **18.** 3,451

Nearest thousand: **19.** 6,732   **20.** 4,891   **21.** 14,078

Use < or > to compare the numbers. (Pages 38–39)

22. 64 ● 47   **23.** 38 ● 314   **24.** 576 ● 567

25. 872 ● 1,243   **26.** 7,013 ● 7,301   **27.** 3,009 ● 3,010

Write in order from least to greatest. (Pages 38–39)

28. 740; 735; 745; 730   **29.** 678; 1,392; 2,914; 258

Write the numbers in standard form. (Pages 40–43)

30. 25 thousand, 638   **31.** 5 million, 289 thousand, 512

Count the money. Write the total. (Pages 44–45)

32.

33.

PROBLEM SOLVING • APPLICATIONS

34. Tom is taller than Martha. Jamie is shorter than Martha and taller than Paul. Who is tallest? (Pages 34–35)

35. Martin bought some pencils for $0.76. He gave the clerk $1.00. How much change does he receive? (Pages 46–47)

COMPUTER APPLICATIONS

Print Commands: + and −

You can make a computer add or subtract numbers. You do this by typing commands on the computer's keyboard. What you type is **input**.

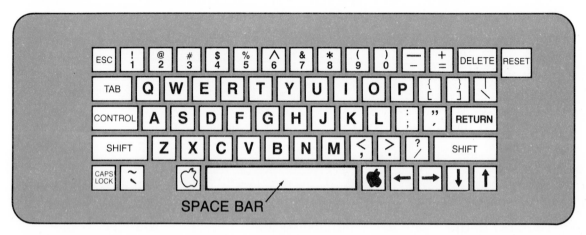

One command you can type is **PRINT 2 + 2.**   Do these steps.

① Type the word **PRINT**. Press one key at a time.

② Press the space bar to make the space between the word **PRINT** and **2 + 2**.

③ Type **2**.

④ To make the + sign, hold down a **SHIFT** key and press the key marked +. You do not have to do this on the Commodore computer.

⑤ Now type the other **2**.

⑥ Press the key marked **RETURN** or **ENTER** or ↵ .

⑦ The computer should show **4**.

   This is the **output**.

PRINT commands are part of the **BASIC** language. Microcomputers "speak" BASIC.

EXERCISES • Write the output from each command.

1. PRINT 1 + 1

2. PRINT 3 + 2

3. PRINT 0 + 6

4. PRINT 7 + 2

5. PRINT 13 − 10

6. PRINT 5 + 1 + 6

7. PRINT 8 + 2 + 4

8. PRINT 9 + 4

9. PRINT 18 − 9

Mixed Practice • Choose the correct answers.

1.   8
   +7

A. 17   **B.** 16
C. 15   **D.** not here

2.   46
   +32

A. 74   **B.** 88
C. 14   **D.** not here

3.   161
   +338

A. 485   **B.** 499
C. 475   **D.** not here

4. What is 474 rounded to the nearest ten?

A. 480   **B.** 470
C. 500   **D.** not here

5. What is 847 rounded to the nearest hundred?

A. 800   **B.** 850
C. 900   **D.** not here

6. What is 4,602 rounded to the nearest thousand?

A. 4,600   **B.** 4,700
C. 4,000   **D.** not here

7.   16
   − 7

A. 8   **B.** 9
C. 11   **D.** not here

8.   78
   −58

A. 30   **B.** 10
C. 20   **D.** not here

9.   438
   −217

A. 229   **B.** 221
C. 219   **D.** not here

10. Bradley rode his bike 48 miles in a week. The next week he rode 16 miles. How many more miles did Bradley ride the first week?

A. 64   **B.** 42
C. 22   **D.** not here

11. There are 33 bike riders in the first race and 25 bike riders in the second race. How many bike riders were in the races?

A. 55   **B.** 58
C. 61   **D.** not here

Addition and Subtraction

Bob is a ham radio operator in San Diego. To talk with his friend in Seattle, he must have other ham operators pass or "patch" his signal to Seattle. The map shows the path of his signal.

● Estimate how many miles the signal travels.

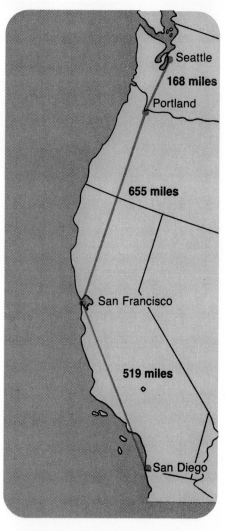

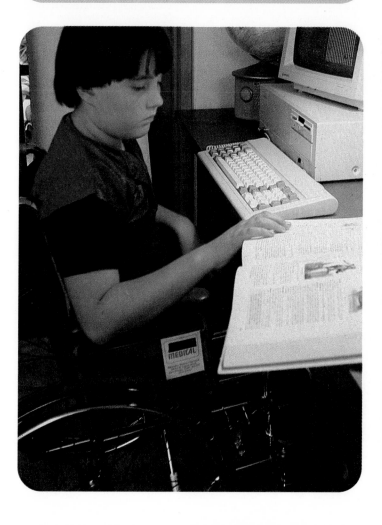

Jeff's computer prints 462 lines a minute. Jill's computer prints 258 lines a minute.

● How many more lines a minute does Jeff's computer print?

55

Adding Two-Digit Numbers

Many years ago, puffs of smoke were used to send messages. Suppose a message used 36 puffs and the reply to the message used 28 puffs.

● How many puffs of smoke were sent in all?

Think You need to find how many puffs of smoke **in all**. So add.

$$36 + 28 = ?$$

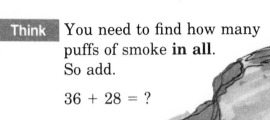

Step 1 Add the ones. **Regroup** 14 ones as 1 ten and 4 ones.

```
  1
  3 6
+ 2 8
    4
```

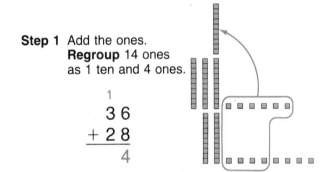

Step 2 Add the tens.

```
  1
  3 6
+ 2 8
  6 4
```

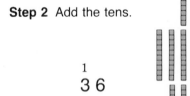
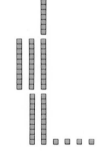

There were **64 puffs of smoke** in all.

More Examples

```
   68          1            1            1
  +21         4 7          6 5          8 6
   89        + 3 7        + 5 7        + 9 5
              8 4         1 2 2        1 8 1
```

PRACTICE • Add.

1. 34
   +63

2. 84
   +15

3. 56
   +21

4. 18
   +70

5. 23
   +74

6. 25
   +32

7. 28
   +45

8. 19
   +61

9. 47
   +33

10. 53
    +29

11. 75
    +18

12. 64
    +29

EXERCISES • Add.

13. 27 $+54$	**14.** 79 $+18$	**15.** 34 $+41$	**16.** 28 $+43$	**17.** 92 $+\ 7$	**18.** 35 $+12$
19. 38 $+51$	**20.** 19 $+79$	**21.** 24 $+26$	**22.** 18 $+45$	**23.** 24 $+62$	**24.** 71 $+\ 4$
25. 29 $+57$	**26.** 27 $+45$	**27.** 48 $+36$	**28.** 27 $+17$	**29.** 30 $+58$	**30.** 65 $+\ 9$
31. 37 $+\ 5$	**32.** 49 $+34$	**33.** 7 $+56$	**34.** 84 $+\ 8$	**35.** 58 $+21$	**36.** 26 $+34$
37. 25 $+45$	**38.** 34 $+43$	**39.** 82 $+\ 9$	**40.** 74 $+19$	**41.** 35 $+44$	**42.** 56 $+19$
43. 69 $+13$	**44.** 43 $+37$	**45.** 15 $+72$	**46.** 45 $+\ 6$	**47.** 29 $+39$	**48.** 33 $+51$

49. $31 + 42 = \underline{\ ?\ }$ **50.** $53 + 14 = \underline{\ ?\ }$ **51.** $63 + 26 = \underline{\ ?\ }$

52. $63 + 8 = \underline{\ ?\ }$ **53.** $26 + 7 = \underline{\ ?\ }$ **54.** $48 + 12 = \underline{\ ?\ }$

★ **55.** $23 + 42 + 13 = \underline{\ ?\ }$ ★ **56.** $52 + 6 + 21 = \underline{\ ?\ }$ ★ **57.** $12 + 23 + 40 + 14 = \underline{\ ?\ }$

PROBLEM SOLVING • APPLICATIONS

58. A bottle containing a message floated 36 miles to an island. It then floated out to sea and traveled 48 more miles. How far did the bottle travel in all?

59. All of the fourth-grade classes made signal flags. Jason's class made 17 flags. Mark's class made 14 flags. How many flags were made in all?

60. Lorie buys a note pad to write letters to her friends. The note pad cost $0.79. She gives the clerk $1.00. She gets back 3 coins. What are the 3 coins?

THINKER'S CORNER

All the missing numbers are the same. Find the missing addends.

$$\begin{array}{r} \square\square \\ +\ \square\square \\ \hline 1\ 3\ 2 \end{array}$$

Adding Three-Digit Numbers

The *Daily Mirror* newspaper owns an office building and a printing plant. The office building has 584 workers. The printing plant has 342 workers.

● How many people work for the *Daily Mirror*?

Think You need to find the **total** number of workers. So add.

$$584 + 342 = ?$$

Step 1
Add the ones.

```
  5 8 4
+ 3 4 2
──────
      6
```

Step 2
Add the tens. Regroup 12 tens as 1 hundred and 2 tens.

```
    1
  5 8 4
+ 3 4 2
──────
    2 6
```

Step 3
Add the hundreds.

```
    1
  5 8 4
+ 3 4 2
──────
  9 2 6
```

The *Daily Mirror* has **926 workers**.

Another Method • Mental Math

● Add: 593 + 324

Think Add the hundreds, tens, and ones separately.

$$
\begin{aligned}
593 &= 500 + 90 + 3 \\
+324 &= 300 + 20 + 4 \\
\hline
&800 + 110 + 7 = \textbf{917}
\end{aligned}
$$

◀ Expanded form

PRACTICE • Add.

1. 129 +634	2. 375 +506	3. 518 +319	4. 384 +215	5. 520 +369	6. 473 +285
7. 628 +190	8. 232 +546	9. 438 + 27	10. 773 +218	11. 219 +437	12. 425 + 82

EXERCISES • Add. Use the method you prefer.

13. 278 +540	14. 179 +208	15. 406 +284	16. 873 + 96	17. 534 +339	18. 284 + 70
19. 372 +543	20. 396 +240	21. 684 + 85	22. 467 +351	23. 93 +670	24. 538 +236
25. 853 + 52	26. 862 + 44	27. 938 + 35	28. 487 +122	29. 708 +210	30. 382 +243
31. 701 +149	32. 19 +570	33. 492 +487	34. 117 +690	35. 42 +875	36. 70 +530
37. 241 +753	38. 38 +961	39. 381 +265	40. 375 +432	41. 419 + 63	42. 365 +454

43. $487 + 306 =$ ___?___

44. $275 + 564 =$ ___?___

45. $914 + 73 =$ ___?___

46. $762 + 128 =$ ___?___

47. $670 + 48 =$ ___?___

48. $358 + 227 =$ ___?___

PROBLEM SOLVING • APPLICATIONS

49. Flora Montez drives a delivery truck for the *Daily Mirror*. On Saturday she delivers 315 bundles of newspapers. On Sunday she delivers 278 bundles of newspapers. How many bundles does she deliver in the two days?

50. Lionel Davies owns the newsstand in the lobby of the *Daily Mirror* building. On Friday he sold 548 newspapers. He returned 61 unsold papers. How many newspapers had he received on Friday?

51. Susie has a paper route in her neighborhood. Susie delivers 16 newspapers to homes on Market Street. She just delivered 9 newspapers. How many more have to be delivered?

THINKER'S CORNER

Arrange seven 4s and four addition signs (+) so that the sum equals 100.

Addition and Subtraction • **59**

Adding: More Than One Regrouping

From 1860 to 1861, Pony Express riders carried mail between Missouri and California. One rider traveled 538 miles one week and 674 miles the next week.

● How far did the rider travel in the two weeks?

Think You need to find the **total** number of miles. So add.

$$538 + 674 = ?$$

Sometimes you need to regroup ones, tens, and hundreds.

Step 1	**Step 2**	**Step 3**
Add the ones. Regroup.	Add the tens. Regroup.	Add the hundreds. Regroup.

Step 1
```
    1
  5 3 8
+ 6 7 4
      2
```

Step 2
```
  1 1
  5 3 8
+ 6 7 4
    1 2
```

Step 3
```
  1 1
  5 3 8
+ 6 7 4
1,2 1 2
```

The rider traveled **1,212 miles** in two weeks.

More Examples

```
  1 1
  4 7 3
+ 2 4 8
  7 2 1
```

```
    1
  6 9 5
+ 8 2 1
1,5 1 6
```

```
  1 1
  9 5 2
+   8 8
1,0 4 0
```

```
  1 1
  6 7 8
+ 3 5 6
1,0 3 4
```

PRACTICE • Add.

1. 657
   +267

2. 768
   + 94

3. 987
   +346

4. 779
   + 83

5. 693
   +835

6. 485
   +349

7. 418
   +793

8. 846
   +457

9. 575
   +666

10. 704
    +599

11. 978
    + 69

12. 898
    +734

EXERCISES • Add.

13. 684 +459	14. 796 +709	15. 985 + 57	16. 394 +638	17. 756 +986	18. 887 +267
19. 569 +769	20. 379 +824	21. 753 +829	22. 716 +761	23. 695 +346	24. 919 +191
25. 125 +878	26. 675 +819	27. 346 +425	28. 629 +152	29. 736 +152	30. 319 +852
31. 421 +535	32. 413 +897	33. 591 +257	34. 637 +906	35. 590 +845	36. 784 + 39
37. 429 +845	38. 952 +783	39. 695 +204	40. 962 + 78	41. 629 +246	42. 881 +714

43. $779 + 441 =$ ___?___

44. $578 + 851 =$ ___?___

45. $725 + 480 =$ ___?___

46. $406 + 387 =$ ___?___

47. $857 + 296 =$ ___?___

48. $984 + 65 =$ ___?___

PROBLEM SOLVING • APPLICATIONS

CHOOSE • mental math • pencil and paper • calculator | SOLVE

49. Bart traveled 476 miles one week and 635 miles the next week. How far did Bart travel in the two weeks?

50. Wes traveled 423 miles the first week. Brad rode 88 miles farther than Wes. How far did Brad ride?

51. John rode more miles than Paul and fewer than Tom. Paul rode more miles than Ray. Who rode the greater number of miles?

52. Greg carried a 19-pound bag of mail 118 miles. Rick carried the bag another 126 miles. How far was the bag carried in all?

THINKER'S CORNER

Find the missing digits.

a.
```
  6 7 ▢
+ 9 7 6
───────
1,▢ 5 4
```

b.
```
  7 5 ▢
+ 8 ▢ 9
───────
1,6 3 3
```

c.
```
  9 5 ▢
+   4 8
───────
1,0 ▢ 5
```

d.
```
  6 4 2
+ ▢ 7 8
───────
▢,5 2 0
```

Estimating Sums

It is a good idea to estimate an answer in order to check if the exact answer is reasonable.

Chris and Karen are news reporters. Chris reports 514 minutes of national news on television each month. Karen reports 382 minutes of local news each month.

● How many minutes of news do they report each month?

   1️⃣ **Estimate** the answer.

     Think Round each number to the nearest hundred and add.

   2️⃣ Find the exact answer.

   3️⃣ Compare the exact answer with the estimate to check whether the exact answer is reasonable.

1️⃣ **Estimate**	2️⃣ **Exact Answer**	3️⃣ **Compare.**
$514 \rightarrow 500$ $382 \rightarrow +400$ $\overline{900}$	514 $+382$ $\overline{896}$	Since the estimate is 900, 896 is a reasonable answer.

Chris and Karen reported **896 minutes** of news each month.

Ⓔ PRACTICE • Estimate each sum. Find the exact answer. Compare.

To estimate, first round each addend to the nearest ten.

1.	2.	3.	4.	5.
72 +36	18 +31	27 +31	59 +74	31 +65

To estimate, first round each addend to the nearest hundred.

6.	7.	8.	9.	10.
158 +319	527 +362	751 +837	692 +785	351 +948

To estimate, first round each addend to the nearest thousand.

11.	12.	13.	14.	15.
3,185 +2,962	4,327 +3,910	2,492 +1,523	8,316 +9,721	3,500 +3,951

EXERCISES • Estimate each sum. Find the exact answer. Compare.

To estimate, first round each addend to the nearest ten.

16. 39	17. 56	18. 24	19. 43	20. 73
+88	+41	+65	+29	+68

To estimate, first round each addend to the nearest hundred.

21. 767	22. 673	23. 426	24. 806	25. 750
+113	+218	+382	+177	+342

To estimate, first round each addend to the nearest thousand.

26. 7,869	27. 3,785	28. 3,005	29. 2,840	30. 6,015
+6,284	+6,373	+1,743	+1,562	+2,534

To estimate, first round each addend to the nearest dollar.

31. $2.16	32. $4.86	33. $5.64	34. $6.14	35. $4.25
+ 3.57	+ 2.22	+ 2.81	+ 3.73	+ 5.79

PROBLEM SOLVING • APPLICATIONS

Estimate each answer. Find the exact answer. Compare.

36. The station has 417 full-time employees. There are also 176 part-time employees. How many employees are there in all?

37. Station WSIR gave away 2,323 television schedule magazines in one week. The next week another 2,644 were given away. How many magazines were given away in all?

CALCULATOR • Estimating Sums

EXERCISES • 1 Estimate the sum.

2 Use a calculator to find the exact answer.

3 Compare the exact answer with the estimate.

1. 7,305 + 1,671

2. 4,286 + 3,753

3. 2,176 + 3,202

4. 6,824 + 2,789

5. 3,421 + 7,589

6. 6,915 + 8,274

7. 4,389 + 6,913

8. 7,213 + 1,694

9. 2,165 + 3,227

Adding Greater Numbers

Machines are used in many post offices to cancel stamps. This prevents the stamps from being used again. In ten minutes, 2,516 stamps are cancelled. In another ten minutes, 2,479 stamps are cancelled.

● How many stamps were cancelled?

Think First **estimate** your answer. Add. Compare.

Estimate	Exact Answer	Compare.
2,516 ⟶ 3,000	2,516	The estimate is
2,479 ⟶ +2,000	+2,479	5,000. So 4,995 is a
5,000	4,995	reasonable answer.

So **4,995 stamps** are cancelled.

More Examples

$$\begin{array}{r} {\scriptstyle 1\ 1} \\ 6{,}7\,5\,4 \\ +\ 8{,}0\,7\,9 \\ \hline 1\,4{,}8\,3\,3 \end{array}$$

$$\begin{array}{r} {\scriptstyle 1\ 1} \\ 7\,4{,}8\,3\,2 \\ +\ 6\,5{,}9\,0\,1 \\ \hline 1\,4\,0{,}7\,3\,3 \end{array}$$

$$\begin{array}{r} {\scriptstyle 1\ 1\ 1\ 1} \\ 5\,9{,}3\,6\,4 \\ +\ \ \ 2{,}7\,8\,6 \\ \hline 6\,2{,}1\,5\,0 \end{array}$$

E **PRACTICE** • Estimate each answer. Add. Compare.

1. 6,779 +1,834	**2.** 6,945 +3,746	**3.** 4,967 +3,645	**4.** 3,852 +1,948	**5.** 43,463 + 8,597
6. 4,397 +8,056	**7.** 3,947 + 874	**8.** 65,693 +31,876	**9.** 53,207 +80,895	**10.** 17,654 + 7,899

EXERCISES • Add.

11. 3,805
    +4,778

12. 6,784
    +8,522

13. 2,411
    +6,729

14. 3,528
    +2,497

15. 42,896
    +39,107

16. 3,469
    +4,578

17. 1,046
    +5,997

18. 2,964
    +7,092

19. 28,358
    + 4,629

20. 1,894
    +3,406

21. 2,180
    +7,609

22. 9,619
    +93,624

23. 3,227
    +6,349

24. 67,282
    +32,744

25. 9,479
    +3,824

26. 35,821
    + 4,978

27. 4,207
    +3,945

28. 4,352
    +65,437

29. 2,432
    +6,059

30. 9,832
    +7,045

31. 2,955
    +3,786

32. 7,480
    +10,656

33. 99,695
    +87,367

34. 78,906
    +43,697

35. 55,937
    +48,065

36. $4{,}829 + 1{,}361 = $ ___?___

37. $1{,}281 + 7{,}039 = $ ___?___

38. $96{,}421 + 3{,}592 = $ ___?___

39. $8{,}942 + 72{,}059 = $ ___?___

★40. $481{,}206 + 299{,}854 = $ ___?___

★41. $763{,}907 + 454{,}095 = $ ___?___

PROBLEM SOLVING • APPLICATIONS

Use the table to answer the questions.

42. What was the total number of magazines and packages delivered?

43. What was the total number of letters and postcards delivered?

44. How many letters and magazines altogether were delivered?

45. How many pieces of mail were delivered in all?

LAST WEEK'S MAIL DELIVERIES	
letters	64,763
postcards	21,546
magazines	12,488
packages	9,326

More Than Two Addends

Bob is a *ham radio operator* in San Diego. He wants to talk with his friend in Seattle. Bob's radio signal is not powerful enough to reach Seattle. He must have other ham radio operators pass or "patch" his signal through to Seattle. The map shows the path his signal travels.

● About how many miles does his signal travel?

Think You can add to find the total number of miles. To **estimate**, first round to the nearest hundred.

$$
\begin{array}{r}
519 \longrightarrow 500 \\
655 \longrightarrow 700 \\
+168 \longrightarrow +200 \\
\hline
1,400 \quad \blacktriangleleft \text{ Estimate}
\end{array}
$$

The signal travels about **1,400 miles**.

● What is the exact number of miles his signal travels?

519 + 655 + 168 = ?

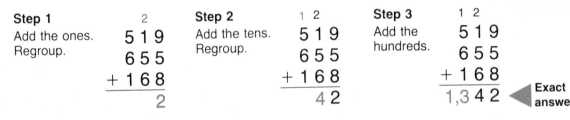

Step 1
Add the ones.
Regroup.

```
  2
  5 1 9
  6 5 5
+ 1 6 8
───────
      2
```

Step 2
Add the tens.
Regroup.

```
  1 2
  5 1 9
  6 5 5
+ 1 6 8
───────
    4 2
```

Step 3
Add the hundreds.

```
  1 2
  5 1 9
  6 5 5
+ 1 6 8
───────
1,3 4 2   ◀ Exact answer
```

The radio signal travels **1,342 miles**.

Compare the exact answer with the estimate.
Since the estimate is 1,400 miles, 1,342 miles is a reasonable answer.

More Examples

```
    2
   6 7
   5 6
 + 2 9
───────
 1 5 2
```

```
  1 1 2
  7,4 0 8
    3 8 5
+ 5,6 2 9
─────────
1 3,4 2 2
```

```
    2 2
    1 7 9
    6 3 5
    7 7 7
 + 9 4 2
─────────
  2,5 3 3
```

PRACTICE • Add.

| 1. | 24
51
+13 | 2. | 76
63
+98 | 3. | 836
979
+ 13 | 4. | 2,703
144
+ 32 | 5. | 854
825
+945 | 6. | 35
835
+735 |

| 7. | 528
788
+ 47 | 8. | 807
605
+796 | 9. | 73
93
+1,856 | 10. | 378
245
+876 | 11. | 3,667
79
+ 974 | 12. | 475
35
+715 |

EXERCISES • Add.

| 13. | 23
32
+37 | 14. | 83
62
+79 | 15. | 62
15
+21 | 16. | 35
47
+98 | 17. | 86
737
+458 | 18. | 94
374
+667 |

| 19. | 709
82
+269 | 20. | 98
609
+295 | 21. | 341
10
+527 | 22. | 583
363
+ 72 | 23. | 670
580
+ 66 | 24. | 893
74
+844 |

| 25. | 269
348
253
+315 | 26. | 973
84
63
+4,216 | 27. | 106
4,867
2,431
+ 353 | 28. | 7,458
535
647
+5,238 | 29. | 8,326
24
3,215
+ 83 | 30. | 43
4,273
9,683
+ 13 |

31. $462 + 711 + 98 = $ ___?___

32. $909 + 7 + 9,901 = $ ___?___

33. $5,000 + 2,278 + 99 = $ ___?___

34. $2,365 + 1,707 + 833 = $ ___?___

PROBLEM SOLVING • APPLICATIONS

35. A club for ham radio operators has three chapters. There are 38 members in one chapter, 46 in another, and 43 in the third. How many members are there?

36. Louise keeps a weekly log of the number of hours she talks on her radio. She talked 28 hours, 35 hours, 21 hours, and 32 hours. How many hours did she talk in all?

37. Draw a picture to find the path this ham radio signal travels. The signal begins in San Francisco. Denver comes before Atlanta. Chicago comes between Denver and Atlanta. Miami comes after Atlanta.

THINKER'S CORNER

Jamie bought a bicycle for $60.00 and sold it for $70.00. She bought it back for $80.00 and sold it again for $90.00. How much money did she make or lose in buying and selling the bicycle?

MID-CHAPTER REVIEW

Add. (Pages 56–61)

1. 72	2. 52	3. 492	4. 629	5. 693
+15	+29	+467	+182	+228

Estimate the sum. Find the actual answer. Compare. (Pages 62–63)
To estimate, first round to the nearest

ten.	hundred.	dollar.	hundred.	thousand.
6. 58	7. 426	8. $6.16	9. 669	10. 7,376
+47	+388	+ 2.85	+236	+1,023

Add. (Pages 64–67)

11. 2,926	12. 36,821	13. 53,798	14. 88	15. 4,273
+4,736	+ 1,359	+38,065	764	2,368
			+438	+ 147

Solve.

16. Ms. Hart watched 25 minutes of national news and 18 minutes of local news. How many minutes of news did she watch?
(Pages 56–57)

17. Roberto delivered 16,253 letters one week and 12,877 letters the next week. How many letters did he deliver? (Pages 64–65)

MAINTENANCE • MIXED PRACTICE

In the number 4,728, what number is in the

1. tens place?

2. thousands place?

3. hundreds place?

Use < or > to compare the numbers.

4. 88 ⬤ 82

5. 643 ⬤ 649

6. 286 ⬤ 806

7. 7,423 ⬤ 4,794

Write in order from least to greatest.

8. 4,305; 4,350; 4,310; 4,301

9. 6,115; 327; 43; 698

Solve.

10. Alice needs 17 animal cards to complete her collection. She has 9. How many more cards does she need?

11. Jake spent $0.63 at the store. He gave the clerk $1.00. His change was 2 pennies, 1 nickel, and some dimes. How many dimes did he receive?

CAREER APPLICATIONS

Store Clerk

Ellen is a store clerk. She marks the price for each item using a **code**. She uses a shape to stand for a number.

Code ⌐ = 1   ⌐⌐ = 2   ∟ = 3

⌐ = 4   □ = 5   ⌐ = 6

⌐ = 7   ⊓ = 8   ⌐ = 9   0 = 0

This computer code gives the price of the milk.

Example 1 Write the code for each price.

    a. $134   **b.** $2,059

Solutions: **a.** 1 = ⌐   **b.** 2 = ⊔

               3 = ∟   0 = 0

               4 = ⌐   5 = □

         $134 = ⌐∟⌐   9 = ⌐

                            $2,059 = ⊔ 0 □⌐

Example 2 A computer is coded ⌐□⊔ 0.

          A printer is coded ⌐⌐∟□.

          What is the total price of both?

Solution: Computer: ⌐ = 4   □ = 5   ⊔ = 2   0 = 0

             Price: $4,520

            Printer: ⌐ = 1   ⌐ = 1   ∟ = 3   □ = 5

              Price: $1,135

      Total Price: $4,520
                 + 1,135
                 $5,655

EXERCISES • Write the code for each price.

1. $9,201   **2.** $4,358   **3.** $2,976   **4.** $9,015

5. A television set is coded ⌐⌐⌐ . A television stand is coded ⌐⊓⊓.

    What is the total price for both?

PROJECT Make up a similar code. Use it to write addition and subtraction exercises. Give your exercises to a friend to decode and solve.

Subtracting Two-Digit Numbers

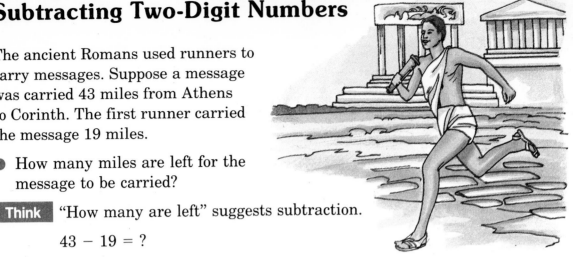

The ancient Romans used runners to carry messages. Suppose a message was carried 43 miles from Athens to Corinth. The first runner carried the message 19 miles.

● How many miles are left for the message to be carried?

Think "How many are left" suggests subtraction.

$$43 - 19 = ?$$

Step 1 Regroup 4 tens 3 ones as 3 tens 13 ones.

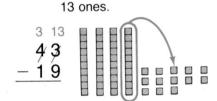

Step 2 Subtract the ones.

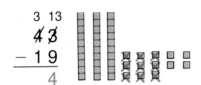

Step 3 Subtract the tens.

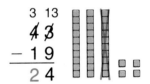

There are **24 miles** left for the message to be carried.

● You can use addition to check your answer. $24 + 19 = 43$

Another Method • Mental Math

● Subtract: $84 - 17$

Think Subtracting 17 is the same as subtracting 20 and then adding 3.

$$84 - 17 = 84 - 20 + 3$$
$$= 64 + 3$$
$$= \mathbf{67}$$

PRACTICE • Subtract. Check your answers by adding.

1.	97 −45	2.	53 −27	3.	48 −34	4.	79 −25	5.	97 −49	6.	62 − 5

7.	72 −25	8.	56 −42	9.	98 −26	10.	83 −76	11.	58 −51	12.	50 −18

EXERCISES • Subtract. Check your answers by adding.

13. 93
    −21

14. 47
    −15

15. 98
    −69

16. 68
    −36

17. 71
    −68

18. 52
    − 7

19. 91
    −34

20. 84
    −50

21. 59
    −29

22. 60
    −41

23. 84
    − 6

24. 92
    −58

25. 89
    −77

26. 64
    −59

27. 66
    −34

28. 70
    −65

29. 84
    −38

30. 76
    − 9

31. 48
    −19

32. 84
    −54

33. 68
    −61

34. 37
    −18

35. 48
    −29

36. 76
    −47

37. 99
    −78

38. 56
    −37

39. 81
    −26

40. 62
    −26

41. 49
    −38

42. 62
    −38

43. 73
    −47

44. 95
    −69

45. 57
    −28

46. 71
    −23

47. 52
    −25

48. 85
    −38

49. 59 − 21 = ___?___

50. 38 − 17 = ___?___

51. 68 − 49 = ___?___

52. 84 − 15 = ___?___

53. 78 − 40 = ___?___

54. 91 − 32 = ___?___

★ 55. 78 − ___?___ = 49

★ 56. 47 − ___?___ = 22

★ 57. 92 − ___?___ = 78

PROBLEM SOLVING • APPLICATIONS

58. In many offices, short notes called memos are used to send messages. This week Janet typed 46 memos. Last week she typed 28 memos. How many more did she type this week?

59. Mrs. Casper keeps all her office memos. In one file, she has 92 memos. In another file, she has 78 memos. How many more memos are in the first file?

60. Mr. Goldstein made 37 local calls and 18 long distance calls last month. Mr. Shay made 73 phone calls last month. Who made more calls? How many more?

THINKER'S CORNER

Find the missing numbers. They are all the same.

```
  1 7 6
−  □ □
   □ □
```

Try to make up a subtraction problem like this one. Give it to a friend to solve.

Subtracting Three-Digit Numbers

Personal computers were first introduced in 1970. Today, many people own computers. Jeff's computer prints 462 lines a minute. Jill's computer prints 258 lines a minute.

● How many more lines a minute does Jeff's computer print?

Think "How many more" suggests subtraction.

462 − 258 = ?

Step 1
Regroup.
Subtract the ones.

```
   5 12
 4 6 2
− 2 5 8
───────
       4
```

Step 2
Subtract the tens.

```
   5 12
 4 6 2
− 2 5 8
───────
     0 4
```

Step 3
Subtract the hundreds.

```
   5 12
 4 6 2
− 2 5 8
───────
   2 0 4
```

Use addition to check your answer.

```
     1
   2 0 4
 + 2 5 8
───────
   4 6 2
```

Jeff's computer prints **204 more lines** a minute.

More Examples

```
  2 12              1
  3 2 7  ←        1 7 5
− 1 5 2          + 1 5 2
───────          ───────
  1 7 5  └→        3 2 7
```

```
  5 13              1
  5 6 3  ←        3 2 6
− 2 3 7          + 2 3 7
───────          ───────
  3 2 6  └→        5 6 3
```

PRACTICE • Subtract. Check your answers.

1.	237	2.	428	3.	895	4.	628	5.	781	6.	545
	−146		−136		−457		−432		−334		−253

7.	746	8.	195	9.	621	10.	643	11.	875	12.	712
	−696		− 37		−503		− 73		−380		− 41

EXERCISES • Subtract.

13. 126
    − 53

14. 867
    −473

15. 132
    − 92

16. 592
    −283

17. 926
    − 73

18. 216
    −136

19. 457
    −453

20. 161
    − 52

21. 425
    − 31

22. 752
    −160

23. 825
    − 71

24. 653
    −516

25. 968
    −778

26. 840
    −250

27. 764
    −342

28. 853
    − 5

29. 661
    −490

30. 938
    −625

31. 653
    −291

32. 128
    − 43

33. 639
    −352

34. 617
    −502

35. 469
    −264

36. 815
    −482

37. 655
    −207

38. 582
    −350

39. 817
    −127

40. 985
    −271

41. 704
    −302

42. 811
    −405

43. 637
    −293

44. 531
    −209

45. 957
    −486

46. 319
    −224

47. 375
    −141

48. 498
    −259

49. $395 - 162 = $ ___?___

50. $776 - 427 = $ ___?___

51. $327 - 47 = $ ___?___

52. $882 - 491 = $ ___?___

53. $657 - 429 = $ ___?___

54. $519 - 74 = $ ___?___

Find the missing digits.

★55.   8 3 ▨
     − 7 0 4
     ─────
       1 ▨ 1

★56.   ▨ 9 9
     −   6 ▨
     ─────
       9 3 6

★57.   8 ▨ 9
     − ▨ 0 7
     ─────
       5 3 2

★58.   5 6 ▨
     −   ▨ 7
     ─────
       5 3 1

PROBLEM SOLVING • APPLICATIONS

59. A computer operates the bank's automatic teller machine. In one week 893 people used the machine. The next week 747 people used the machine. How many more people used the machine the first week?

60. In 1978 Wiztec Computer Company had 273 employees. Since then the company has hired 427 new employees. How many employees does Wiztec have today?

PROBLEM SOLVING · STRATEGIES

Choosing the Operation

The words in a problem are the clues that tell you whether to add or subtract.

Clues	Think
Find the **sum**. How many **in all**? How many **altogether**? Find the **total** amount. Find five **more than** eight. Find thirteen **plus** twelve.	**ADD**
Find the **difference**. How many **are left**? **How many more** are there? **How many fewer** are there? Find ten **minus** six. Find fifteen **less** nine.	**SUBTRACT**

PROBLEMS • Write **ADD** or **SUBTRACT**.

1. **How many more** calculators are used than computers?

2. What is the **total** number of computers?

3. How many computers **are left**?

4. How many computers are there **in all**?

5. **How many fewer** printers are there?

6. How many calculators are there **altogether**?

Solve each problem.

7. Tri-City Cable Company has 763 customers. Cable-View has 162 more customers than Tri-City. How many customers do they have altogether?

Look for clue words.

---

8. The Wiz-3 computer prints 365 lines per minute. The Wiz-5 computer prints 125 more lines per minute than the Wiz-3. How many lines per minute does the Wiz-5 computer print?

9. The radio signal for Station WWKA can travel 275 miles. The signal for Station WWDZ can travel 325 miles. How many more miles can the WWDZ signal travel than the WWKA signal?

10. The MYT Telephone Company has 176 employees at one store and 924 employees at another store. How many employees are there in all?

11. Mia is a telephone operator. She receives 624 calls in the morning and 683 calls in the afternoon. How many total calls does Mia receive that day?

12. The All-Electric Company has 342 telephone jacks in stock. The clerk sells 215 of them. How many are left?

13. The *Daily Mirror* has 218 part-time employees. It has 423 full-time employees. How many employees are there altogether?

Sometimes there are no clue words.

---

14. Doris sells 15 computers in May and 38 computers in June. How many computers does she sell in both May and June?

15. Janice has 12 printers in her store. She sells 8 printers. How many does she have now?

Estimating Differences

It is a good idea to estimate an answer in order to check if the exact answer is reasonable.

Station KDKA in Pittsburgh was the first radio station in the United States. Today, the station has 85 employees. Suppose there were 18 employees when the station began in 1920.

● How many more employees are there today than in 1920?

   1️⃣ **Estimate** the answer.

     Think Round each number to the nearest ten and subtract.

   2️⃣ Find the exact answer.

   3️⃣ Compare the exact answer with the estimate to check whether the exact answer is reasonable.

1️⃣ **Estimate**	2️⃣ **Exact Answer**	3️⃣ **Compare.**
$85 \rightarrow\ \ 90$ $18 \rightarrow -20$ $\overline{\quad\ \ 70}$	$\ \ 85$ -18 $\overline{\ \ 67}$	Since the estimate is 70, 67 is a reasonable answer.

There are **67 more employees** today.

Ⓔ PRACTICE • Estimate each difference. Find the exact answer. Compare.

To estimate, round each addend to the nearest ten.

1. 45	**2.** 38	**3.** 71	**4.** 85	**5.** 76
-27	-19	-43	-39	-58

To estimate, round each addend to the nearest hundred.

6. 529	**7.** 652	**8.** 863	**9.** 548	**10.** 917
-347	-275	-491	-239	-549

To estimate, round each addend to the nearest thousand.

11. 7,652	**12.** 9,364	**13.** 8,596	**14.** 5,284	**15.** 7,685
$-1,538$	$-6,179$	$-2,941$	$-1,386$	$-2,594$

EXERCISES • Estimate each difference. Find the exact answer. Compare.

To estimate, first round each number to the nearest ten.

16. 68	17. 47	18. 73	19. 86	20. 44
−27	−19	−56	−45	−28

To estimate, first round each number to the nearest hundred.

21. 922	22. 634	23. 736	24. 515	25. 863
−546	−295	−488	−275	−184

To estimate, first round each number to the nearest thousand.

26. 5,683	27. 3,493	28. 7,725	29. 6,245	30. 2,838
−4,148	−1,507	−2,184	−3,112	−1,217

To estimate, first round each number to the nearest dollar.

31. $8.67	32. $4.64	33. $6.81	34. $3.86	35. $8.12
−3.94	−2.83	−2.24	−1.51	−5.26

PROBLEM SOLVING • APPLICATIONS

Estimate each answer. Then find the exact answer.

36. The station plans to air 227 commercials on Friday and 416 on Saturday. How many more will be aired on Saturday?

37. An AM radio sells for $14.35. An AM-FM radio costs $18.95. How much more does the AM-FM radio cost?

CALCULATOR • Estimating Differences

EXERCISES • Estimate each answer. Then use a calculator to find the exact answer. Compare.

1. 7,426 − 3,863 = __?__

2. 4,263 − 1,427 = __?__

3. 5,317 − 2,611 = __?__

4. 6,755 − 4,189 = __?__

5. 9,438 − 3,729 = __?__

6. 8,125 − 2,057 = __?__

7. 4,836 − 1,927 = __?__

8. 3,894 − 1,785 = __?__

9. 9,436 − 6,871 = __?__

10. 3,842 − 1,649 = __?__

Subtracting: More Than One Regrouping

The first television was made in 1929. Color television was introduced in 1953. Today, most people have color televisions. Suppose there are 932 color televisions and 343 black-and-white televisions in one town.

● **Estimate** to find how many more color televisions there are.

Think "How many more" suggests subtraction. To estimate, first round each number to the nearest hundred.

$$932 \longrightarrow 900$$
$$-343 \longrightarrow -300$$
$$\overline{600} \blacktriangleleft \text{ Estimate}$$

There are about **600 more** color televisions.

● Exactly how many more color televisions are there?

$932 - 343 = ?$

Step 1	**Step 2**	**Step 3**
Regroup. Subtract the ones.	Regroup. Subtract the tens.	Subtract the hundreds.

2 12	12 8 2 12	12 8 2 12
9 3 2	9 3 2	9 3 2
− 3 4 3	− 3 4 3	− 3 4 3
9	8 9	5 8 9 ◀ Exact answer

There are exactly **589 more** color televisions.
Compare the exact answer with the estimate. Since the estimate is 600 televisions, 589 televisions is a reasonable answer.

More Examples

13	14	15
4 3 13	8 4 16	6 5 11
5 4 3	9 5 6	7 6 1
− 2 9 7	− 7 8 8	− 3 8 5
2 4 6	1 6 8	3 7 6

E PRACTICE • Estimate the differences. Then subtract.

1. 357 −169	2. 518 −329	3. 734 −498	4. 952 −687	5. 874 −189	6. 675 −298
7. 946 −847	8. 522 −275	9. 516 −289	10. 734 − 87	11. 342 −206	12. 711 −368

EXERCISES • Subtract.

13. 561 −478	14. 787 −389	15. 635 − 57	16. 532 −346	17. 438 −359	18. 843 −367
19. 654 −295	20. 872 −584	21. 635 −286	22. 721 −429	23. 585 −387	24. 443 −284
25. 918 −239	26. 567 −248	27. 673 −389	28. 721 − 78	29. 911 −325	30. 734 −304
31. 698 −199	32. 919 −129	33. 821 −352	34. 675 −462	35. 453 −179	36. 782 −487
37. 868 −165	38. 341 −162	39. 639 −447	40. 785 −289	41. 857 −278	42. 593 −497

43. $531 - 478 = $?   44. $842 - 49 = $?   45. $658 - 342 = $?

46. $782 - 389 = $?   47. $561 - 473 = $?   48. $582 - 283 = $?

49. $421 - 208 = $?   50. $973 - 385 = $?   51. $844 - 348 = $?

PROBLEM SOLVING • APPLICATIONS

52. Ted sold 221 color televisions in May. Marilyn sold 152 color televisions in May. How many more did Ted sell than Marilyn?

53. Mr. Thompson buys a remote control channel selector for his television. He receives 2 quarters, 1 dime, 1 nickel, and 2 pennies as his change. How much does he receive?

Zeros in Subtraction

Most television signals are sent through the air. Television station WCBA is 704 miles from Betty's house. Television station WXYZ is 236 miles from her house.

● About how many more miles does the WCBA signal travel than the WXYZ signal? **Estimate.**

Think "How many more" suggests subtraction. Round. Then subtract.

$$
\begin{array}{ccc}
704 & \longrightarrow & 700 \\
-236 & \longrightarrow & -200 \\
\hline
& & 500 \blacktriangleleft \ \text{Estimate}
\end{array}
$$

The WCBA signal travels about **500 more miles.**

● How many more miles does the WCBA signal actually travel?

$$704 - 236 = ?$$

Step 1
Regroup the hundreds.

$$
\begin{array}{r}
\overset{6\ 10}{\cancel{7}\ 0\ 4} \\
-2\ 3\ 6 \\
\hline
\end{array}
$$

Step 2
Regroup the tens.

$$
\begin{array}{r}
\overset{\ \ \ \ 9}{\overset{6\ \cancel{10}\ 14}{\cancel{7}\ \cancel{0}\ \cancel{4}}} \\
-2\ 3\ 6 \\
\hline
\end{array}
$$

Step 3
Subtract.

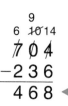

$$
\begin{array}{r}
\overset{\ \ \ \ 9}{\overset{6\ \cancel{10}\ 14}{\cancel{7}\ \cancel{0}\ 4}} \\
-2\ 3\ 6 \\
\hline
4\ 6\ 8
\end{array}
\blacktriangleleft \ \text{Exact answer}
$$

The WCBA signal travels **468 more miles.**

Compare the exact answer with the estimate.
Since the estimate is 500 miles, 468 miles is a reasonable answer.

Ⓔ **PRACTICE** • Estimate the differences. Then subtract.

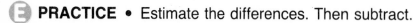

1. 905 −349	**2.** 502 −194	**3.** 504 −399	**4.** 307 −108	**5.** 604 −357	**6.** 804 −421
7. 400 −182	**8.** 506 − 37	**9.** 800 − 45	**10.** 304 −197	**11.** 607 −169	**12.** 500 −329

EXERCISES • Subtract.

13. 204
  − 59

14. 907
  −438

15. 600
  −415

16. 304
  −127

17. 800
  −405

18. 805
  −143

19. 600
  −457

20. 208
  − 39

21. 506
  −397

22. 700
  −298

23. 300
  −127

24. 905
  −807

25. 405
  −296

26. 500
  −357

27. 731
  −429

28. 908
  −149

29. 439
  −241

30. 309
  −128

31. 822
  −419

32. 702
  −405

33. 400
  − 85

34. 943
  −162

35. 615
  −229

36. 908
  −429

37. 739
  −487

38. 508
  −339

39. 819
  −185

40. 492
  −189

41. 900
  −892

42. 707
  −509

43. 818
  −399

44. 603
  −494

45. 819
  −120

46. 300
  −113

47. 590
  −327

48. 430
  −257

49. 420 − 195 = __?__

50. 504 − 309 = __?__

51. 611 − 422 = __?__

52. 717 − 409 = __?__

53. 800 − 309 = __?__

54. 650 − 362 = __?__

55. 502 − 119 = __?__

★ 56. 2,304 − 759 = __?__

★ 57. 8,003 − 494 = __?__

PROBLEM SOLVING • APPLICATIONS

58. Cable TV brings television to the home by way of cables. Tri-City Cable connected 187 homes one week and 305 homes the next week. How many more homes were connected the second week?

59. Dave is a new salesman for Tri-City Cable. He got 194 new customers his first month and 212 new customers his second month. How many new customers has he signed up in the two months?

Subtracting Greater Numbers

Some people have newspapers delivered daily to their homes. Other people buy papers from newspaper boxes. On Sunday, 6,740 papers were placed in boxes around town. During the day, 3,198 papers were bought from the boxes.

● How many papers were left in the newspaper boxes?

Think First estimate your answer. Subtract. Compare.

Estimate		Exact Answer	Compare.
6,740 ⟶	7,000	6,740	Since the estimate is 4,000,
3,198 ⟶	−3,000	−3,198	3,542 is a reasonable answer.
	4,000	3,542	

So **3,542 papers** were left in the newspaper boxes.

More Examples

$$
\begin{array}{r}
\scriptstyle 6\ 10\ 3\ 12 \\
7{,}0\,4\,2 \\
-\ 5{,}3\,3\,8 \\
\hline
1{,}7\,0\,4
\end{array}
\qquad
\begin{array}{r}
\scriptstyle 4\ 12\ 8\ 14 \\
5\,2{,}9\,4\,1 \\
-\ 2\,4{,}7\,5\,0 \\
\hline
2\,8{,}1\,9\,1
\end{array}
\qquad
\begin{array}{r}
\scriptstyle 3\ 18\ 2\ 12 \\
7\,4{,}8\,3\,2 \\
-\quad 3{,}9\,0\,6 \\
\hline
7\,0{,}9\,2\,6
\end{array}
\qquad
\begin{array}{r}
\scriptstyle 4\ 9\ 9\ 10 \\
2\,5{,}0\,0\,0 \\
-\qquad 4\,9\,6 \\
\hline
2\,4{,}5\,0\,4
\end{array}
$$

Ｅ **PRACTICE** • Estimate the differences. Subtract. Compare.

1. 6,079 −3,504	**2.** 2,910 −1,786	**3.** 7,805 −3,688	**4.** 3,264 −1,576	**5.** 8,721 −2,645
6. 9,325 −7,264	**7.** 4,070 −3,648	**8.** 27,025 −14,892	**9.** 18,754 − 5,936	**10.** 65,768 −32,889

EXERCISES • Subtract

11. 5,763 −2,697	**12.** 6,438 −4,659	**13.** 4,253 −⠀⠀⠀6	**14.** 8,346 −⠀⠀79	**15.** 5,374 −⠀685
16. 3,954 −1,876	**17.** 6,745 −3,868	**18.** 7,242 −2,567	**19.** 1,760 −⠀357	**20.** 7,239 −1,807
21. 8,462 −⠀789	**22.** 7,146 −6,687	**23.** 6,899 −2,798	**24.** 5,321 −4,563	**25.** 5,697 −5,286
26. 5,093 −⠀785	**27.** 9,432 −4,984	**28.** 17,804 −⠀5,921	**29.** 36,847 −⠀2,603	**30.** 54,926 −⠀7,957

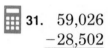

31. 59,026 −28,502	**32.** 74,070 −46,921	**33.** 41,005 −⠀⠀426	**34.** 30,320 −⠀1,857	**35.** 83,000 −14,162

36. 8,704 − 1,325 = _⠀?⠀_

37. 9,005 − 1,236 = _⠀?⠀_

38. 7,400 − 6,592 = _⠀?⠀_

39. 13,572 − 4,906 = _⠀?⠀_

40. 63,000 − 14,521 = _⠀?⠀_

41. 70,009 − 41,035 = _⠀?⠀_

PROBLEM SOLVING • APPLICATIONS

CHOOSE • estimation • mental math • pencil and paper • calculator SOLVE

42. Sunday's newspaper had 5,765 classified ads. Monday's paper had 3,937 ads. How many more ads were in Sunday's paper?

43. On Sunday, 23,734 copies of the *Daily Herald* and 17,429 copies of the *Daily Mirror* were sold. How many more copies of the *Daily Herald* were sold?

44. There were 38,415 papers printed on Monday. Of these, 31,279 papers were sold How many papers were not sold?

45. There were 19,348 papers sold on Monday and 18,792 papers sold on Tuesday. How many papers were sold in all?

46. Martha's monthly bill for home delivery of her newspaper is $8.96. She pays with a ten-dollar bill. How much change does she receive?

★ **47.** At least 300 papers are sold each day at the newsstand. During February 8,435 papers were sold. During March 9,789 papers were sold. How many more papers were sold during March?

Adding and Subtracting Money

Today phone companies are offering many new services. One new service is *Call Waiting*. Mr. Simmons pays $9.95 each month for basic telephone service. He pays an extra $2.35 each month for *Call Waiting*.

● How much does Mr. Simmons pay each month for both services?

Think To find *both,* you add.

$9.95 + $2.35 = ?

Line up the cents point. Add.

```
  $9.95
+  2.35
 $12.30
```
◄ Write a dollar sign and cents point.

Mr. Simmons pays **$12.30** each month for both services.

Mrs. Jamison wants to buy a wall telephone for $36.95 and a telephone jack for $3.99. She has $40.00.

● Does she have enough money?

Think The total must be less than $40.00. **Estimate** the sum. Round to the nearest dollar.

```
$36.95 →   $37.00
$ 3.99 → +  4.00
           $41.00
```

Since $41.00 is greater than $40.00, Mrs. Jamison **does not have enough money.**

Ms. Jackson has *Call Waiting* and several other services. She pays $17.85 each month.

● How much more does Ms. Jackson pay than Mr. Simmons?

Think To find *how much more,* you subtract.

$17.85 − $12.30 = ?

Line up the cents point. Subtract.

```
  $17.85
−  12.30
 $ 5.55
```
◄ Write a dollar sign and cents point.

Ms. Jackson pays **$5.55** more than Mr. Simmons.

PRACTICE • Add.

1. $8.92
  + 6.09

2. $6.74
  + 6.92

3. $0.49
  + 8.76

4. $34.76
  + 74.75

5. $80.17
  + 58.90

Subtract.

6. $66.57
  − 8.68

7. $50.05
  − 38.97

8. $51.13
  − 23.48

9. $46.52
  − 6.86

10. $18.00
  − 9.43

EXERCISES • Add.

11. $60.46
  + 9.97

12. $ 9.47
  + 83.62

13. $69.73
  + 94.43

14. $78.45
  + 49.27

15. $ 6.39
  + 38.59

16. $73.28
  + 85.72

17. $93.42
  + 1.93

18. $63.11
  + 75.89

19. $33.37
  + 81.70

20. $32.43
  + 0.86

21. $61.06
  + 5.35

22. $85.80
  + 76.42

23. $29.40
  + 2.12

★ 24. $358.45
  + 419.73

★ 25. $583.25
  + 236.95

Subtract.

26. $61.18
  − 8.59

27. $16.56
  − 8.21

28. $94.66
  − 39.87

29. $90.05
  − 26.46

30. $73.44
  − 69.65

31. $53.67
  − 7.22

32. $87.33
  − 27.37

33. $91.13
  − 6.75

34. $51.02
  − 42.94

35. $63.73
  − 14.21

36. $50.03
  − 35.49

37. $84.36
  − 34.29

38. $60.00
  − 25.52

★ 39. $637.21
  − 22.78

★ 40. $472.82
  − 256.15

PROBLEM SOLVING • APPLICATIONS

41. Ms. Thomas pays $17.85 each month for phone service. In January she also paid $35.67 for long distance calls. How much was her total January bill?

42. Mr. Powell bought a kitchen phone for $49.37. He also bought a desk phone for $54.95. How much more was the desk phone?

43. Mrs. Kim has $40.00. She wants to buy a wall telephone for $36.95 and some telephone wire for $4.99. Does she have enough money?

★ 44. Mr. Caruso has $50.00. He wants to buy a desk telephone for $36.95 and two telephone jacks for $3.99 each. Does he have enough money?

NON-ROUTINE PROBLEM SOLVING

Sometimes solving problems involves making choices. The choice you make depends on what is best for you in a given situation.

Trish uses the telephone to order her lunch from McLean's Diner. She wants to choose one item from each of the four basic food groups.

Four Basic Food Groups

Milk Group

Fruit and Vegetable Group

Meat Group

Bread and Cereal Group

LUNCH McLEAN'S DINER

Ham	$2.29	Baked Potato	$0.67	Green Beans	$0.65
Turkey	$2.19	Mashed Potato	$0.55	Broccoli	$0.69
Roast Beef	$2.75	Macaroni and		Lima Beans	$0.59
Chicken	$2.09	Cheese	$0.67	Peas	$0.59
Hamburger	$1.95	Roll	$0.21	Squash	$0.65
		Salad	$0.79	Pudding	$0.75
		Jello	$0.77	Pie	$0.69
		Apple	$0.85	Milk	$0.45

Trish can choose her meal from this menu. She can spend up to $4.00 for her meal. She listed three possible choices.

Choice 1	**Choice 2**	**Choice 3**
Ham	Turkey	Chicken
Broccoli	Salad, Roll	Mashed Potato
Milk	Milk	Peas
Roll	Pudding	Milk

Finding the Cost

1. **Choice 1**
   a. How much does Choice 1 cost?
   b. Is Choice 1 greater than or less than $4.00?
   c. Is Choice 1 a balanced meal?

2. **Choice 2**
   a. How much does Choice 2 cost?
   b. Is Choice 2 greater than or less than $4.00?
   c. Is Choice 2 a balanced meal?

3. **Choice 3**
   a. How much does Choice 3 cost?
   b. Is Choice 3 greater than or less than $4.00?
   c. Is Choice 3 a balanced meal?

Making a Choice

4. If you were Trish, what choice would you make?

5. Suppose you could add a food to Choice 3. What food could you add to make a balanced meal? Would the meal cost less than $4.00?

6. Suppose you took away a food item in Choice 2. What food could you take away and still have a balanced meal? Would the meal cost less than $4.00?

7. Suppose your family went to McLean's Diner for lunch. Choose a different balanced meal for each member of your family. Each person can spend $6.00 for the meal.

CHAPTER REVIEW

Part 1: VOCABULARY

For Exercises 1–5, choose from the box at the right the word that completes the sentence.

1. An answer that is close to the exact answer is an ___?___. (Page 62)

2. In the problem at the right, you cannot subtract 3 from 1. So you must ___?___. (Page 70)

$$\begin{array}{r} 71 \\ -23 \end{array}$$

3. To check the answer to a subtraction problem, you ___?___. (Page 70)

4. In the problem at the right, 13 ones are regrouped as one ___?___ and 3 ones. (Page 56)

$$\begin{array}{r} 1 \\ 28 \\ +45 \\ \hline 3 \end{array}$$

5. Before you estimate a sum, you should ___?___ each addend. (Page 62)

add
estimate
hundred
regroup
round
subtract
ten

Part 2: SKILLS

Add. (Pages 56–61, 64–67)

6. $\begin{array}{r} 45 \\ +32 \\ \hline \end{array}$ 7. $\begin{array}{r} 203 \\ +\ 92 \\ \hline \end{array}$ 8. $\begin{array}{r} 174 \\ +314 \\ \hline \end{array}$ 9. $\begin{array}{r} 8,117 \\ +\ 562 \\ \hline \end{array}$ 10. $\begin{array}{r} 24,366 \\ +20,613 \\ \hline \end{array}$

11. $\begin{array}{r} 37 \\ +48 \\ \hline \end{array}$ 12. $\begin{array}{r} 62 \\ +78 \\ \hline \end{array}$ 13. $\begin{array}{r} 482 \\ +\ 37 \\ \hline \end{array}$ 14. $\begin{array}{r} 170 \\ +694 \\ \hline \end{array}$ 15. $\begin{array}{r} 957 \\ +255 \\ \hline \end{array}$

16. $\begin{array}{r} 3,664 \\ +3,918 \\ \hline \end{array}$ 17. $\begin{array}{r} 18,253 \\ +57,198 \\ \hline \end{array}$ 18. $\begin{array}{r} 75 \\ 46 \\ +91 \\ \hline \end{array}$ 19. $\begin{array}{r} 261 \\ 58 \\ +542 \\ \hline \end{array}$ 20. $\begin{array}{r} 3,097 \\ 232 \\ +1,654 \\ \hline \end{array}$

Estimate the sum. Find the exact answer. Compare. (Pages 62–63)
To estimate, first round to the nearest

ten.   hundred.   hundred.   dollar.   thousand.

21. $\begin{array}{r} 54 \\ +35 \\ \hline \end{array}$ ___   22. $\begin{array}{r} 260 \\ +425 \\ \hline \end{array}$ ___   23. $\begin{array}{r} 819 \\ +376 \\ \hline \end{array}$ ___   24. $\begin{array}{r} \$2.95 \\ +\ 4.59 \\ \hline \end{array}$ ___   25. $\begin{array}{r} 6,247 \\ +1,398 \\ \hline \end{array}$ ___

Subtract. (Pages 70–73, 78–83)

26. 76	27. 285	28. 639	29. 9,448	30. 25,662
−31	− 65	−514	−1,231	−14,251

31. 83	32. 356	33. 423	34. 937	35. 607
−64	−129	−271	−268	− 92

36. 800	37. 5,466	38. 1,901	39. 32,009	40. 75,007
−315	−1,878	− 763	−1,451	−48,216

Estimate the difference. Find the exact answer. Compare. (Pages 76–77)
To estimate, first round to the nearest

ten.	hundred.	hundred.	dollar.	thousand.
41. 47	42. 716	43. 652	44. $9.25	45. 4,610
−23	−284	−143	− 5.49	−1,786

Add or subtract. (Pages 84–85)

46. $49.95	47. $10.50	48. $93.83	49. $13.65	50. $85.00
− 6.25	+ 24.69	− 72.96	− 3.78	− 58.32

Part 3: PROBLEM SOLVING • APPLICATIONS

51. The owner of Sights and Sounds has 27 black and white televisions in the store. He also has 44 color televisions. How many more color televisions than black and white televisions does the store have? (Pages 74–75)

52. A television signal travels 173 miles to a satellite. It then travels 439 more miles. How far does the signal travel in all?
(Pages 74–75)

53. The manager at Wiztez Computer Company has 428 computers. He sells 319 of them. How many are left? (Pages 74–75)

54. David has $60.00. He wants to buy a telephone for $48.95 and a phone jack for $6.88. Does he have enough money? (Pages 84–85)

55. Casey wants to buy a record album and two cassette tapes. He has $25.00. An album costs $12.95. A cassette tape costs $8.99. Does he have enough money? (Pages 84–85)

56. Mrs. Chin budgets $26.00 for monthly telephone service. In October, her bill was $18.49 for service and $7.89 for long distance calls. Does she have enough money budgeted to pay the bill?
(Pages 84–85)

Addition and Subtraction • **89**

CHAPTER TEST

Add.

1. 16
  +72

2. 406
  +275

3. 625
  +197

4. 7,359
  +1,812

5. 718
  264
  +193

6. 28 + 35 = ___?___

7. 318 + 493 = ___?___

8. $17.84 + $38.92 = ___?___

Estimate each sum. Find the exact answer. Compare. To estimate, first round to the nearest

ten.

hundred.

dollar.

9. 36 + 43 = ___?___

10. 781 + 234 = ___?___

11. $23.14 + $57.68 = ___?___

Subtract.

12. 82
  −51

13. 926
  −417

14. 318
  −149

15. 500
  −261

16. 8,346
  −1,907

17. 95 − 38 = ___?___

18. 908 − 319 = ___?___

Estimate each difference. Find the exact answer. Compare. To estimate, first round to the nearest

ten.

hundred.

dollar.

19. 87 − 39 = ___?___

20. 513 − 291 = ___?___

21. $43.72 − $18.59 = ___?___

Solve

22. Maxine used her computer 30 hours one week. She used it 42 hours the next week. How many total hours did Maxine use her computer during those two weeks?

23. On Tuesday, Ron delivered 215 newspapers and Jack delivered 324 newspapers. How many more newspapers did Jack deliver than Ron?

24. The *Daily Sun* has 138 part-time employees. It has 467 full-time employees. How many employees are there altogether?

25. Jack has 1,842 newspapers. He delivers 1,285 of them. How many are left?

ENRICHMENT

Palindromes

A **palindrome** is a word or a number that reads the same forward or backward.

MOM and TOOT are word palindromes.
4,774, and 58,985 are number palindromes.

Follow these steps to get a palindrome.

1. Write a number. —————————→ 847
2. Reverse the digits. —————————→ +748
3. Add. —————————————→ 1,595
4. Reverse these digits. —————————→ +5,951
5. Add. —————————————→ 7,546
6. Continue until you get   +6,457
   a palindrome.   14,003
                            +30,041
   Palindrome —————————→   44,044

EXERCISES • Use these numbers to get palindromes.

1. 27   2. 38   3. 349   4. 518   5. 685

6. 728   7. 843   8. 994   9. 3,259   10. 5,482

ADDITIONAL PRACTICE

SKILLS

Add. (Pages 56–61, 64–67)

1. 52 +14	**2.** 47 +16	**3.** 534 +339	**4.** 381 +259	**5.** 879 +486
6. 7,650 +5,793	**7.** 72,509 + 8,492	**8.** 217 86 +459	**9.** 528 788 +947	**10.** 4,685 6,194 +5,352

Subtract. (Pages 70–73, 78–81)

11. 86 −42	**12.** 75 −38	**13.** 875 −380	**14.** 787 −389	**15.** 443 −384
16. 506 −168	**17.** 900 −162	**18.** 9,325 −7,264	**19.** 2,371 − 856	**20.** 73,805 −48,697

Estimate the sum or difference. Find the exact answer. Compare. (Pages 62–63, 76–77)
To estimate, first round to the nearest

ten.	hundred.	thousand.	hundred.	dollar.
21. 62 +25	**22.** 721 +474	**23.** 3,027 +4,398	**24.** 893 −430	**25.** $6.05 − 5.29

Add or subtract. (Pages 84–85)

26. $6.98 + 8.59	**27.** $42.89 + 77.32	**28.** $7.46 − 3.48	**29.** $25.32 − 18.75	**30.** $50.00 − 32.87

PROBLEM SOLVING • APPLICATIONS

31. The newsstand received 1,465 papers to sell. There were 1,248 papers sold. How many papers are left? (Pages 74–75)

32. The post office sold 12,463 stamps one morning and 14,962 that afternoon. How many stamps were sold altogether? (Pages 74–75)

33. Rico delivered 148 papers. Jason delivered 212 papers. How many more papers did Jason deliver than Rico? (Pages 74–75)

34. Caren wants to buy two tapes for $6.99 each. She has $15.00. Does she have enough money? (Pages 84–85)

PROBLEM SOLVING MAINTENANCE

Solve.

1. Roland had 15 goldfish in his bowl. He gave 7 goldfish to his friend. How many goldfish did he have left? (Page 12)

2. Jacques had 7 goldfish and 6 guppies in his aquarium. He bought 4 angelfish to put in the aquarium. How many fish does he have in all? (Page 12)

3. Pauline went to the pet store to buy fish for her aquarium. She wanted to buy 12 fish. She found 4 goldfish and 5 guppies. How many more fish does she need? (Page 16)

4. Sarah bought 11 cans of dog food for her dog. She used 3 of them. How many cans are left? (Page 16)

5. The pet shop has 4 puppies. The poodle weighs less than the boxer. The spaniel weighs more than the boxer. The beagle weighs more than the boxer but less than the spaniel. Which dog weighs the most? (Page 34)

6. Matthew bought his cat a ball for $0.77. He gave the clerk $1.00. His change was 3 pennies, 1 dime and one other coin. What was the other coin? (Page 46)

7. Jacob gave the clerk $1.00 for $0.47 worth of fish food. The clerk gave Jacob 3 pennies, 2 nickels, and some dimes. How many dimes did he receive? (Page 46)

8. The pet store has 652 rawhide bones in stock. The clerk ordered 838 more rawhide bones. How many bones will the store have altogether? (Page 74)

9. The pet store has 200 parakeet cages and 47 parrot cages. How many more parakeet cages than parrot cages does the store have? (Page 74)

10. The pet store sold 786 dogs in 1984. They sold 1,279 dogs in 1985. How many dogs were sold in all? (Page 74)

Mixed Practice • Choose the correct answers.

1. $9 + 9 + 9 + 9 =$ ___?___

A. 36   B. 27
C. 32   D. not here

2. $7 + 7 + 7 + 7 =$ ___?___

A. 48   B. 35
C. 42   D. not here

3. $6 + 6 + 6 + 6 =$ ___?___

A. 18   B. 24
C. 21   D. not here

4. Choose the correct sign.

9 ● 11

A. =   B. <
C. >   D. not here

5. Choose the correct sign.

61 ● 21

A. =   B. <
C. >   D. not here

6. Choose the correct sign.

$8 + 7 + 4$ ● 19

A. >   B. =
C. <   D. not here

7. $10 + \underline{\ \ ?\ \ } = 21$

A. 11   B. 12
C. 10   D. not here

8. $28 - \underline{\ \ ?\ \ } = 11$

A. 18   B. 16
C. 17   D. not here

9. $47 + \underline{\ \ ?\ \ } = 64$

A. 27   B. 17
C. 23   D. not here

10. The telephone repairman repaired 27 telephones on Monday. On Tuesday he repaired 34. How many telephones did he repair in all?

A. 63   B. 7
C. 61   D. not here

11. The appliance store sold 147 black and white televisions and 339 color televisions in one week. How many more color televisions did the store sell?

A. 192   B. 112
C. 486   D. not here

Multiplication and Division Facts

Hawaiians often use *double outrigger* canoes to travel from island to island. Each canoe has 2 outriggers.

A group of canoes has 18 outriggers.

● How many canoes are there?

A dog sled is a dependable way to travel in the Arctic. Each sled is pulled by 4 dogs.

● How many sleds can be pulled by 20 dogs?

95

2 and 3 as Factors

In 1871, James Starley invented the bicycle. The word
bicycle has the prefix **bi** which means **two**.

● How many wheels are there on 6 bicycles?

Think You can count by 2's. 2 4 6 8 10 12

You can add. 2 + 2 + 2 + 2 + 2 + 2 = 12

Each bicycle has 2 wheels. Multiply.

$$6 \times 2 = 12$$

factor factor product

$$\begin{array}{r} 2 \leftarrow \text{factor} \\ \times 6 \leftarrow \text{factor} \\ \hline 12 \leftarrow \text{product} \end{array}$$

There are **12 wheels** on 6 bicycles.

The first tricycle had two huge wheels in front and one small wheel
behind. Tricycle has the prefix **tri** which means **three**.

● How many wheels are there on 4 tricycles?

Think Each tricycle has 3 wheels.
Multiply

$$4 \times 3 = 12 \qquad \begin{array}{r} 3 \\ \times 4 \\ \hline 12 \end{array}$$

There are **12 wheels.**

PRACTICE • Find the products.

1.
$$\begin{array}{r} 2 \\ \times 1 \end{array} \quad \begin{array}{r} 2 \\ \times 2 \end{array} \quad \begin{array}{r} 2 \\ \times 3 \end{array} \quad \begin{array}{r} 2 \\ \times 4 \end{array} \quad \begin{array}{r} 2 \\ \times 5 \end{array} \quad \begin{array}{r} 2 \\ \times 6 \end{array} \quad \begin{array}{r} 2 \\ \times 7 \end{array} \quad \begin{array}{r} 2 \\ \times 8 \end{array} \quad \begin{array}{r} 2 \\ \times 9 \end{array}$$

2.
$$\begin{array}{r} 3 \\ \times 1 \end{array} \quad \begin{array}{r} 3 \\ \times 2 \end{array} \quad \begin{array}{r} 3 \\ \times 3 \end{array} \quad \begin{array}{r} 3 \\ \times 4 \end{array} \quad \begin{array}{r} 3 \\ \times 5 \end{array} \quad \begin{array}{r} 3 \\ \times 6 \end{array} \quad \begin{array}{r} 3 \\ \times 7 \end{array} \quad \begin{array}{r} 3 \\ \times 8 \end{array} \quad \begin{array}{r} 3 \\ \times 9 \end{array}$$

Multiply.

3. $2 \times 2 =$ ___?___   **4.** $4 \times 2 =$ ___?___   **5.** $6 \times 3 =$ ___?___   **6.** $4 \times 3 =$ ___?___

7. $\begin{array}{r} 3 \\ \times 2 \\ \hline \end{array}$ **8.** $\begin{array}{r} 3 \\ \times 9 \\ \hline \end{array}$ **9.** $\begin{array}{r} 2 \\ \times 7 \\ \hline \end{array}$ **10.** $\begin{array}{r} 3 \\ \times 7 \\ \hline \end{array}$ **11.** $\begin{array}{r} 2 \\ \times 5 \\ \hline \end{array}$ **12.** $\begin{array}{r} 3 \\ \times 8 \\ \hline \end{array}$ **13.** $\begin{array}{r} 2 \\ \times 1 \\ \hline \end{array}$

EXERCISES • Multiply.

14. $6 \times 3 =$ ___?___   **15.** $8 \times 2 =$ ___?___   **16.** $9 \times 3 =$ ___?___   **17.** $7 \times 3 =$ ___?___

18. $3 \times 2 =$ ___?___   **19.** $9 \times 2 =$ ___?___   **20.** $8 \times 2 =$ ___?___   **21.** $9 \times 3 =$ ___?___

22. $3 \times 3 =$ ___?___   **23.** $4 \times 2 =$ ___?___   **24.** $6 \times 2 =$ ___?___   **25.** $9 \times 2 =$ ___?___

26. $\begin{array}{r} 2 \\ \times 5 \\ \hline \end{array}$ **27.** $\begin{array}{r} 2 \\ \times 4 \\ \hline \end{array}$ **28.** $\begin{array}{r} 3 \\ \times 5 \\ \hline \end{array}$ **29.** $\begin{array}{r} 2 \\ \times 6 \\ \hline \end{array}$ **30.** $\begin{array}{r} 2 \\ \times 8 \\ \hline \end{array}$ **31.** $\begin{array}{r} 2 \\ \times 7 \\ \hline \end{array}$

32. $\begin{array}{r} 3 \\ \times 4 \\ \hline \end{array}$ **33.** $\begin{array}{r} 3 \\ \times 8 \\ \hline \end{array}$ **34.** $\begin{array}{r} 3 \\ \times 6 \\ \hline \end{array}$ **35.** $\begin{array}{r} 2 \\ \times 2 \\ \hline \end{array}$ **36.** $\begin{array}{r} 3 \\ \times 4 \\ \hline \end{array}$ **37.** $\begin{array}{r} 2 \\ \times 3 \\ \hline \end{array}$

38. $\begin{array}{r} 3 \\ \times 5 \\ \hline \end{array}$ **39.** $\begin{array}{r} 3 \\ \times 7 \\ \hline \end{array}$ **40.** $\begin{array}{r} 3 \\ \times 3 \\ \hline \end{array}$ **41.** $\begin{array}{r} 2 \\ \times 5 \\ \hline \end{array}$ **42.** $\begin{array}{r} 2 \\ \times 9 \\ \hline \end{array}$ **43.** $\begin{array}{r} 3 \\ \times 9 \\ \hline \end{array}$

Complete. Work inside the parentheses first.

★ **44.** $(4 + 2) \times 3 =$ ___?___   ★ **45.** $(14 - 9) \times 2 =$ ___?___   ★ **46.** $5 \times (7 - 4) =$ ___?___

PROBLEM SOLVING • APPLICATIONS

47. A bicycle "built for two" can carry 2 people. How many people can ride on 8 bicycles built for two?

48. Jim's bicycle has 3 plastic streamers on each hand grip. How many plastic streamers are on Jim's bicycle?

★ **49.** There are 3 girls with bicycles. Each bicycle has 2 reflectors on each wheel. How many reflectors are there in all?

THINKER'S CORNER

There are bicycles and tricycles in the bike rack. There are 12 wheels in all. How many bicycles are there?

4 and 5 as Factors

In 1908, the *Model T* became the first car ever made on an assembly line. The Model T had 4 cylinders in the engine.

● How many cylinders are there in 3 Model T's?

Think There are 4 cylinders in one car. Multiply to find how many are in 3 cars.

$$3 \times 4 = 12$$

$$\begin{array}{r} 4 \\ \times 3 \\ \hline 12 \end{array}$$

There are **12 cylinders** in 3 Model T's.

Each Model T can carry 5 people.

● How many people can ride in 3 Model T's?

Think 5 people can ride in one Model T. Multiply to find how many can ride in 3 Model T's.

$$3 \times 5 = 15$$

$$\begin{array}{r} 5 \\ \times 3 \\ \hline 15 \end{array}$$

So, **15 people** can ride in 3 Model T's.

PRACTICE • Find the products.

1.
$\begin{array}{r} 4 \\ \times 1 \\ \hline \end{array}$
$\begin{array}{r} 4 \\ \times 2 \\ \hline \end{array}$
$\begin{array}{r} 4 \\ \times 3 \\ \hline \end{array}$
$\begin{array}{r} 4 \\ \times 4 \\ \hline \end{array}$
$\begin{array}{r} 4 \\ \times 5 \\ \hline \end{array}$
$\begin{array}{r} 4 \\ \times 6 \\ \hline \end{array}$
$\begin{array}{r} 4 \\ \times 7 \\ \hline \end{array}$
$\begin{array}{r} 4 \\ \times 8 \\ \hline \end{array}$
$\begin{array}{r} 4 \\ \times 9 \\ \hline \end{array}$

2.
$\begin{array}{r} 5 \\ \times 1 \\ \hline \end{array}$
$\begin{array}{r} 5 \\ \times 2 \\ \hline \end{array}$
$\begin{array}{r} 5 \\ \times 3 \\ \hline \end{array}$
$\begin{array}{r} 5 \\ \times 4 \\ \hline \end{array}$
$\begin{array}{r} 5 \\ \times 5 \\ \hline \end{array}$
$\begin{array}{r} 5 \\ \times 6 \\ \hline \end{array}$
$\begin{array}{r} 5 \\ \times 7 \\ \hline \end{array}$
$\begin{array}{r} 5 \\ \times 8 \\ \hline \end{array}$
$\begin{array}{r} 5 \\ \times 9 \\ \hline \end{array}$

3. $7 \times 4 = $ ___?___   **4.** $5 \times 5 = $ ___?___   **5.** $6 \times 4 = $ ___?___   **6.** $8 \times 5 = $ ___?___

7.	**8.**	**9.**	**10.**	**11.**	**12.**	**13.**
4	5	4	5	3	5	4
$\times 5$	$\times 7$	$\times 9$	$\times 6$	$\times 5$	$\times 9$	$\times 1$

EXERCISES • Multiply

14. $2 \times 4 = $ ___?___   **15.** $8 \times 4 = $ ___?___   **16.** $4 \times 4 = $ ___?___   **17.** $2 \times 5 = $ ___?___

18. $4 \times 5 = $ ___?___   **19.** $3 \times 4 = $ ___?___   **20.** $6 \times 5 = $ ___?___   **21.** $8 \times 5 = $ ___?___

22. $6 \times 4 = $ ___?___   **23.** $3 \times 2 = $ ___?___   **24.** $5 \times 4 = $ ___?___   **25.** $9 \times 2 = $ ___?___

26.	**27.**	**28.**	**29.**	**30.**	**31.**	**32.**
5	4	5	2	3	4	5
$\times 3$	$\times 3$	$\times 7$	$\times 6$	$\times 5$	$\times 6$	$\times 6$

33.	**34.**	**35.**	**36.**	**37.**	**38.**	**39.**
5	5	4	2	3	2	3
$\times 5$	$\times 4$	$\times 4$	$\times 4$	$\times 8$	$\times 5$	$\times 4$

40.	**41.**	**42.**	**43.**	**44.**	**45.**	**46.**
4	5	3	3	4	3	4
$\times 7$	$\times 9$	$\times 3$	$\times 6$	$\times 9$	$\times 7$	$\times 8$

Write a multiplication fact for the product. Use 4 or 5 as
one of the factors.

★ **47.** 12 ★ **48.** 20 ★ **49.** 36 ★ **50.** 40 ★ **51.** 28 ★ **52.** 45

PROBLEM SOLVING • APPLICATIONS

53. Each Model T has 5 lights. How many lights are on 7 Model T's?

54. Ruben sells car batteries. He has 4 shelves with 5 batteries on each shelf. How many batteries are on the shelves?

55. A parking lot has 35 cars in the front lot and 28 in the back lot. How many more cars are in the front lot than in the back lot?

★ **56.** Each car has 4 tires and 1 spare tire. How many tires are needed for 6 cars?

6 and 7 as Factors

Trucks can be used to provide door-to-door freight service. A truck brings cars from the factory directly to the car dealer.

One truck can carry 6 vans.

● How many vans can 8 trucks carry?

Think Each truck can carry 6 vans. Multiply to find how many 8 trucks can carry.

$$8 \times 6 = 48 \qquad \begin{array}{r} 6 \\ \times 8 \\ \hline 48 \end{array}$$

The 8 trucks can carry **48 vans.**

Logging trucks carry logs from the forest to the saw mill. One truck can carry 7 logs.

● How many logs can 6 trucks carry?

Think Each truck can carry 7 logs. Multiply to find how many 6 trucks can carry.

$$6 \times 7 = 42 \qquad \begin{array}{r} 7 \\ \times 6 \\ \hline 42 \end{array}$$

The 6 trucks can carry **42 logs.**

PRACTICE • Find the products.

1. $\begin{array}{r} 6 \\ \times 1 \\ \hline \end{array}$ $\begin{array}{r} 6 \\ \times 2 \\ \hline \end{array}$ $\begin{array}{r} 6 \\ \times 3 \\ \hline \end{array}$ $\begin{array}{r} 6 \\ \times 4 \\ \hline \end{array}$ $\begin{array}{r} 6 \\ \times 5 \\ \hline \end{array}$ $\begin{array}{r} 6 \\ \times 6 \\ \hline \end{array}$ $\begin{array}{r} 6 \\ \times 7 \\ \hline \end{array}$ $\begin{array}{r} 6 \\ \times 8 \\ \hline \end{array}$ $\begin{array}{r} 6 \\ \times 9 \\ \hline \end{array}$

2. $\begin{array}{r} 7 \\ \times 1 \\ \hline \end{array}$ $\begin{array}{r} 7 \\ \times 2 \\ \hline \end{array}$ $\begin{array}{r} 7 \\ \times 3 \\ \hline \end{array}$ $\begin{array}{r} 7 \\ \times 4 \\ \hline \end{array}$ $\begin{array}{r} 7 \\ \times 5 \\ \hline \end{array}$ $\begin{array}{r} 7 \\ \times 6 \\ \hline \end{array}$ $\begin{array}{r} 7 \\ \times 7 \\ \hline \end{array}$ $\begin{array}{r} 7 \\ \times 8 \\ \hline \end{array}$ $\begin{array}{r} 7 \\ \times 9 \\ \hline \end{array}$

3. $6 \times 7 = $ _?_   4. $9 \times 6 = $ _?_   5. $4 \times 7 = $ _?_   6. $3 \times 6 = $ _?_

7. $\begin{array}{r} 7 \\ \times 8 \\ \hline \end{array}$ 8. $\begin{array}{r} 7 \\ \times 2 \\ \hline \end{array}$ 9. $\begin{array}{r} 6 \\ \times 6 \\ \hline \end{array}$ 10. $\begin{array}{r} 6 \\ \times 8 \\ \hline \end{array}$ 11. $\begin{array}{r} 7 \\ \times 3 \\ \hline \end{array}$ 12. $\begin{array}{r} 6 \\ \times 5 \\ \hline \end{array}$ 13. $\begin{array}{r} 7 \\ \times 9 \\ \hline \end{array}$

14. $7 \times 6 = $ _?_ **15.** $4 \times 6 = $ _?_ **16.** $2 \times 6 = $ _?_ **17.** $5 \times 7 = $ _?_

18. $7 \times 7 = $ _?_ **19.** $9 \times 7 = $ _?_ **20.** $6 \times 5 = $ _?_ **21.** $7 \times 3 = $ _?_

22. $1 \times 6 = $ _?_ **23.** $7 \times 4 = $ _?_ **24.** $4 \times 6 = $ _?_ **25.** $6 \times 6 = $ _?_

26. $\begin{array}{r} 6 \\ \times 9 \\ \hline \end{array}$ **27.** $\begin{array}{r} 4 \\ \times 6 \\ \hline \end{array}$ **28.** $\begin{array}{r} 5 \\ \times 7 \\ \hline \end{array}$ **29.** $\begin{array}{r} 6 \\ \times 8 \\ \hline \end{array}$ **30.** $\begin{array}{r} 4 \\ \times 7 \\ \hline \end{array}$ **31.** $\begin{array}{r} 5 \\ \times 7 \\ \hline \end{array}$ **32.** $\begin{array}{r} 6 \\ \times 8 \\ \hline \end{array}$

33. $\begin{array}{r} 7 \\ \times 6 \\ \hline \end{array}$ **34.** $\begin{array}{r} 2 \\ \times 6 \\ \hline \end{array}$ **35.** $\begin{array}{r} 7 \\ \times 9 \\ \hline \end{array}$ **36.** $\begin{array}{r} 7 \\ \times 7 \\ \hline \end{array}$ **37.** $\begin{array}{r} 4 \\ \times 3 \\ \hline \end{array}$ **38.** $\begin{array}{r} 7 \\ \times 8 \\ \hline \end{array}$ **39.** $\begin{array}{r} 7 \\ \times 9 \\ \hline \end{array}$

40. $\begin{array}{r} 5 \\ \times 4 \\ \hline \end{array}$ **41.** $\begin{array}{r} 3 \\ \times 6 \\ \hline \end{array}$ **42.** $\begin{array}{r} 2 \\ \times 7 \\ \hline \end{array}$ **43.** $\begin{array}{r} 5 \\ \times 3 \\ \hline \end{array}$ **44.** $\begin{array}{r} 4 \\ \times 8 \\ \hline \end{array}$ **45.** $\begin{array}{r} 3 \\ \times 7 \\ \hline \end{array}$ **46.** $\begin{array}{r} 6 \\ \times 6 \\ \hline \end{array}$

Multiply. Then write $>$ or $<$.

★ **47.** 7×8 ⬤ 59 ★ **48.** 24 ⬤ 7×3 ★ **49.** 43 ⬤ 6×7

★ **50.** 5×6 ⬤ 7×4 ★ **51.** 9×3 ⬤ 8×4 ★ **52.** 4×6 ⬤ 5×5

PROBLEM SOLVING • APPLICATIONS

53. A factory ships washing machines to its customers by truck. One truck can carry 6 machines. How many machines would be on 9 trucks?

54. A bookmobile is a truck containing library books. There are 3 shelves with 7 books on each shelf. How many books are there?

55. There are 4 vehicles stopped at the light. The pickup truck is behind the van and in front of the taxi. The taxi is between the pickup truck and the car. Which is first in line?

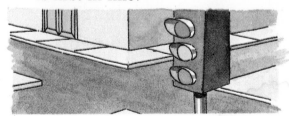

THINKER'S CORNER

Use these clues to find the digits on Bob's license plate. His plate has his name, followed by the last two digits of the year he was born.

Clue 1: Their sum is 9.
Clue 2: Their product is 18.
Clue 3: The first number is twice the second.

8 and 9 as Factors

The railroad played a very important part in the settling of the West. In 1878, the trip from coast to coast could be made by train in 8 days.

● How many meals would you eat during the trip if you ate 3 meals a day?

Think You eat 3 meals one day. So multiply to find how many meals you would eat in 8 days.

$$3 \times 8 = 24 \qquad \begin{array}{r} 8 \\ \times 3 \\ \hline 24 \end{array}$$

You would eat **24 meals** during the trip.

The Concord Coach could carry 9 passengers in its carriage. The baggage was carried on top of the coach. Suppose 9 people were going on a trip and each person had 2 bags.

● How many bags were carried on top of the coach?

Think Each person had 2 bags. So multiply to find how many bags for 9 persons.

$$2 \times 9 = 18 \qquad \begin{array}{r} 9 \\ \times 2 \\ \hline 18 \end{array}$$

There would be **18 bags** carried on top of the coach.

PRACTICE • Find the products.

1. $\begin{array}{r} 8 \\ \times 1 \end{array}$ $\begin{array}{r} 8 \\ \times 2 \end{array}$ $\begin{array}{r} 8 \\ \times 3 \end{array}$ $\begin{array}{r} 8 \\ \times 4 \end{array}$ $\begin{array}{r} 8 \\ \times 5 \end{array}$ $\begin{array}{r} 8 \\ \times 6 \end{array}$ $\begin{array}{r} 8 \\ \times 7 \end{array}$ $\begin{array}{r} 8 \\ \times 8 \end{array}$ $\begin{array}{r} 8 \\ \times 9 \end{array}$

2. $\begin{array}{r} 9 \\ \times 1 \end{array}$ $\begin{array}{r} 9 \\ \times 2 \end{array}$ $\begin{array}{r} 9 \\ \times 3 \end{array}$ $\begin{array}{r} 9 \\ \times 4 \end{array}$ $\begin{array}{r} 9 \\ \times 5 \end{array}$ $\begin{array}{r} 9 \\ \times 6 \end{array}$ $\begin{array}{r} 9 \\ \times 7 \end{array}$ $\begin{array}{r} 9 \\ \times 8 \end{array}$ $\begin{array}{r} 9 \\ \times 9 \end{array}$

3. $4 \times 8 = \underline{\ ?\ }$ 4. $9 \times 2 = \underline{\ ?\ }$ 5. $8 \times 7 = \underline{\ ?\ }$ 6. $3 \times 9 = \underline{\ ?\ }$

7. $\begin{array}{r} 8 \\ \times 5 \end{array}$ 8. $\begin{array}{r} 8 \\ \times 9 \end{array}$ 9. $\begin{array}{r} 9 \\ \times 6 \end{array}$ 10. $\begin{array}{r} 9 \\ \times 5 \end{array}$ 11. $\begin{array}{r} 3 \\ \times 8 \end{array}$ 12. $\begin{array}{r} 8 \\ \times 8 \end{array}$ 13. $\begin{array}{r} 9 \\ \times 9 \end{array}$

EXERCISES • Multiply.

14. $6 \times 8 = $? **15.** $7 \times 9 = $? **16.** $4 \times 9 = $? **17.** $2 \times 8 = $?

18. $8 \times 9 = $? **19.** $7 \times 8 = $? **20.** $9 \times 9 = $? **21.** $1 \times 9 = $?

22. $9 \times 6 = $? **23.** $3 \times 8 = $? **24.** $3 \times 5 = $? **25.** $8 \times 5 = $?

26. $9 \times 4 = $? **27.** $9 \times 5 = $? **28.** $6 \times 7 = $? **29.** $2 \times 9 = $?

30. $\begin{array}{r}3\\ \times 9\\ \hline\end{array}$	**31.** $\begin{array}{r}8\\ \times 7\\ \hline\end{array}$	**32.** $\begin{array}{r}4\\ \times 8\\ \hline\end{array}$	**33.** $\begin{array}{r}5\\ \times 9\\ \hline\end{array}$	**34.** $\begin{array}{r}8\\ \times 6\\ \hline\end{array}$	**35.** $\begin{array}{r}7\\ \times 9\\ \hline\end{array}$	**36.** $\begin{array}{r}9\\ \times 8\\ \hline\end{array}$
37. $\begin{array}{r}6\\ \times 8\\ \hline\end{array}$	**38.** $\begin{array}{r}4\\ \times 9\\ \hline\end{array}$	**39.** $\begin{array}{r}3\\ \times 4\\ \hline\end{array}$	**40.** $\begin{array}{r}1\\ \times 8\\ \hline\end{array}$	**41.** $\begin{array}{r}4\\ \times 6\\ \hline\end{array}$	**42.** $\begin{array}{r}5\\ \times 8\\ \hline\end{array}$	**43.** $\begin{array}{r}6\\ \times 9\\ \hline\end{array}$
44. $\begin{array}{r}7\\ \times 7\\ \hline\end{array}$	**45.** $\begin{array}{r}8\\ \times 3\\ \hline\end{array}$	**46.** $\begin{array}{r}9\\ \times 3\\ \hline\end{array}$	**47.** $\begin{array}{r}7\\ \times 8\\ \hline\end{array}$	**48.** $\begin{array}{r}1\\ \times 1\\ \hline\end{array}$	**49.** $\begin{array}{r}9\\ \times 4\\ \hline\end{array}$	**50.** $\begin{array}{r}8\\ \times 2\\ \hline\end{array}$

Multiply a number by 1, 2, 3, and so on.
Each product is a **multiple** of that number.
3, 6, 9, and 12 are multiples of 3.

$3 \times 1 = 3$
$3 \times 2 = 6$
$3 \times 3 = 9$
$3 \times 4 = 12$

Mental Math • TRUE or FALSE.

51. 11 is a multiple of 2.

52. 24 is a multiple of 3.

53. 10 is a multiple of 3.

54. Even numbers are multiples of 2.

PROBLEM SOLVING • APPLICATIONS

CHOOSE • mental math • pencil and paper • calculator SOLVE

55. One train has 8 freight cars. Each freight car has 8 wheels. How many wheels are there in all?

56. The Concord Coach could carry 9 passengers. If the coach made 6 trips, how many people could it carry?

57. The Rucker family traveled 705 miles by coach and 2,245 miles by train to reach California. How many miles did they travel in all?

★ **58.** Each Concord Coach was pulled by 4 horses. There were 5 passengers on board. How many horses did it take to pull 8 coaches?

Properties of Multiplication

In some jungle areas, dugout canoes are the best way to travel. Each canoe holds 1 person. Suppose there are 3 canoes.

● How many people can ride in 3 canoes?

$3 \times 1 = 3$ There are **3 people** in 3 canoes.

This illustrates the following property of multiplication.

Property of 1 for Multiplication When one of two factors is 1, the product equals the other factor.	$1 \times 3 = 3$ $5 \times 1 = 5$

● Here are some other properties of multiplication.

Zero Property for Multiplication When a factor is 0, the product is 0.	$3 \times 0 = 0$ $0 \times 7 = 0$
Order Property of Multiplication You can multiply two factors in either order. The product is always the same.	$2 \times 3 = 3 \times 2$ $6 \ = \ 6$
Grouping Property of Multiplication You can group factors differently. The product is always the same.	$(3 \times 2) \times 4 = ?$ $\quad 3 \times (2 \times 4) = ?$ $6 \ \times 4 = 24 \quad 3 \times \ 8 \ = 24$

PRACTICE • Find the products.

1. $0 \times 4 = \underline{\ ?\ }$

2. $1 \times 3 = \underline{\ ?\ }$

3. $2 \times 7 = \underline{\ ?\ }$

4. $1 \times 5 = \underline{\ ?\ }$

5. $3 \times 0 = \underline{\ ?\ }$

6. $1 \times 0 = \underline{\ ?\ }$

7. $6 \times 5 = \underline{\ ?\ }$

8. $7 \times 1 = \underline{\ ?\ }$

9. $(1 \times 5) \times 8 = \underline{\ ?\ }$

10. $1 \times (5 \times 8) = \underline{\ ?\ }$

11. $(4 \times 2) \times 3 = \underline{\ ?\ }$

12. $4 \times (2 \times 3) = \underline{\ ?\ }$ **13.** $(3 \times 0) \times 9 = \underline{\ ?\ }$ **14.** $3 \times (0 \times 9) = \underline{\ ?\ }$

15. 0 $\times 2$	**16.** 4 $\times 8$	**17.** 3 $\times 0$	**18.** 3 $\times 1$	**19.** 0 $\times 0$	**20.** 7 $\times 4$	**21.** 9 $\times 0$

EXERCISES • Multiply.

22. $3 \times 3 = \underline{\ ?\ }$ **23.** $6 \times 0 = \underline{\ ?\ }$ **24.** $5 \times 7 = \underline{\ ?\ }$ **25.** $0 \times 9 = \underline{\ ?\ }$

26. $9 \times 7 = \underline{\ ?\ }$ **27.** $1 \times 2 = \underline{\ ?\ }$ **28.** $4 \times 4 = \underline{\ ?\ }$ **29.** $1 \times 8 = \underline{\ ?\ }$

30. $4 \times 0 = \underline{\ ?\ }$ **31.** $8 \times 7 = \underline{\ ?\ }$ **32.** $9 \times 1 = \underline{\ ?\ }$ **33.** $0 \times 7 = \underline{\ ?\ }$

34. $(6 \times 1) \times 5 = \underline{\ ?\ }$ **35.** $6 \times (1 \times 5) = \underline{\ ?\ }$ **36.** $(2 \times 4) \times 2 = \underline{\ ?\ }$

37. $2 \times (4 \times 2) = \underline{\ ?\ }$ **38.** $(0 \times 9) \times 9 = \underline{\ ?\ }$ **39.** $0 \times (9 \times 9) = \underline{\ ?\ }$

40. 1 $\times 1$	**41.** 0 $\times 3$	**42.** 7 $\times 3$	**43.** 2 $\times 0$	**44.** 6 $\times 4$	**45.** 4 $\times 7$	**46.** 7 $\times 0$
47. 3 $\times 5$	**48.** 8 $\times 4$	**49.** 9 $\times 3$	**50.** 7 $\times 6$	**51.** 1 $\times 6$	**52.** 4 $\times 6$	**53.** 6 $\times 8$
54. 1 $\times 3$	**55.** 4 $\times 1$	**56.** 9 $\times 8$	**57.** 5 $\times 0$	**58.** 0 $\times 8$	**59.** 9 $\times 5$	**60.** 7 $\times 7$

Write $>$, $<$, or $=$.

★ **61.** $(0 \times 4) \times 8 \ \bullet \ 3 \times (7 \times 0)$ ★ **62.** $(2 \times 3) \times 2 \ \bullet \ 3 \times (1 \times 3)$

★ **63.** $(7 \times 1) \times 9 \ \bullet \ 7 \times (1 \times 9)$ ★ **64.** $(4 \times 2) \times 3 \ \bullet \ 4 \times (4 \times 1)$

PROBLEM SOLVING • APPLICATIONS

Complete each number sentence. Then tell what property is shown by each number sentence.

65. $2 \times 5 = \underline{\ ?\ } \times 2$ **66.** $8 \times \underline{\ ?\ } = 8$

67. $\underline{\ ?\ } \times 4 = 0$ **68.** $(4 \times 2) \times 3 = 4 \times (\underline{\ ?\ } \times 3)$

Write a word problem for each number sentence.

★ **69.** $1 \times 6 = 6$ ★ **70.** $9 \times 0 = 0$

Multiplication Facts

Find each product.

1. $\begin{array}{r}3\\ \times5\\\hline\end{array}$	2. $\begin{array}{r}9\\ \times9\\\hline\end{array}$	3. $\begin{array}{r}7\\ \times5\\\hline\end{array}$	4. $\begin{array}{r}3\\ \times1\\\hline\end{array}$	5. $\begin{array}{r}7\\ \times2\\\hline\end{array}$	6. $\begin{array}{r}0\\ \times8\\\hline\end{array}$
7. $\begin{array}{r}5\\ \times8\\\hline\end{array}$	8. $\begin{array}{r}9\\ \times4\\\hline\end{array}$	9. $\begin{array}{r}5\\ \times1\\\hline\end{array}$	10. $\begin{array}{r}6\\ \times4\\\hline\end{array}$	11. $\begin{array}{r}0\\ \times5\\\hline\end{array}$	12. $\begin{array}{r}4\\ \times8\\\hline\end{array}$
13. $\begin{array}{r}7\\ \times7\\\hline\end{array}$	14. $\begin{array}{r}5\\ \times3\\\hline\end{array}$	15. $\begin{array}{r}1\\ \times7\\\hline\end{array}$	16. $\begin{array}{r}4\\ \times5\\\hline\end{array}$	17. $\begin{array}{r}5\\ \times5\\\hline\end{array}$	18. $\begin{array}{r}1\\ \times8\\\hline\end{array}$
19. $\begin{array}{r}0\\ \times0\\\hline\end{array}$	20. $\begin{array}{r}3\\ \times0\\\hline\end{array}$	21. $\begin{array}{r}3\\ \times4\\\hline\end{array}$	22. $\begin{array}{r}5\\ \times7\\\hline\end{array}$	23. $\begin{array}{r}9\\ \times3\\\hline\end{array}$	24. $\begin{array}{r}1\\ \times0\\\hline\end{array}$
25. $\begin{array}{r}0\\ \times2\\\hline\end{array}$	26. $\begin{array}{r}7\\ \times6\\\hline\end{array}$	27. $\begin{array}{r}9\\ \times0\\\hline\end{array}$	28. $\begin{array}{r}2\\ \times8\\\hline\end{array}$	29. $\begin{array}{r}8\\ \times3\\\hline\end{array}$	30. $\begin{array}{r}1\\ \times5\\\hline\end{array}$
31. $\begin{array}{r}3\\ \times2\\\hline\end{array}$	32. $\begin{array}{r}3\\ \times9\\\hline\end{array}$	33. $\begin{array}{r}8\\ \times6\\\hline\end{array}$	34. $\begin{array}{r}2\\ \times2\\\hline\end{array}$	35. $\begin{array}{r}1\\ \times9\\\hline\end{array}$	36. $\begin{array}{r}6\\ \times1\\\hline\end{array}$
37. $\begin{array}{r}8\\ \times5\\\hline\end{array}$	38. $\begin{array}{r}7\\ \times9\\\hline\end{array}$	39. $\begin{array}{r}8\\ \times0\\\hline\end{array}$	40. $\begin{array}{r}2\\ \times7\\\hline\end{array}$	41. $\begin{array}{r}9\\ \times8\\\hline\end{array}$	42. $\begin{array}{r}4\\ \times2\\\hline\end{array}$
43. $\begin{array}{r}0\\ \times7\\\hline\end{array}$	44. $\begin{array}{r}3\\ \times7\\\hline\end{array}$	45. $\begin{array}{r}1\\ \times3\\\hline\end{array}$	46. $\begin{array}{r}9\\ \times5\\\hline\end{array}$	47. $\begin{array}{r}2\\ \times3\\\hline\end{array}$	48. $\begin{array}{r}8\\ \times1\\\hline\end{array}$
49. $\begin{array}{r}6\\ \times7\\\hline\end{array}$	50. $\begin{array}{r}2\\ \times1\\\hline\end{array}$	51. $\begin{array}{r}8\\ \times8\\\hline\end{array}$	52. $\begin{array}{r}9\\ \times6\\\hline\end{array}$	53. $\begin{array}{r}8\\ \times2\\\hline\end{array}$	54. $\begin{array}{r}1\\ \times4\\\hline\end{array}$
55. $\begin{array}{r}5\\ \times9\\\hline\end{array}$	56. $\begin{array}{r}7\\ \times0\\\hline\end{array}$	57. $\begin{array}{r}2\\ \times5\\\hline\end{array}$	58. $\begin{array}{r}6\\ \times9\\\hline\end{array}$	59. $\begin{array}{r}0\\ \times4\\\hline\end{array}$	60. $\begin{array}{r}2\\ \times4\\\hline\end{array}$
61. $\begin{array}{r}9\\ \times2\\\hline\end{array}$	62. $\begin{array}{r}6\\ \times6\\\hline\end{array}$	63. $\begin{array}{r}0\\ \times1\\\hline\end{array}$	64. $\begin{array}{r}1\\ \times6\\\hline\end{array}$	65. $\begin{array}{r}4\\ \times9\\\hline\end{array}$	66. $\begin{array}{r}7\\ \times1\\\hline\end{array}$
67. $\begin{array}{r}6\\ \times3\\\hline\end{array}$	68. $\begin{array}{r}1\\ \times1\\\hline\end{array}$	69. $\begin{array}{r}6\\ \times5\\\hline\end{array}$	70. $\begin{array}{r}6\\ \times0\\\hline\end{array}$	71. $\begin{array}{r}9\\ \times7\\\hline\end{array}$	72. $\begin{array}{r}5\\ \times2\\\hline\end{array}$

Find each product without using paper or pencil.

73. 7
    ×8

74. 5
    ×4

75. 4
    ×6

76. 0
    ×3

77. 8
    ×9

78. 2
    ×6

79. 4
    ×1

80. 7
    ×3

81. 4
    ×7

82. 6
    ×2

83. 5
    ×0

84. 8
    ×4

85. 3
    ×6

86. 1
    ×2

87. 0
    ×9

88. 8
    ×7

89. 4
    ×0

90. 5
    ×6

91. 4
    ×3

92. 2
    ×9

93. 0
    ×6

94. 9
    ×1

95. 3
    ×3

96. 6
    ×8

97. 4
    ×4

98. 2
    ×0

99. 3
    ×8

100. 7
    ×4

CALCULATOR • Repeated Addition

You can find a product by using repeated addition.
Use your calculator to help you.

$4 \times 8 = \underline{\quad ? \quad}$

	Group 1	Group 2	Group 3	Group 4

Press ⑧ ⊕ ⑧ ⊕ ⑧ ⊕ ⑧ ⊜ ⎡ 32. ⎤

Multiply to check. Press ④ ⊗ ⑧ ⊜ ⎡ 32. ⎤

Now find 8 groups of 4 by addition.

④ ⊕ ④ ⊕ ④ ⊕ ④ ⊕ ④ ⊕ ④ ⊕ ④ ⊕ ④ ⊜ _?_

What does your calculator show? __?__

Multiply to check. Press ⑧ ⊗ ④ ⊜ __?__

MID-CHAPTER REVIEW

Multiply. (Pages 96–103)

1. $\begin{array}{r} 6 \\ \times 2 \\ \hline \end{array}$	2. $\begin{array}{r} 7 \\ \times 7 \\ \hline \end{array}$	3. $\begin{array}{r} 4 \\ \times 4 \\ \hline \end{array}$	4. $\begin{array}{r} 7 \\ \times 6 \\ \hline \end{array}$	5. $\begin{array}{r} 3 \\ \times 8 \\ \hline \end{array}$	6. $\begin{array}{r} 7 \\ \times 3 \\ \hline \end{array}$
7. $\begin{array}{r} 7 \\ \times 4 \\ \hline \end{array}$	8. $\begin{array}{r} 5 \\ \times 5 \\ \hline \end{array}$	9. $\begin{array}{r} 6 \\ \times 8 \\ \hline \end{array}$	10. $\begin{array}{r} 8 \\ \times 2 \\ \hline \end{array}$	11. $\begin{array}{r} 6 \\ \times 9 \\ \hline \end{array}$	12. $\begin{array}{r} 4 \\ \times 6 \\ \hline \end{array}$
13. $\begin{array}{r} 9 \\ \times 3 \\ \hline \end{array}$	14. $\begin{array}{r} 3 \\ \times 5 \\ \hline \end{array}$	15. $\begin{array}{r} 7 \\ \times 9 \\ \hline \end{array}$	16. $\begin{array}{r} 6 \\ \times 3 \\ \hline \end{array}$	17. $\begin{array}{r} 5 \\ \times 7 \\ \hline \end{array}$	18. $\begin{array}{r} 9 \\ \times 8 \\ \hline \end{array}$

Multiply. (Pages 104–105)

19. $1 \times 8 = \underline{\ ?\ }$

20. $4 \times 0 = \underline{\ ?\ }$

21. $0 \times 1 = \underline{\ ?\ }$

22. $2 \times 5 = \underline{\ ?\ } \times 2$

23. $(4 \times 2) \times 3 = 4 \times (2 \times \underline{\ ?\ })$

Solve.

24. There are 3 bicycle racks at school. Each rack has 9 bicycles. How many bicycles are in the racks? (Pages 96–97)

25. The bank parking lot has 5 parking spaces in each row. There are 9 rows. How many parking spaces are there in all? (Pages 98–99)

MAINTENANCE • MIXED PRACTICE

Add or subtract.

1. $\begin{array}{r} 39 \\ +85 \\ \hline \end{array}$	2. $\begin{array}{r} 294 \\ +\ 61 \\ \hline \end{array}$	3. $\begin{array}{r} 3,467 \\ +2,825 \\ \hline \end{array}$	4. $\begin{array}{r} 78 \\ -43 \\ \hline \end{array}$	5. $\begin{array}{r} 205 \\ -\ 97 \\ \hline \end{array}$	6. $\begin{array}{r} 510 \\ -\ 12 \\ \hline \end{array}$
7. $\begin{array}{r} \$54.09 \\ +\ 28.98 \\ \hline \end{array}$	8. $\begin{array}{r} \$54.09 \\ -\ 28.98 \\ \hline \end{array}$	9. $\begin{array}{r} \$90.05 \\ +\ 47.66 \\ \hline \end{array}$	10. $\begin{array}{r} \$90.05 \\ -\ 47.66 \\ \hline \end{array}$	11. $\begin{array}{r} \$55.56 \\ +\ 46.57 \\ \hline \end{array}$	12. $\begin{array}{r} \$55.56 \\ -\ 46.57 \\ \hline \end{array}$

Round each number to the nearest ten, the nearest hundred, and the nearest thousand.

13. 7,354   14. 6,193   15. 2,907   16. 3,512   17. 4,175   18. 5,637

19. Holly bought a basket that costs $16.95 for her bicycle. She gave the clerk $20.00. How much change did she receive?

20. Juan bought a new tire for his bicycle for $5.76. He gave the clerk $6.00. His change was 2 dimes and some pennies. How many pennies did he receive?

Telephone

Telephone lines can be thought of as
a form of transportation because they
"carry" messages. Some phone companies
charge the customer message units for phone calls.

Example   Jonah made a phone call from Los Angeles to
Sun Valley. The call lasted 8 minutes.
How many message units did it cost?

1   Find Sun Valley on the map. Read the number.

4 ⟵—— This is the number of message units for 3 minutes.

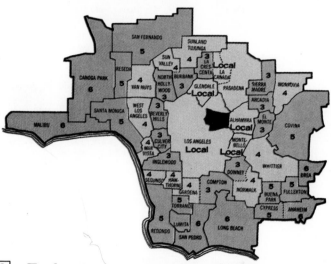

2   Each minute over three minutes costs 2 message units.
The call lasted 8 minutes. So there are 5 **overtime** minutes.

$$5 \times 2 = 10 \text{ message units for overtime}$$

3   Add the message units.   **4 + 10 = 14 message units.**

EXERCISES • Find the number of message units
for each call from Los Angeles.

1. To Downey, for 5 minutes
2. To Gardena, for 6 minutes
3. To Brea, for 10 minutes
4. To Covina, for 8 minutes
5. To Pasadena, for 9 minutes
6. To Burbank, for 9 minutes

Missing Factors

The product of two numbers is 35.
One of the factors is 5.

● Find the **missing factor.**

Think   5 times what number equals 35?

$$5 \times 4 = 20 \longleftarrow \text{too small}$$
$$5 \times 5 = 25 \longleftarrow \text{too small}$$
$$5 \times 6 = 30 \longleftarrow \text{too small}$$
$$5 \times 7 = 35 \quad \checkmark \quad \text{exactly right}$$

The missing factor is 7.

A dog sled is a dependable way to travel
in the Arctic. Each sled is usually
pulled by 4 dogs.

● How many sleds can be pulled by 20 dogs?

Think   4 times what number equals 20?

$$4 \times ? = 20$$
$$4 \times 3 = 12 \longleftarrow \text{too small}$$
$$4 \times 4 = 16 \longleftarrow \text{too small}$$
$$4 \times 5 = 20 \quad \checkmark \quad \text{exactly right!}$$
The missing factor is 5.

So **5 sleds** can be pulled by 20 dogs.

PRACTICE • Find the missing factors.

1. $\underline{\ ?\ } \times 4 = 16$ 2. $\underline{\ ?\ } \times 9 = 27$ 3. $6 \times \underline{\ ?\ } = 24$

4. $\underline{\ ?\ } \times 2 = 18$ 5. $3 \times \underline{\ ?\ } = 21$ 6. $\underline{\ ?\ } \times 5 = 40$

EXERCISES • Find the missing factors.

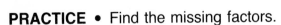

7. $\underline{\ ?\ } \times 2 = 16$ 8. $4 \times \underline{\ ?\ } = 36$ 9. $\underline{\ ?\ } \times 9 = 63$

10. $\underline{\ ?\ } \times 8 = 32$ 11. $9 \times \underline{\ ?\ } = 54$ 12. $6 \times \underline{\ ?\ } = 18$

13. $5 \times \underline{\ ?\ } = 25$ 14. $\underline{\ ?\ } \times 7 = 49$ 15. $\underline{\ ?\ } \times 6 = 36$

16. $4 \times \underline{\ ?\ } = 12$ 17. $3 \times \underline{\ ?\ } = 24$ 18. $7 \times \underline{\ ?\ } = 28$

19. $8 \times \underline{} = 72$ **20.** $7 \times \underline{} = 56$ **21.** $\underline{} \times 6 = 30$

22. $\underline{} \times 9 = 81$ **23.** $5 \times \underline{} = 45$ **24.** $7 \times \underline{} = 42$

Follow the rules to find the **INPUT**.

★ **25.** Rule: **Multiply by 6.** ★ **26.** Rule: **Multiply by 8.** ★ **27.** Rule: **Multiply by 4.**

INPUT	OUTPUT
?	42
?	24
?	36
?	54

INPUT	OUTPUT
?	24
?	56
?	32
?	64

INPUT	OUTPUT
?	36
?	8
?	24
?	20

PROBLEM SOLVING • APPLICATIONS

28. Pack animals are used to carry goods over desert areas. A camel can carry 3 bundles. How many camels are needed to carry 18 bundles?

29. Oxen are sometimes used to carry goods through the mountains. Each oxen can carry 3 sacks. How many oxen are needed to carry 9 sacks?

30. The American Indians used a horse to pull a *travois* (trə-'vȯi) to move equipment and supplies. They traveled 12 miles one day. The next day they traveled 8 miles more than the first day. How many miles did they travel in two days?

31. The product is 28. One factor is 7. What is the other factor?

a. The product is 63. The sum of the two factors is 16. Their difference is 2. What are the factors?

b. The product is 36. The sum of the two factors is 13. What is their difference?

Dividing by 2 and 3

Hawaiians often use double outrigger canoes to travel from island to island. There are 2 outriggers on each canoe. There are 18 outriggers.

● How many canoes are there?

Think There are 18 outriggers in all. You need to find how many groups of 2 are in 18. So divide.

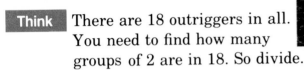

in all · on each canoe · number of canoes

There are **9 canoes.**

● Division can be shown in two ways.

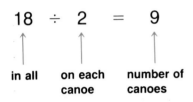

quotient
divisor
dividend

$$27 \div 3 = 9 \qquad 3\overline{)27}$$

● $21 \div 3 = ?$

Think You can use a multiplication fact to help you find the quotient.

$$? \times 3 = 21 \text{ Since } 7 \times 3 = 21,$$
$$21 \div 3 = 7.$$

PRACTICE • Find the quotients.

1. $18 \div 3 = $ ___?___

   Think: $? \times 3 = 18$

2. $8 \div 2 = $ ___?___

   Think: $? \times 2 = 8$

3. $12 \div 3 = $ ___?___

   Think: $? \times 3 = 12$

4. $2\overline{)8}$
5. $3\overline{)9}$
6. $2\overline{)16}$
7. $2\overline{)12}$
8. $3\overline{)27}$
9. $2\overline{)10}$

EXERCISES • Divide.

10. $6 \div 3 = \underline{\quad?\quad}$ **11.** $12 \div 2 = \underline{\quad?\quad}$ **12.** $6 \div 2 = \underline{\quad?\quad}$

13. $24 \div 3 = \underline{\quad?\quad}$ **14.** $15 \div 3 = \underline{\quad?\quad}$ **15.** $14 \div 2 = \underline{\quad?\quad}$

16. $4 \div 2 = \underline{\quad?\quad}$ **17.** $10 \div 2 = \underline{\quad?\quad}$ **18.** $16 \div 2 = \underline{\quad?\quad}$

19. $3\overline{)6}$ **20.** $2\overline{)18}$ **21.** $3\overline{)3}$ **22.** $2\overline{)10}$ **23.** $3\overline{)27}$ **24.** $2\overline{)4}$

25. $2\overline{)8}$ **26.** $3\overline{)9}$ **27.** $2\overline{)16}$ **28.** $3\overline{)12}$ **29.** $2\overline{)12}$ **30.** $2\overline{)6}$

31. $2\overline{)2}$ **32.** $2\overline{)14}$ **33.** $3\overline{)21}$ **34.** $3\overline{)18}$ **35.** $3\overline{)24}$ **36.** $3\overline{)15}$

37. $2\overline{)18}$ **38.** $2\overline{)8}$ **39.** $3\overline{)18}$ **40.** $3\overline{)9}$ ★ **41.** $2\overline{)20}$ ★ **42.** $3\overline{)30}$

PROBLEM SOLVING • APPLICATIONS

43. There are 3 seats in a small canoe. Suppose you count 21 seats in these small canoes. How many canoes are there?

44. There are 12 people waiting to rent a canoe. Each canoe holds 2 people. How many canoes are needed?

45. It costs $13.75 for a one-hour canoe ride. Jane gave the clerk $15.00. How much change did she receive?

★ **46.** Boats often were powered by teams of rowers in ancient times. Suppose there were 16 rowers on *each* side of the boat. It took 2 people to handle each oar. How many oars were there on the boat?
(Hint: There are oars on both sides.)

Dividing by 4 and 5

A subway is an underground railway. There are 4 doors on each car of a subway train. This train has 32 doors.

● How many cars are there?

Think There are 32 doors in all. You need to find how many groups of 4 are in 32. So divide.

$$32 \div 4 = ?$$

Think You can use a multiplication fact to help you find the quotient.

$$? \times 4 = 32 \quad \text{Since } 8 \times 4 = 32,$$
$$32 \div 4 = 8.$$

There are **8 subway cars** on the train.

● $35 \div 5 = ?$

Think You can use a multiplication fact to help you find the quotient.

$$? \times 5 = 35 \quad \text{Since } 7 \times 5 = 35,$$
$$35 \div 5 = 7.$$

PRACTICE • Find the quotients.

1. $16 \div 4 = \underline{\quad?\quad}$

   Think: $? \times 4 = 16$.

2. $30 \div 5 = \underline{\quad?\quad}$

   Think: $? \times 5 = 30$.

3. $20 \div 4 = \underline{\quad?\quad}$

   Think: $? \times 4 = 20$.

Divide.

4. $5\overline{)10}$ 5. $4\overline{)24}$ 6. $5\overline{)25}$ 7. $5\overline{)35}$ 8. $5\overline{)0}$ 9. $4\overline{)28}$

EXERCISES • Divide.

10. $8 \div 4 = \underline{\quad?\quad}$

11. $24 \div 4 = \underline{\quad?\quad}$

12. $25 \div 5 = \underline{\quad?\quad}$

13. $15 \div 5 = \underline{\quad?\quad}$

14. $36 \div 4 = \underline{\quad?\quad}$

15. $32 \div 4 = \underline{\quad?\quad}$

16. $18 \div 3 = \underline{?}$　　　　**17.** $12 \div 3 = \underline{?}$　　　　**18.** $45 \div 5 = \underline{?}$

19. $4\overline{)24}$　　**20.** $5\overline{)20}$　　**21.** $4\overline{)36}$　　**22.** $4\overline{)0}$　　**23.** $4\overline{)8}$　　**24.** $5\overline{)40}$

25. $5\overline{)35}$　　**26.** $4\overline{)16}$　　**27.** $3\overline{)27}$　　**28.** $4\overline{)12}$　　**29.** $5\overline{)25}$　　**30.** $5\overline{)20}$

31. $4\overline{)28}$　　**32.** $2\overline{)14}$　　**33.** $2\overline{)10}$　　**34.** $5\overline{)35}$　　**35.** $5\overline{)45}$　　**36.** $5\overline{)15}$

37. $5\overline{)15}$　　**38.** $3\overline{)15}$　　**39.** $2\overline{)12}$　　**40.** $5\overline{)5}$　　**41.** $4\overline{)20}$　　**42.** $3\overline{)21}$

43. $5\overline{)40}$　　**44.** $4\overline{)8}$　　**45.** $5\overline{)30}$　　**46.** $3\overline{)15}$　　**47.** $5\overline{)20}$　　**48.** $2\overline{)16}$

Name the missing numbers.

★ **49.** $\underline{?} \div 4 = 9$　　　★ **50.** $\underline{?} \div 3 = 8$　　　★ **51.** $\underline{?} \div 5 = 7$

★ **52.** $4\overline{)?}^{\,8}$　　　★ **53.** $6\overline{)?}^{\,9}$　　　★ **54.** $8\overline{)?}^{\,7}$

PROBLEM SOLVING • APPLICATIONS

55. People often ride from the parking lot to the football stadium on a shuttle bus. Each bench in the bus holds 5 people. There are 30 people. How many benches are needed to seat these people?

56. The local metro bus makes 45 stops in 5 days. The bus makes the same number of stops each day. How many stops does it make each day?

 CALCULATOR • Repeated Subtraction

EXERCISES • You can find a quotient by using repeated subtraction.

$$27 \div 9 = \underline{?}$$

Use your calculator to help you. Count how many times you press 9 until you reach 0.

Press: ② ⑦ ⊖ ⑨ ⊜ `18.`　　You pressed 9 three times.

① ⑧ ⊖ ⑨ ⊜ `9.`　　So $27 \div 9 = 3$.

⑨ ⊖ ⑨ ⊜ `0.`

Check your answers to Exercises 37–48 by using repeated subtraction.

PROBLEM SOLVING • STRATEGIES

Understanding the Operation/ Two Uses of Division

In the lessons on pages 112–115, you saw one use of division.

● To find how many groups there are.

There is a second use of division.

● To find how many are in each group.

Example 1

Standard-sized automobiles are shipped to market in groups of 12 on special railroad cars. There are 4 automobiles on each deck.

● How many decks are on the railroad car?

Divide to find how many groups.

$$\begin{array}{r} 3 \text{ decks} \\ \text{cars per } 4\overline{)12} \text{ cars} \\ \text{deck} \quad \underline{-12} \\ 0 \end{array}$$

There are **3 decks** on each railroad car.

Example 2

Standard-sized automobiles are shipped to market in groups of 12 on special railroad cars. There are 3 decks on the railroad car. The same number of cars are on each deck.

● How many automobiles are on each deck of the railroad car?

Divide to find how many in each group.

$$\begin{array}{r} 4 \text{ cars per deck} \\ \text{decks } 3\overline{)12} \text{ cars} \\ \underline{-12} \\ 0 \end{array}$$

There are **4 automobiles** on each deck.

PROBLEMS • Decide what the problem is asking: how many groups or how many in each group. Then solve.

1. Taillights are sold in packages of 4. There are 32 taillights in all. How many packages are there?

2. There are 8 packages of taillights. There are 32 taillights in all. The same number are in each package. How many taillights are in each package?

Use division to find how many groups or how many in each group.

3. A large car in the 1970's could get about 9 miles to the gallon. Suppose you traveled 81 miles. How many gallons of gas would you use?

4. Manuel counts 42 tires in all on the trucks in the parking lot. There are 7 trucks. Each truck has the same number of tires. How many tires are on each truck?

5. Mrs. Roehn drives the company car to work 5 days each week. She drives a total of 40 miles. She drives the same number of miles each day. How many miles does she drive each day?

6. A steam-powered car in 1770 could travel 3 miles in one hour. Suppose it traveled 15 miles. How many hours did it take?

7. Each Model T has 5 lights. Suppose you count 35 Model T lights in the parking lot. How many Model T's are there?

Write Your Own Problem

a. Write a story problem like Example 1 to find how many groups.

b. Write a story problem like Example 2 to find how many in each group.

Dividing by 6 and 7

Between 1969 and 1972, 18 astronauts made 6 trips to the moon. The same number of astronauts went on each flight.

● How many astronauts went on each flight?

Think There were 18 astronauts in all. You need to find how many were in each group. So divide.

$18 \div 6 = ?$

Think You can use a multiplication fact to help you find the quotient.

$? \times 6 = 18$ Since $3 \times 6 = 18$, $18 \div 6 = 3$.

There were **3 astronauts** on each flight.

PRACTICE • Find the quotients.

1. $48 \div 6 = \underline{\ ?\ }$

Think: $? \times 6 = 48.$

2. $36 \div 6 = \underline{\ ?\ }$

Think: $? \times 6 = 36.$

3. $14 \div 7 = \underline{\ ?\ }$

Think: $? \times 7 = 14.$

Divide.

4. $7\overline{)28}$ **5.** $6\overline{)24}$ **6.** $7\overline{)21}$ **7.** $7\overline{)35}$ **8.** $6\overline{)12}$ **9.** $6\overline{)30}$

EXERCISES • Divide.

10. $18 \div 6 = \underline{\ ?\ }$ **11.** $56 \div 7 = \underline{\ ?\ }$ **12.** $63 \div 7 = \underline{\ ?\ }$

13. $42 \div 6 = \underline{\ ?\ }$ **14.** $24 \div 6 = \underline{\ ?\ }$ **15.** $49 \div 7 = \underline{\ ?\ }$

16. $48 \div 6 = \underline{\ ?\ }$ **17.** $54 \div 6 = \underline{\ ?\ }$ **18.** $35 \div 7 = \underline{\ ?\ }$

19. $6\overline{)36}$ **20.** $6\overline{)6}$ **21.** $7\overline{)42}$ **22.** $7\overline{)14}$ **23.** $4\overline{)4}$ **24.** $6\overline{)54}$

25. $7\overline{)21}$ **26.** $6\overline{)42}$ **27.** $7\overline{)49}$ **28.** $4\overline{)32}$ **29.** $7\overline{)21}$ **30.** $7\overline{)63}$

31. $7\overline{)56}$ **32.** $7\overline{)7}$ **33.** $5\overline{)25}$ **34.** $7\overline{)35}$ **35.** $5\overline{)40}$ **36.** $6\overline{)48}$

37. $7\overline{)28}$ **38.** $6\overline{)12}$ **39.** $7\overline{)56}$ **40.** $6\overline{)18}$ **41.** $4\overline{)20}$ **42.** $5\overline{)30}$

43. $6\overline{)24}$ **44.** $4\overline{)32}$ **45.** $6\overline{)30}$ **46.** $7\overline{)63}$ **47.** $6\overline{)36}$ **48.** $6\overline{)12}$

Complete.

	Pairs	Operation	Result
★ 49.	6, 7	_____?_____	42
★ 50.	18, _?_	Subtraction	12
★ 51.	_?_ , 7	Division	8

PROBLEM SOLVING • APPLICATIONS

52. There are 30 engines needed to make the 6 trips to the moon. Each Apollo spacecraft used the same number of engines. How many engines were used for each trip to the moon?

53. The astronauts on Apollo 15 explored the moon in a small battery-powered vehicle. Suppose they could go 7 miles on one battery. How many batteries would they need to travel 14 miles?

54. There were 7 pilots chosen for the first group to train as astronauts. There were two times as many chosen for the second group. How many were there in the two groups?

★ **55.** Parachutes were used to slow the command module as it headed for splashdown. Each command module used 3 parachutes. There were 4 frogmen waiting to help the astronauts out of the spacecraft. How many parachutes were used for the 6 moon trips?

Multiplication and Division Facts • **119**

Dividing by 8 and 9

In 1865, Jules Verne designed a "moon train" with 9 cars. On one trip, the train carried 72 people. The same number of people were in each car.

● How many people were in each car?

Think	There are 72 people in all. You need to find how many are in each car. Divide.

$$72 \div 9 = ?$$

Think	You can use a multiplication fact to help you find the quotient.

$? \times 9 = 72$ Since $8 \times 9 = 72$,
$$72 \div 9 = 8.$$

There would be 8 people in each car.

● $81 \div 9 = ?$

Think	You can use a multiplication fact to help you find the quotient.

$? \times 9 = 81$ Since $9 \times 9 = 81$,
$$81 \div 9 = 9.$$

● Multiplication and division facts form **fact families**.

Use 8, 9, and 72. You can make two multiplication sentences and two division sentences.

$$8 \times 9 = 72 \qquad 72 \div 9 = 8$$
$$9 \times 8 = 72 \qquad 72 \div 8 = 9$$

PRACTICE • Find the quotients.

1. $64 \div 8 = \underline{\ ?\ }$

Think: $? \times 8 = 64.$

2. $32 \div 8 = \underline{\ ?\ }$

Think: $? \times 8 = 32.$

3. $36 \div 9 = \underline{\ ?\ }$

Think: $? \times 9 = 36.$

Divide.

4. $9\overline{)45}$ **5.** $8\overline{)56}$ **6.** $8\overline{)40}$ **7.** $9\overline{)63}$ **8.** $8\overline{)16}$ **9.** $8\overline{)48}$

Complete the fact families.

10. $4 \times 8 = 32$
$32 \div 8 = 4$

11. $24 \div 3 = 8$
$8 \times 3 = 4$

12. $9 \times 2 = 18$
$18 \div 2 = 9$

EXERCISES • Divide.

13. $24 \div 8 = $ __?__

14. $27 \div 9 = $ __?__

15. $9 \div 9 = $ __?__

16. $72 \div 8 = $ __?__

17. $54 \div 9 = $ __?__

18. $72 \div 9 = $ __?__

19. $42 \div 7 = $ __?__

20. $81 \div 9 = $ __?__

21. $56 \div 8 = $ __?__

22. $63 \div 9 = $ __?__

23. $16 \div 4 = $ __?__

24. $18 \div 9 = $ __?__

25. $9\overline{)36}$ **26.** $8\overline{)32}$ **27.** $8\overline{)8}$ **28.** $9\overline{)54}$ **29.** $8\overline{)64}$ **30.** $9\overline{)45}$

31. $8\overline{)72}$ **32.** $6\overline{)36}$ **33.** $8\overline{)40}$ **34.** $9\overline{)27}$ **35.** $9\overline{)9}$ **36.** $5\overline{)30}$

37. $9\overline{)81}$ **38.** $8\overline{)8}$ **39.** $3\overline{)24}$ **40.** $6\overline{)48}$ **41.** $9\overline{)18}$ **42.** $8\overline{)48}$

43. $4\overline{)28}$ **44.** $8\overline{)24}$ **45.** $9\overline{)36}$ **46.** $9\overline{)63}$ **47.** $8\overline{)40}$ **48.** $9\overline{)72}$

Complete the fact families.

49. $9 \times 3 = 27$
$27 \div 3 = 9$

50. $56 \div 7 = 8$
$8 \times 7 = 56$

51. $9 \times 8 = 72$
$72 \div 8 = 9$

Name the missing numbers.

★ **52.** __?__ $\div 3 = 9$

★ **53.** __?__ $\div 8 = 6$

★ **54.** __?__ $\div 9 = 5$

PROBLEM SOLVING • APPLICATIONS

55. One day, 56 people ride a space shuttle to the space station. Each shuttle holds 8 people. How many shuttles are needed?

56. Each space station has 63 crew members. They work in teams with 7 members on each team. How many teams are there?

Properties of Division

Snowmobiles are designed to ride on ice or snow. There are 6 snowmobiles and there are 6 people.

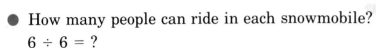

● How many people can ride in each snowmobile?

$6 \div 6 = ?$

 $6 \div 6 = ?$ means $6 \times ? = 6$
Since $6 \times 1 = 6$, $6 \div 6 = \mathbf{1}$.

There is **1 person** in each snowmobile.

This illustrates the following property of division.

Any number except 0 that is divided by itself is 1.	$6 \div 6 = 1$ $1 \times 6 = 6$

● Here are some other properties of division.

Any number divided by 1 is that number.	$8 \div 1 = 8$ $8 \times 1 = 8$
Zero divided by any number except 0 is 0.	$0 \div 2 = 0$ $0 \times 2 = 0$
Never divide by 0. $\quad 5 \div 0 = ?$ $\qquad\qquad\qquad\quad ? \times 0 = 5$	**No number will make the sentence true.**

PRACTICE • Divide

1. $7 \div 1 = \underline{\ ?\ }$ **2.** $0 \div 9 = \underline{\ ?\ }$ **3.** $1 \div 1 = \underline{\ ?\ }$ **4.** $0 \div 2 = \underline{\ ?\ }$

EXERCISES • Divide.

5. $9 \div 1 = \underline{\ ?\ }$ **6.** $5 \div 5 = \underline{\ ?\ }$ **7.** $0 \div 1 = \underline{\ ?\ }$ **8.** $3 \div 3 = \underline{\ ?\ }$

9. $4 \div 4 = \underline{\ ?\ }$ ★ **10.** $13 \div 1 = \underline{\ ?\ }$ ★ **11.** $0 \div 21 = \underline{\ ?\ }$ ★ **12.** $39 \div 1 = \underline{\ ?\ }$

13. $8\overline{)8}$ **14.** $1\overline{)2}$ **15.** $2\overline{)0}$ **16.** $5\overline{)5}$ **17.** $1\overline{)10}$

18. $1\overline{)9}$ **19.** $1\overline{)0}$ **20.** $9\overline{)9}$ ★ **21.** $1\overline{)35}$ ★ **22.** $1\overline{)45}$

Division Facts

Find each quotient.

1. $5\overline{)35}$ 2. $3\overline{)18}$ 3. $4\overline{)20}$ 4. $8\overline{)16}$ 5. $1\overline{)7}$ 6. $6\overline{)24}$

7. $9\overline{)36}$ 8. $2\overline{)0}$ 9. $7\overline{)49}$ 10. $4\overline{)28}$ 11. $6\overline{)42}$ 12. $1\overline{)2}$

13. $5\overline{)25}$ 14. $8\overline{)48}$ 15. $3\overline{)0}$ 16. $7\overline{)35}$ 17. $9\overline{)54}$ 18. $2\overline{)16}$

19. $3\overline{)12}$ 20. $7\overline{)7}$ 21. $2\overline{)6}$ 22. $4\overline{)24}$ 23. $9\overline{)63}$ 24. $6\overline{)30}$

25. $5\overline{)0}$ 26. $8\overline{)32}$ 27. $1\overline{)4}$ 28. $8\overline{)56}$ 29. $4\overline{)8}$ 30. $7\overline{)21}$

31. $1\overline{)8}$ 32. $5\overline{)10}$ 33. $3\overline{)24}$ 34. $2\overline{)14}$ 35. $6\overline{)36}$ 36. $9\overline{)27}$

37. $6\overline{)18}$ 38. $5\overline{)30}$ 39. $3\overline{)6}$ 40. $9\overline{)9}$ 41. $7\overline{)28}$ 42. $4\overline{)12}$

43. $8\overline{)0}$ 44. $1\overline{)5}$ 45. $2\overline{)10}$ 46. $7\overline{)42}$ 47. $9\overline{)72}$ 48. $5\overline{)45}$

49. $3\overline{)3}$ 50. $2\overline{)8}$ 51. $6\overline{)48}$ 52. $1\overline{)6}$ 53. $4\overline{)16}$ 54. $7\overline{)56}$

55. $2\overline{)18}$ 56. $9\overline{)81}$ 57. $8\overline{)8}$ 58. $7\overline{)0}$ 59. $4\overline{)4}$ 60. $5\overline{)15}$

61. $6\overline{)54}$ 62. $3\overline{)21}$ 63. $1\overline{)0}$ 64. $9\overline{)18}$ 65. $2\overline{)2}$ 66. $8\overline{)64}$

67. $6\overline{)0}$ 68. $1\overline{)9}$ 69. $8\overline{)72}$ 70. $3\overline{)27}$ 71. $5\overline{)5}$ 72. $4\overline{)32}$

73. $1\overline{)1}$ 74. $7\overline{)14}$ 75. $6\overline{)12}$ 76. $2\overline{)14}$ 77. $8\overline{)24}$ 78. $9\overline{)0}$

79. $5\overline{)20}$ 80. $4\overline{)0}$ 81. $3\overline{)9}$ 82. $6\overline{)6}$ 83. $9\overline{)45}$ 84. $4\overline{)36}$

85. $5\overline{)40}$ 86. $2\overline{)12}$ 87. $1\overline{)3}$ 88. $3\overline{)15}$ 89. $8\overline{)40}$ 90. $7\overline{)63}$

Quotients and Remainders

One section of a wide-bodied jet has 32 seats in its first-class section. Each complete row has 6 seats.

- How many complete rows are there?

- How many seats are left over?

Think There are 32 seats in all. You need to find how many groups of 6 are in 32. So divide. The remainder tells how many are left over.

$$32 \div 6 = ?$$

Think You can use a multiplication fact to help you find the quotient. How many 6's are there in 32?

$$? \times 6 = 32$$
Try 4: $4 \times 6 = 24$ ◀ **24 is too small.**
Try 5: $5 \times 6 = 30$
Try 6: $6 \times 6 = 36$ ◀ **36 is too big.**

Use the multiplication fact $5 \times 6 = 30$ to divide.

Step 1
Write 5 above the 2 in 32.

$$6\overline{)32}^{\,5}$$

Step 2
Multiply.
$5 \times 6 = 30$

$$\begin{array}{r} 5 \\ 6\overline{)32} \\ 30 \end{array}$$

Step 3
Subtract.
$32 - 30 = 2$

$$\begin{array}{r} 5 \\ 6\overline{)32} \\ -30 \\ \hline 2 \end{array}$$

The **remainder** is the number left over.

Step 4
Show the remainder in the answer

$$\begin{array}{r} 5 \text{ r2} \\ 6\overline{)32} \\ -30 \\ \hline 2 \end{array}$$

The remainder must be less than the divisor.

There are **5 rows** with **2 seats** left over.

PRACTICE • Find the quotients and the remainders.

1. $3\overline{)23}$ 2. $5\overline{)19}$ 3. $7\overline{)26}$ 4. $6\overline{)33}$ 5. $8\overline{)44}$ 6. $7\overline{)47}$

7. $8\overline{)52}$ 8. $4\overline{)27}$ 9. $9\overline{)30}$ 10. $6\overline{)49}$ 11. $6\overline{)19}$ 12. $8\overline{)29}$

EXERCISES • Find the quotients and the remainders.

13. $9\overline{)29}$ 14. $8\overline{)73}$ 15. $4\overline{)37}$ 16. $8\overline{)26}$ 17. $6\overline{)23}$ 18. $3\overline{)16}$

19. $5\overline{)27}$ 20. $4\overline{)23}$ 21. $7\overline{)45}$ 22. $9\overline{)47}$ 23. $3\overline{)28}$ 24. $2\overline{)15}$

25. $3\overline{)25}$ 26. $7\overline{)17}$ 27. $4\overline{)34}$ 28. $2\overline{)17}$ 29. $5\overline{)38}$ 30. $8\overline{)43}$

31. $3\overline{)22}$ 32. $4\overline{)17}$ 33. $8\overline{)15}$ 34. $6\overline{)39}$ 35. $3\overline{)11}$ 36. $8\overline{)49}$

37. $7\overline{)58}$ 38. $4\overline{)33}$ 39. $6\overline{)45}$ 40. $7\overline{)51}$ 41. $9\overline{)77}$ 42. $6\overline{)57}$

43. $50 \div 9 = \underline{\ ?\ }$ 44. $20 \div 7 = \underline{\ ?\ }$ 45. $39 \div 5 = \underline{\ ?\ }$

46. $23 \div 8 = \underline{\ ?\ }$ 47. $52 \div 7 = \underline{\ ?\ }$ 48. $60 \div 8 = \underline{\ ?\ }$

★ 49. $43 = (9 \times \underline{\ ?\ }) + 7$ ★ 50. $34 = (8 \times \underline{\ ?\ }) + 2$ ★ 51. $67 = (9 \times \underline{\ ?\ }) + 4$

PROBLEM SOLVING • APPLICATIONS   CHOOSE   • mental math   • pencil and paper   • calculator   SOLVE

52. A wide-bodied jet needs a crew of 5 flight attendants. On Tuesday, 46 flight attendants reported to work. How many crews is this? How many are left over?

53. A flight attendant for Jet-Away Airlines fills souvenir bags for children. She has 35 items. She puts 4 items in each bag. How many souvenir bags can she fill? How many items are left over?

54. Joe wants to watch the movie while he is on the airplane. He rents a headset for $2.00. He gives the attendant $5.00. How much change should he receive?

55. The flight attendant placed 27 ham sandwiches and 46 roast beef sandwiches in the plane's serving kitchen. There were 98 passengers on board the plane. How many more sandwiches must the flight attendant order?

PROBLEM SOLVING · STRATEGIES

Choosing the Operation

The words in a problem are the clues that tell you whether to multiply or divide.

Clues	Think
Find the **product**. How many **in all**? How many **altogether**? Find the **total**. Find five **times** seven.	**MULTIPLY**
Find the **quotient**. How many **groups**? How many **in each group**? How many for **each** person? How much **per** day? Find six **divided by** two.	**DIVIDE**

PROBLEMS • Write **MULTIPLY** or **DIVIDE**.

1. How many students **in all** attended?

2. How many tickets did **each** student have?

3. What was the **total** number of tickets?

4. How many students were **in each group?**

5. How many miles were traveled **altogether**?

6. How many tickets **per** day were sold?

Solve each problem.

Look for clues.

7. The fourth grade is taking a bus to the airport for a field trip. Each bus has 4 tires. There are 6 buses. How many tires are there altogether?

8. The students see buses parked in rows at the airport. There are 5 rows with 2 buses in each row. How many buses in all did they see?

9. The students are put in groups with 9 students in each group. There are 63 students in all. How many groups of students are there?

The words *in all*, *altogether*, and *total* are also clues for addition. So be careful!

---

10. The lunch trays are stacked and ready to be put on the plane. There are 7 stacks with 8 trays in each stack. How many lunch trays are there in all?

11. There were 6 students on one minibus. There were 11 students on another minibus. How many students were there in all?

12. There are many people at the ticket counters in the terminal. At one airline counter, there are 4 ticket lines with 9 people in each line. What is the total number of people in line?

13. The airport has hangars to store and repair aircraft. The students saw 7 hangars with 3 airplanes in each hangar. What is the total number of airplanes in these hangars?

Sometimes there are no clue words.

---

14. The ticket agent also gives tickets for baggage. Each bag must have 2 tickets on it before it can be put on the plane. One man has 8 tickets. How many bags can he put tickets on?

15. The airport has 4 passenger terminals. There are 20 airplanes in all. Each passenger terminal has the same number of planes. How many planes are at each terminal?

Write Your Own Problem

Write a story problem about people at an airport. Have clues in the problem to tell whether to multiply or divide. Underline the clues.

CHAPTER REVIEW

Part 1: VOCABULARY

For Exercises 1–7, choose the word from the box at the right that completes each statement.

1. In a multiplication problem, the numbers you multiply are called __?__. (Page 96)

2. The answer to a division problem is called the __?__. (Page 112)

3. The answer when 2 factors are multiplied is called the __?__. (Page 96)

4. $(2 \times 3) \times 4 = 2 \times (3 \times 4)$ is an example of the __?__ property. (Page 104)

5. In a division problem, the number left over is the __?__. (Page 124)

6. $6 \times 4 = 4 \times 6$ is an example of the __?__ property. (Page 104)

7. When you find how many groups something is separated into, you __?__. (Page 122)

divide
dividend
divisor
fact family
factors
grouping
multiple
multiply
order
product
quotient
remainder
zero property

Part 2: SKILLS

Multiply. (Pages 96–105)

8. $6 \times 2 =$ __?__

9. $4 \times 3 =$ __?__

10. $6 \times 5 =$ __?__

11. $7 \times 4 =$ __?__

12. $8 \times 8 =$ __?__

13. $9 \times 6 =$ __?__

14. $\begin{array}{r} 3 \\ \times 8 \\ \hline \end{array}$

15. $\begin{array}{r} 3 \\ \times 9 \\ \hline \end{array}$

16. $\begin{array}{r} 4 \\ \times 6 \\ \hline \end{array}$

17. $\begin{array}{r} 8 \\ \times 4 \\ \hline \end{array}$

18. $\begin{array}{r} 5 \\ \times 9 \\ \hline \end{array}$

19. $\begin{array}{r} 6 \\ \times 7 \\ \hline \end{array}$

20. $\begin{array}{r} 9 \\ \times 8 \\ \hline \end{array}$

21. $\begin{array}{r} 7 \\ \times 0 \\ \hline \end{array}$

22. $\begin{array}{r} 7 \\ \times 7 \\ \hline \end{array}$

23. $\begin{array}{r} 8 \\ \times 5 \\ \hline \end{array}$

24. $\begin{array}{r} 1 \\ \times 8 \\ \hline \end{array}$

25. $\begin{array}{r} 0 \\ \times 1 \\ \hline \end{array}$

Write the missing factors. (Pages 110–111)

26. $\underline{?} \times 8 = 24$

27. $6 \times \underline{?} = 30$

28. $9 \times \underline{?} = 63$

29. $\underline{?} \times 6 = 42$

30. $\underline{?} \times 7 = 35$

31. $5 \times \underline{?} = 40$

32. $8 \times \underline{?} = 32$

33. $4 \times \underline{?} = 28$

34. $\underline{?} \times 3 = 21$

Divide. (Pages 112–115, 118–123)

35. $28 \div 7 = \underline{?}$

36. $18 \div 3 \underline{?}$

37. $16 \div 2 = \underline{?}$

38. $21 \div 7 = \underline{?}$

39. $56 \div 8 = \underline{?}$

40. $20 \div 4 = \underline{?}$

41. $3\overline{)9}$ **42.** $7\overline{)42}$ **43.** $8\overline{)0}$ **44.** $9\overline{)36}$ **45.** $3\overline{)12}$ **46.** $9\overline{)9}$

47. $6\overline{)30}$ **48.** $5\overline{)45}$ **49.** $1\overline{)5}$ **50.** $9\overline{)72}$ **51.** $1\overline{)0}$ **52.** $7\overline{)63}$

Find the quotients and the remainders. (Pages 124–125)

53. $2\overline{)15}$ **54.** $5\overline{)29}$ **55.** $4\overline{)38}$ **56.** $7\overline{)20}$ **57.** $9\overline{)30}$ **58.** $6\overline{)51}$

Part 3: PROBLEM SOLVING • APPLICATIONS

59. There are 56 people in all in a rowboat race. There are 8 people in each rowboat. How many rowboats are in the race? (Pages 116–117)

60. There are 56 people in all in a rowboat race. There are 7 boats. How many people are in each rowboat? (Pages 116–117)

61. One parking garage in the city has 3 levels for parking. Suppose there are 8 cars on each level. How many cars in all are parked in the garage? (Pages 126–127)

62. A truck delivers 72 television sets in all to the warehouse. The sets are unloaded and put on a dolly. Each dolly carries 8 sets. How many trips must be made to unload the sets? (Pages 126–127)

Multiplication and Division Facts • **129**

CHAPTER TEST

Multiply.

1. $\begin{array}{r} 4 \\ \times 3 \\ \hline \end{array}$ 2. $\begin{array}{r} 6 \\ \times 0 \\ \hline \end{array}$ 3. $\begin{array}{r} 7 \\ \times 4 \\ \hline \end{array}$ 4. $\begin{array}{r} 6 \\ \times 7 \\ \hline \end{array}$ 5. $\begin{array}{r} 2 \\ \times 8 \\ \hline \end{array}$ 6. $\begin{array}{r} 6 \\ \times 9 \\ \hline \end{array}$

Write the missing factor.

7. $9 \times \underline{\quad?\quad} = 63$ 8. $\underline{\quad?\quad} \times 8 = 56$ 9. $3 \times 4 = \underline{\quad?\quad} \times 3$

Divide.

10. $36 \div 9 = \underline{\quad?\quad}$ 11. $72 \div 8 = \underline{\quad?\quad}$ 12. $0 \div 4 = \underline{\quad?\quad}$

13. $1\overline{)8}$ 14. $8\overline{)24}$ 15. $4\overline{)32}$ 16. $6\overline{)45}$ 17. $9\overline{)77}$ 18. $3\overline{)22}$

19. $52 \div 7 = \underline{\quad?\quad}$ 20. $39 \div 5 = \underline{\quad?\quad}$ 21. $33 \div 4 = \underline{\quad?\quad}$

Solve.

22. The dealership in Athens sells only motor homes. Each motor home has 6 tires. A salesman counted 42 tires in all. How many motor homes does he have?

23. Memorial Hospital has 8 ambulances to use in the county. On Saturday, each ambulance made 4 emergency runs. How many trips were made for the day?

24. There are 35 people waiting in line to take a balloon ride. The balloon makes 7 trips. An equal number of people ride each time. How many people are in the balloon for each trip?

25. A dump truck can carry 3 tons of dirt. It carries 9 full loads of dirt from the construction site. How many tons of dirt does it carry altogether?

ENRICHMENT

Prime Numbers

A **prime number** has exactly two factors: itself and 1.

THE NUMBER 1 IS NOT A PRIME NUMBER BECAUSE IT ONLY HAS ONE FACTOR

2 is a prime number.
Its factors are 1 and 2. $1 \times 2 = 2$

3 is a prime number.
Its factors are 1 and 3. $1 \times 3 = 3$

4 is not a prime number.
Its factors are 1, 2, and 4. $1 \times 4 = 4$ and $2 \times 2 = 4$

EXERCISES • Copy and complete the table.

1.

Number	Factors
2	1, 2
3	1, 3
4	1, 2, 4
5	
6	
7	
8	
9	1, 3, 9
10	

2.

Number	Factors
11	
12	1, 2, 3, 4, 6, 12
13	
14	
15	
16	1, 2, 4, 8, 16
17	
18	
19	

3. Make a table to show the prime numbers between 20 and 50.

ADDITIONAL PRACTICE

SKILLS

Multiply. (Pages 96–105).

1. $4 \times 3 = $ ___?___
2. $5 \times 7 = $ ___?___
3. $9 \times 2 = $ ___?___
4. $0 \times 6 = $ ___?___

5. $3 \times 8 = $ ___?___
6. $7 \times 4 = $ ___?___
7. $1 \times 9 = $ ___?___
8. $6 \times 6 = $ ___?___

9. $\begin{array}{r} 8 \\ \times 8 \\ \hline \end{array}$
10. $\begin{array}{r} 4 \\ \times 5 \\ \hline \end{array}$
11. $\begin{array}{r} 3 \\ \times 9 \\ \hline \end{array}$
12. $\begin{array}{r} 7 \\ \times 6 \\ \hline \end{array}$
13. $\begin{array}{r} 9 \\ \times 5 \\ \hline \end{array}$
14. $\begin{array}{r} 6 \\ \times 9 \\ \hline \end{array}$

Find the missing factors. (Pages 110–111)

15. ___?___ $\times 6 = 30$
16. $4 \times$ ___?___ $= 0$
17. ___?___ $\times 8 = 48$

18. $7 \times$ ___?___ $= 49$
19. ___?___ $\times 9 = 81$
20. $9 \times$ ___?___ $= 72$

Divide. (Pages 112–115, 118–123)

21. $56 \div 7 = $ ___?___
22. $0 \div 9 = $ ___?___
23. $35 \div 7 = $ ___?___
24. $32 \div 8 = $ ___?___

25. $5 \div 5 = $ ___?___
26. $14 \div 2 = $ ___?___
27. $63 \div 9 = $ ___?___
28. $24 \div 6 = $ ___?___

29. $4\overline{)28}$
30. $3\overline{)21}$
31. $5\overline{)40}$
32. $2\overline{)18}$
33. $7\overline{)7}$
34. $9\overline{)27}$

35. $8\overline{)16}$
36. $4\overline{)12}$
37. $7\overline{)0}$
38. $5\overline{)25}$
39. $9\overline{)45}$
40. $6\overline{)54}$

Find the quotient and the remainder. (Pages 124–125)

41. $5\overline{)8}$
42. $9\overline{)70}$
43. $7\overline{)60}$
44. $8\overline{)75}$
45. $6\overline{)32}$
46. $3\overline{)4}$

PROBLEM SOLVING • APPLICATIONS

47. At each airport, 6 planes land each hour. How many planes land in 8 hours? (Pages 102–103)

48. A small airplane can carry 4 people. How many people can ride in 6 small airplanes? (Pages 98–99)

49. There are 54 people on the Sky Train. The Sky Train has 6 cars. The same number of people are in each car. How many people are in each car? (Pages 116–117)

50. Jodi drives a delivery truck. Last week she worked 32 hours. She worked 8 hours each day. How many days did she work? (Pages 120–121)

COMMON ERRORS

Each of these problems contains a common error.

a. Find the correct answer.

b. Find the error.

1. Write the number.

4 hundreds 0 tens 8 ones = **480**

2. Write the expanded form for 312.

300 + 12

3. 2,492 rounded to the nearest thousand is **3,000.**

4. Write > or <.

725 ● 1,325

725 **>** 1,325

5.
```
   7
 +9
 ‾‾‾
  15
```

6.
```
   2
   5
 +4
 ‾‾‾
   7
```

7. 3 + __?__ = 7

3 + **10** = 7

8.
```
  2
 65
+17
‾‾‾
 91
```

9.
```
  1 1 1
  7,2 3 5
+ 3,1 4 6
‾‾‾‾‾‾‾‾‾
1 1,4 8 1
```

10. 375 + 6 + 15 = __?__

```
  375
    6
 +15
‾‾‾‾‾
1,125
```

11.
```
  6,352
 −2,947
 ‾‾‾‾‾‾
  4,615
```

12.
```
  3 1010
  4,0̸ 0̸ 7
 − 2,1 4 3
 ‾‾‾‾‾‾‾‾
   1,9 6 4
```

13.
```
   8
  ×7
 ‾‾‾
  54
```

14.
```
   0
  ×9
 ‾‾‾
   9
```

15.
```
    9
 3)‾1‾8‾
   18
   ‾‾
    0
```

16.
```
    6
 8)‾5‾0‾
   48
   ‾‾
    2
```

CUMULATIVE REVIEW
Chapters 1 through 4

Choose the correct answers.

1. 8 + 7 = _____?_____

A. 16   B. 14
C. 15   D. not here

2.   7
          4
        +3

A. 14   B. 15
C. 13   D. not here

3.   16
        − 7

A. 8   B. 9
C. 11   D. not here

4. Choose a number sentence that belongs to the same family of facts.

> 13 − 6 = 7
> 6 + 7 = 13

A. 13 + 6 = 19
B. 7 − 6 = 1
C. 13 − 7 = 6
D. not here

5. Choose the standard form for:

2,000 + 10

A. 2,100
B. 2,010
C. 2,101
D. not here

6. What is 3,089 rounded to the nearest hundred?

A. 3,090
B. 3,100
C. 3,000
D. not here

7. In 12,486 what digit is in the thousands place?

A. 8
B. 4
C. 1
D. not here

8. Choose the standard form for sixteen million, four hundred 5 thousand, two hundred ten.

A. 16,405,210
B. 16,450,201
C. 16,4005,210
D. not here

9. Which sign is missing?

1,406 ● 1,460

A. =
B. >
C. <
D. not here

10. Seanda needs 17 stickers to complete her sticker collection. She found 7 at the drugstore and 4 more at the card store. How many more stickers does Seanda need?

A. 10   B. 13
C. 28   D. 6

11. Erasers cost $0.11 each. Andy buys 3 erasers. He gives the clerk $0.50. What is his change?

A. $0.39   B. $0.27
C. $0.17   D. $0.13

12. 864
+375

A. 1,229 **B.** 1,139
C. 1,129 **D.** not here

13. $1,654 + 318 + 64 = \underline{\quad?\quad}$

A. 2,138 **B.** 2,036
C. 2,028 **D.** not here

14. $14.86
− 6.97

A. $8.79 **B.** $7.89
C. $7.81 **D.** not here

15. 3,600
−1,747

A. 1,853 **B.** 1,863
C. 1,963 **D.** not here

16. 4,587
−2,694

A. 2,193 **B.** 1,883
C. 1,893 **D.** not here

17. $8 \times \underline{\quad?\quad} = 56$

A. 6 **B.** 8
C. 7 **D.** not here

18. $18 = (2 \times \underline{\quad?\quad}) \times 3$

A. 3 **B.** 6
C. 1 **D.** not here

19. $64 \div 8 = \underline{\quad?\quad}$

A. 9 **B.** 6
C. 7 **D.** not here

20. $6\overline{)57}$

A. 9 r3 **B.** 8 r9
C. 9 r2 **D.** not here

21. $7\overline{)0}$

A. 1 **B.** 7
C. 0 **D.** not here

22. $37 \div 4 = \underline{\quad?\quad}$

A. 8 r5 **B.** 9 r1
C. 9 r4 **D.** not here

23. $9 \times \underline{\quad?\quad} = 63$

A. 7 **B.** 8
C. 6 **D.** not here

24. The store clerk counted 1,697 pencils on the shelf. He sold 498 on Monday. How many pencils were left?

A. 1,299 **B.** 1,199
C. 1,009 **D.** 1,099

25. There were 42 parakeets in the pet store. The store had 6 large cages. How many birds could be put in each cage?

A. 8 **B.** 7
C. 36 **D.** 48

MAINTENANCE
Chapters 1 through 4

Mixed Practice • Choose the correct answers.

1.
$$\begin{array}{r} 11 \\ +\ 8 \\ \hline \end{array}$$

A. 18   **B.** 19
C. 17   **D.** not here

2.
$$\begin{array}{r} 24 \\ +18 \\ \hline \end{array}$$

A. 32   **B.** 42
C. 34   **D.** not here

3. $17 + 4 + 8 = \underline{\ ?\ }$

A. 21   **B.** 19
C. 28   **D.** not here

4.
$$\begin{array}{r} 81 \\ 76 \\ 34 \\ +25 \\ \hline \end{array}$$

A. 216   **B.** 205
C. 206   **D.** not here

5. $18 - 9 = \underline{\ ?\ }$

A. 8   **B.** 11
C. 9   **D.** not here

6.
$$\begin{array}{r} 67 \\ -38 \\ \hline \end{array}$$

A. 39   **B.** 29
C. 31   **D.** not here

7.
$$\begin{array}{r} 300 \\ -\ 87 \\ \hline \end{array}$$

A. 127   **B.** 313
C. 213   **D.** not here

8.
$$\begin{array}{r} 218 \\ -149 \\ \hline \end{array}$$

A. 69   **B.** 169
C. 131   **D.** not here

9. ◖ = 3 tennis balls

◖◖◖ = $\underline{\ ?\ }$ tennis balls

A. 3   **B.** 9
C. 6   **D.** not here

10. Joseph counted the books each afternoon. He counted 32 reading books, 34 math books, 27 spelling books, and 18 science books. How many books did he count in all?

A. 91   **B.** 102
C. 110   **D.** not here

11. Martha counted the rulers and scissors in the classroom. She counted 96 rulers and 79 pairs of scissors. How many more rulers than scissors did she count?

A. 27   **B.** 17
C. 18   **D.** not here

Graphing

The students in a science class counted the number of times their hearts beat in one minute. They made the bar graph below to show the data.

- How many more heartbeats did Dawn count than Cathy?

Kinds of Collections

Collections

Model Cars
Sea Shells
Stamps
Dolls

0 1 2 3 4 5 6 7 8
Number of Students

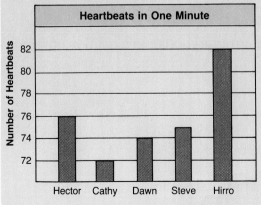

Heartbeats in One Minute

Number of Heartbeats

82
80
78
76
74
72

Hector Cathy Dawn Steve Hirro

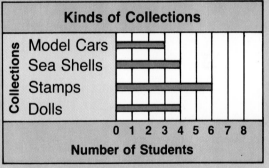

The students in Room 27 made the bar graph above to show the kinds of collections they have.

- How many students have stamp collections?

Bar Graphs

Mrs. Taylor asked the students in her class to choose their favorite subject. They made a **bar graph** to show the results.

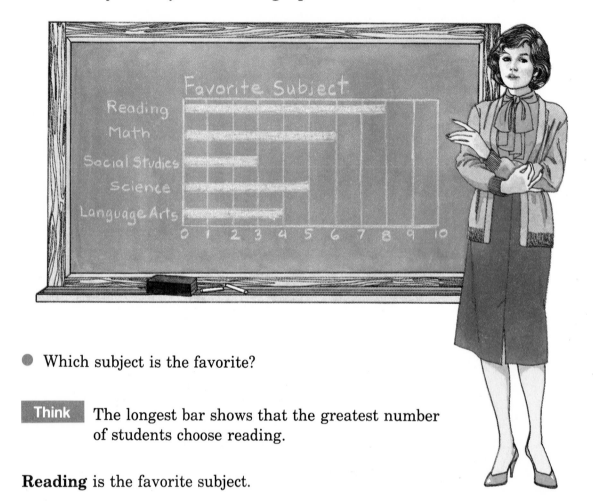

● Which subject is the favorite?

Think   The longest bar shows that the greatest number of students choose reading.

Reading is the favorite subject.

PRACTICE • Use the graph for Exercises 1–7.

Did more students choose

1. science or math?

2. language arts or social studies?

How many students chose

3. math?

4. science?

5. language arts?

How many more students chose

6. reading than science?

7. math than language arts?

EXERCISES • Use the graph for Exercises 8–12.

All of the students chose an after-school activity. They made a bar graph.

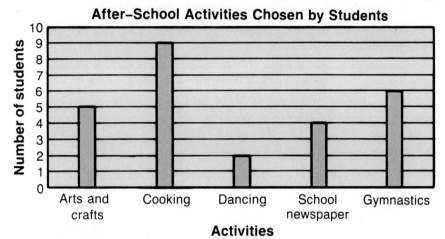

8. Which activity was chosen by the most students? the fewest?

Did more students choose

9. cooking or school newspaper?   10. school newspaper or dancing?

How many students chose   11. arts and crafts?   12. dancing?

Use this bar graph for Exercises 13–20.

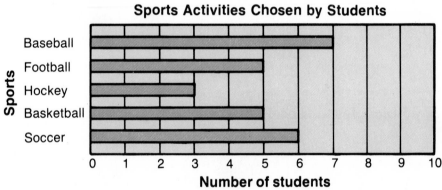

13. Which sport was chosen by the most students? the fewest?

Did more students choose   14. baseball or soccer?   15. basketball or hockey?

How many students chose   16. football?   17. hockey?   18. soccer?

PROBLEM SOLVING • APPLICATIONS

19. How many more students choose football than hockey?

20. How many more students choose soccer than hockey?

Pictographs

For one week Althea counted the number of bicycles that students rode to school each day. She made a **pictograph** to show this information.

Bicycles Students Ride to School Key: Each 🚲 stands for 10 bicycles.	
Monday	🚲 🚲 🚲 🚲
Tuesday	🚲 🚲 🚲 🚲 🚲
Wednesday	🚲 🚲 🚲 🚲
Thursday	🚲 🚲 🚲 🚲 🚲 🚲
Friday	🚲 🚲

● How many bicycles were at school on Wednesday?

Think The **key** shows that each 🚲 stands for 10 bicycles.

So each 🚲 stands for 5 bicycles.

$$10 + 10 + 10 = 30$$ ◀ Count the number of 🚲.
Count 10 for each bicycle.

$$30 + 5 = 35$$ ◀ Add 🚲.

There were **35 bicycles** at school on Wednesday.

PRACTICE • Use the graph for Exercises 1–7.

1. On which day were the most bicycles at school?

2. On which day were the fewest bicycles at school?

3. Were more bicycles at school on Tuesday or on Wednesday?

4. Were more bicycles at school on Tuesday or on Thursday?

How many bicycles were at school

5. on Monday?   6. on Tuesday?   7. on Friday?

EXERCISES • Use the graph for Exercises 8–13.

Herlis Miller owns a bicycle shop. He made a pictograph to show the number of tires he sold in six months.

Tires Sold in Six Months Key: Each ◯ stands for 20 tires.	
July	◯ ◯ ◯
August	◯ ◯ ◯ ◯ ◯
September	◯ ◯ ◖
October	◯ ◖
November	◯ ◯ ◯
December	◯ ◯ ◯ ◯ ◯ ◖

8. In which month were the most tires sold?

9. In which month were the fewest tires sold?

10. Were more tires sold in September or in November?

11. In which two months were the same number of tires sold?

12. How many tires were sold in August?   13. in September?

Use the graph for Exercises 14 and 15.

14. Who read the fewest books?

15. How many books did Sara read?

Student	Number of Books Read Key: Each ⌂ stands for 1 book.
Joe	⌂ ⌂ ⌂
Sara	⌂ ⌂ ⌂ ⌂ ⌂
Karl	⌂

PROBLEM SOLVING • APPLICATIONS

Suppose the key for the picture graph were changed so that each ⌂ stands for 6 books.

16. How many books were read by Joe?   17. by Sarah?   18. by Karl?

19. How many more books did Sarah read than Joe?

20. How many more books did Sarah read than Joe and Karl together?

PROBLEM SOLVING · STRATEGIES

Collecting Data to Make Graphs

Graphs are used to show and compare data or facts.

Example 1 The mathematics teacher did a survey of the class to find out how each student used each day. Each student made a table of the data. Then each student made a pictograph of this data. Here is Martha's table and graph.

Activity	Number of Hours Spent Each Day
Sleeping	9
Playing	2
Television	4
School	6
Homework	1
Eating	1
Other	1

How Martha Uses Her School Day	
Sleeping	▲▲▲▲▲▲▲▲▲
Playing	▲▲
Television	▲▲▲▲
School	▲▲▲▲▲▲
Homework	▲
Eating	▲
Other Things	▲

Key: ▲ stands for 1 hour

Example 2 The students in science class did an experiment. The students counted the number of times their heart beats in one minute. They made a table of this data. Then they made a bar graph of this data.

Name	Number of Heartbeats
Hector	76
Cathy	72
Dawn	74
Steve	75
Hirro	82

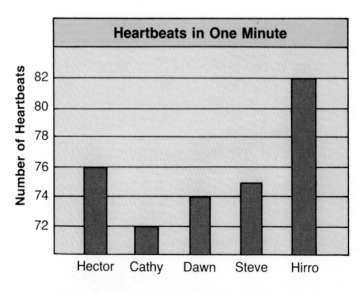

PROBLEMS • Use the pictograph in Example 1 to solve Problems 1–4.

1. How many hours did Martha spend in school?

2. How many hours did she spend doing homework?

3. How many hours did she spend altogether each day at school and doing homework?

4. How many more hours did she spend playing than in doing homework?

A graph should always have a title.

---

5. Make a pictograph to show how Suzie uses her day.

   Let ▩ stand for 2 hours.

Suzie's Table	
Activity	**Number of Hours Spent Each Day**
Sleeping	8
Playing	1
Television	3
School	6
Homework	1
Eating	2
Other	3

Use the bar graph in Example 2 to solve Problems 6–9.

6. How many heartbeats did Hirro count?

7. How many heartbeats did Dawn count?

8. How many more heartbeats did Hirro count than Dawn?

9. How many more heartbeats did Hector count than Steve?

10. Make a bar graph of this data.

Name	Number of Heartbeats
Maria	78
Blane	77
Betty	74
Tim	79

PROJECT Do the experiment. Make a table and a bar graph.

Experiment

● Count the number of breaths you take in one minute.

● Jog in place for one minute.

● Then count again the number of breaths you take in one minute.

Write a word problem based on the information in the graph.

Line Graphs

The students in Mr. Watt's class made a **line graph** showing the temperature at noon for one week. A line graph is used to show change.

● On what day was the temperature the highest?

Think The highest point on the graph shows the highest temperature.

The highest temperature was on **Tuesday**.

PRACTICE • Use the graph for Exercises 1–7.

1. Which day had the lowest temperature?

2. Which two days were the warmest?

3. Was the temperature on Monday higher or lower than the temperature on Thursday?

What was the temperature on

4. Wednesday?   5. Sunday?   6. Friday?

7. On which day was the temperature 20°C?

EXERCISES • Use the line graph below for Exercises 8–12.

The students in the class made a line graph to show how the number of students in the fourth grade changed during a period of six years.

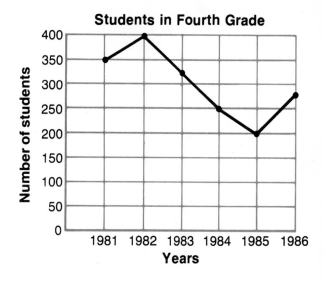

Students in Fourth Grade

8. During which year were there the most students in the fourth grade? the fewest?

9. Were there more or fewer students in 1982 than 1984?

10. During which two years did the number of students go up?

11. How many students were there in 1981?

12. in 1984?

Use this line graph for Exercises 13–19.

13. In what year did a school lunch cost $0.70?

14. In what year did the price go up the most?

15. In what two years did the price stay the same?

16. What was the price of a school lunch in 1981?

17. What was the price of a school lunch in 1984?

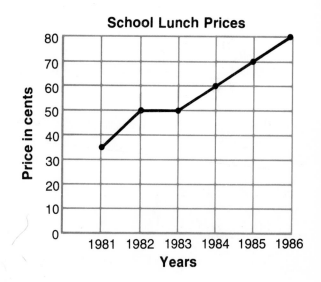

School Lunch Prices

PROBLEM SOLVING • APPLICATIONS

18. How much did the lunch prices increase from 1981 to 1984?

19. Write a word problem based on the information in the graph.

Locating Points on a Grid

Mrs. Lowry, the mathematics teacher, uses an **ordered pair** of numbers to locate the desk for each student. She made this grid on graph paper. Each seat is a point, and each point is named by a letter.

● Which point is located by the ordered pair (2, 4)?

Step 1 Start at 0.

Step 2 Move 2 spaces to the right.

Step 3 Move 4 spaces up.

Point A is located by the ordered pair (2, 4).

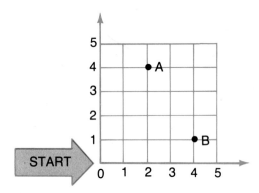

● Which ordered pair tells the location of point B?

Think B is located 4 spaces to the right of zero and 1 space up from zero.

The ordered pair **(4, 1)** tells the location of point B.

PRACTICE • Use the grid below for Exercises 1–24.
What letter does each ordered pair stand for?

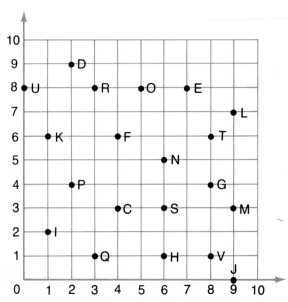

1. (6, 3)   **2.** (1, 6)   **3.** (5, 8)

4. (4, 6)   **5.** (3, 1)   **6.** (9, 0)

7. (6, 1)   **8.** (2, 9)   **9.** (2, 4)

10. (0, 8)   **11.** (8, 1)   **12.** (9, 7)

Which ordered pair tells the location of the point?

13. M   **14.** R   **15.** I   **16.** C   **17.** G   **18.** E

19. N   **20.** T   **21.** K   **22.** U   **23.** H   **24.** J

EXERCISES • Use this grid for Exercises 25–42. Which letter is at each point?

25. (2, 2)   **26.** (4, 8)   **27.** (7, 1)

28. (0, 5)   **29.** (3, 4)   **30.** (8, 7)

31. (9, 10)   **32.** (5, 0)   **33.** (1, 9)

What ordered pair tells the location of the point?

34. A   **35.** E   **36.** G

37. R   **38.** H   **39.** X

40. K   **41.** V   **42.** Z

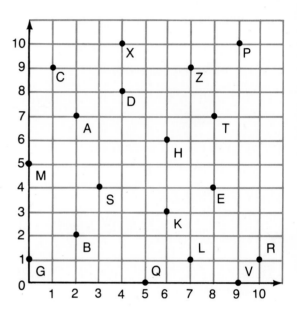

PROBLEM SOLVING • APPLICATIONS

Use the letters at the points to answer the riddles. Move right and up to find each letter.

43. What are raised in Brazil during the rainy season?
(8, 4) (10, 5) (9, 6) (5, 8) (6, 5) (7, 1) (7, 1) (5, 2) (10, 9)

44. Which side of a chicken has the most feathers?
(3, 2) (2, 6) (6, 5) (2, 4) (8, 4) (3, 2) (10, 9) (7, 9) (9, 2) (6, 5)

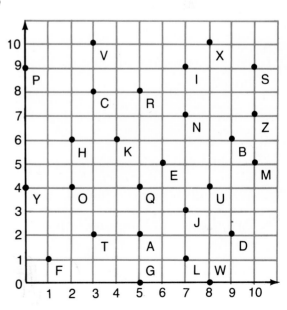

CHAPTER REVIEW

Part 1: VOCABULARY

For Exercises 1–5, choose from the box at the right the word that completes each statement.

1. A picture or symbol is used to represent numbers in a ___?___. (Page 140)

2. A ___?___ is used in a pictograph to show how many each object represents. (Page 140)

3. The length or height of a bar represents a number in a ___?___ graph. (Page 138)

4. A graph in which a line is used to show a change is a ___?___ graph. (Page 144)

5. A pair of numbers used to locate points on a grid is called an ___?___ pair. (Page 146)

| bar |
| circle |
| key |
| line |
| ordered |
| pictograph |

Part 2: SKILLS

Use the bar graph to answer Exercises 6–11. (Pages 138–139)

6. Which drink is chosen by the most students?

7. Which drink is chosen by the fewest students?

8. Do more students choose milk or chocolate milk?

9. How many students choose apple juice?

10. How many students choose orange juice?

11. How many more students choose apple juice than orange juice?

Use the pictograph to answer Exercises 12–17. (Pages 140–141)

12. Which club has the most members?

13. Which club has the fewest members?

14. Are there more members in the science club or in the crafts club?

15. How many music club members are there?

School Clubs Each ☺ stands for 10 members.	
Science club	☺ ☺ ☺
Crafts club	☺ ☺ ☺
Bowling club	☺ ☺ ☺ ☺
Chess club	☺ ☺
Music club	☺ ☺

16. How many chess club members are there?

17. How many more members are in the music club than the chess club?

Use the line graph to answer Exercises 18–23. (Pages 144–145)

18. Which day has the highest average temperature?

19. Which day has the lowest average temperature?

20. On which day is the average temperature 4°C?

21. What is the average temperature on Monday?

22. What is the average temperature on Tuesday?

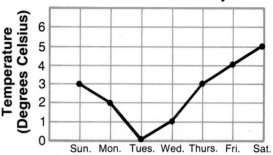

Average Temperature for One Week in January

23. How much higher is the average temperature on Friday than on Wednesday?

Use the grid to answer Exercises 24–35. (Pages 146–147)

What letter does each ordered pair stand for?

24. (10, 3)   **25.** (2, 2)   **26.** (4, 7)
27. (3, 1)   **28.** (8, 0)   **29.** (6, 4)

What ordered pair tells the location of the point?

30. F   **31.** B   **32.** H
33. K   **34.** N   **35.** J

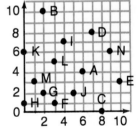

Part 3: PROBLEM SOLVING • APPLICATIONS

36. Make a bar graph to show the favorite pets chosen most often by Mrs. Taylor's class. Use this data. (Page 142)

Type of animal	Number of votes
Dog	10
Cat	8
Hamster	6
Fish	4
Bird	2

Graphing • **149**

CHAPTER TEST

Use the bar graph for Exercises 1–3.

1. Which collection do the most students have?

2. Do more students have a collection of model cars or dolls?

3. How many students collect stamps?

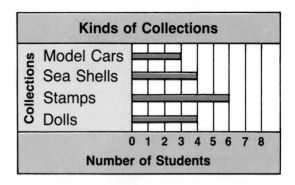

Use the pictograph for Exercises 4–6.

4. Which team has the fewest number of students?

5. Which team has more students than the basketball team?

6. How many students are on the hockey team?

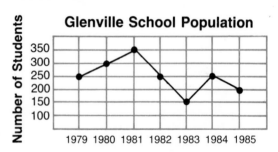

Use the line graph for Exercises 7–9.

7. In which year were there the most students?

8. In which year were there more students, 1980 or 1982?

9. How many students were in Glenville School in 1981?

Use the grid for Exercises 10–12.

10. Which letter is at point (5, 4)?

11. Which letter is at point (3, 1)?

12. Which ordered pair tells the location of point D?

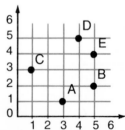

13. Make a bar graph to show the favorite books chosen most often by Miss Carr's class. Use the data at the right.

Type of Book	Number of Votes
Biography	8
Sports	4
Mystery	5
Fiction	3

ENRICHMENT

Graphing Ordered Pairs

John made a picture by graphing these ordered pairs.

a. (3, 2)   **b.** (3, 4)   **c.** (5, 4)   **d.** (7, 4)   **e.** (7, 6)   **f.** (5, 6)

g. (3, 6)   **h.** (5, 9)   **i.** (7, 12)   **j.** (7, 9)   **k.** (7, 6)   **l.** (7, 4)

m. (9, 4)   **n.** (11, 4)   **o.** (9, 2)   **p.** (6, 2)   **q.** (3, 2)

First he numbered a grid. Then he located (3,2).

| Think | Move 3 points to the right and 2 points up.

Next he located (3,4).

| Think | Move 3 points to the right and 4 points up. Connect the dots.

Then he completed the picture by graphing the ordered pairs and connecting the dots in order.

What did John draw?

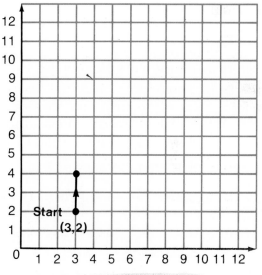

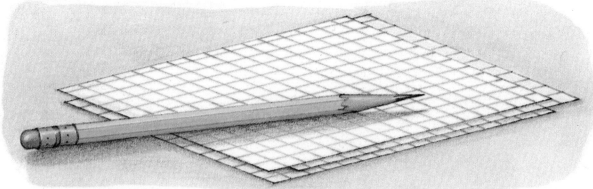

EXERCISES • Locate the points for each ordered pair and draw a dot. Then connect the dots in order. Tell what picture you graphed.

1. (1, 6)   **2.** (4, 7)   **3.** (3, 9)   **4.** (5, 8)   **5.** (6, 12)   **6.** (7, 8)

7. (9, 9)   **8.** (8, 7)   **9.** (11, 6)   **10.** (8, 5)   **11.** (9, 3)   **12.** (7, 4)

13. (6, 0)   **14.** (5, 4)   **15.** (3, 3)   **16.** (4, 5)   **17.** (1, 6)

ADDITIONAL PRACTICE

Martha made a bar graph to show how many tickets
each fourth-grade class sold to a spaghetti dinner.

Use the bar graph to answer Exercises 1–4.
(Pages 138–139)

1. Which room sold the most tickets?

2. Which room sold the fewest tickets?

3. Did Room A or Room B sell more tickets?

4. How many more tickets did Room C sell
than Room D?

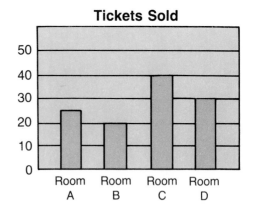

Mr. James, the physical education teacher, made a
pictograph to show the results of the baseball games.

Use the pictograph to answer Exercises 5–8. (Pages 140–141)

5. How many games did room D win?

6. Which room won the most games?

7. Which room won the fewest games?

8. How many more games did Room
B win than Room D?

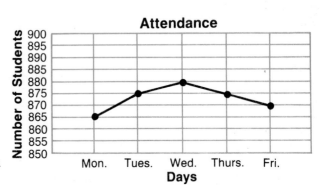

Mrs. Campbell made a line graph to show the change
in attendance at Oak Knoll Elementary in a week.

Use the line graph to answer Exercises 9–11.
(Pages 144–145)

9. On what day of the week was
the attendance the highest?

10. On which days was the
attendance the same?

11. How many more students were
in school on Wednesday than on
Friday?

COMPUTER APPLICATIONS
Print Commands: * and /

The symbol for multiplication in BASIC is *.
On most computers, you must hold down a shift key
to type *. (You may have to do this for + also.)
Type this command.

PRINT 3*2 — **Press the space bar to make this space.**

Now press **RETURN** or **ENTER** or ←⏎
Does the computer show 6?

 RETURN

 ENTER

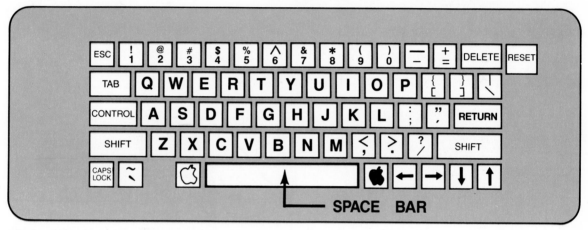

SPACE BAR

The symbol for division in BASIC is /.
To type / you do **not** have to hold down a shift key.
Remember! What you type is **input**. What the computer shows is **output**.

Your input	PRINT 7 + 6	PRINT 14 − 7	PRINT 7 * 6	PRINT 42 / 7
Computer's output	13	7	42	6

EXERCISES • What is the computer's output?

1. PRINT 9 + 5
2. PRINT 14 − 9
3. PRINT 7 * 8
4. PRINT 56/7
5. PRINT 18 − 6
6. PRINT 12 + 6
7. PRINT 9 * 6
8. PRINT 54/6
9. PRINT 9 + 6
10. PRINT 9 − 3
11. PRINT 9 * 3
12. PRINT 27/3

MAINTENANCE

Mixed Practice • Choose the correct answers.

1. 9
  ×8

A. 76   B. 72
C. 74   D. not here

2. 7 × 6 = __?__

A. 45   B. 35
C. 42   D. not here

3. $0.08
  ×   6

A. $0.48   B. $0.56
C. 48   D. not here

4. 8
  ×8

A. 16   B. 72
C. 64   D. not here

5. (4 × 8) + 6 = __?__

A. 37   B. 38
C. 33   D. not here

6. (9 × 7) + 8 = __?__

A. 71   B. 70
C. 64   D. not here

7. (7 × 8) + 8 = __?__

A. 54   B. 64
C. 63   D. not here

8. 4 × __?__ = 36

A. 8   B. 7
C. 9   D. not here

9. 9 × __?__ = 54

A. 3   B. 30
C. 1   D. not here

10. A computer has 4 rows of keys. Each row has 8 keys. How many keys are there in all?

A. 15   B. 32
C. 44   D. not here

11. At the animal exhibit there are 9 pens. Each pen holds 6 animals. How many animals are there in all?

A. 45   B. 15
C. 56   D. not here

Multiplying by One-Digit Numbers

Martin buys some tickets for rides at the fair. He receives $0.43 in change. The clerk gives him a quarter, a dime, 3 pennies, and one other coin.

● What is the other coin?

The bumper cars at the fair are crowded. There are 3 lines of people waiting to ride. Each line has 23 people.

● How many people are waiting in all?

155

Multiplying Two-Digit Numbers

The merry-go-round is one of the most popular rides at the fair. There are 12 horses in each row around the merry-go-round. There are 3 rows of horses.

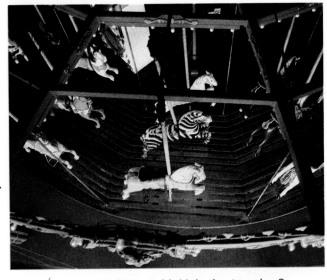

● How many horses are there?

Think There are 3 groups of 12. So multiply.

$3 \times 12 = ?$

Step 1 Multiply the ones by 3.

$$\begin{array}{r} 12 \\ \times\ 3 \\ \hline 6 \end{array}$$

Step 2 Multiply the tens by 3.

$$\begin{array}{r} 12 \\ \times\ 3 \\ \hline 36 \end{array}$$ ◀ Product

There are **36 horses** on the merry-go-round.

PRACTICE • Multiply.

1. $\begin{array}{r} 21 \\ \times\ 4 \\ \hline \end{array}$
2. $\begin{array}{r} 41 \\ \times\ 2 \\ \hline \end{array}$
3. $\begin{array}{r} 13 \\ \times\ 3 \\ \hline \end{array}$
4. $\begin{array}{r} 32 \\ \times\ 3 \\ \hline \end{array}$
5. $\begin{array}{r} 33 \\ \times\ 2 \\ \hline \end{array}$
6. $\begin{array}{r} 42 \\ \times\ 2 \\ \hline \end{array}$

7. $\begin{array}{r} 31 \\ \times\ 2 \\ \hline \end{array}$
8. $\begin{array}{r} 24 \\ \times\ 2 \\ \hline \end{array}$
9. $\begin{array}{r} 23 \\ \times\ 3 \\ \hline \end{array}$
10. $\begin{array}{r} 44 \\ \times\ 2 \\ \hline \end{array}$
11. $\begin{array}{r} 21 \\ \times\ 3 \\ \hline \end{array}$
12. $\begin{array}{r} 12 \\ \times\ 3 \\ \hline \end{array}$

EXERCISES • Multiply.

13. $\begin{array}{r} 14 \\ \times\ 2 \\ \hline \end{array}$
14. $\begin{array}{r} 21 \\ \times\ 2 \\ \hline \end{array}$
15. $\begin{array}{r} 11 \\ \times\ 3 \\ \hline \end{array}$
16. $\begin{array}{r} 31 \\ \times\ 3 \\ \hline \end{array}$
17. $\begin{array}{r} 34 \\ \times\ 2 \\ \hline \end{array}$
18. $\begin{array}{r} 41 \\ \times\ 1 \\ \hline \end{array}$

19. $\begin{array}{r} 33 \\ \times\ 3 \\ \hline \end{array}$
20. $\begin{array}{r} 11 \\ \times\ 7 \\ \hline \end{array}$
21. $\begin{array}{r} 43 \\ \times\ 2 \\ \hline \end{array}$
22. $\begin{array}{r} 34 \\ \times\ 1 \\ \hline \end{array}$
23. $\begin{array}{r} 12 \\ \times\ 4 \\ \hline \end{array}$
24. $\begin{array}{r} 13 \\ \times\ 2 \\ \hline \end{array}$

25. $\begin{array}{r} 20 \\ \times\ 2 \\ \hline \end{array}$
26. $\begin{array}{r} 10 \\ \times\ 2 \\ \hline \end{array}$
27. $\begin{array}{r} 12 \\ \times\ 2 \\ \hline \end{array}$
28. $\begin{array}{r} 20 \\ \times\ 4 \\ \hline \end{array}$
29. $\begin{array}{r} 25 \\ \times\ 1 \\ \hline \end{array}$
30. $\begin{array}{r} 20 \\ \times\ 3 \\ \hline \end{array}$

31. 11 × 5	32. 30 × 2	33. 10 × 9	34. 10 × 6	35. 22 × 4	36. 11 × 8
37. 10 × 3	38. 22 × 3	39. 30 × 3	40. 23 × 2	41. 40 × 2	42. 10 × 5

Mental Math Give the products.

43. $4 \times 11 = $ __?__

44. $8 \times 10 = $ __?__

45. $2 \times 22 = $ __?__

46. $3 \times 12 = $ __?__

47. $9 \times 11 = $ __?__

48. $2 \times 14 = $ __?__

49. $3 \times 13 = $ __?__

50. $2 \times 34 = $ __?__

51. $2 \times 32 = $ __?__

Write > or <.

★ 52. $11 \times 2 \times 3$ ● $10 \times 3 \times 2$

★ 53. $11 \times 2 \times 4$ ● $21 \times 2 \times 2$

PROBLEM SOLVING • APPLICATIONS

CHOOSE • mental math • pencil and paper • calculator **SOLVE**

54. The bumper cars are crowded. There are 3 lines of people waiting to ride. Each line has 23 people. How many people are waiting?

55. The fair has 4 trains to carry visitors. Each train holds 12 people. How many people will the trains hold?

★ 57. The tea cup ride is busy. There are 114 people in line. Each of the 22 cups hold 4 people. After loading for the next ride, how many people will still be in line?

56. The sky rocket ride seats 48 people in all. There are 6 rockets on it. How many people will each rocket seat?

Multiplying by One-Digit Numbers • 157

Regrouping Ones

Through the years, many new inventions have been exhibited at fairs. Among these were the telephone in 1876, the early automobiles in 1904, and the television in 1939.

The state fair has 3 large exhibition tents. Each tent has room for 29 exhibits.

● How many exhibits are shown in all?

Think There are 3 groups of 29. So multiply.

$$3 \times 29 = ?$$

Step 1 Multiply the ones.
$3 \times 9 = 27$
Regroup 27 as
2 tens and 7 ones.

```
  2
  2 9
×   3
─────
    7
```

Step 2 Multiply the tens.
$3 \times 2 \text{ tens} = 6 \text{ tens}$
Add the 2 tens.
$6 \text{ tens} + 2 \text{ tens} = 8 \text{ tens}$

```
  2
  2 9
×   3
─────
  8 7
```

Another Method • Mental Math

Use the **distributive property.**

$$3 \times 29 = 3 \times (20 + 9)$$
$$= (3 \times 20) + (3 \times 9)$$
$$= 60 + 27$$
$$= \mathbf{87}$$

There are **87 exhibits** in all.

PRACTICE • Multiply.

1. $\begin{array}{r} 14 \\ \times\ 3 \\ \hline \end{array}$	2. $\begin{array}{r} 26 \\ \times\ 3 \\ \hline \end{array}$	3. $\begin{array}{r} 16 \\ \times\ 5 \\ \hline \end{array}$	4. $\begin{array}{r} 27 \\ \times\ 3 \\ \hline \end{array}$	5. $\begin{array}{r} 38 \\ \times\ 2 \\ \hline \end{array}$	6. $\begin{array}{r} 46 \\ \times\ 2 \\ \hline \end{array}$
7. $\begin{array}{r} 24 \\ \times\ 4 \\ \hline \end{array}$	8. $\begin{array}{r} 18 \\ \times\ 4 \\ \hline \end{array}$	9. $\begin{array}{r} 19 \\ \times\ 5 \\ \hline \end{array}$	10. $\begin{array}{r} 28 \\ \times\ 2 \\ \hline \end{array}$	11. $\begin{array}{r} 39 \\ \times\ 2 \\ \hline \end{array}$	12. $\begin{array}{r} 17 \\ \times\ 5 \\ \hline \end{array}$
13. $\begin{array}{r} 27 \\ \times\ 2 \\ \hline \end{array}$	14. $\begin{array}{r} 39 \\ \times\ 2 \\ \hline \end{array}$	15. $\begin{array}{r} 48 \\ \times\ 2 \\ \hline \end{array}$	16. $\begin{array}{r} 13 \\ \times\ 7 \\ \hline \end{array}$	17. $\begin{array}{r} 24 \\ \times\ 3 \\ \hline \end{array}$	18. $\begin{array}{r} 25 \\ \times\ 3 \\ \hline \end{array}$

EXERCISES • Multiply. Use the method you prefer.

19. 36 × 2	20. 14 × 7	21. 26 × 3	22. 37 × 2	23. 47 × 2	24. 13 × 6

25. 18 × 5	26. 15 × 6	27. 20 × 4	28. 14 × 6	29. 35 × 2	30. 32 × 3

31. 43 × 2	32. 27 × 3	33. 45 × 2	34. 16 × 3	35. 25 × 2	36. 10 × 7

37. 41 × 2	38. 19 × 4	39. 49 × 2	40. 30 × 3	41. 38 × 2	42. 48 × 2

43. $5 \times 14 =$ __?__   44. $2 \times 26 =$ __?__   45. $3 \times 28 =$ __?__

46. $2 \times 46 =$ __?__   47. $5 \times 13 =$ __?__   48. $3 \times 32 =$ __?__

Mental Math Give the missing factors.

49. $5 \times$ __?__ $= 50$ 50. $3 \times$ __?__ $= 30$ 51. $9 \times$ __?__ $= 90$

52. $2 \times$ __?__ $= 22$ 53. $4 \times$ __?__ $= 44$ 54. $9 \times$ __?__ $= 99$

PROBLEM SOLVING • APPLICATIONS

55. Inside the energy exhibit, there are 6 large tables. Each table has 18 chairs. How many people will this exhibit hold?

56. The computer exhibit is in 2 sections. Each section has 26 computers. How many computers are there in all?

THINKER'S CORNER

Three children lined up to take turns at the dart throw. Each child made 3 times as many points as the child before him. Ted was the first to throw his five darts. Alice was last. How many points did John have?

Regrouping Ones and Tens

Students from Garden Elementary School are going to the fair. They are riding in 4 buses. Each bus carries 32 students.

● How many students are going to the fair?

Think There are 4 groups of 32. So multiply.

$$4 \times 32 = ?$$

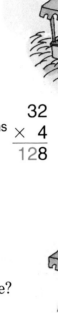

Step 1
Multiply the ones.
$4 \times 2 = 8$

$$\begin{array}{r} 32 \\ \times\ 4 \\ \hline 8 \end{array}$$

Step 2
Multiply the tens.
4×3 tens $= 12$ tens

$$\begin{array}{r} 32 \\ \times\ 4 \\ \hline 128 \end{array}$$

There are **128 students** going to the fair.

There are 6 booths on the midway. Each booth has 27 different prizes.

● How many different prizes are there?

Think There are 6 groups of 27. So multiply.

$$6 \times 27 = ?$$

Step 1
Multiply the ones.
$6 \times 7 = 42$
Regroup 42 ones as 4 tens and 2 ones

$$\begin{array}{r} \overset{4}{2}7 \\ \times\ 6 \\ \hline 2 \end{array}$$

Step 2
Multiply the tens.
6×2 tens $= 12$ tens
Add the 4 tens.
12 tens $+ 4$ tens $= 16$ tens

$$\begin{array}{r} \overset{4}{2}7 \\ \times\ 6 \\ \hline 162 \end{array}$$

There are **162 different prizes**.

PRACTICE • Multiply.

1. $\begin{array}{r} 27 \\ \times\ 6 \end{array}$

2. $\begin{array}{r} 35 \\ \times\ 4 \end{array}$

3. $\begin{array}{r} 42 \\ \times\ 9 \end{array}$

4. $\begin{array}{r} 81 \\ \times\ 5 \end{array}$

5. $\begin{array}{r} 42 \\ \times\ 4 \end{array}$

6. $\begin{array}{r} 63 \\ \times\ 3 \end{array}$

7. $\begin{array}{r} 54 \\ \times\ 3 \end{array}$

8. $\begin{array}{r} 62 \\ \times\ 4 \end{array}$

9. $\begin{array}{r} 37 \\ \times\ 8 \end{array}$

10. $\begin{array}{r} 52 \\ \times\ 4 \end{array}$

11. $\begin{array}{r} 91 \\ \times\ 6 \end{array}$

12. $\begin{array}{r} 45 \\ \times\ 8 \end{array}$

EXERCISES • Multiply.

13. 39
× 3

14. 37
× 7

15. 28
× 5

16. 46
× 9

17. 67
× 2

18. 76
× 6

19. 59
× 4

20. 36
× 8

21. 44
× 6

22. 27
× 8

23. 92
× 8

24. 94
× 5

25. 82
× 7

26. 42
× 4

27. 70
× 5

28. 52
× 9

29. 32
× 3

30. 68
× 9

31. 35
× 9

32. 56
× 4

33. 41
× 6

34. 89
× 3

35. 27
× 3

36. 39
× 7

37. 48
× 4

38. 37
× 2

39. 52
× 6

40. 49
× 8

41. 63
× 5

42. 84
× 3

43. 57
× 4

44. 28
× 7

45. 48
× 2

46. 95
× 8

47. 67
× 9

48. 78
× 5

49. $6 \times 53 =$ ___?___

50. $7 \times 56 =$ ___?___

51. $5 \times 16 =$ ___?___

52. $4 \times 47 =$ ___?___

53. $7 \times 98 =$ ___?___

54. $9 \times 67 =$ ___?___

★ 55. $(3 + 6) \times 16 =$ ___?___

★ 56. $7 \times (16 + 10) =$ ___?___

★ 57. $7 \times (52 - 15) =$ ___?___

PROBLEM SOLVING • APPLICATIONS

58. Bill won 4 bags of marbles on the midway. Each bag has 38 marbles. How many marbles did he win?

59. Carlos won 3 boxes of baseball cards. There were 18 cards in each box. How many cards did he win?

60. Lisa used 28 tickets at midway booths. Jill used 18 tickets along the midway. How many more tickets did Lisa use than Jill?

★ 61. At the softball toss, John knocked down 19 milk cartons in 5 tries. Ted knocked down 2 times as many as John. How many did Ted knock down?

Multiplying Three-Digit Numbers

The roller coaster at the state fair has 3 tunnels. Each tunnel measures 254 feet long.

● What is the total length for all 3 tunnels?

Think The 3 tunnels measure the same length. So multiply to find the total length.

$$3 \times 254 = ?$$

Step 1 Multiply the ones. Regroup 12 ones as 1 ten 2 ones.

$$\begin{array}{r} 1 \\ 254 \\ \times \quad 3 \\ \hline 2 \end{array}$$

Step 2 Multiply the tens. Add the 1 ten. Regroup 16 tens as 1 hundred 6 tens.

$$\begin{array}{r} 1\ 1 \\ 254 \\ \times \quad 3 \\ \hline 62 \end{array}$$

Step 3 Multiply the hundreds. Add the 1 hundred.

$$\begin{array}{r} 1\ 1 \\ 254 \\ \times \quad 3 \\ \hline 762 \end{array}$$

The total length of the 3 tunnels is **762 feet.**

More Examples

With Regrouping

$$\begin{array}{r} 1 \\ 409 \\ \times \quad 2 \\ \hline 818 \end{array} \qquad \begin{array}{r} 2\ 1 \\ 176 \\ \times \quad 3 \\ \hline 528 \end{array}$$

Without Regrouping

$$\begin{array}{r} 234 \\ \times \quad 2 \\ \hline 468 \end{array} \qquad \begin{array}{r} 312 \\ \times \quad 3 \\ \hline 936 \end{array}$$

PRACTICE • Multiply.

1. $\begin{array}{r} 325 \\ \times \ \ 3 \\ \hline \end{array}$
2. $\begin{array}{r} 264 \\ \times \ \ 2 \\ \hline \end{array}$
3. $\begin{array}{r} 423 \\ \times \ \ 2 \\ \hline \end{array}$
4. $\begin{array}{r} 425 \\ \times \ \ 2 \\ \hline \end{array}$
5. $\begin{array}{r} 324 \\ \times \ \ 2 \\ \hline \end{array}$
6. $\begin{array}{r} 413 \\ \times \ \ 2 \\ \hline \end{array}$

7. $\begin{array}{r} 481 \\ \times \ \ 2 \\ \hline \end{array}$
8. $\begin{array}{r} 325 \\ \times \ \ 3 \\ \hline \end{array}$
9. $\begin{array}{r} 151 \\ \times \ \ 4 \\ \hline \end{array}$
10. $\begin{array}{r} 148 \\ \times \ \ 6 \\ \hline \end{array}$
11. $\begin{array}{r} 319 \\ \times \ \ 3 \\ \hline \end{array}$
12. $\begin{array}{r} 272 \\ \times \ \ 3 \\ \hline \end{array}$

EXERCISES • Multiply.

13. 413
× 2

14. 243
× 3

15. 326
× 3

16. 146
× 5

17. 182
× 4

18. 309
× 3

19. 170
× 5

20. 218
× 4

21. 252
× 3

22. 124
× 7

23. 412
× 2

24. 317
× 2

25. 158
× 6

26. 192
× 3

27. 209
× 4

28. 178
× 4

29. 405
× 2

30. 183
× 5

31. 315
× 3

32. 147
× 6

33. 308
× 3

34. 153
× 4

35. 192
× 4

36. 224
× 4

37. $7 \times 128 =$ ___?___

38. $4 \times 209 =$ ___?___

39. $2 \times 304 =$ ___?___

40. $3 \times 248 =$ ___?___

41. $6 \times 143 =$ ___?___

★ 42. $4 \times 187 =$ ___?___

PROBLEM SOLVING • APPLICATIONS

43. The largest carousel can carry 115 people. How many people will ride if it is filled 5 times?

44. The roller-coaster can carry 132 people. How many people will ride if it is filled 6 times?

45. Martin buys some tickets for fair rides. He receives $0.43 in change. The clerk gives him 1 quarter, 1 dime, 3 pennies, and 1 other coin. What is the other coin?

★ 46. The ferris wheel has 36 gondolas. Each gondola holds 6 people. The ferris wheel is filled 8 times every hour. How many people can ride the ferris wheel in one hour?

Make up a story problem to go with the numbers. Then solve.

★ 47. $4 \times 215 =$ ___?___

★ 48. $3 \times 324 =$ ___?___

THINKER'S CORNER

What are the next two numbers in the pattern?

a. | 2 | 8 | 32 | ? | ? |

b. | 6 | 18 | 54 | ? | ? |

Greater Products

Saturday is student day at the state fair. Each of the 7 local schools were given 246 free passes to give to the students.

● How many free passes were given?

Think There are 7 groups of 246 students.
So multiply.

$7 \times 246 = ?$

Step 1
Multiply the ones.
Regroup 42 ones
as 4 tens 2 ones.

$$
\begin{array}{r}
{\scriptstyle 4} \\
2\,4\,6 \\
\times\quad 7 \\
\hline
2 \\
\end{array}
$$

Step 2
Multiply the tens.
Add the 4 tens.
Regroup 32 tens
as 3 hundreds 2
tens.

$$
\begin{array}{r}
{\scriptstyle 3}\,{\scriptstyle 4} \\
2\,4\,6 \\
\times\quad 7 \\
\hline
2\,2 \\
\end{array}
$$

Step 3
Multiply the hundreds.
Add the 3 hundreds.

$$
\begin{array}{r}
{\scriptstyle 3}\,{\scriptstyle 4} \\
2\,4\,6 \\
\times\quad 7 \\
\hline
1,7\,2\,2 \\
\end{array}
$$

There were **1,722 free passes** given to the students.

PRACTICE • Multiply.

1. 923 × 6	2. 465 × 2	3. 724 × 7	4. 248 × 4	5. 823 × 8	6. 673 × 6
7. 195 × 3	8. 369 × 2	9. 135 × 9	10. 827 × 6	11. 435 × 3	12. 563 × 5

EXERCISES • Multiply.

13. 276 × 5	14. 365 × 7	15. 556 × 4	16. 726 × 9	17. 758 × 2	18. 179 × 6
19. 456 × 8	20. 247 × 7	21. 323 × 4	22. 179 × 8	23. 986 × 3	24. 498 × 9

25. 145	**26.** 758	**27.** 904	**28.** 413	**29.** 376	**30.** 640
× 5	× 6	× 9	× 2	× 3	× 8

31. 428	**32.** 203	**33.** 607	**34.** 513	**35.** 398	**36.** 938
× 4	× 3	× 6	× 2	× 3	× 5

Mental Math Give the products.

37. $3 \times 400 =$ ___?___

38. $8 \times 300 =$ ___?___

39. $2 \times 200 =$ ___?___

40. $7 \times 600 =$ ___?___

41. $4 \times 200 =$ ___?___

42. $2 \times 300 =$ ___?___

PROBLEM SOLVING • APPLICATIONS

43. The rodeo arena holds 865 people. The arena is full for 3 shows each day. How many people see the rodeo each day?

★**44.** The tent can hold 150 people. It was full for the first two shows. There were 13 empty seats at the third show. How many people saw the three shows?

CALCULATOR • Estimation

The box office at the fair sold 667 tickets for each of the 6 nights of the fair. Use your calculator to find how many tickets have been sold for this period of time.

Press: The calculator shows: ⟨ 4002. ⟩

Estimate to see if the answer makes sense.

Think	700	◀ Round 667 to the nearest hundred. Multiply by 6.
	× 6	
	4,200	◀ Estimated answer

Since 4,200 is close to 4,002, the answer makes sense.

Ⓔ EXERCISES • Estimate each answer. Use your calculator to find the exact answer. Compare.

1. 209	**2.** 281	**3.** 412	**4.** 435	**5.** 843	**6.** 568
× 3	× 5	× 6	× 4	× 3	× 2

PROBLEM SOLVING · STRATEGIES

Using Tables

Example 1

One of the largest educational exhibits at this year's fair is the recycling exhibit. People bring items to be recycled by the U.S.A. Recycling Company.

Jack and Carol handle the aluminum recycling. They know that 24 aluminum cans weigh about 1 pound.

● How much do 72 cans weigh?

They use a table to help them find the answers quickly.

Cans	24	48	72	96	120	144	168	?	216	240
Pounds	1	2	3	4	5	6	7	8	9	10

The 72 cans weigh about **3 pounds.**

PROBLEMS • Use the table for Problems 1 and 2.

1. How much do 168 cans weigh?

2. How many cans weigh 9 pounds?

3. Jack and Carol use multiplication to make the table.

Number of pounds	×	Number of cans per pound	=	Number of cans
1	×	24	=	24

Complete this number sentence.

Number of pounds	×	Number of cans per pound	=	Number of cans
6	×	24	=	?

Use the table to check your answer.

4. Write a number sentence to find the number of cans in 8 pounds.

Example 2

After Jack and Carol know the weight of the aluminum, they must pay the person for it. They pay $0.30 for each pound. They use a second table to help them. Jack and Carol use multiplication to make this table.

Number of pounds	×	Amount paid per pound	=	Total paid
1	×	$0.30	=	$0.30

Pounds	1	2	3	4	5	6	7	8	9	10
Total Paid	$0.30	$0.60	$0.90	$1.20	$1.50	$1.80	?	$2.40	$2.70	$3.00

PROBLEMS

5. Write a number sentence to find the amount paid for 7 pounds of cans.

6. How much would you be paid for 4 pounds?

7. How many pounds would you need to sell in order to receive $2.70?

Example 3

Kevin and Susan handle the recycling of newspapers. They weigh the papers and bundle them in 50-pound stacks. The people are then paid $0.65 for each stack. Kevin and Susan use multiplication and make a table. They know:

Number of stacks	×	Price per stack	=	Amount paid
1	×	$0.65	=	$0.65

PROBLEMS

8. Complete their table.

Amount paid	$0.65	$1.30	$1.95	$2.60	?	?	?	?	?	?
Number of stacks	1	2	3	4	5	6	7	8	9	10

9. How much money would you receive for 6 stacks?

10. How much money would you receive for 9 stacks?

MID-CHAPTER REVIEW

Multiply.

(Pages 156–159)

1. 12
$\times$ 3

2. 13
$\times$ 3

3. 25
$\times$ 3

4. 32
$\times$ 3

5. 49
$\times$ 2

(Pages 160–161)

6. 32
$\times$ 4

7. 27
$\times$ 6

8. 56
$\times$ 4

9. 94
$\times$ 5

10. 84
$\times$ 3

(Pages 162–163)

11. 254
$\times$ 3

12. 209
$\times$ 2

13. 192
$\times$ 3

14. 185
$\times$ 5

15. 234
$\times$ 2

(Pages 164–165)

16. 246
$\times$ 7

17. 823
$\times$ 8

18. 513
$\times$ 2

19. 376
$\times$ 3

20. 759
$\times$ 8

21. The sky rocket ride has 4 rockets. Each rocket holds 12 people. How many people can ride at one time? (Pages 156–157)

22. There is a big tent with tables behind the food stands. There are 24 tables each with 4 chairs. How many chairs are there? (Pages 158–159)

MAINTENANCE • MIXED PRACTICE

Use this bar graph for Exercises 1–6. It shows the different forms of transportation the students in Seymour use to get to school.

1. How many students ride in a car to school?

2. How many students walk to school?

3. How many students ride the bus to school?

4. How do most students get to school?

5. How many more students walk than ride the bus to school?

6. How many students in all attend school?

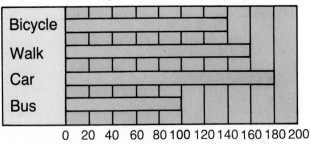

Transportation to School

Bicycle
Walk
Car
Bus

0 20 40 60 80 100 120 140 160 180 200

Number of Students

CAREER APPLICATIONS

Chefs

Charlie and Susan are chefs. One of their best recipes is for clam chowder. They make sure that each bowl has 5 clams. How many clams do they need for 2 bowls? 5 bowls? 7 bowls?

They make a table to help them find the answers quickly.

Bowls	1	2	3	4	5	6	7	8	9
Clams	5	10	15	20	25	30	35	40	45

To read the table   **Step 1** Find the number of bowls across the top.
Step 2 Find the number of clams across the bottom.

The table shows that there are **10 clams in 2 bowls.**
There are **25 clams in 5 bowls** and **35 clams in 7 bowls.**

EXERCISES • Use tables A and B below to answer Exercises 1 through 3.

Soup

A. Milk	2	4	6	8	10	12	14	16
Corn	3	6	9	12	15	18	21	24

Pudding

B. Milk	1	2	3	4	5	6	7	8
Corn	4	8	12	16	20	24	28	32

1. Susan's corn soup is tasty. She uses 3 cups of corn for every 2 cups of milk. If she uses 15 cups of corn, how much milk should she use?

2. Susan uses table B to make some corn pudding. She uses 3 cups of milk. How many cups of corn does she need?

3. Susan can make either soup or pudding. She uses 4 cups of milk. Will she use more corn with table A or with table B?

PROJECT   Make a table to show the ingredients needed to make lemonade for 2 cups, 4 cups, 6 cups, and 8 cups.

Multiplying Four-Digit Numbers

Each day the juice machine makes 1,125 frozen yogurt bars. The yogurt bars are sold in a booth in the exhibit tent.

● How many yogurt bars does the machine make in 6 days?

Think The same number are made each day. So multiply.

$$6 \times 1,125 = ?$$

Step 1
Multiply the ones.
Regroup 30 ones as
3 tens 0 ones.

```
    3
1,1 2 5
×     6
      0
```

Step 2
Multiply the tens.
Add. Regroup
15 tens as
1 hundred 5 tens.

```
  1 3
1,1 2 5
×     6
     5 0
```

Step 3
Multiply the hundreds.
Add.

```
  1 3
1,1 2 5
×     6
    7 5 0
```

Step 4
Multiply the thousands.

```
  1 3
1,1 2 5
×     6
  6,7 5 0
```

The yogurt machine makes **6,750 yogurt** bars in 6 days.

More Examples

```
  2 1 1
  1,7 3 4
×       4
  6,9 3 6
```

```
  1 2 2
  2,3 6 7
×       3
  7,1 0 1
```

```
    1 2
  5,0 4 8
×       3
 1 5,1 4 4
```

```
  2   1
  3,6 2 4
×       4
 1 4,4 9 6
```

PRACTICE • Multiply.

1. 1,178
   × 7

2. 8,113
   × 9

3. 5,903
   × 8

4. 7,027
   × 6

5. 6,723
   × 4

6. 2,468
   × 5

7. 2,736
   × 3

8. 1,234
   × 7

9. 7,210
   × 5

10. 1,752
    × 9

EXERCISES • Multiply.

11. 4,857
$\times$ 4

12. 7,039
$\times$ 3

13. 4,595
$\times$ 4

14. 5,563
$\times$ 4

15. 4,371
$\times$ 9

16. 5,046
$\times$ 8

17. 5,926
$\times$ 7

18. 7,348
$\times$ 4

19. 5,489
$\times$ 7

20. 8,572
$\times$ 8

21. 9,342
$\times$ 7

22. 7,653
$\times$ 5

23. 8,315
$\times$ 4

24. 3,040
$\times$ 8

25. 8,104
$\times$ 2

26. 4,296
$\times$ 4

27. 2,341
$\times$ 2

28. 8,509
$\times$ 8

29. 3,324
$\times$ 2

30. 9,367
$\times$ 6

31. $6 \times 1,806 =$ _?_

32. $7 \times 4,538 =$ _?_

33. $2 \times 2,130 =$ _?_

34. $3 \times 4,982 =$ _?_

35. $4 \times 8,147 =$ _?_

36. $9 \times 2,654 =$ _?_

Mental Math Give the products.

37. $5 \times 8,000 =$ _?_

38. $3 \times 3,000 =$ _?_

39. $7 \times 7,000 =$ _?_

★ **40.** $4 \times 9,000 =$ _?_

★ **41.** $8 \times 20,000 =$ _?_

★ **42.** $6 \times 60,000 =$ _?_

PROBLEM SOLVING • APPLICATIONS

43. Apples are a popular food at the fair. About 2,350 apples are eaten a day. How many apples are eaten in 4 days?

44. Rico has $4.00. He wants to buy 2 hotdogs. The hotdogs cost $1.89 each. What is his change?

THINKER'S CORNER

Complete this problem.

The missing digits are all the same.

There are two different answers.

Multiplying Money

Mr. Johnson decides to buy state fair T-shirts for his family of 7. Each T-shirt costs $3.49.

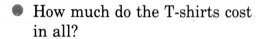

● How much do the T-shirts cost in all?

Think You know the cost of one T-shirt. Multiply to find the cost of seven T-shirts.

$7 \times \$3.49 = ?$

Multiply amounts of money as if you were multiplying whole numbers. Remember to write the dollar sign and cents point in the answer.

Step 1
Multiply as whole numbers.

$$\begin{array}{r} \overset{3\ 6}{\$3.4\,9} \\ \times \quad 7 \\ \hline 2\,4\,4\,3 \end{array}$$

Step 2
Write a dollar sign and cents point.

$$\begin{array}{r} \overset{3\ 6}{\$3.4\,9} \\ \times \quad 7 \\ \hline \$2\,4.4\,3 \end{array}$$

The T-shirts cost **$24.43.**

More Examples

$$\begin{array}{r} \overset{4}{\$0.2\,9} \\ \times \quad 5 \\ \hline \$1.4\,5 \end{array}$$

$$\begin{array}{r} \overset{2\ 2\ 1}{\$1\,8.9\,5} \\ \times \quad 3 \\ \hline \$5\,6.8\,5 \end{array}$$

$$\begin{array}{r} \overset{3\ \ 4}{\$2\,5.0\,7} \\ \times \quad 6 \\ \hline \$1\,5\,0.4\,2 \end{array}$$

PRACTICE • Multiply.

1. $\begin{array}{r} \$3.65 \\ \times \quad 7 \\ \hline \end{array}$

2. $\begin{array}{r} \$7.06 \\ \times \quad 9 \\ \hline \end{array}$

3. $\begin{array}{r} \$0.89 \\ \times \quad 4 \\ \hline \end{array}$

4. $\begin{array}{r} \$34.56 \\ \times \quad 8 \\ \hline \end{array}$

5. $\begin{array}{r} \$0.84 \\ \times \quad 3 \\ \hline \end{array}$

EXERCISES • Multiply.

6. $8.39
   × 4

7. $0.97
   × 8

8. $4.68
   × 6

9. $2.76
   × 9

10. $1.09
    × 7

11. $1.79
    × 6

12. $23.98
    × 3

13. $16.45
    × 8

14. $3.96
    × 2

15. $0.98
    × 9

16. $0.45
    × 3

17. $3.24
    × 2

18. $52.04
    × 7

19. $6.37
    × 2

20. $67.26
    × 5

21. $0.45
    × 5

22. $7.58
    × 6

23. $19.84
    × 9

24. $7.57
    × 2

25. $53.76
    × 3

26. $8 × \$2.35 = $?

27. $3 × \$1.95 = $?

28. $2 × \$3.09 = $?

29. $9 × \$17.85 = $?

30. $6 × \$0.84 = $?

31. $5 × \$4.05 = $?

E **Mental Math** — Estimate. To estimate, first round to the nearest dollar.

★ 32. $4.07
      × 4

★ 33. $3.53
      × 6

★ 34. $1.48
      × 7

★ 35. $2.54
      × 5

★ 36. $6.79
      × 3

PROBLEM SOLVING • APPLICATIONS

CHOOSE — • estimation • mental math • pencil and paper • calculator — SOLVE

37. Mr. Henderson buys 4 baseball caps at the fair. Each cap costs $1.49. About how much does he pay in all?

38. Mrs. Alvarez buys 2 large stuffed animals for her daughters. Each animal costs $6.75. How much does she pay in all?

39. Jane has $5.00. She buys one admission ticket. How much change does she receive?

★ 40. Mr. Davidson takes his 4 children to the fair. He pays the fair admission and buys 5 tickets for each child. How much does he spend on the children?

Admission $2.25
Tickets 25¢

PROBLEM SOLVING • STRATEGIES

Too Much Information

Sometimes more facts are given than
are needed to solve a problem.

Example

There are 12 rides and 8 ticket
booths at the fair. Marsha bought 3
tickets for each ride.

● How many tickets did she buy
altogether?

Think Find the key facts:

- Number of rides (12)
- Number of tickets Marsha
  bought for each ride (3)

The number of ticket booths
is not needed.

Then multiply.

$$12 \times 3 = 36$$

Marsha bought **36 tickets.**

PROBLEMS

List the key facts. Then solve the problem.

1. Bill spends $0.50 for 5 balls at
the softball throw. He knocks
down 7 milk bottles with each
ball. How many bottles does he
knock down?

2. There are 12 cars on the space
shuttle ride. Each car holds 6
people. Jose rides the space
shuttle 4 times. How many
people can the ride carry when
full?

SOLVE.

3. There are 63 people in line for the teacup ride. The gates open at 9:00 A.M. There are 22 cups. Each cup holds 4 people. How many people can ride at one time?

4. John wins 4 bags of marbles with 32 marbles in each bag. He also wins 3 boxes of pencils with 15 pencils in each box. How many marbles does he win?

5. The owner of a concession stand orders 9 cases of hotdog buns and 12 cases of hamburger buns. There are 24 hotdog buns in a case. How many hotdog buns were ordered?

Use only the facts you need to answer the problem.

---

6. On Friday, 55 people ate lunch at Tony's Stand. Tony cooked over 150 hamburgers that day. On Saturday, 95 people ate lunch at Tony's Stand. How many people ate lunch at Tony's Stand on Friday and Saturday?

7. There will be 3 shows in the computer exhibit today. After the 45-minute class, all the computers are used by the visitors. There are 15 tables with 6 computers on each table. How many computers are there?

8. Wednesday is Scout Day at the fair. There are 8 Brownie troops with 23 girls each. The Girl Scouts have 27 girls in each of 6 troops. How many Brownies go to the fair?

9. The roller coaster has 8 cars. Each car rides on 16 small wheels. The ride lasts about 3 minutes. There are 6 people in each car on the roller coaster. How many people are on the ride?

Write Your Own Problem

Write a story problem about the circus. Include one more fact than you need to solve the problem. Underline the fact that is not needed.

CHAPTER REVIEW

Part 1: VOCABULARY

For Exercises 1–4, choose from the box at the right the word that completes each statement.

1. When you change 12 ones to 1 ten and 2 ones, you __?__ the ones. (Page 158)

2. If you had 3 equal groups and wanted to find the total, you would __?__. (Page 156)

3. In a multiplication problem, the answer is called the __?__. (Page 156)

4. To help you find answers quickly, you might use a __?__. (Page 166)

| multiply |
| product |
| regroup |
| table |

Part 2: SKILLS

Multiply. (Pages 156–157)

| 5. 32
× 2 | 6. 11
× 9 | 7. 12
× 3 | 8. 41
× 1 | 9. 21
× 3 |

(Pages 158–159)

| 10. 19
× 4 | 11. 25
× 2 | 12. 37
× 2 | 13. 43
× 2 | 14. 18
× 5 |

(Pages 160–161)

| 15. 36
× 8 | 16. 78
× 5 | 17. 41
× 6 | 18. 56
× 4 | 19. 35
× 9 |

(Pages 162–163)

| 20. 192
× 3 | 21. 153
× 4 | 22. 412
× 2 | 23. 326
× 3 | 24. 183
× 5 |

(Pages 164–165)

| 25. 247
× 7 | 26. 758
× 2 | 27. 323
× 4 | 28. 607
× 6 | 29. 904
× 9 |

Multiply.

(Pages 170–171)

30. 7,653	**31.** 4,538	**32.** 9,367	**33.** 5,046	**34.** 4,595
× 5	× 7	× 6	× 8	× 4

(Pages 172–173)

35. $1.35	**36.** $7.57	**37.** $4.06	**38.** $16.45	**39.** $53.76
× 7	× 2	× 3	× 8	× 3

Part 3: *PROBLEM SOLVING* • *APPLICATIONS*

Jack and Carol began this table to help them
find the number of aluminum cans per pound. (Pages 166–167)

Number of cans	24	48	?	96	?	144	?	?	?	?
Pounds	1	2	3	4	5	6	7	8	9	10

40. How many cans are needed to weigh 4 pounds?

41. How much do 144 cans weigh?

42. How many cans are needed to weigh 3 pounds?

43. How much do 96 cans weigh?

44. Write a number sentence to find the number of cans in 9 pounds.

List the key facts. Then solve the problem. (Pages 174–175)

45. Tuesday is Scout Day at the fair. There are 6 Cub Scout troops with 24 boys in each troop. There are 9 buses of scouts. How many Cub Scouts are going to the fair?

46. There are 56 people in line for the roller coaster. The gates open at 9:00. There are 8 roller coaster cars. Each car holds 6 people. How many people can ride on the roller coaster at one time?

47. The teacup ride has 22 cups. Each cup holds 4 people. The ticket man has punched 144 tickets. How many people can ride at one time?

48. Lashanda knocks down 3 milk bottles each time she throws a ball. She throws the ball 6 times. The balls are 3 for 75¢. How many bottles does she knock down?

CHAPTER TEST

Multiply.

1. 23
× 2

2. 32
× 2

3. 14
× 4

4. 35
× 2

5. 18
× 4

6. 60
× 3

7. 54
× 2

8. 29
× 5

9. 217
× 3

10. 152
× 4

11. 209
× 4

12. 526
× 5

13. 294
× 6

14. 129
× 7

15. 5,119
× 7

16. 1,688
× 6

17. 4,706
× 5

18. $14.40
× 7

19. $37.05
× 9

20. $82.16
× 5

21. 4,178 × 8 = __?__

22. $49.84 × 7 = __?__

Karen and Jason began this table to help them find
the price for large balloons.

Price	$0.75	$1.50	$2.25	$3.00	$3.75	?	$5.25	$6.00	$6.75	$7.50
Number of Balloons	1	2	3	4	5	6	7	8	9	10

23. How much would you pay for 6 balloons?

24. How many balloons would you receive for $2.25?

List the key facts. Then solve the problem.

25. There are 7 judges at the art
fair. They will give out 5 prizes
at the end of the day. Each
judge will look at 14 art
projects. How many art projects
are at the fair?

ENRICHMENT

Even and Odd Products

Even numbers end in 0, 2, 4, 6, or 8. **Odd numbers** end in 1, 3, 5, 7, or 9.

EXERCISES

1. List the even numbers between 11 and 19.

2. List the odd numbers between 10 and 20.

Copy and complete the multiplication tables.

3.

×	3	9	27
5			
7			
1			

4.

×	2	6	48
4			
8			
0			

5.

×	5	9	63
2			
6			
8			

Write EVEN or ODD.

6. In Exercise 3 all the products are _____ numbers.

7. In Exercises 4 and 5 all the products are _____ numbers.

8. The product of two odd numbers is always an _____ number.

9. The product of two even numbers is always an _____ number.

10. The product of an odd number and an even number is always an

_____ number.

Copy and complete the table.
Use it to write EVEN or ODD
for each product.

Multiply to check your answers.

×	E	O
E		
O		

E = EVEN
O = ODD

11. $8 \times 42 = $ ___?___

12. $9 \times 57 = $ ___?___

13. $7 \times 73 = $ ___?___

14. $3 \times 68 = $ ___?___

15. $6 \times 89 = $ ___?___

16. $4 \times 91 = $ ___?___

ADDITIONAL PRACTICE

SKILLS

Multiply. (Pages 156–159)

1. 12	2. 23	3. 28	4. 19	5. 36
$\times\ 2$	$\times\ 2$	$\times\ 2$	$\times\ 5$	$\times\ 2$

(Pages 160–163)

6. 28	7. 31	8. 143	9. 236	10. 477
$\times\ 6$	$\times\ 6$	$\times\ 4$	$\times\ 3$	$\times\ 2$

(Pages 164–165, 170–171)

11. 623	12. 668	13. 7,653	14. 4,371	15. 5,046
$\times\ 4$	$\times\ 2$	$\times\ 5$	$\times\ 9$	$\times\ 8$

(Pages 172–173)

16. $3.96	17. $0.98	18. $3.09	19. $9 \times \$19.84 = \underline{\quad ?\quad}$
$\times\ 2$	$+\ \ 5$	$\times\ 4$	20. $6 \times \$\ 2.76 = \underline{\quad ?\quad}$

PROBLEM SOLVING • APPLICATIONS

The man who works at the baseball throw made this table so players would find the information quickly. (Pages 166–167)

Number of Tickets	1	2	3	4	5
Number of Balls	3	6	9	12	15

21. How many balls would you receive for 3 tickets?

22. How many tickets would you need for 15 balls?

23. Write a number sentence to find the number of balls for 2 tickets.

List the key facts. Then solve the problem.

24. Mr. King buys 2 baseball caps at the fair. Each cap costs $1.49. The stuffed animals are $6.75. How much does he pay in all?

(Page 174–175)

25. Mr. Davidson buys 5 tickets for each child. There are 3 children. Each ticket cost $0.25. How many tickets does Mr. Davidson buy?

(Pages 174–175)

PROBLEM SOLVING MAINTENANCE

Solve.

1. In the animal exhibit at the fair, there were 17 brown cows and 12 white cows. There were 11 cows that won prize ribbons. How many cows did not win a prize ribbon? (Page 16)

2. There was a baseball throwing contest at the fair. Mark threw his ball farther than Heidi. Kristi did not throw the ball as far as Mark, but farther than Heidi. Manuel threw his ball farther than Mark. Who threw the farthest ball? (Page 34)

3. Miguel bought $1.36 worth of tickets for the rides. He gave the clerk $2.00. He received 4 pennies and some dimes for change. How many dimes did he receive? (Page 46)

4. The fair had 137 exhibits last year. This year there were 176 exhibits. How many more exhibits were there this year? (Page 74)

5. There were 56 pigs at the fair. There were 8 pig pens. How many pigs could be put in each pen? (Page 116)

6. The 4-H Club members brought in 27 guinea pigs to exhibit. Three guinea pigs can be put in a cage How many cages are needed? (Page 116)

7. There were 5 shelves of canned vegetables in the food exhibit. Each shelf held 12 jars. How many jars in all were on the shelves? (Page 126)

8. The 4-H Club members counted the number of visitors to the animal exhibits. They made a table of this data. Using the table, make a pictograph of the data. (Page 142)

Day of The Week	Number of Visitors
Monday	120
Tuesday	110
Wednesday	100
Thursday	130
Friday	160

9. Steven knew that 1 pig ate 4 pounds of food. He used a table to find out how much food he needed to feed the pigs at the fair. Complete the table. (Page 166)

Number of pigs	1	2	3	4	5	?	7	8
Pounds of food	4	8	12	?	20	24	?	?

How many pounds of food are needed for 8 pigs?

10. Robbie used 15 tickets for 5 rides at the fair. He stayed at the fair for 3 hours. How many tickets did he use for each ride? (Page 174)

MAINTENANCE

Chapters 1 through 6

Mixed Practice • Choose the correct answers.

1. $64 \div 8 = \underline{\ ?\ }$

A. 7 **B.** 9
C. 8 **D.** not here

2. $3\overline{)24}$

A. 7 **B.** 8
C. 9 **D.** not here

3. $81 \div 8 = \underline{\ ?\ }$

A. 9 **B.** 18
C. 7 **D.** not here

4. $\begin{array}{r} 49 \\ \times\ 7 \\ \hline \end{array}$

A. 333 **B.** 283
C. 343 **D.** not here

5. $(67 \times 6) + 7 = \underline{\ ?\ }$

A. 409 **B.** 369
C. 419 **D.** not here

6. $(86 \times 4) + 9 = \underline{\ ?\ }$

A. 344 **B.** 363
C. 358 **D.** not here

7. $17 + 8 + 79 = \underline{\ ?\ }$

A. 113 **B.** 104
C. 914 **D.** not here

8. Round 750 to the nearest hundred.

A. 700 **B.** 750
C. 800 **D.** not here

9. Round 1,964 to the nearest thousand.

A. 1,900 **B.** 2,000
C. 1,000 **D.** not here

10. There are 48 suitcases to be put on the jet plane. There were 7 racks on the plane. How many suitcases would be on each rack? How many suitcases would be left over?

A. 6, 6 left over
B. 6, 7 left over
C. 7, 0 left over
D. not here

11. The ticket agent had sold 64 tickets for 8 flights. She sold an equal number of tickets for each flight. How many tickets did she sell for each flight?

A. 11
B. 9
C. 12
D. not here

Dividing by One-Digit Numbers

7

Jon Silvereagle has 320 seeds to plant. He places 3 seeds in each hole.

● How many holes does he dig?

On Friday, Lily's scores for the first two games were 150 and 160. Her average for the 3 games was 155.

● What was her score for the third game?

Two-Digit Quotients

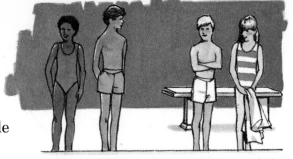

All campers that go swimming must swim with a "buddy group." There are 2 swimmers in each buddy group.

● How many buddy groups can be made from 27 campers?

● How many campers will not have a buddy?

Think Each group has 2 swimmers. Divide to find how many 2's there are in 27. The remainder tells how many are left over.

$$27 \div 2 = ?$$

Step 1 Divide the tens.

Think: $2\overline{)2}$

$$
\begin{array}{r}
1 \\
2\overline{)27} \\
-2 \quad\leftarrow \text{ Multiply: } 1 \times 2 \\
\hline
0 \quad\leftarrow \text{ Subtract: } 2 - 2
\end{array}
$$

↑ This must be less than the divisor 2

Step 2 Bring down the 7. Divide the ones.

Think: $2\overline{)7}$

$$
\begin{array}{r}
13 \text{ r1} \quad\leftarrow \text{ Show the remainder.} \\
2\overline{)27} \\
-2\downarrow \\
\hline
7 \\
-6 \quad\leftarrow \text{ Multiply: } 3 \times 2 \\
\hline
1 \quad\leftarrow \text{ Subtract: } 7 - 6
\end{array}
$$

There will be **13 buddy groups.** There is **1 camper** without a buddy.

● Check your answer.

Think **quotient × divisor + remainder = dividend**

Multiply the quotient by the divisor. ——→

$$
\begin{array}{r}
13 \\
\times\ 2 \\
\hline
26
\end{array}
$$

Add the remainder. ——→

$$
\begin{array}{r}
+\ 1 \\
\hline
27
\end{array}
$$

◀ This should equal the dividend.

PRACTICE • Divide. Check your answers.

1. $3\overline{)36}$ 2. $5\overline{)57}$ 3. $8\overline{)88}$ 4. $4\overline{)87}$ 5. $7\overline{)77}$

6. $4\overline{)48}$ 7. $3\overline{)97}$ 8. $3\overline{)39}$ 9. $8\overline{)89}$ 10. $2\overline{)85}$

11. $8\overline{)16}$ **12.** $7\overline{)28}$ **13.** $6\overline{)36}$ **14.** $5\overline{)45}$ **15.** $9\overline{)54}$

EXERCISES • Divide.

16. $3\overline{)95}$ **17.** $2\overline{)29}$ **18.** $7\overline{)79}$ **19.** $6\overline{)68}$ **20.** $4\overline{)89}$

21. $6\overline{)69}$ **22.** $4\overline{)49}$ **23.** $3\overline{)35}$ **24.** $2\overline{)65}$ **25.** $2\overline{)28}$

26. $3\overline{)37}$ **27.** $4\overline{)88}$ **28.** $4\overline{)86}$ **29.** $2\overline{)43}$ **30.** $3\overline{)39}$

31. $4\overline{)47}$ **32.** $3\overline{)34}$ **33.** $3\overline{)98}$ **34.** $2\overline{)62}$ **35.** $3\overline{)99}$

36. $63 \div 2 = \underline{\quad?\quad}$ **37.** $99 \div 9 = \underline{\quad?\quad}$ **38.** $85 \div 4 = \underline{\quad?\quad}$

39. $94 \div 3 = \underline{\quad?\quad}$ **40.** $67 \div 2 = \underline{\quad?\quad}$ **41.** $58 \div 5 = \underline{\quad?\quad}$

42. $67 \div 3 = \underline{\quad?\quad}$ **43.** $46 \div 4 = \underline{\quad?\quad}$ **44.** $89 \div 2 = \underline{\quad?\quad}$

45. $47 \div 2 = \underline{\quad?\quad}$ **46.** $84 \div 4 = \underline{\quad?\quad}$ **47.** $56 \div 5 = \underline{\quad?\quad}$

48. $(24 \div 2) + 52 = \underline{\quad?\quad}$ **49.** $(96 \div 3) - 14 = \underline{\quad?\quad}$ **50.** $(44 \div 4) \times 7 = \underline{\quad?\quad}$

PROBLEM SOLVING • APPLICATIONS

51. Together, Raoul, Tammy, and Nathan swam 39 lengths of the pool. Each swam the same number of lengths. How many lengths did each swim?

52. A camp lifeguard has 23 swim fins. She gives 2 fins to each swimmer. How many swimmers get fins? How many fins are left over?

53. The campers have a swim meet with 12 relay teams. Each team has 4 swimmers. How many campers in all are on relay teams?

★**54.** Camp Pinetree has 57 life jackets for its 5 boats. Two of the boats have 1 more life jacket than the other boats have. How many life jackets are on each boat?

More 2-Digit Quotients

Camp Pinetree's stable has 73 horses.
Each guide is assigned 5 horses.

● How many guides are needed?

● How many horses are left over?

Think Each guide has 5 horses. Divide
to find how many 5's there are in
73. The remainder tells how many
are left over.

$$73 \div 5 = ?$$

Step 1 Divide the tens.

Think:  5)7

$$
\begin{array}{r}
1 \\
5)\overline{73} \\
-5 \leftarrow 1 \times 5 \\
\hline
2 \leftarrow 7 - 5
\end{array}
$$

↑
**Is this less than
the divisor?**

Step 2 Bring down the 3.

Think: 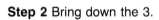 5)23

$$
\begin{array}{r}
14 \; r\, 3 \\
5)\overline{73} \\
-5 \downarrow \\
\hline
23 \\
-20 \leftarrow 4 \times 5 \\
\hline
3 \leftarrow 23 - 20
\end{array}
$$

Show the remainder.

The camp needs **14 guides.** There are **3 horses** left over.

● Check your answer.

Think quotient × divisor + remainder = dividend

Multiply the quotient ——→ 14
by the divisor. ————→ × 5
                          ——
                          70
Add the remainder. ———→ + 3
                          ——
                          73 ◄ **Does this equal
                                the dividend?**

PRACTICE • Divide.

1. $2\overline{)56}$ **2.** $6\overline{)75}$ **3.** $2\overline{)47}$ **4.** $5\overline{)76}$ **5.** $4\overline{)56}$

6. $5\overline{)69}$ **7.** $6\overline{)74}$ **8.** $3\overline{)72}$ **9.** $7\overline{)84}$ **10.** $4\overline{)67}$

EXERCISES • Divide.

11. $7\overline{)96}$ **12.** $8\overline{)95}$ **13.** $2\overline{)57}$ **14.** $4\overline{)95}$ **15.** $3\overline{)73}$

16. $4\overline{)94}$ **17.** $3\overline{)57}$ **18.** $7\overline{)90}$ **19.** $5\overline{)75}$ **20.** $6\overline{)89}$

21. $2\overline{)32}$ **22.** $2\overline{)93}$ **23.** $6\overline{)72}$ **24.** $9\overline{)99}$ **25.** $5\overline{)74}$

26. $4\overline{)59}$ **27.** $7\overline{)79}$ **28.** $2\overline{)51}$ **29.** $4\overline{)86}$ **30.** $6\overline{)82}$

31. $5\overline{)62}$ **32.** $2\overline{)91}$ **33.** $6\overline{)80}$ **34.** $3\overline{)69}$ **35.** $7\overline{)85}$

36. $45 \div 3 = \underline{\ ?\ }$ **37.** $74 \div 2 = \underline{\ ?\ }$ **38.** $50 \div 4 = \underline{\ ?\ }$

39. $97 \div 8 = \underline{\ ?\ }$ **40.** $59 \div 5 = \underline{\ ?\ }$ **41.** $76 \div 2 = \underline{\ ?\ }$

42. $87 \div 7 = \underline{\ ?\ }$ **43.** $75 \div 3 = \underline{\ ?\ }$ **44.** $80 \div 5 = \underline{\ ?\ }$

Complete.

★ **45.** $\underline{\ ?\ } \div 9 = 10 \text{ r}4$ ★ **46.** $\underline{\ ?\ } \div 3 = 28 \text{ r}1$ ★ **47.** $\underline{\ ?\ } \div 2 = 37$

★ **48.** $\underline{\ ?\ } \div 7 = 13 \text{ r}2$ ★ **49.** $\underline{\ ?\ } \div 5 = 13 \text{ r}3$ ★ **50.** $\underline{\ ?\ } \div 8 = 11 \text{ r}7$

PROBLEM SOLVING • APPLICATIONS

51. Gordon cleans 81 bridles. He puts 6 bridles on each post. How many posts does he use? How many bridles are left over?

52. Rita is putting away 54 saddles. She puts 4 saddles in each stack. How many stacks does she make? How many saddles are left over?

53. Jackie, Marcia, Jeff, and Lily are riding horses on the trail. Jeff is behind Jackie. Lily is between Jeff and Marcia. Who is first in line?

★ **54.** There are 96 campers. Five campers clean the stables. The rest form riding groups. Each riding group has 8 campers. How many groups do they make? How many campers are left over?

Three-Digit Quotients

Jenna and Karla work in the supply cabin. The cabin contains 684 boxes of dried fruit. Each carton contains 5 boxes.

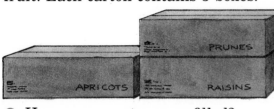

● How many cartons are filled?

● How many boxes are left over?

Think Each carton has 5 boxes. Divide to find how many 5's there are in 684. The remainder tells how many are left over.

$$684 \div 5 = ?$$

Step 1
Divide the hundreds.

Think: 5)6

```
    1
5)684
 -5  ← 1 × 5
  1  ← 6 - 5
```

Step 2
Bring down the 8 tens.

Think: 5)18

```
   13
5)684
 -5↓
  18
 -15  ← 3 × 5
   3  ← 18 - 15
```

Step 3
Bring down the 4 ones.

Think: 5)34

```
   136 r4
5)684
 -5 |
  18 |
 -15↓
  34
 -30  ← 6 × 5
   4  ← 34 - 30
```

The check is left for you to do.

There are **136 full cartons.** There are **4 boxes** left over.

PRACTICE • Divide. Check your answers.

1. 2)497   2. 4)608   3. 3)644   4. 6)797   5. 4)879

6. 7)807   7. 6)774   8. 5)738   9. 3)738   10. 2)855

EXERCISES • Divide. Check your answers.

11. 3)773   12. 2)702   13. 3)535   14. 4)705   15. 6)792

16. 7)944   17. 8)998   18. 6)852   19. 2)573   20. 4)974

21. 5)779   22. 3)730   23. 7)865   24. 8)986   25. 3)684

26. 3)965   27. 4)609   28. 5)568   29. 2)745   30. 4)567

31. 7)857   32. 6)753   33. 4)752   34. 7)848   35. 5)627

36. 849 ÷ 6 = ___?___   37. 344 ÷ 2 = ___?___   38. 745 ÷ 5 = ___?___

39. 524 ÷ 3 = ___?___   40. 926 ÷ 7 = ___?___   41. 617 ÷ 4 = ___?___

★ 42. 6,728 ÷ 5 = ___?___   ★ 43. 4,954 ÷ 3 = ___?___   ★ 44. 8,509 ÷ 7 = ___?___

Mental Math What is the greatest possible remainder for each exercise?
Do not use pencil or paper. Do not divide.

★ 45. 8)991   ★ 46. 6)809   ★ 47. 3)743   ★ 48. 7)902   ★ 49. 2)897

PROBLEM SOLVING • APPLICATIONS

50. There are 500 bags of wheat flour.
Jenna packs 3 bags in each box.
How many boxes does she pack?
How many bags are left over?

51. Karl moves 876 crates to a
storage area. The cart he uses
can hold 6 crates. How many
trips does he have to make if he
fills the cart each time?

CALCULATOR • Using a Formula

Example   Use the formula below to find the dividend.   → ? ÷ 6 = 138 r 5

Formula: quotient × divisor + remainder = dividend

138   ×   6   +   5   =   ?

The quotient
is 833.

EXERCISES • Use the formula to find each dividend.

1. 7)?   132 r6   2. 4)?   159 r2   3. 2)?   268 r1   4. 4)?   179 r1   5. 2)?   384 r1

Placing the First Digit

On Saturday, a new group of 120 campers arrive. They line up behind 8 counselors. The same number of campers are assigned to each counselor.

● How many campers are assigned to each counselor?

Think Each counselor has the same number of campers. Divide 120 by 8 to find how many are in each group.

$$120 \div 8 = ?$$

Step 1 There is one digit in the divisor.
Draw a line after the first digit in the dividend.

$8\overline{)1\,20}$ Since 1 is less than 8, draw a new line.

$8\overline{)12\,0}$ Since 12 is greater than 8, the first digit goes over the 2.

Step 2 Divide the tens.

Think: $8\overline{)12}$

$$
\begin{array}{r}
1 \\
8\overline{)120} \\
-8 \quad \leftarrow 1 \times 8 \\
\hline
4 \quad \leftarrow 12 - 8
\end{array}
$$

Write the 1 over the 2.

Step 3 Bring down the 0.

Think: $8\overline{)40}$

$$
\begin{array}{r}
15 \\
8\overline{)120} \\
-8\downarrow \\
\hline
40 \\
-40 \quad \leftarrow 5 \times 8 \\
\hline
0 \quad \leftarrow 40 - 40
\end{array}
$$

Check the answer.

These should be equal.

$$
\begin{array}{r}
15 \\
\times\ 8 \\
\hline
120 \\
+\ 0 \\
\hline
120
\end{array}
$$

There are **15 campers** assigned to each counselor.

PRACTICE • Write an X to show where to place the first digit in the quotient. The first one has been done for you.

1. $\overset{\text{X}}{4\overline{)304}}$ 2. $8\overline{)512}$ 3. $7\overline{)748}$ 4. $9\overline{)579}$ 5. $6\overline{)810}$

Divide. Check your answers.

6. $5\overline{)393}$ 7. $6\overline{)157}$ 8. $4\overline{)274}$ 9. $5\overline{)186}$ 10. $2\overline{)195}$

EXERCISES • Divide.

11. 4)299   **12.** 6)443   **13.** 2)133   **14.** 3)102   **15.** 5)475

16. 5)408   **17.** 4)186   **18.** 6)397   **19.** 4)234   **20.** 3)148

21. 8)384   **22.** 3)498   **23.** 3)115   **24.** 6)350   **25.** 5)479

26. 4)169   **27.** 5)459   **28.** 2)151   **29.** 4)889   **30.** 3)265

31. 6)752   **32.** 4)358   **33.** 8)694   **34.** 5)238   **35.** 8)514

36. 9)529   **37.** 5)917   **38.** 7)409   **39.** 7)848   **40.** 5)238

41. $505 \div 6 = \underline{\ ?\ }$ **42.** $747 \div 8 = \underline{\ ?\ }$ **43.** $485 \div 7 = \underline{\ ?\ }$

44. $193 \div 2 = \underline{\ ?\ }$ **45.** $437 \div 3 = \underline{\ ?\ }$ **46.** $605 \div 9 = \underline{\ ?\ }$

★ **47.** $1{,}243 \div 5 = \underline{\ ?\ }$ ★ **48.** $1{,}439 \div 8 = \underline{\ ?\ }$ ★ **49.** $3{,}629 \div 7 = \underline{\ ?\ }$

PROBLEM SOLVING • APPLICATIONS

50. During Camp Pinetree's second session, there are 180 campers. The campers are divided into 4 groups for activities. Each group has the same number of campers. How many campers are in each group?

51. The camp has 255 pup tents in 3 sheds. The same number of tents are stored in each shed. How many tents are stored in each shed?

52. On Wednesday afternoon, 40 campers go on a canoe trip. A group of 25 campers go hiking and 15 campers go horseback riding. Make a bar graph to show this data.

THINKER'S CORNER

Aaron works in the camp craft shop. He can saw a board into 2 pieces in 2 minutes. How long will it take Aaron to saw the board into 3 pieces?

Finding Averages

Camp Pinetree has several bowling teams. This table shows the bowling scores for one week.

Bowler	Day	Game 1	Game 2	Game 3
Katie	Sat.	122	138	157
Tisa	Sat.	147	163	176
Utina	Mon.	155	139	162
Utina	Thurs.	187	173	195
Nova	Thurs.	161	158	170
Isaac	Tues.	179	182	170
Yoko	Wed.	163	171	125
Pablo	Tues.	154	164	147
Pablo	Wed.	173	162	151
Kim	Sat.	158	174	166
Lily	Fri.	150	160	

● What was Katie's average score on Saturday?

Step 1
Find Katie's scores in the table.
Add the scores.

$122 + 138 + 157 = 417$ ← Sum of the scores

Step 2
Divide the sum by the number of scores.

Number of scores → $3\overline{)417}$ ← Sum of the scores, 139 ← Average

Katie's average score on Saturday was **139**.

PRACTICE • Find the average for each set of numbers.

1. 45, 30 and 15

2. 65, 41 and 14

3. 23, 651 and 79

4. 436, 839, 396 and 329

5. Nova's scores were 161, 158, and 170.

6. Isaac's scores were 179, 182, and 170.

EXERCISES • Find each answer.

7. What is Yoko's average score for the 3 games she bowled on Wednesday?

8. What is Utina's average score for the 3 games she bowled on Monday?

9. What is Pablo's average score for Games 1 and 2 that he bowled on Tuesday?

10. What is Katie's average score for Games 1 and 2 that she bowled on Saturday?

11. What is Kim's average score for the 3 games she bowled on Saturday?

12. What is Pablo's average score for Games 1 and 3 that he bowled on Wednesday?

PROBLEM SOLVING • APPLICATIONS

13. On Thursday afternoon, Nova bowled the 3 games shown in the table. That evening she bowled 1 game and scored 147. What is her average score for all 4 games?

14. Who had the higher average score on Saturday, Tisa or Kim?

PROJECT Ask a friend to count the number of times you can jump rope before missing. Do this 5 different times. Make a table and record the number of jumps each time. Find your average. Note: If you have a remainder of 1 or 2 after dividing, drop the remainder. If you have a remainder of 3 or 4, drop the remainder and add 1 to your answer.

15. On Friday, Lily's score for Game 3 was not shown in the table. Her average for the 3 games was 155. What was her score for Game 3?

NON-ROUTINE PROBLEM SOLVING

Sheila attends the Camp Pinetree Craft Club for 6 days. She may choose 3 projects to make.

Sheila must pay for the materials to be used in each project. She has $3.50 to spend on the projects.

PROJECTS	DAYS TO COMPLETE PROJECT	COST
Clothespin dolls	2	$1.50
Macrame plant hangers	3	0.95
Beaded necklaces	1	0.80
Paper-mache animals	3	1.25
Kites	2	0.75
Clay vases	1	1.15

Sheila listed three possible choices.

Choice 1

Clothespin doll

Macrame plant hanger

Clay vase

Choice 2

Paper-mache animal

Kite

Beaded necklace

Choice 3

Macrame plant hanger

Clothespin doll

Kite

Finding the Cost

1. **Choice 1**

   a. How much does Choice 1 cost?

   b. Is Choice 1 greater than or less than $3.50?

   c. Can Sheila finish the projects given for Choice 1 in 6 days?

2. **Choice 2**

   a. How much does Choice 2 cost?

   b. Is Choice 2 greater than or less than $3.50?

   c. Can Sheila finish the projects given for Choice 2 in 6 days?

3. **Choice 3**

   a. How much does Choice 3 cost?

   b. Is Choice 3 greater than or less than $3.50?

   c. Can Sheila finish the projects given for Choice 3 in 6 days?

Making a Choice

4. What choice can Sheila make?

6. Suppose you decided to make a clay vase instead of a clothespin doll in Choice 3. Could you still finish all the projects in 6 days? Would the cost be less than $3.50?

5. Suppose you decided to make a beaded necklace instead of a clay vase in Choice 1. Could you still finish all the projects in 6 days? Would the cost be less than $3.50?

7. Suppose you went to the Craft Club for 4 days. You have $2.15 to spend on the projects. What projects would you choose?

MID-CHAPTER REVIEW

Divide. (Pages 184–187)

1. $2\overline{)27}$ 2. $3\overline{)39}$ 3. $2\overline{)67}$ 4. $85 \div 4 = \underline{\ ?\ }$

(Pages 184–187)

5. $5\overline{)73}$ 6. $7\overline{)90}$ 7. $3\overline{)73}$ 8. $76 \div 2 = \underline{\ ?\ }$

(Pages 188–189)

9. $5\overline{)684}$ 10. $2\overline{)745}$ 11. $4\overline{)609}$ 12. $926 \div 7 = \underline{\ ?\ }$

(Pages 190–191)

13. $8\overline{)120}$ 14. $2\overline{)195}$ 15. $3\overline{)264}$ 16. $605 \div 9 = \underline{\ ?\ }$

Camp Pinetree keeps a record of the number of campers attending each two-week session.

Campers	Session I	Session II	Session III
Boys	81	83	79
Girls	82	88	76

Use the table to answer these questions. (Pages 192–193)

17. What is the average attendance of boys for all 3 Sessions?

18. What is the average attendance of girls for all 3 Sessions?

MAINTENANCE • MIXED PRACTICE

1. Write the expanded form for 23,542.

2. Write the number for 4,000 + 200 + 6.

3. Round 5,483 to the nearest hundred.

4. Round 8,256 to the nearest thousand.

5. $\begin{array}{r} 42 \\ \times\ 2 \\ \hline \end{array}$ 6. $\begin{array}{r} 56 \\ +\ 4 \\ \hline \end{array}$ 7. $\begin{array}{r} 312 \\ \times\ \ 2 \\ \hline \end{array}$ 8. $\begin{array}{r} 807 \\ -342 \\ \hline \end{array}$ 9. $\begin{array}{r} 4,326 \\ \times\ \ \ \ 4 \\ \hline \end{array}$

10. $\begin{array}{r} \$1.37 \\ \times\ \ \ 7 \\ \hline \end{array}$ 11. $\begin{array}{r} \$26.40 \\ +\ 56.35 \\ \hline \end{array}$ 12. $\begin{array}{r} \$82.33 \\ -\ 51.68 \\ \hline \end{array}$ 13. $\begin{array}{r} 2,480 \\ -\ \ 156 \\ \hline \end{array}$ 14. $\begin{array}{r} 8,927 \\ +\ 842 \\ \hline \end{array}$

15. Kiyoshi needs 9 packages of gravel for his fish tank. He has 2 packages. How many more packages does he need?

16. The fourth grade is taking a bus to the airport. There are 18 seats with 3 students in each seat. How many students are on the bus?

CAREER APPLICATIONS

Food Services

Martin Bloom stores the food at Camp Pinetree. The following list shows the number of cans of vegetables that he has on each shelf.

Item	Shelf				
	A	B	C	D	E
Carrots	68	72	49	65	70
Corn	45	73	62	56	48
Peas	87	90	88	73	69
String Beans	61	86	95	83	87
Tomatoes	24	19	36	28	40

EXERCISES • Use paper and pencil, or your calculator, to solve each exercise.

Find the total number of cans of each vegetable.

1. Carrots

2. Corn

3. Peas

Find the total number of cans on each shelf.

4. Shelf A

5. Shelf C

6. Shelf E

7. Mr. Bloom moved the carrots to 4 shelves. He put the same number of cans on each shelf. How many cans are on each shelf?

8. Mr. Bloom used 3 shelves to store all the tomatoes. He put the same number of cans on each shelf. How many cans are on each shelf?

Zero in the Quotient

Jon Silvereagle works in the camp garden. He has 320 seeds to plant. He places 3 seeds in each hole.

● How many holes does he dig?

● How many seeds are left over?

Think Jon is placing 320 seeds into groups of 3. To find how many groups, divide. The number of groups equals the number of holes.

$$320 \div 3 = ?$$

Step 1 Find where to place the first digit in the quotient.

Think: $3\overline{)3\,20}$ Since $3 \div 3 = 1$, write the first digit over the 3.

Step 2 Divide the hundreds.

Think: $3\overline{)3}$
Write 1 over the 3

$$
\begin{array}{r}
1 \\
3\overline{)320} \\
-3 \leftarrow 1 \times 3 \\
\hline
0 \leftarrow 3-3
\end{array}
$$

Step 3 Divide the tens.

Think: $3\overline{)2}$
Write 0 over the 2.

$$
\begin{array}{r}
10 \\
3\overline{)320} \\
-3\downarrow \\
\hline
02 \\
-0 \leftarrow 0 \times 3 \\
\hline
2 \leftarrow 2-0
\end{array}
$$

Step 4 Divide the ones.

Think: $3\overline{)20}$
Write 6 over the 0.

$$
\begin{array}{r}
106 \text{ r2} \\
3\overline{)320} \\
-3\downarrow \\
\hline
2 \\
-0\downarrow \\
\hline
20 \\
-18 \leftarrow 6 \times 3 \\
\hline
2 \leftarrow 20-18
\end{array}
$$

Jon digs **106 holes.** There are **2 seeds** left over.

● $165 \div 8 = ?$

Find where to place the first digit.

$8\overline{)1\,65} \leftarrow 1 < 8$ $\qquad$ $8\overline{)1\,6\,5} \leftarrow 16 > 8$

Divide.

$$
\begin{array}{r}
20 \text{ r5} \\
8\overline{)165} \\
-16 \\
\hline
05 \leftarrow 8\overline{)5} \\
-0 \\
\hline
5
\end{array}
$$

PRACTICE • Divide. Check your answers.

1. $4\overline{)83}$
2. $7\overline{)75}$
3. $5\overline{)352}$
4. $5\overline{)545}$
5. $8\overline{)242}$

6. $5\overline{)550}$
7. $4\overline{)480}$
8. $2\overline{)215}$
9. $3\overline{)914}$
10. $7\overline{)425}$

EXERCISES • Divide. Check your answers.

11. $2\overline{)61}$
12. $6\overline{)483}$
13. $3\overline{)120}$
14. $7\overline{)717}$
15. $5\overline{)253}$

16. $6\overline{)665}$
17. $4\overline{)920}$
18. $4\overline{)835}$
19. $9\overline{)547}$
20. $9\overline{)969}$

21. $5\overline{)403}$
22. $9\overline{)769}$
23. $4\overline{)838}$
24. $2\overline{)603}$
25. $7\overline{)514}$

26. $4\overline{)671}$
27. $6\overline{)185}$
28. $7\overline{)938}$
29. $7\overline{)563}$
30. $5\overline{)527}$

31. $87 \div 8 = \underline{\quad?\quad}$
32. $959 \div 8 = \underline{\quad?\quad}$
33. $563 \div 8 = \underline{\quad?\quad}$

34. $645 \div 6 = \underline{\quad?\quad}$
35. $811 \div 2 = \underline{\quad?\quad}$
36. $517 \div 5 = \underline{\quad?\quad}$

PROBLEM SOLVING • APPLICATIONS

37. Brandon picks 641 tomatoes. He puts the tomatoes in baskets to sell. He puts 6 tomatoes in each basket. How many baskets does he fill? How many tomatoes are left over?

38. Sandra has 515 strawberry plants. She is planting 5 rows of strawberries. She plants the same number in each row. How many plants does she put in each row?

39. Lamont bags peaches for the camp fruit stand. There are 460 peaches. He puts 4 peaches in each bag. Each bag will sell for $1.69. How many bags does he fill?

★ 40. Tod puts 8 flowering plants on each of 54 shelves. Each plant sells for $1.29. How many plants did Tod put on the shelves?

THINKER'S CORNER

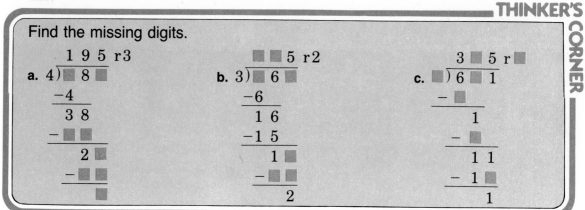

Find the missing digits.

a.
```
    1 9 5 r3
  4) ■ 8 ■
    -4
    3 8
   -■ ■
     2 ■
    -■ ■
      ■
```

b.
```
      ■ ■ 5 r2
  3) ■ 6 ■
    -6
    1 6
   -1 5
     1 ■
    -■ ■
      2
```

c.
```
      3 ■ 5 r■
  ■) 6 ■ 1
    -■
     1
    -■
    1 1
   -1 ■
    1
```

Dividing by One-Digit Numbers • **199**

Four-Digit Quotients

Camp Pinetree has several cooks in the kitchen.
They prepare 3,516 meals in 3 days.

● How many meals are prepared each day?

Think You need to find how
many groups of 3 there are
in 3,516. So divide.

$$3,516 \div 3 = ?$$

Check the
answer.

```
   1,172
3)3,516  ←
 −3 ↓
   5
  −3↓
   21
  −21↓
    6
   −6
    0
```

These
should
be equal.

```
  1,172
×     3
  3,516
```

There were **1,172 meals** prepared each day.

Sometimes the first digit of the quotient is in the hundreds place.

● $1,482 \div 5 = ?$

Think 5)1,|482 Since 1 < 5, draw a new line.

5)1,4|82 Since 14 > 5, the first digit goes over the 4.

```
    296 r2
5)1,482  ←
 −1 0↓
   48
  −45↓
   32
  −30
    2
```

Check your answer.

```
   296
 ×   5
 1,480
 +   2
 1,482
```

Does this equal
the dividend?

1. $\overset{\text{X}}{3\overline{)4,970}}$ 2. $4\overline{)6,218}$ 3. $6\overline{)3,251}$ 4. $7\overline{)9,211}$ 5. $6\overline{)5,469}$

6. $2\overline{)1,799}$ 7. $5\overline{)4,381}$ 8. $9\overline{)3,654}$ 9. $8\overline{)9,506}$ 10. $5\overline{)3,773}$

EXERCISES • Divide. Check your answers.

11. $6\overline{)8,215}$ 12. $4\overline{)5,448}$ 13. $2\overline{)1,546}$ 14. $3\overline{)9,504}$ 15. $7\overline{)4,615}$

16. $8\overline{)5,321}$ 17. $9\overline{)8,145}$ 18. $6\overline{)7,543}$ 19. $5\overline{)5,906}$ 20. $7\overline{)8,582}$

21. $4\overline{)2,890}$ 22. $6\overline{)9,367}$ 23. $4\overline{)5,714}$ 24. $4\overline{)4,927}$ 25. $6\overline{)8,450}$

26. $5\overline{)5,309}$ 27. $4\overline{)5,028}$ 28. $3\overline{)4,767}$ 29. $5\overline{)9,462}$ 30. $8\overline{)6,390}$

31. $4,218 \div 5 = $ __?__   32. $3,602 \div 3 = $ __?__   33. $9,301 \div 8 = $ __?__

34. $5,006 \div 4 = $ __?__   35. $7,325 \div 2 = $ __?__   36. $6,900 \div 7 = $ __?__

37. $6,084 \div 9 = $ __?__   38. $2,994 \div 6 = $ __?__   39. $4,321 \div 4 = $ __?__

PROBLEM SOLVING • APPLICATIONS   CHOOSE   • mental math   • pencil and paper   • calculator   SOLVE

40. There are 1,656 frozen hamburgers to be put in boxes. Each box holds 8 hamburgers. How many boxes are needed?

41. There are 1,656 eggs in the supply cabin. The eggs are stored in 9 containers. Each container holds the same number of eggs. How many eggs are in each container?

42. When the camping season opens, the camp director buys 2,142 forks and 3,150 spoons. How many more spoons than forks are there?

★ 43. The camp cooks make 1,049 hamburgers for a barbecue. There are 187 people who eat 2 hamburgers each. Another 216 people eat 3 hamburgers each. How many hamburgers are left over?

THINKER'S CORNER

Divide. Use paper and pencil or a calculator.

a. $19,998 \div 2$ b. $29,997 \div 3$ c. $39,996 \div 4$

What pattern do you see in the answers?

Dividing Money

Samantha and Danielle sell clothespin
dolls in the camp craft store. At
the end of the day, they have earned
$2.90. They share the money equally.

● How much money does each receive?

Think Since they share the money
equally, divide the amount by 2.

$$\$2.90 \div 2 = ?$$

Divide amounts of money as if you were
dividing whole numbers.
Remember! Write the dollar sign and
the cents point in the answer.

```
                145                    $1.45
Think:     2) 290      Write:     2) $2.90
            -2↓                       -2 ↓
             9                         9
            -8↓                       -8↓
            10                        10
           -10                       -10
             0                         0
```

They each receive **$1.45.**

More Examples

```
      $ .24              $1.20              $1.05
   8) $1.92           7) $8.40           4) $4.20
   - 16                - 7                - 4
     32                 1 4                2
    -32                -1 4               -0
      0                 00                 20
                       - 0               -20
                         0                 0
```

PRACTICE • Divide.

1. 6) $7.92   2. 4) $2.60   3. 3) $5.34   4. 5) $2.95   5. 7) $3.57

6. 8) $9.92   7. 2) $2.16   8. 5) $7.75   9. 6) $1.32   10. 3) $9.30

EXERCISES • Divide.

11. $7\overline{)\$9.38}$ **12.** $6\overline{)\$8.52}$ **13.** $3\overline{)\$7.29}$ **14.** $4\overline{)\$9.72}$ **15.** $7\overline{)\$6.65}$

16. $5\overline{)\$4.80}$ **17.** $6\overline{)\$5.04}$ **18.** $8\overline{)\$8.56}$ **19.** $7\overline{)\$9.80}$ **20.** $2\overline{)\$1.58}$

21. $6\overline{)\$3.12}$ **22.** $9\overline{)\$8.37}$ **23.** $5\overline{)\$5.95}$ **24.** $7\overline{)\$7.49}$ **25.** $8\overline{)\$5.76}$

26. $6\overline{)\$9.00}$ **27.** $4\overline{)\$9.44}$ **28.** $3\overline{)\$3.21}$ **29.** $9\overline{)\$1.98}$ **30.** $8\overline{)\$8.64}$

31. $\$5.18 \div 7 = \underline{\quad?\quad}$ **32.** $\$8.25 \div 3 = \underline{\quad?\quad}$ **33.** $\$6.54 \div 6 = \underline{\quad?\quad}$

34. $\$4.80 \div 4 = \underline{\quad?\quad}$ **35.** $\$6.23 \div 7 = \underline{\quad?\quad}$ **36.** $\$7.11 \div 3 = \underline{\quad?\quad}$

★ **37.** $\$63.65 \div 5 = \underline{\quad?\quad}$ ★ **38.** $\$15.84 \div 9 = \underline{\quad?\quad}$ ★ **39.** $\$87.56 \div 4 = \underline{\quad?\quad}$

PROBLEM SOLVING • APPLICATIONS

40. The two girls share equally the cost of the clothespins. One package costs $2.30. How much does each girl pay?

41. The girls buy a bag of buttons to use as hats on some of the dolls. The bag costs $1.44. There are 6 buttons in the bag. How much does each button cost?

42. At the end of the week the girls have $15.60. They spent $3.74 for the clothespins and the buttons. How much money did each girl earn?

43. A clothespin doll can be made in 4 minutes. Samantha makes 12 dolls in one day. How many minutes does she spend making dolls?

44. One counselor spends $4.72 at the craft store. He pays with a 5-dollar bill and receives 4 coins in change. What four coins does he receive as change?

THINKER'S CORNER

Grant keeps all the craft sticks in one box. He has 15 wood sticks and 12 plastic sticks. If he reaches in the box without looking, what is the least number of sticks he can take out to be sure he gets two sticks that are different?

PROBLEM SOLVING • STRATEGIES

Using Estimation

Sometimes you only need to know about how many. You can estimate to find about how many.

Follow this rule.

> Round any number greater than 10 so that it has only one digit that is not zero.

Example 1   2,631 + 7,184

Think   Round each number to the nearest thousand.

$$\begin{array}{r} 2{,}631 \longrightarrow 3{,}000 \\ +7{,}184 \longrightarrow 7{,}000 \\ \hline 10{,}000 \end{array}$$ ◀ Estimated answer

Example 2   418 − 294

Think   Round each number to the nearest hundred.

$$\begin{array}{r} 418 \longrightarrow 400 \\ -294 \longrightarrow -300 \\ \hline 100 \end{array}$$ ◀ Estimated answer

Example 3   827 × 6

Think   Round 827 to the nearest hundred.

$$\begin{array}{r} 827 \longrightarrow 800 \\ \times\ 6 \longrightarrow \times\ 6 \\ \hline 48{,}000 \end{array}$$ ◀ Estimated answer

Example 4   213 ÷ 5

Think   Round 213 to the nearest hundred.

$$5\overline{)213} \longrightarrow 5\overline{)200}$$ 40 ◀ Estimated answer

E   **PROBLEMS** • Choose the best estimate. Choose **a**, **b**, or **c**.

1. 87 + 62	**a.** 80 + 60	**b.** 90 + 70	**c.** 90 + 60
2. 514 + 793	**a.** 500 + 700	**b.** 500 + 800	**c.** 600 + 800
3. 3,903 + 4,217	**a.** 3,000 + 4,000	**b.** 4,000 + 4,000	**c.** 4,000 + 5,000
4. 609 − 213	**a.** 600 − 200	**b.** 600 − 300	**c.** 700 − 200
5. 8,994 − 5,210	**a.** 9,000 − 6,000	**b.** 8,000 − 6,000	**c.** 9,000 − 5,000
6. 710 × 4	**a.** 700 × 4	**b.** 800 × 4	**c.** 1,000 × 4
7. 589 ÷ 6	**a.** 1,200 ÷ 6	**b.** 500 ÷ 6	**c.** 600 ÷ 6

E Choose the best estimate. Choose **a**, **b**, or **c**.

8. 93 + 78

  a. 160   **b.** 170   **c.** 180

9. 601 − 499

  a. 100   **b.** 200   **c.** 300

10. 402 × 9

  a. 5,400   **b.** 4,500   **c.** 3,600

11. 63 ÷ 5

  a. 10   **b.** 12   **c.** 20

12. Last week there were about 62 packages of hot dog buns in the supply room. Since then, 13 packages have been used. About how many packages are left?

  a. 60 − 20 **b.** 60 − 10 **c.** 70 − 10

13. On Wednesday afternoon, about 42 boys went swimming. Later 28 girls also went swimming. About how many campers went swimming in all?

  a. 50 + 20 **b.** 40 + 20 **c.** 40 + 30

14. Camp Pinetree has 21 large tents. Each tent has 9 bunk beds. About how many bunk beds are there in the tents?

  a. 20 × 9 **b.** 30 × 9 **c.** 10 × 9

15. Camp Pinetree has about 88 canoe paddles. There are 11 broken paddles. About how many paddles are not broken?

  a. 90   **b.** 80   **c.** 70

16. The first session at Camp Pinetree had 97 campers. The second session had about 23 more campers than the first session. About how many campers were in the second session?

  a. 100   **b.** 110   **c.** 120

17. Camp Pinetree is building 18 new cabins. Each cabin can hold about 8 campers. About how many campers will the new buildings hold?

  a. 80   **b.** 100   **c.** 160

CHAPTER REVIEW

Part 1: VOCABULARY

For Exercises 1–5, choose from the box at the right the word(s) that completes each statement.

1. The remainder must be less than the ___?___ (Page 184)

2. To find how many equal groups there are you can ___?___. (Page 184)

3. The quotient in a division problem is the ___?___. (Page 184)

4. To check a division problem, you multiply the ___?___ by the divisor. (Page 184)

5. After you check a division problem, the answer should equal the ___?___. (Page 184)

> answer
> divide
> dividend
> divisor
> product
> quotient

Part 2: SKILLS

Divide. (Pages 184–185)

6. $5\overline{)57}$ 7. $3\overline{)39}$ 8. $4\overline{)49}$ 9. $2\overline{)89}$ 10. $3\overline{)94}$

(Pages 186–187)

11. $7\overline{)84}$ 12. $4\overline{)94}$ 13. $6\overline{)80}$ 14. $2\overline{)76}$ 15. $3\overline{)75}$

(Pages 188–189)

16. $4\overline{)608}$ 17. $7\overline{)848}$ 18. $5\overline{)684}$ 19. $2\overline{)573}$ 20. $6\overline{)792}$

(Pages 190–191)

21. $4\overline{)274}$ 22. $3\overline{)29}$ 23. $3\overline{)102}$ 24. $5\overline{)408}$ 25. $8\overline{)694}$

(Pages 198–199)

26. $4\overline{)83}$ 27. $7\overline{)425}$ 28. $4\overline{)835}$ 29. $5\overline{)515}$ 30. $2\overline{)811}$

(Pages 200 –201)

31. $3\overline{)4,970}$ 32. $6\overline{)7,543}$ 33. $4\overline{)4,321}$ 34. $2\overline{)1,546}$ 35. $8\overline{)5,321}$

(Pages 202–203)

36. $7\overline{)\$8.47}$ 37. $3\overline{)\$9.30}$ 38. $9\overline{)\$1.98}$ 39. $6\overline{)\$6.54}$ 40. $7\overline{)\$5.18}$

Part 3: PROBLEM SOLVING • APPLICATIONS

Solve.

41. The nature group will plant 324 acorns. They will plant 9 rows of trees. How many trees will be in each row? (Pages 190–191)

42. Tracey collected 78 acorns. She bags the acorns for storage. Each bag holds 5 acorns. How many bags will she fill? How many acorns will be left over? (Pages 186–187)

Choose the best estimate.

43. A group of 68 campers are going into town. One adult counselor is needed for every 12 campers. About how many adults will be needed? (Pages 204–205)

    a. $60 \div 10$ **b.** $70 \div 10$
    c. $60 \div 20$ **d.** $70 \div 20$

44. On Friday afternoon 46 boys went out in the canoes. Later 32 girls went in the canoes. About how many campers went canoeing in all? (Pages 204–205)

    a. $50 + 40$ **b.** $40 + 30$
    c. $40 + 40$ **d.** $50 + 30$

Each week the campers at Camp Pinetree take a test for their water safety badge.

Use the table to find the averages. (Pages 192–193)

45. What is Pam's average test score?

46. What is Joe's average test score?

47. What is Carlos's average test score?

48. What is Rosa's average test score?

49. Who has the highest average test score?

	week 1	week 2	week 3
Joe	98	83	95
Pam	95	89	98
Carlos	87	92	94
Rosa	90	85	95

CHAPTER TEST

Divide.

1. $4\overline{)89}$ 2. $7\overline{)98}$ 3. $4\overline{)936}$ 4. $3\overline{)749}$

5. $5\overline{)592}$ 6. $4\overline{)651}$ 7. $2\overline{)133}$ 8. $5\overline{)375}$

9. $8\overline{)243}$ 10. $2\overline{)616}$ 11. $8\overline{)2,095}$ 12. $4\overline{)3,281}$

13. $6\overline{)9,237}$ 14. $6\overline{)\$9.30}$ 15. $7\overline{)\$5.74}$ 16. $3\overline{)\$7.50}$

17. $96 \div 3 =$ __?__   18. $424 \div 6 =$ __?__   19. $\$8.00 \div 5 =$ __?__

Camp Pinetree has several basketball teams. This table shows
the basketball scores for the month.

Team	Game 1	Game 2	Game 3	Game 4
Red Robins	96	65	53	74
Cardinals	84	78	81	57
Eagles	54	80	102	63

20. What is the average score for the first two games played by the Cardinals?

21. What is the average score for all 4 games played by the Red Robins?

Choose the best estimate. Choose **a**, **b**, or **c**.

22. On Tuesday, 37 campers went on a hike. Two days later, 42 campers went on another hike. About how many campers went hiking?

    a. 30 + 40 **b.** 40 + 40 **c.** 40 + 50

23. The camp has 4 archery teams. There are 21 campers on each team. About how many campers altogether are on an archery team?

    a. 100   **b.** 125   **c.** 80

24. Susan earned 85 badges at Camp Pinetree. David earned 56 badges. About how many more badges did Susan earn than David?

    a. 90 − 60 **b.** 90 − 50 **c.** 80 − 50

25. The camp cook worked 68 hours the first week. About how many hours does the cook work in 6 weeks?

    a. 360   **b.** 420   **c.** 490

ENRICHMENT

Divisibility Rules for 2, 3, and 5

Divide one number by another. If the remainder is 0, then the first number **is divisible by** the second.

$$2\overline{)12} \quad \begin{array}{r} 6 \\ -12 \\ \hline 0 \end{array}$$

12 is divisible by 2.

$$2\overline{)13} \quad \begin{array}{r} 6 \\ -12 \\ \hline 1 \end{array}$$

13 is not divisible by 2.

Divisibility rules can help you decide if one number is divisible by another without dividing.

If a number is an even number, it is divisible by 2.	132 is divisible by 2. 349 is not divisible by 2.
If there is a 0 or a 5 in the ones place, then the number is divisible by 5.	135 is divisible by 5. 276 is not divisible by 5.
If the sum of the digits of a number is divisible by 3, then the number is divisible by 3.	Is 216 divisible by 3? $216 \rightarrow 2 + 1 + 6 = 9$ Since 9 is divisible by 3, 216 is divisible by 3.

EXERCISES • Is the number divisible by 2? Write YES or NO.

1. 92   **2.** 158   **3.** 710   **4.** 1,823   **5.** 2,385

Is the number divisible by 5? Write YES or NO.

6. 49   **7.** 105   **8.** 450   **9.** 1,275   **10.** 8,944

Is the number divisible by 3? Write YES or NO.

11. 78   **12.** 263   **13.** 854   **14.** 3,549   **15.** 6,252

ADDITIONAL PRACTICE

SKILLS

(Pages 184–187)

1. $3\overline{)37}$ **2.** $2\overline{)48}$ **3.** $4\overline{)96}$ **4.** $7\overline{)86}$ **5.** $5\overline{)65}$

(Pages 188–191)

6. $6\overline{)846}$ **7.** $2\overline{)925}$ **8.** $4\overline{)272}$ **9.** $8\overline{)168}$ **10.** $9\overline{)298}$

(Pages 198–201)

11. $5\overline{)52}$ **12.** $4\overline{)839}$ **13.** $2\overline{)612}$ **14.** $6\overline{)8,557}$ **15.** $5\overline{)2,825}$

(Pages 202–203)

16. $3\overline{)\$3.90}$ **17.** $5\overline{)\$1.55}$ **18.** $7\overline{)\$8.40}$ **19.** $6\overline{)\$6.24}$ **20.** $4\overline{)\$9.48}$

PROBLEM SOLVING • APPLICATIONS

21. The campers are to store their supplies in lockers. Each locker is assigned to 3 campers. How many lockers are needed for 597 campers? (Pages 188–189)

22. The cook made 535 cups of punch. He gave each camper 2 cups. How many campers did he serve? How many cups were left over? (Pages 188–189)

23. The Redskin archery team scored 183, 192, and 210. What is their average score for all 3 games? (Pages 192–193)

24. Jonathan's scores in the archery game were 45, 37, 62, and 48. Find his average score. (Pages 192–193)

Choose the best estimate. Choose **a**, **b**, or **c**.

25. On Saturday 492 campers traveled to Camp Pinetree by car. Another 112 traveled by bus. About how many campers altogether arrived in Camp Pinetree on Saturday? (Pages 204–205)

  a. 500 **b.** 600 **c.** 700

26. The camp buses can hold 52 campers. About how many campers can travel on 9 buses? (Pages 204–205)

  a. 50×9 **b.** 50×10 **c.** 60×9

Each of these problems contains a common error.

a. Find the correct answer.

b. Find the error.

1. Each  stands for 10 cars sold.

How many cars were sold?

3 cars

2. Name the ordered pair that locates point F.

(1, 3)

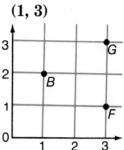

3. How many students like cats best?

3

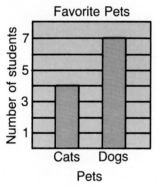

4. In what year did the price go up?

1985

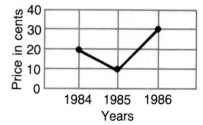

5.   347
    × 6
  ‾‾‾‾‾
  1,842

6.   ⁵ ⁶
    207
    × 9
  ‾‾‾‾‾‾
  2,343

7. $14.63
    ×   5
  ‾‾‾‾‾‾‾
  7,3 15

8. 7)331   46 r9
     28
   ‾‾‾‾
     51
     42
   ‾‾‾‾
      9

9. 6)253   49
     24
   ‾‾‾‾
    229
     54
   ‾‾‾‾
    175

10. 4)817   24 r1
      8
   ‾‾‾‾
    017
     16
   ‾‾‾‾
      1

CUMULATIVE REVIEW

Chapters 1 through 7

Choose the correct answers.

1. What is 6,410 rounded to the nearest thousand?

   A. 6,000 B. 6,400
   C. 7,000 D. not here

2. $$\begin{array}{r} \$17.89 \\ +\ 13.47 \\ \hline \end{array}$$

   A. $30.36 B. $31.38
   C. $31.26 D. not here

3. $$\begin{array}{r} 3{,}870 \\ -2{,}987 \\ \hline \end{array}$$

   A. 887 B. 883
   C. 893 D. not here

4. $$\begin{array}{r} 9{,}003 \\ -6{,}744 \\ \hline \end{array}$$

   A. 2,251 B. 2,259
   C. 2,359 D. not here

5. $27 = (3 \times 3) \times \underline{\ ?\ }$

   A. 2 B. 9
   C. 6 D. not here

6. $8\overline{)84}$

   A. 8 r9 B. 9 r2
   C. 9 r3 D. not here

7.  = 5 People

    = ? People

   A. 4 B. 15
   C. 10 D. not here

8. $$\begin{array}{r} 17 \\ \times\ 5 \\ \hline \end{array}$$

   A. 85 B. 75
   C. 55 D. not here

9. $$\begin{array}{r} 624 \\ \times\ \ 4 \\ \hline \end{array}$$

   A. 2,498 B. 2,596
   C. 2,486 D. not here

10. Lance had $5.00 in his wallet. He bought 3 rolls of film for $0.89 each. How much did the film cost?

    A. $2.67 B. $2.47
    C. $2.33 D. $2.65

11. On Monday 44 children tried out for the track team. On Tuesday 75 children tried out. About how many children tried out in all?

    A. 110 B. 119
    C. 130 D. 120

12. 807
  × 8

A. 6,348   **B.** 6,456
C. 6,356   **D.** not here

13. 6,492
  × 7

A. 45,444   **B.** 44,454
C. 45,434   **D.** not here

14. $12.89
  × 2

A. $24.78   **B.** $25.68
C. $25.78   **D.** not here

15. $64.83 × 3 = ___?___

A. $194.49
B. $193.49
C. $194.59
D. not here

16. 75 ÷ 2 = ___?___

A. 36 r2
B. 37 r1
C. 38
D. not here

17. 6)‾70‾

A. 11 r4
B. 11 r3
C. 12
D. not here

18. 4)‾687‾

A. 121 r3
B. 161 r3
C. 171 r3
D. not here

19. 2)‾810‾

A. 450
B. 405
C. 404
D. not here

20. 7)‾$18.41‾

A. $2.73
B. $2.63
C. $2.53
D. not here

21. 4)‾252‾

A. 58
B. 63
C. 62
D. not here

22. 9)‾397‾

A. 54 r1
B. 43 r1
C. 44 r1
D. not here

23. 4)‾6,589‾

A. 1,647 r1
B. 1,747 r1
C. 1,649
D. not here

24. Use the bar graph to answer the question.

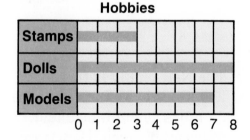

Hobbies

How many students chose models and dolls as hobbies?

A. 11   **B.** 15
C. 10   **D.** 18

25. Mary filled bottles with orange juice. She knew one bottle held 5 ounces. She made a table to find out how much orange juice she needed. Complete the table.

Bottles	1	2	3	4	5	6	?
Juice	5	10	?	20	?	?	35

How many ounces of juice are needed for 6 bottles?

A. 15   **B.** 7
C. 30   **D.** 25

Mixed Practice • Choose the correct answers.

1. 100
 × 7

A. 70   **B.** 707
C. 700   **D.** not here

2. 1,000
 × 9

A. 900   **B.** 9,000
C. 1,009   **D.** not here

3. $8 + 9 + 11 = $ ___?___

A. 28   **B.** 218
C. 35   **D.** not here

4. $8 \times 9 = $ ___?___

A. 64   **B.** 73
C. 81   **D.** not here

5. $6 \times 4 \times 2 = $ ___?___

A. 48   **B.** 46
C. 38   **D.** not here

6. $7 \times 6 \times 3 = $ ___?___

A. 116   **B.** 123
C. 126   **D.** not here

7. $12 \times 9 = $ ___?___

A. 118   **B.** 98
C. 108   **D.** not here

8. $36 \div 3 = $ ___?___

A. 12   **B.** 13
C. 11   **D.** not here

9. What time is it?

A. 3:55   **B.** 4:55
C. 11:20   **D.** not here

10. Tyrone left home at 8:17. He walked for 38 minutes. At what time did he finish his walk?

A. 8:45   **B.** 9:05
C. 8:56   **D.** not here

11. The Neil family is traveling 260 miles to Miami. They drove 87 miles before lunch, and 118 miles after lunch. How many more miles do they have to travel?

A. 55   **B.** 205
B. 60   **D.** not here

Measurement

Diane took 8 pictures of the Mississippi River on Monday and 18 pictures on Tuesday. One roll of film takes 36 pictures.

- How many pictures are left on the roll?

On Tuesday, Alex arrives at Baton Rouge at 8:15 A.M. The next riverboat for New Orleans leaves at 8:40 A.M.

- How long does he have to wait for the riverboat?

Centimeter

A **centimeter** is a metric unit used to measure length.

- The grain of rice is **1 centimeter (cm)** long.

The Mississippi River begins as a stream. It begins at Lake Itasca in Minnesota. The Chippewa Indians still grow wild rice there.

After cutting the stalks of rice, the Indians tie a number of stalks together.

- What is the length of this "tie" to the nearest centimeter?

Think   The length is between 4 and 5 centimeters. It is closer to 5 centimeters. Thus, the length of the tie is **5 centimeters** to the nearest centimeter.

PRACTICE • Measure the length of each "tie" to the nearest centimeter.

1.

2.

3.

4.

5.

6.

EXERCISES • Measure the length of each tie to the nearest centimeter.

7.

8.

9.

10.

11.

12.

13.

Draw each segment. Use your ruler.

14. 5 cm   **15.** 8 cm   **16.** 12 cm   **17.** 15 cm   **18.** 19 cm

PROBLEM SOLVING • APPLICATIONS

19. A rice plant is 82 cm high. Two months ago, it measured 38 cm. How many centimeters did the rice plant grow in two months?

20. Nadia's rice plant measured 43 cm high. Her brother's rice plant measured 69 cm. How many centimeters tall are the two rice plants together?

E **PROJECT**   Copy the table below. Estimate the length of each object that you find around your home. Then measure each to the nearest centimeter. Find the difference between the estimate and the measurement.

object	Estimate	Measure	Difference
Toothbrush			
Comb			
Toothpick			
Pencil			
Book			

Meter and Kilometer

A **meter** is another metric unit used to measure length.

1 meter (m) = 100 centimeters (cm)

Spread your arms apart and measure the distance from one hand to the other. The distance is about 1 meter.

In some places, the Mississippi River is only 3 meters deep.

● How many centimeters is this?

Think   Since 1 m = 100 cm, multiply 100 by 3. ⟶ 3 × 100 = 300
3 m = 300 cm

The width of the Mississippi at Cairo, Illinois, is 1 kilometer. The prefix **kilo** means 1000.

1 kilometer (km) = 1000 meters (m)

● How many meters is 8 kilometers?

Think   Since 1 km = 1000 m, multiply 1000 by 8. ⟶ 8 × 1000 = 8000
8 km = 8,000 m

PRACTICE • Is it more than a meter? Write YES or NO. Use a meter stick to check your answers.

1. the width of your desk

2. the height of your desk

3. your height

4. the length of the chalkboard

Which unit of measure would you use for each?

Write CENTIMETER, METER, or KILOMETER.

5. the length of your shoe

6. the distance across your state

7. the distance you can throw a ball

8. the height of a building

9. the width of a football field

10. the length of a pencil

EXERCISES • Is it more than a meter? Write YES or NO.

11. the length of a car

12. the length of an ant

13. the length of a pen

14. the distance you can walk in 5 minutes

Which unit of measure would you use for each?

Write CENTIMETER, METER, or KILOMETER.

15. the length of a soccer field

16. the distance across an ocean

17. the width of a book

18. the height of a flower

19. the length of your classroom

20. the width of your hand

21. the distance to the moon

22. the width of the school playground

23. the height of your classroom

24. the length of a shoestring

Complete.

25. 3 m = __?__ cm

26. 6 m = __?__ cm

27. __?__ cm = 9 m

28. __?__ cm = 8 m

29. 7 m = __?__ cm

30. __?__ cm = 10 m

★ **31.** 40 m = __?__ cm

★ **32.** __?__ m = 1,500 cm

★ **33.** __?__ m = 2,500 cm

Complete.

34. 2 km = __?__ m

35. 5 km = __?__ m

36. __?__ m = 4 km

37. __?__ m = 7 km

38. 8 km = __?__ m

39. __?__ m = 1 km

★ **40.** __?__ km = 26,000 m

★ **41.** __?__ km = 85,000 m

★ **42.** 24 km = __?__ m

PROBLEM SOLVING • **APPLICATIONS**

43. Bob is 3 meters away from the Mississippi River. Brenda is 335 centimeters away. Who is closer to the River? How much closer?

44. Moira lives 2 kilometers from Susan. Angela lives 1,800 meters from Susan. Which girl lives closer to Susan? How much closer?

Perimeter

> **The distance around a figure is the perimeter.**

A riverboat that cruises the Mississippi River has a pool on the sun deck. The fence around the pool forms a four-sided figure.

● What is the perimeter of this four-sided figure?

Think   Perimeter is the distance around.
So add the lengths of the four sides.

$$10 + 7 + 10 + 7 = 34$$

The perimeter is **34 meters**.

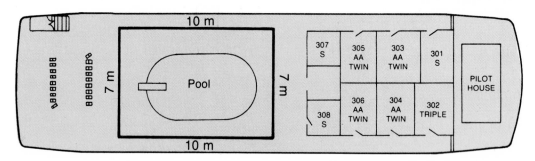

PRACTICE • Find each perimeter.

1.

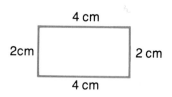

4 cm
2cm   2 cm
4 cm

2.

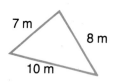

7 m   8 m
10 m

3.

9 cm
9 cm   9 cm
9 cm

4.

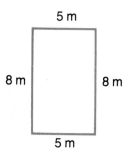

5 m
8 m   8 m
5 m

5.

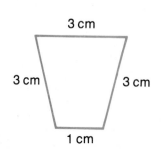

3 cm
3 cm   3 cm
1 cm

6.

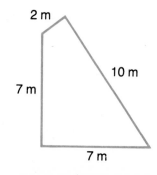

2 m
7 m   10 m
7 m

EXERCISES • Find each perimeter.

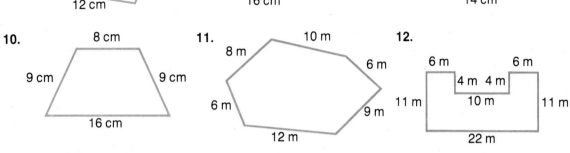

7.

18 cm
10 cm
12 cm

8.

16 cm
12 cm
12 cm
16 cm

9.

14 cm
14 cm
14 cm
14 cm

10.

8 cm
9 cm
9 cm
16 cm

11.

10 m
8 m
6 m
6 m
9 m
12 m

12.

6 m   6 m
4 m 4 m
11 m   10 m   11 m
22 m

Measure each side to the nearest centimeter.
Find the perimeter for each.

13.

14.

PROBLEM SOLVING • APPLICATIONS

Use the drawing of the riverboat for Exercise 15.

15. The railing around the pilot house forms a four-sided figure. Two sides are each 3 meters. The other two sides are each 6 meters. How much railing is needed?

16. One of the decks has a lounge area. It has three sides. Each side is 6 meters long. How much railing is needed to enclose the lounge area?

THINKER'S CORNER

Draw a square that has 4 centimeters on each side. Find the perimeter. Draw 3 different four-sided figures that have the same perimeter.

Area

The planners of the riverboat made a diagram of each stateroom. They want to know the number of *square units* of surface in the stateroom.

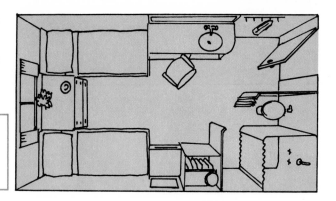

> **The number of square units that covers a surface is the area of the surface.**

● A **square centimeter** is a metric unit of area.

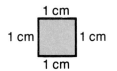

You can count the number of square centimeters to find the area of the surface.

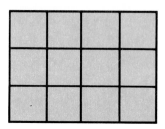

The area is **12 square centimeters**.

● Other metric units of area are the **square meter** and **square kilometer**.

PRACTICE ● Find each area in square centimeters.

1.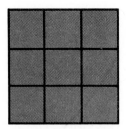

2.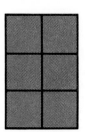

3.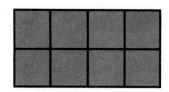

4.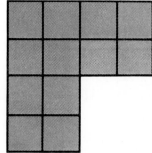

5.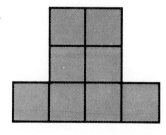

6.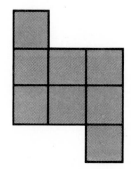

EXERCISES • Find each area in square centimeters.

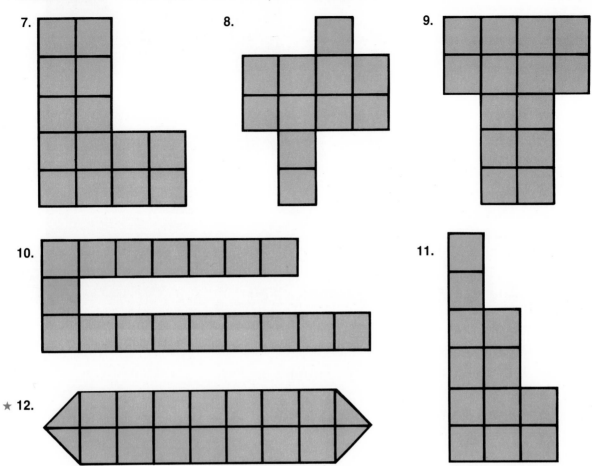

7.

8.

9.

10.

11.

★ 12.

PROBLEM SOLVING • APPLICATIONS

Use the pictures to help you solve the problems.
Each ☐ stands for 1 square meter.

13. This is the floor plan for Stateroom B. What is the area of Stateroom B?

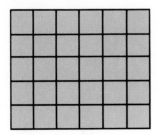

★ 14. This is the floor plan for the New Orleans Lounge. The yellow section is for seating. The center section is for dancing. What is the area of the seating section? What is the area of the dance floor?

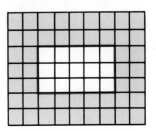

Multiplying to Find Area

Concrete blocks are used on the banks of the Mississippi River to hold back the earth. One section of blocks is 5 meters long and 3 meters wide. Each block is 1 meter long and 1 meter wide.

● What is the area of this section?

Think Draw a picture of the section. There are 3 rows with 5 blocks in each row. So multiply.

$3 \times 5 = 15$

The area is **15 square meters.**

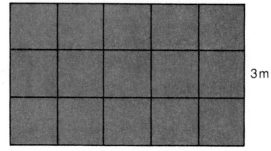

5m

3m

Rectangle

● You can find the area of a rectangle by multiplying the length by the width.

Area = length × width

PRACTICE • Multiply to find each area in square centimeters.

1.
2 cm
4 cm

2.

3 cm
7 cm

3.
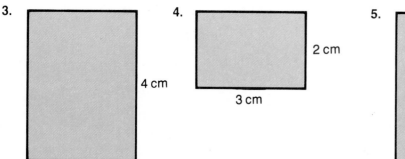
4 cm
3 cm

4.
2 cm
3 cm

5.
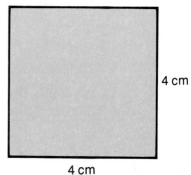
4 cm
4 cm

EXERCISES • Multiply to find each area in square centimeters.

6.

4 cm

5 cm

7.

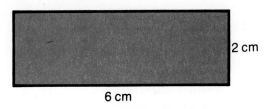

2 cm

6 cm

9.

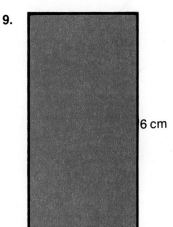

6 cm

3 cm

8.

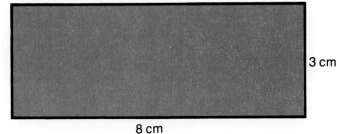

3 cm

8 cm

Find the area.

★ **10.** length = 6 meters
width = 3 meters

★ **11.** length = 9 centimeters
width = 5 centimeters

★ **12.** length = 8 meters
width = 6 meters

★ **13.** length = 7 centimeters
width = 4 centimeters

PROBLEM SOLVING • **APPLICATIONS**

14. A section of riverbank is 9 meters long and 5 meters wide. How many square meters of stone blocks are needed to cover the section?

15. Engineers place stone blocks along a section of the river bank that is 125 meters long and 8 meters wide. How many square meters of stone blocks do they need?

THINKER'S CORNER

The area of the rectangle is 24 square centimeters. Use centimeter graph paper to draw 3 different rectangles with an area of 24 square centimeters.

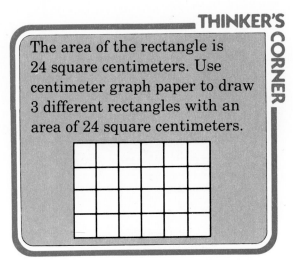

Volume

The Missouri River flows into the Mississippi River near St. Louis. This is where Lewis and Clark began their journey west. In order to pack their supplies into boxes, they had to know the *volume* of each box.

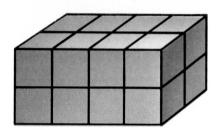

> **The volume of a box is the number of cubic units that will fit inside the box**

● What is the volume of this box?

Think Count the number of cubic units

The volume is **16 cubic units.**

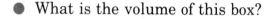

A **cubic centimeter** is a metric unit of volume. Each side has a length of one centimeter.

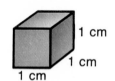

1 cm
1 cm
1 cm

1 cubic centimeter

PRACTICE • Each stands for 1 cubic centimeter. Find the volume of each box in cubic centimeters.

1.

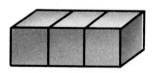

2.

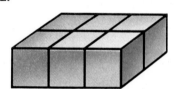

3.

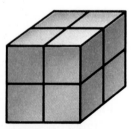

4.

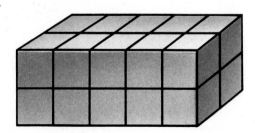

5.

EXERCISES • Each 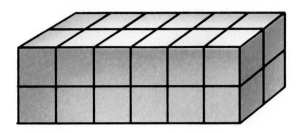 stands for 1 cubic centimeter. Find the volume of each box in cubic centimeters.

6.

7.

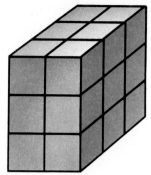

8.

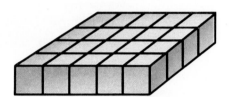

9.

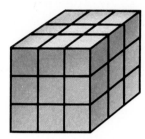

10.

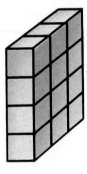

11.

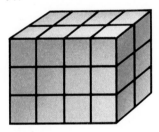

12.

PROBLEM SOLVING • APPLICATIONS

Each stands for 1 cubic centimeter.

13. Ken is putting blocks into this box. Each block is 1 cubic centimeter. How many blocks will fit into this box?

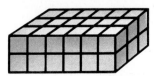

★ **14.** Sheila made this model of a building. How many blocks did she use?

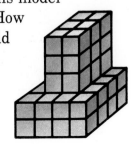

Multiplying to Find Volume

The Mississippi River is our nation's chief inland waterway. Container ships carry goods of all kinds in metal containers. The metal containers are loaded on the ships by cranes and stacked in **cells**.

● What is the volume of the cell at the right?

Think There are 4 × 3 = 12 cubic meters in one layer.

There are 2 layers. So there are

4 × 3 × 2 = **24 cubic meters.**

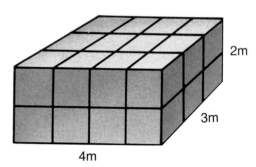

Volume = length × width × height

PRACTICE • Multiply to find the volume of each box in cubic centimeters.

1.

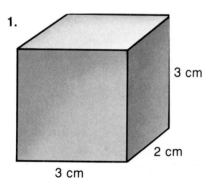

3 cm
2 cm
3 cm

2.

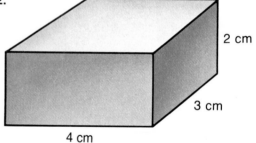

2 cm
3 cm
4 cm

3.

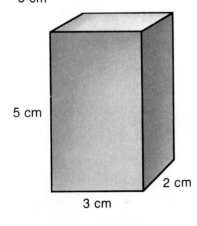

5 cm
2 cm
3 cm

4.

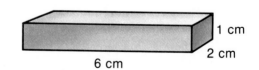

1 cm
2 cm
6 cm

EXERCISES • Multiply to find the volume in cubic centimeters for each box.

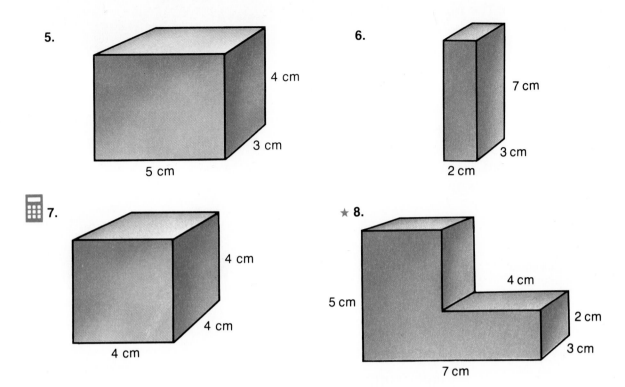

5.
4 cm
3 cm
5 cm

6.
7 cm
3 cm
2 cm

7.
4 cm
4 cm
4 cm

★ 8.
5 cm
4 cm
2 cm
3 cm
7 cm

Complete the table.

	Length	Width	Height	Volume
9.	8 cm	4 cm	6 cm	
10.	7 cm	6 cm	9 cm	
11.	5 cm	8 cm	12 cm	

PROBLEM SOLVING • APPLICATIONS

12. A metal container is 12 meters long, 2 meters wide, and 3 meters high. What is the volume of the metal container?

13. **a.** A special box was made to ship glasses. It is 10 centimeters long, 8 centimeters wide, and 7 centimeters high. What is the volume of the box?

   ★ **b.** Padding was put in the bottom of the box. It is 1 centimeter thick. Now what is the volume inside the box?

Milliliter and Liter

The pollution in the Mississippi River is threatening the fish. They will die if there is not enough oxygen in the water. This sample of river water is being tested for oxygen levels. What unit of measure can scientists use to take samples of the water?

The **milliliter (mL)** and **liter (L)** are metric units used to measure liquids.

Eyedropper
1 milliliter

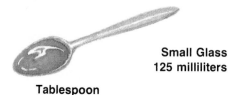
Tablespoon
5 milliliters

Small Glass
125 milliliters

Quart is a little less than 1,000 milliliters.

It would take 1,000 eyedroppers to fill a 1-liter container.

$$1,000 \text{ milliliters (mL)} = 1 \text{ liter (L)}$$

● How many milliliters are in 6 liters?

Think   Since 1,000 mL = 1 L, multiply 1,000 by 6. ⟶ 6 × 1,000 = 6,000

$$6,000 \text{ mL} = 6L$$

PRACTICE • Which unit of measure would you use for each? Write MILLILITER or LITER.

1. water in a straw

2. cocoa in a cup

3. water in a fishtank

4. soup in a spoon

5. gasoline in a car

6. water in a barrel

EXERCISES • Which unit of measure would you use for each? Write MILLILITER or LITER.

7. water in a washing machine

8. milk in a glass

9. punch in a bowl

10. water for a small plant

11. shampoo in a bottle

12. water for a bath

Choose the correct measures.

13.

4 mL or 4 L

14.

240 mL or 240 L

15.

40 mL or 40 L

16.

4 mL or 4 L

17.

65 mL or 65 L

18.

350 mL or 350 L

Complete.

19. 3 L = __?__ mL

20. 8 L = __?__ mL

21. __?__ mL = 2 L

22. __?__ mL = 5 L

23. 6 L = __?__ mL

24. __?__ mL = 1 L

25. 4 L = __?__ mL

26. 9 L = __?__ mL

27. __?__ mL = 7 L

★ 28. 15,000 mL = __?__ L

★ 29. 14,000 mL = __?__ L

★ 30. __?__ mL = 20 L

PROBLEM SOLVING • APPLICATIONS

31. Mrs. Kono collects 4,000 milliliters of river water to test. How many liters is this?

32. Mrs. Kono has two river samples. One contains 500 milliliters. The other contains 350 milliliters. How much more does she need to fill a liter container?

★ 33. A container can hold 250 milliliters. How many liters of river water would Mrs. Kono need to fill 8 containers?

★ 34. Mrs. Kono has 3 liters of river water. She pours 200 milliliters into each test tube. How many test tubes can she fill?

Gram and Kilogram

The marshlands of the Mississippi Delta area provide winter nesting grounds for ducks. Most ducks weigh about 2 *kilograms*.

The **gram (g)** and **kilogram (kg)** are metric units of mass.

A paper clip is about 1 **gram.**   This book is about 1 **kilogram**.

There are 1,000 grams in 1 kilogram.

1,000 grams (g) = 1 kilogram (kg)

● How many grams are in 5 kilograms?

| **Think** | Since 1,000 g = 1 kg, multiply 1,000 by 5. ⟶ $5 \times 1,000 = 5,000$ |

5,000 g = 5 kg

A milliliter of water is about 1 gram.   A liter of water is about 1 kilogram.

PRACTICE • Which unit of measure would you use? Write GRAM or KILOGRAM.

1.

2.

3.

4.

5.

6.

EXERCISES • Which unit of measure would you use?
Write GRAM or KILOGRAM.

7.

8.

9.

10.

11.

12.

Choose the correct measures.

13. a car tire
10 grams or 10 kilograms

14. a bicycle
20 grams or 20 kilograms

15. a flashlight battery
100 grams or 100 kilograms

16. a pencil
5 grams or 5 kilograms

17. a bar of soap
200 grams or 200 kilograms

18. a refrigerator
150 grams or 150 kilograms

Complete.

19. 4 kg = __?__ g

20. 6 kg = __?__ g

21. __?__ g = 3 kg

22. __?__ g = 8 kg

23. 5 kg = __?__ g

24. __?__ g = 7 kg

★ 25. __?__ g = 10 kg

★ 26. 17,000 g = __?__ kg

★ 27. 25,000 g = __?__ kg

PROBLEM SOLVING • APPLICATIONS

28. A small duck has a mass of 1,000 grams. How many kilograms is this?

29. A duck has a mass of 3 kilograms. How many grams is this?

30. A female duck lays 5 eggs. Each egg is 70 grams. What is the mass of all the eggs?

PROBLEM SOLVING • STRATEGIES

Missing Information

Sometimes a problem cannot be solved because there is not enough information.

Example The riverboat that cruises the Mississippi River has a dance floor in the dining room. The dance floor is 5 meters long.

● What is the area of the dance floor?

Think Write a number sentence.

Area = length × width

Area =   5   × __?__

You cannot find the area.

You need to know the **width** of the dance floor.

PROBLEMS • Choose the information you need. Then solve the problem.

1. Roberto is making a rug for the living room of his model home. The width of the rug is 9 centimeters. What is the area of the rug?

   a. The length of the room is 30 centimeters.

   b. The width of the room is 20 centimeters.

   c. The length of the rug is 25 centimeters.

2. Lian buys a souvenir for each member of her family. Each souvenir costs the same amount. She spends $20 in all. How much does each souvenir cost?

   a. Lian bought 5 souvenirs.

   b. Lian spent $30 for food.

   c. Lian received $10 in change.

3. There are 82 passengers on board the riverboat. Some leave when the boat docks. How many are left?

   a. 54 passengers attend a dance.

   b. 38 passengers leave the boat.

   c. 19 passengers played shuffleboard.

Write a number sentence to help you decide if information is missing.

What other information do you need to solve the problem?

4. A special box was made to ship glass figures. The box is 10 centimeters long and 7 centimeters high. What is the volume of the box?

5. Mrs. Kono has two samples of river water. There are 350 milliliters in one sample. How many milliliters of river water does she have in all?

6. In one section of the riverboat there are 8 rows of seats. How many seats are in this section in all?

7. Jim is weighing the different animals found on the marshlands of the Mississippi Delta. A large duck weighs 2 kilograms. How much more does the alligator weigh than the duck?

8. Stateroom A is the largest of the rooms on the riverboat. The length of the room is 4 meters. What is the area of Stateroom A?

9. The Indians grew rice near the Mississippi River. Suppose a rice plant grew 22 centimeters in one month. The next month it grew some more. How many centimeters did the rice plant grow in those months?

10. In some places, the Mississippi River is only 3 meters deep. Its deepest point is at Cairo, Illinois. How much deeper is the river in Cairo?

11. A large bull frog weighs 1 pound. A large crawfish weighs 20 grams. How much more do 20 crawfish weigh than 1 large bullfrog?

12. The riverboat is 50 meters long. The distance from Natchez to New Orleans is 500 kilometers. How long will it take to go from New Orleans to Natchez?

MID-CHAPTER REVIEW

Which unit of measure would you use?
Write CENTIMETER, METER, or KILOMETER. (Pages 216–219)

1. the height of a flagpole

2. the length of the Mississippi River

3. Find the perimeter. (Pages 220–221)

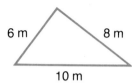

4. Find the area. (Pages 222–225)

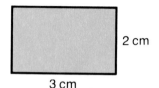

5. Find the volume. (Pages 226–229)

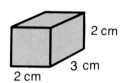

Complete. (Pages 230–233)

6. 2 L = ___?___ mL

7. 4 L = ___?___ mL

8. 7 kg = ___?___ g

Which unit of measure would you use?
Write GRAM or KILOGRAM. (Pages 232–233)

9. a pencil

10. a bicycle

11. an automobile

What other information do you need to solve Exercises 12–13?

12. Stateroom B is the smallest room on the riverboat. The length of the room is 4 meters. What is the area of Stateroom B? (Pages 234–234)

13. Mr. Brice has 2 river samples. One sample has 250 milliliters. How many milliliters does he have in all? (Pages 234–235)

MAINTENANCE • MIXED PRACTICE

Add or subtract. Watch the signs.

1. 4,724 − 189	2. 8,635 +5,947	3. 5,603 +9,610	4. 3,814 −1,406	5. 5,268 − 688

Divide.

6. 4)80   7. 3)99   8. 6)82   9. 4)89   10. 3)94

Solve.

11. Felipe bought tickets for fair rides. He received $0.23 in change. The clerk gave him 3 pennies, 2 nickels, and 1 other coin. What was the other coin?

12. There are 48 people on the Sky Train. The Sky Train has 6 cars. The same number of people are in each car. How many people are in each car?

CONSUMER APPLICATIONS

Reading Maps

The Turner family is visiting Adams County Park.
They find the entrance and drive **north** to the ranger
station. They want to go to the campgrounds first.

● In which direction are the campgrounds from the ranger station?

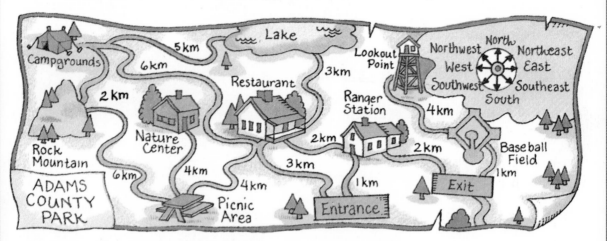

The campgrounds are **northwest** of the ranger station.

● How far must they travel from the ranger station?

To find how far they must travel, add.

$$
\begin{array}{r}
2 \text{ km} \\
+6 \text{ km} \\
\hline
8 \text{ km}
\end{array}
$$

← ranger station to the restaurant
← restaurant to the campgrounds

The total distance is **8 kilometers.**

EXERCISES • Use the map to help you find the direction.
How far is the distance traveled in each exercise?

1. From the restaurant to the picnic area

2. From the baseball field to Lookout Point

3. From the restaurant to the exit

4. From the campgrounds to the picnic area

5. From the campgrounds to the lake

6. From the nature center to the restaurant

PROJECT Make a map to show how to go from your house to school.

Degrees Celsius

The waters that flow through the Mississippi River Drainage Basin form part of the longest cave system in the world. The temperature inside Mammoth Flint Ridge Cave is always about 20° *Celsius*.

A **degree Celsius (°C)** is a metric unit used to measure temperature.

This is a **Celsius thermometer**. Each mark stands for 2 degrees Celsius. The temperature is **20 degrees Celsius above zero**. Another way to write this is **20°C**.

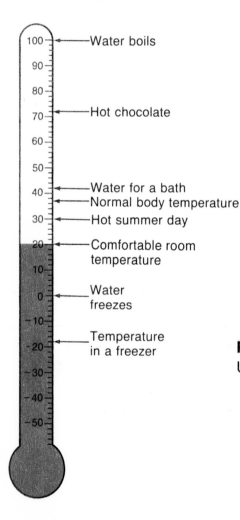

● Suppose the temperature falls 30 degrees. The new temperature would be **10 degrees Celsius below zero**. Another way to write this is **−10°C**.

PRACTICE • What is the temperature for each? Use the thermometer.

1. water freezes
2. water for a bath
3. body temperature
4. a summer day
5. hot chocolate
6. inside a freezer
7. room temperature
8. water boils

EXERCISES • Choose the correct temperatures.

9. swimming weather

   2°C or 32°C

10. ice cubes

    10°C or −20°C

11. hot soup

    15°C or 75°C

12. ice skating weather

    30°C or −5°C

13. spring day

    15°C or 60°C

14. snowball

    30°C or 0°C

15. fever temperature

    39°C or 100°C

16. winter day

    0°C or 35°C

17. a cold drink

    40°C or 5°C

18. soccer weather

    25°C or 60°C

19. office temperature

    20°C or 40°C

20. swimming pool

    15°C or 70°C

PROBLEM SOLVING • APPLICATIONS

Use the table to answer the questions.

Air Temperature at Mammoth Cave National Park		
Month	High Temperature	Low Temperature
January	7°C	−3°C
April	19°C	7°C
July	32°C	19°C
October	22°C	8°C

21. What is the high temperature in October?

22. What is the low temperature in January?

23. During which month is the low temperature the same as the high temperature in January?

Time

Mark Twain wrote many books about life on the Mississippi River. Mr. Barnes's class went on a 60-minute tour of the Mark Twain Museum in Hannibal, Missouri.

- There are 60 minutes (**min**) in 1 hour.

- There are 24 hours (**h**) in 1 day.

Clocks show the hours and minutes of each day.

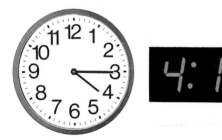

Read: **fifteen minutes after four** or **four-fifteen** or **quarter after four**

Write: **4:15**

Read: **thirty minutes after four** or **four-thirty** or **half past four**

Write: **4:30**

Read: **forty-seven minutes after four** or **four-forty-seven** or **thirteen minutes to five**

Write: **4:47**

Read: **fifty minutes after four** or **four-fifty** or **ten minutes to five**

Write: **4:50**

We use **A.M.** or **P.M.** to tell what part of the day it is.

A.M. means the hours between midnight and noon.

P.M. means the hours between noon and midnight.

PRACTICE • Write the time for each.

1.
2.
3.

4. eight minutes after six

5. quarter to nine

EXERCISES • Write the time for each.

6.
7.
8.

9. three minutes after eleven

10. half past six

11. twenty-one minutes to seven

12. eight-thirty

13. quarter to twelve

14. quarter after five

15. ten past seven

16. seventeen minutes to twelve

17. three-thirty-five

18. eleven-twenty

Write **A.M.** or **P.M.**

19. Go to gym class at 1:45 __?__ .

20. Eat lunch at 12:14 __?__ .

21. Practice baseball at 4:30 __?__ .

22. Wake up at 7:45 __?__ .

★ **23.** One hour before noon is 11:00 __?__ .

★ **24.** One hour after noon is 1:00 __?__ .

PROBLEM SOLVING • **APPLICATIONS**

Write the times using **A.M.** and **P.M.**

25. The bus leaves the school for the museum at ten minutes after nine.

26. The bus leaves the museum at eleven-thirty-five.

PROJECT Record the temperatures at 9:00 A.M. AND 2:00 P.M. for each day of the week. Make a table to show this information.

Time Intervals

Large ships can travel the entire Mississippi River by using canal locks. These locks allow the ships to avoid shallow areas and waterfalls along the River.

A ship enters this lock at 2:15 P.M. It is filled with water at 2:50 P.M.

● How many minutes did it take to fill the lock?

Think Count by fives from 2:15 P.M. to 2:50 P.M.

There are **35 minutes** from 2:15 P.M. to 2:50 P.M.

A ship enters this lock at 3:30 P.M. It takes 40 minutes to empty the water.

● What time was the lock empty?

Think Start at 3:30 P.M. Count by fives to 40.

40 minutes later than 3:30 P.M. is **4:10 P.M.**

PRACTICE • How many minutes from

1. 3:00 to 3:30?

2. 4:25 to 4:40?

3. 2:05 to 2:45?

Write the time for each.

4. 10 minutes later than 1:20

5. 30 minutes later than 6:10

6. 45 minutes later than 5:15

EXERCISES • How many minutes from

7. 11:00 to 11:45?

8. 10:10 to 10:50?

9. 8:20 to 9:10?

10. 7:05 to 7:35?

11. 12:15 to 12:35?

12. 5:40 to 6:00?

13. 4:50 to 5:10?

★ **14.** 8:20 to 8:47?

★ **15.** 3:20 to 3:53?

Write the time for each.

16. 30 minutes later than 2:10

17. 20 minutes earlier than 8:40

18. 15 minutes earlier than 7:25

19. 15 minutes later than 1:05

20. 30 minutes earlier than 11:30

21. 20 minutes later than 9:55

★ **22.** 14 minutes earlier than 12:05

PROBLEM SOLVING • APPLICATIONS

23. The gates will be ready to open in 20 minutes. It is now 5:15. What time will the gates be opened?

24. A ship left port at 1:40 P.M. It arrived at McAlpine Locks at 2:35 P.M. How long did it take to get to McAlpine Locks?

25. An engineer arrives at the control station at 4:30 P.M. He inspects the equipment at the power station until 5:45 P.M. How long did it take the engineer to inspect the equipment?

PROBLEM SOLVING • STRATEGIES

Using a Schedule

A schedule helps you find information. This is a schedule for the riverboat cruises along the Mississippi River. It shows the times that the riverboats are available from Baton Rouge to New Orleans.

Example   Jonathan wants to take a cruise along the Mississippi River on Tuesday. He wants to arrive in New Orleans close to 12:30 P.M.

● Which riverboat should he take?

● At what time will he arrive?

Step 1 Look at the column labeled

Arrives at New Orleans.

Read down to find the riverboat that arrives close to 12:30 P.M.

Step 2 Read across the column labeled

Riverboat Cruises.

Does the riverboat run on Tuesday?

Step 3 Look at the column labeled

Leaves Baton Rouge.

At what time does the riverboat leave?

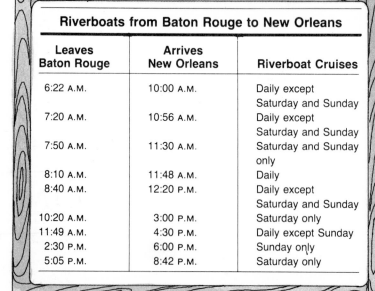

Schedule:

Riverboats from Baton Rouge to New Orleans

Leaves Baton Rouge	Arrives New Orleans	Riverboat Cruises
6:22 A.M.	10:00 A.M.	Daily except Saturday and Sunday
7:20 A.M.	10:56 A.M.	Daily except Saturday and Sunday
7:50 A.M.	11:30 A.M.	Saturday and Sunday only
8:10 A.M.	11:48 A.M.	Daily
8:40 A.M.	12:20 P.M.	Daily except Saturday and Sunday
10:20 A.M.	3:00 P.M.	Saturday only
11:49 A.M.	4:30 P.M.	Daily except Sunday
2:30 P.M.	6:00 P.M.	Sunday only
5:05 P.M.	8:42 P.M.	Saturday only

Jonathan can take the **8:40 A.M.** riverboat from Baton Rouge.
He will arrive in New Orleans at **12:20 P.M.**

PROBLEMS • Use the schedule to answer the questions.

1. Mrs. Karas wants to go to New Orleans on Friday. Which riverboat must she take to arrive by 11:00 A.M.?

Check the hours to see if they are A.M. or P.M.

---

2. Mr. Turner is taking his class for a cruise on Saturday. They will need to be in New Orleans by 3:00 P.M. Which riverboat should they take from Baton Rouge?

3. Lee Anne takes the 8:40 A.M. riverboat from Baton Rouge. At what time should she arrive in New Orleans?

4. Thelma wants to be in New Orleans by 4:30 P.M. on Sunday. What is the last riverboat she can take from Baton Rouge?

5. How many riverboats leave Baton Rouge for New Orleans on Sunday mornings?

6. How many riverboats go from Baton Rouge to New Orleans on Saturday mornings?

7. How long does it take the 10:20 A.M. riverboat to go from Baton Rouge to New Orleans?

8. Fran will take the first riverboat leaving Baton Rouge on Sunday. At what time will she arrive in New Orleans?

9. On Tuesday Alex arrives at Baton Rouge at 8:15 A.M. How long does he have to wait for the next riverboat to New Orleans?

10. The 8:10 A.M. riverboat is 11 minutes late. At what time should it now arrive in New Orleans?

Write Your Own Problem

Use the schedule on page 244 to write 2 story problems.

Write one problem like Problem 2 and one problem like Problem 7.

Inch

An **inch (in.)** is a customary unit used to measure length.

Cotton is grown along the Mississippi River. The fibers from each cotton ball are about 1 inch long.

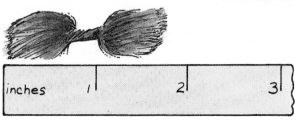

● What is the length of this cotton fiber to the nearest inch?

Think The length of this cotton fiber is between 1 and 2 inches. It is nearer to 2 inches. The length is **2 inches** to the nearest inch.

● Inch rulers are sometimes marked to show $\frac{1}{2}$ inches, $\frac{1}{4}$ inches, and $\frac{1}{8}$ inches.

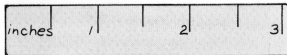

This ruler is marked to show $\frac{1}{2}$ inches. The cotton fiber is $1\frac{1}{2}$ **inches** long to the nearest $\frac{1}{2}$ inch.

This ruler is marked to show $\frac{1}{4}$ inches. The cotton fiber is $1\frac{3}{4}$ **inches** long to the nearest $\frac{1}{4}$ inch.

This ruler is marked to show $\frac{1}{8}$ inches. The cotton fiber is $1\frac{7}{8}$ **inches** long to the the nearest $\frac{1}{8}$ inch.

PRACTICE • Measure each length to the nearest inch, $\frac{1}{2}$ inch, $\frac{1}{4}$ inch, and $\frac{1}{8}$ inch.

1.
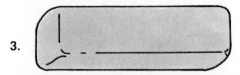

2.

EXERCISES • Measure each length to the nearest inch, $\frac{1}{2}$ inch, $\frac{1}{4}$ inch, and $\frac{1}{8}$ inch.

3.

4.

5.

6.

Draw each line segment. Use your ruler.

7. 5 in.

8. $3\frac{1}{2}$ in.

9. $7\frac{1}{2}$ in.

10. $6\frac{1}{4}$ in.

11. $4\frac{3}{4}$ in.

12. $8\frac{3}{8}$ in.

13. $5\frac{7}{8}$ in.

14. $4\frac{1}{8}$ in.

E **PROJECT**   Copy the table below. Estimate the length of each object that you find around your home. Then measure each to the nearest inch. Find the difference between the estimate and the measurement.

Object	Estimate	Measure	Difference
Toothbrush			
Comb			
Toothpick			
Pencil			

Foot, Yard, and Mile

Memphis, Tennessee, stretches along the banks of the Mississippi River. It is the largest hardwood lumber center in the world. Lumber is measured in *board feet*. One **board foot** is 1 foot long and 1 foot wide.

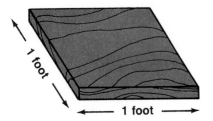

● The **foot (ft), yard (yd),** and **mile (mi)** are other customary units used to measure length.

● The distance from your elbow to your fingertips is about **1 foot.**

● The length of a baseball bat is about **1 yard.**

● A car traveling at 60 miles an hour takes about 1 minute to go 1 mile. This sign shows how these units are related.

● How many inches are in 8 feet?

Think | Since 12 in. = 1 ft, multiply 12 by 8.

$8 \times 12 = 96$ ◄ **8 ft = 96 in.**

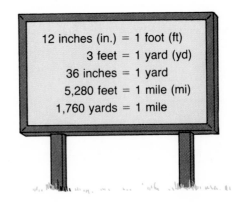

12 inches (in.) = 1 foot (ft)
3 feet = 1 yard (yd)
36 inches = 1 yard
5,280 feet = 1 mile (mi)
1,760 yards = 1 mile

● How many inches are in 4 yards?

Think | Since 36 in. = 1 yd, multiply 36 by 4.

$4 \times 36 = 144$ ◄ **4 yd = 144 in.**

PRACTICE • Choose the correct measures.

1. the length of a paper clip
2 inches or 2 feet

2. the length of a bicycle
5 feet or 5 yards

3. the width of a stamp
1 inch or 1 foot

4. the distance across the United States
2,800 yards or 2,800 miles

5. the length of a car
10 feet or 10 yards

6. the width of a jumbo jet
185 inches or 185 feet

EXERCISES • Choose the correct measures.

7. the height of a room
8 inches or 8 feet

8. the height of a desk
1 foot or 1 yard

9. the length of a toothbrush
6 inches or 6 feet

10. the length of a school bus
12 feet or 12 yards

11. the height of a tree
15 inches or 15 feet

12. the distance across Texas
770 yards or 770 miles

Complete.

	13.	**14.**	**15.**	**16.**	**17.**
feet	1	2	3	4	5	6
inches	12	?	?	?	?	?

	18.	**19.**	**20.**	**21.**	**22.**
yards	1	2	3	4	5	6
feet	3	?	?	?	?	?

Complete.

23. 4 ft = __?__ in.

24. 7 ft = __?__ in.

25. 5 yd = __?__ ft

26. 7 yd = __?__ ft

27. 6 ft = __?__ in.

28. 4 yd = __?__ ft

29. 2 yd = __?__ in.

30. 1 mi = __?__ ft

31. 1 mi = __?__ yd

★ **32.** 15 ft = __?__ in.

★ **33.** 24 ft = __?__ yd

★ **34.** 180 in. = __?__ yd

PROBLEM SOLVING • APPLICATIONS

35. A piece of hardwood lumber is 5 feet long. How many inches is this?

36. The width of the Mississippi River, near Memphis, is about 1 mile. How many yards is this?

37. A piece of oak is 3 yards long. A piece of birch is 3 feet long. How much longer is the piece of oak?

★ **38.** A piece of maple is 72 inches long. How many feet is this? How many yards is this?

Perimeter and Area

Roberto is building a model of this home found along the Mississippi River. He made a window for the model.

● What is the perimeter of this window?

Think Add to find the perimeter.

$$4 + 2 + 4 + 2 = 12$$

The perimeter is **12 inches.**

A **square inch** is a customary unit of area.

● What is the area of the window?

Think You can count each square inch or multiply to find the area.

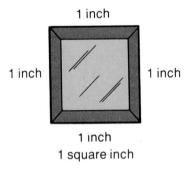

1 inch

1 inch   1 inch

1 inch
1 square inch

Area = length × width
Area = 4 × 2

The area of the window is **8 square inches.** A **square foot** and **square yard** are also customary units of area.

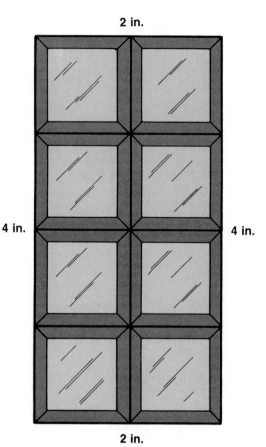

2 in.

4 in.   4 in.

2 in.

PRACTICE • Each ▢ stands for 1 square inch. Find the perimeter and area.

1.   4 in.

3 in.   3 in.

4 in.

2.   3 in.

3 in.   3 in.

5 in.   5 in.

3 in.

3.   2 in.

4 in.   4 in.

2 in.

EXERCISES • Each 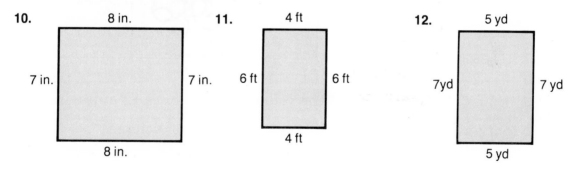 stands for 1 square inch. Find the perimeter and area.

4.
4 in.
5 in.   5 in.
4 in.

5.
3 in.
3 in.   3 in.
3 in.

6.
2 in.
5 in.   5 in.
2 in.

7.
4 in.
4 in.   4 in.
4 in.

8.
6 in.
3 in.   4 in.
6 in.

9.
4 in.
2 in.   2 in.
3 in.
4 in.

Find the perimeter and area.

10.
8 in.
7 in.   7 in.
8 in.

11.
4 ft
6 ft   6 ft
4 ft

12.
5 yd
7 yd   7 yd
5 yd

PROBLEM SOLVING • APPLICATIONS

13. The living room of the model home is 12 inches long and 18 inches wide. What is the perimeter of the living room?

14. Roberto makes an area rug from yarn. The rug is 8 inches long and 6 inches wide. What is the area of the rug?

★ **15.** A bedroom is in the shape of a rectangle. Its area is 54 square inches. Its perimeter is 30 inches. What is the bedroom's length and width?

Volume

The Turner family likes to camp near the mouth of the Wisconsin River. It was here that Marquette and Jolliet first explored the Mississippi River in 1673.

The volume of Ted's backpack determines how many supplies will fit in it.

● What is the volume of this box?

Think You can count or multiply to find the volume.

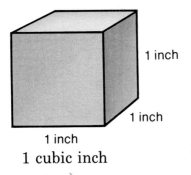

1 inch

1 inch

1 inch

1 cubic inch

A **cubic inch** is a customary unit of volume.

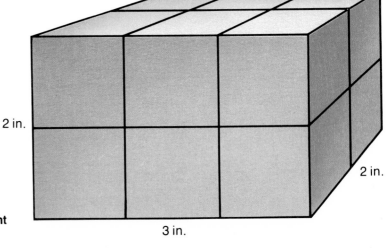

2 in.

2 in.

3 in.

Volume = length × width × height
Volume = 3 × 2 × 2
Volume = 12 cubic inches

The volume of this box is **12 cubic inches.**

A **cubic foot** and **cubic yard** are also customary units of volume.

PRACTICE • Each ▭ stands for 1 cubic inch. Find the volume.

1.

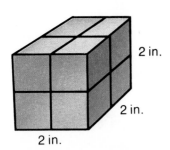

2 in.

2 in.

2 in.

2.

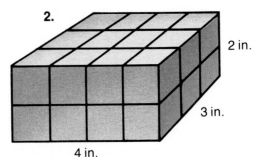

2 in.

3 in.

4 in.

EXERCISES • Find the volume.

3.

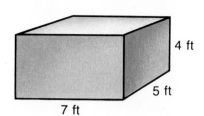

4 ft
5 ft
7 ft

4.

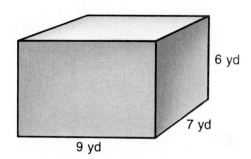

6 yd
7 yd
9 yd

5.

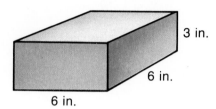

3 in.
6 in.
6 in.

6.

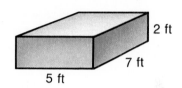

2 ft
7 ft
5 ft

PROBLEM SOLVING • APPLICATIONS

7. Mr. Turner has his camera in a steel box. The box is approximately 7 inches high, 6 inches wide, and 10 inches long. What is the volume?

8. Ted's plastic backpack is 22 inches high, 15 inches wide and 9 inches deep. What is the volume?

9. The Turners keep their food in a cooler. How many 2-inch cubes will fit inside this cooler?

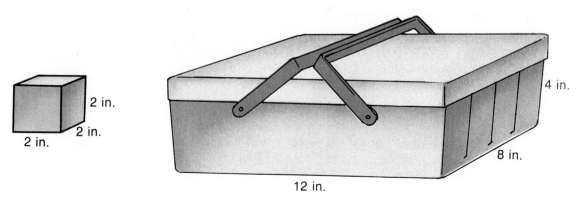

2 in.
2 in.
2 in.

4 in.
8 in.
12 in.

10. How many 4-inch cubes will fit inside the box?

Cup, Pint, Quart, and Gallon

After taking a long hike, the
Turner family rests for a while at
the camp. Ted pours 4 cups of water
from their quart thermos bottle.

● The **cup (c)**, **pint (pt)**, **quart
(qt)**, and **gallon (gal)** are
customary units used to measure
liquids.

1 cup

2 cups = 1 pint

2 pints = 1 quart

4 quarts = 1 gallon

PRACTICE • Complete.

		1.	2.	3.	4.	5.	6.	7.
Quarts	1	2	3	4	5	6	7	8
Pints	2	?	?	?	?	?	?	?
Cups	4	?	?	?	?	?	?	?

8. 2 pt = __?__ c

9. 3 qt = __?__ pt

10. 7 qt = __?__ pt

11. 4 pt = __?__ c

12. 5 qt = __?__ pt

13. 8 qt = __?__ pt

14. 2 gal = __?__ qt

15. 4 gal = __?__ qt

16. 3 gal = __?__ pt

EXERCISES • Complete.

17. 3 pt = _?_ c

18. 2 qt = _?_ pt

19. 2 gal = _?_ qt

20. 3 qt = _?_ pt

21. 1 gal = _?_ pt

22. 5 pt = _?_ c

23. 4 qt = _?_ pt

24. 2 gal = _?_ qt

25. 6 qt = _?_ pt

26. 4 qt = _?_ c

27. 2 gal = _?_ pt

28. 2 gal = _?_ c

★ **29.** $\frac{1}{2}$ pt = _?_ c

★ **30.** 1 pt = _?_ qt

★ **31.** 1 qt = _?_ gal

Which is greater?

32. 4 c or 3 pt

33. 2 pt or 3 c

34. 7 qt or 1 gal

35. 3 qt or 5 pt

36. 10 qt or 2 gal

37. 6 pt or 4 qt

38. 10 pt or 1 gal

39. 8 c or 3 qt

40. 20 c or 1 gal

Choose the correct measures.

41.

1 c or 1 qt

42.

1 c or 1 qt

43.

2 c or 2 gal

44.

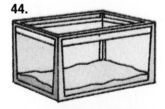

10 c or 10 gal

45.

1 c or 1 qt

46.

2 c or 2 qt

47. Mrs. Turner prepares 12 cups of soup for her family's lunch. How many pints are there in 12 cups?

48. Amy goes to the natural spring at the campground to get 2 gallons of water. How many quarts are in 2 gallons?

49. Mr. Turner's canteen holds 2 pints of water. How many cups can he fill with his canteen?

★ **50.** Ted is making instant juice for breakfast. The directions call for 5 cups of water. Will a 2-quart pitcher hold that amount of water?

Ounce, Pound, and Ton

Farmers use the fertile soil of the Mississippi Delta to produce fruits and vegetables.

A tomato weighs about 6 ounces.

A basket of tomatoes weighs about 2 pounds.

A truck weighs about 1 ton.

● The **ounce (oz), pound (lb),** and **ton (T)** are customary units used to measure weight.

16 ounces (oz) = 1 pound (lb)   **2,000 pounds (lbs) = 1 ton (T)**

PRACTICE • Choose the correct measures.

1.

5 oz or 5 lb

2.

2 oz or 2 lb

3.

1 lb or 1 T

4.

20 oz or 20 lb

5.

4 lb or 4 T

6.

7 oz or 7 lb

EXERCISES • Choose the correct measures.

7.

4 oz or 4 lb

8.

350 lb or 350 T

9.

1 oz or 1 lb

Complete.

		10.	11.	12.	13.	14.	15.	16.
Pounds	1	2	3	4	5	6	7	8
Ounces	16	?	?	?	?	?	?	?

17. 2 lb = ___?___ oz

18. 5 lb = ___?___ oz

19. 3 lb = ___?___ oz

20. 9 lb = ___?___ oz

21. 2 lb = ___?___ oz

22. 9 T = ___?___ lb

23. 2 T = ___?___ lb

24. 5 lb = ___?___ oz

25. 5 T = ___?___ lb

★ **26.** 2 lb 2 oz = ___?___ oz

★ **27.** 4 lb 6 oz = ___?___ oz

★ **28.** 6 lb 14 oz = ___?___ oz

★ **29.** $\frac{1}{2}$ lb = ___?___ oz

★ **30.** $\frac{1}{4}$ lb = ___?___ oz

★ **31.** $\frac{3}{4}$ lb = ___?___ oz

Which is greater?

32. 2 lb or 30 oz

33. 1,000 lb or 1 T

34. 3 lb or 45 oz

35. 2 T or 5,000 lb

36. 60 oz or 3 lb

★ **37.** 7 oz or $\frac{1}{2}$ lb

PROBLEM SOLVING • APPLICATIONS

CHOOSE • mental math • pencil and paper • calculator SOLVE

38. One tomato plant produces 9 pounds of fruit. How many ounces are in 9 pounds?

39. A hybrid tomato weighs 1 pound. A cherry tomato weighs 4 ounces. Which tomato is heavier? How much heavier?

★ **40.** A prize-winning tomato weighs 2 pounds 4 ounces. How many ounces does this tomato weigh?

★ **41.** A harvesting machine picks 1 ton 500 pounds of tomatoes in the morning. It picks 3,000 pounds in the afternoon. Were more pounds picked in the morning or in the afternoon? How much more?

Degrees Fahrenheit

New Orleans is located on the Mississippi Delta. It is not unusual for the temperature on a spring day to reach 80° Fahrenheit.

● A **degree Fahrenheit** (°F) is a customary unit used to measure temperature.

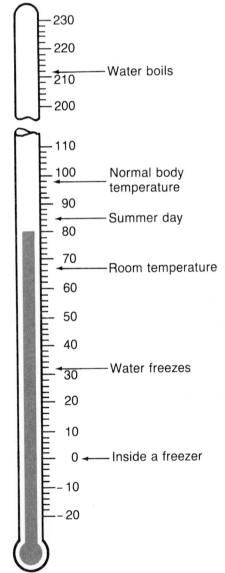

This is a **Fahrenheit thermometer**.
Each mark stands for 2 degrees.
The temperature is **80 degrees Fahrenheit above zero**.

Another way to write this is **80°F**.

Suppose the temperature were 100 degrees less. The new temperature would be **20 degrees Fahrenheit below zero**.

Another way to write this is **−20°F**.

PRACTICE • Use the thermometer.

What is the temperature of each?
1. summer day

2. water boils

3. inside a freezer

4. body temperature

5. room temperature

6. water freezes

EXERCISES • Choose the correct temperatures.

7. water for a bath
40°F or 95°F

8. baseball weather
10°F or 80°F

9. skiing weather
28°F or 50°F

10. spring day
65°F or 30°F

11. hot soup
50°F or 150°F

12. iced tea
35°F or 70°F

13. very cold winter day
−5°F or 70°F

14. swimming weather
90°F or 40°F

15. the ocean
55°F or 150°F

16. fever temperature
98°F or 100°F

17. chilly day
40°F or 65°F

18. house temperature
20°F or 70°F

PROBLEM SOLVING • APPLICATIONS

Each of the cities listed in the chart below are located along the Mississippi River. These high and low temperatures were recorded on the same day in March. Use the chart to answer the questions.

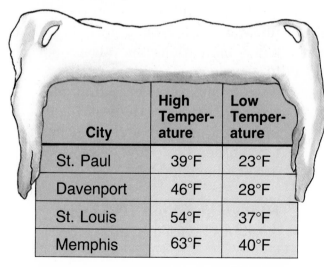

City	High Temperature	Low Temperature
St. Paul	39°F	23°F
Davenport	46°F	28°F
St. Louis	54°F	37°F
Memphis	63°F	40°F

19. Which city had the lowest temperature?

20. Which city had the highest temperature?

21. What is the difference between the highest and lowest temperatures in Davenport? in St. Louis?

22. What is the difference between the high temperatures in St. Paul and Memphis?

PROBLEM SOLVING • STRATEGIES

More Than One Step

Example

A lumber yard in Memphis will cut lumber to any length you want. Marie has a board 10 feet long. She wants 2 pieces each 4 feet in length.

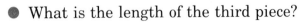

● What is the length of the third piece?

Think To find the length of the third piece, you must first answer this question.

What is the total length of the two pieces?

This is the **hidden question** in the problem.

STEP 1

Find the total length of the 2 pieces.

$$\begin{array}{r} 4 \\ \times 2 \\ \hline 8 \end{array}$$

STEP 2

Find the length of the third piece.

$$\begin{array}{r} 10 \\ -\ 8 \\ \hline 2 \end{array}$$

The third piece of wood is **2 feet** long.

PROBLEMS • Answer the hidden question first. Then solve the problem.

1. The Turner family is traveling 800 miles to Memphis by car. The first day they drive 480 miles. They drive 240 miles before noon the second day. How many miles are left?

   Hidden question: How many miles have they driven in all?

2. Roberto is building a model of a home found along the Mississippi River. He needs 48 inches of wood to make the fence that goes around the house. He uses 14 inches for one side and 10 inches for another side. How much wood does he have left?

   Hidden question: How much wood has he used in all?

3. The Turner family is camping along the Mississippi River. Mary is reading a 250 page book by Mark Twain. She read 50 pages on Monday and 38 pages on Tuesday. How many pages does she have left to read?

   Hidden question: How many pages has Mary read in all?

4. Scott and John are building a raft. They bought 12 boards that are each 8 feet in length. Each boy ties 4 boards together. How many boards are left?

   Hidden question: How many boards have been tied together?

Find the hidden question. Answer the hidden question first. Then solve.

5. Jeff is making lemonade to take along while the family hikes by the river. He pours the lemonade into a gallon jug by using a cup. It will take 16 cups to fill the gallon jug. He pours 8 cups and his sister pours 4 cups. How many cups are left to pour?

6. After taking a long hike, the family rests for a while. Mark pours each person 2 cups of juice. There are 4 people who want juice. How many cups are left in a jug that holds 16 cups?

7. The Turner family buys fruits and vegetables from a road-side stand. Susan buys 4 tomatoes each weighing about 6 ounces and an apple weighing 8 ounces. How many ounces of fruit and vegetables did she buy in all?

8. Dianne takes pictures along the Mississippi River. One roll of film takes 36 pictures. Dianne took 8 pictures on Monday and 18 pictures on Tuesday. How many pictures are left on the roll?

9. There are 1,500 pounds of tomatoes to be picked. The harvesting machine picks 500 pounds in the morning and 800 pounds in the afternoon. How many pounds are left to be picked?

CHAPTER REVIEW

Part 1: VOCABULARY

For Exercises 1–10, choose the word(s) from the box at the right that completes each statement.

1. To measure length, the metric unit is the __?__.
   (Page 218)

2. The distance around a figure is the __?__. (Page 220)

3. The number of square units that cover a surface is the __?__ of the surface. (Page 222)

4. To find the area of a rectangle, you multiply the length times the __?__. (Page 224)

5. The number of cubic units that will fit inside the box is the __?__. (Page 226)

6. To find the volume, you multiply the length times the width, times the __?__. (Page 228)

7. To measure liquids, the metric unit is the __?__.
   (Page 230)

8. The metric unit for mass is the __?__. (Page 232)

9. The metric unit to measure temperature is __?__.
   (Page 238)

10. The customary unit to measure temperature is __?__. (Page 258)

area
degrees Celsius
degrees Fahrenheit
gram
height
inches
liter
meter
perimeter
pound
volume
width

Part 2: SKILLS

Measure each length to the nearest centimeter. (Pages 216–217)

11.

12.

Complete. (Pages 218–219, 230–233)

13. 4 m = __?__ cm
14. 5 km = __?__ m
15. 3 m = __?__ cm

16. 1 L = __?__ mL
17. 9 L = __?__ mL
18. 3 L = __?__ mL

19. 1 kg = __?__ g
20. 4 kg = __?__ g
21. 3 kg = __?__ g

Choose the correct measures. (Pages 230–233, 238–239)

22. glass of water
250 mL or 250 L

23. bowling ball
6 g or 6 kg

24. frozen lake
0°C or 32°C

Write the time for each. (Pages 240–243)

25. quarter to eleven

26. ten past five

27. 20 minutes later
than 3:15

Measure each length to the nearest $\frac{1}{8}$ inch. (Pages 246–247)

28. _____

29. _____

Complete. (Pages 254–255, 256–257)

30. 2 qt = __?__ pt

31. 2 gal = __?__ qt

32. 5 lb = __?__ oz

Part 3: PROBLEM SOLVING • APPLICATIONS

What other information do you need to solve each problem?
Write the missing information.

33. The dining room on the riverboat
is getting new carpet. The width
of the room is 5 meters. What is
the area of the room? (Pages 234–235)

34. The picture of a riverboat needs
to have a frame. What is the
perimeter of the picture? (Pages
234–235)

Answer the hidden question first. Then solve the problem.

35. Mr. Turner has a roll of film
that takes 24 pictures. He takes
8 pictures by the river and 7
pictures in town. How many
pictures are left on the roll?
(Pages 260–261)

36. Jill has a piece of lumber 18
feet long. She has two pieces
cut. Each piece is 8 feet long.
How much lumber is left?
(Pages 260–261)

Use the schedule to answer the questions.

37. John wants to be in New
Orleans by 11:00. What time
will he leave Baton Rouge?
(Pages 244–245)

38. Dianne needs to leave Baton
Rouge after 7:40. What time
will she arrive in New Orleans?
(Pages 244–245)

Riverboat Cruises	
Leaves Baton Rouge	Arrives New Orleans
7:20 A.M.	10:56 A.M.
7:50 A.M.	11:30 A.M.

CHAPTER TEST

Measure each length to the nearest centimeter.

1. [image of bar]

2. [image of bar]

Complete.

3. 6 m = __?__ cm

4. __?__ cm = 3 m

5. 2 km = __?__ m

6. 2 ft = __?__ in.

7. 3 pt = __?__ c

8. __?__ oz = 2 lb

9. 5 yd = __?__ ft

10. __?__ qt = 4 gal

Choose the correct measures.

11. a golf ball
50 g or 50 kg

12. a glass of water
250 mL or 250 L

13. a can of soup
350 mL or 350 L

14. ice skating weather
30°C or −20°C

15. hot soup
50°F or 150°F

Measure each length to the nearest $\frac{1}{4}$ inch.

16.

17.

18. Find the perimeter.

5 ft 6 ft
8 ft

19. Find the area.

3 m
5 m

20. Find the volume.

3 cm
4 cm
3 cm

Write the time for each.

21. ten minutes to nine

22. 35 minutes later than 7:45

Solve.

23. What information do you need to solve the problem? Stateroom A is 13 feet wide. What is the area?

24. There are 43 apples in the basket. Tim and Jan each ate 3 apples. How many apples are left?

25. Joe will take the first boat leaving Baton Rouge on Sunday. At what time will he arrive in New Orleans?

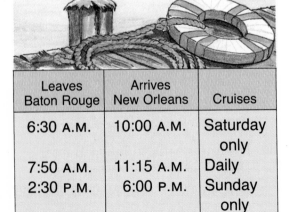

Leaves Baton Rouge	Arrives New Orleans	Cruises
6:30 A.M.	10:00 A.M.	Saturday only
7:50 A.M.	11:15 A.M.	Daily
2:30 P.M.	6:00 P.M.	Sunday only

ENRICHMENT

Fractional Areas

This is a piece of centimeter graph paper.
Each box has an area of 1 square centimeter.
The area of the blue figure
is $\frac{1}{2}$ of a square centimeter.

Use this to help you find the area of
the green figure.

The area of the green figure is $5\frac{1}{2}$
square centimeters.

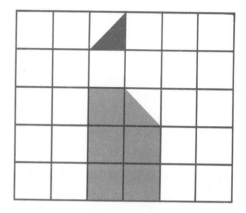

EXERCISES • Find the area of each figure.

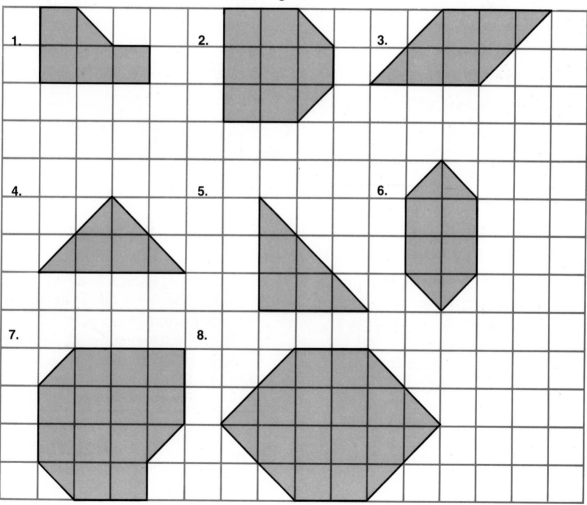

1.

2.

3.

4.

5.

6.

7.

8.

ADDITIONAL PRACTICE

SKILLS

Complete. (Pages 218–219, 230–233)

1. 4 m = __?__ cm

2. 5 m = __?__ cm

3. 3 km = __?__ m

4. 7 km = __?__ m

5. 8 L = __?__ mL

6. 7 kg = __?__ g

Find the perimeter and area of each figure. (Pages 220–225, 250–251)

7. 2 in. [7 in.] 2 in.
       7 in.

8.   6 yd
    6 yd [ ] 6 yd
          6 yd

Find each volume in cubic centimeters. (Pages 226–229)

9.

10.

11.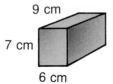
9 cm
7 cm
6 cm

Choose the correct temperature. (Pages 238–239, 258–259)

12. a cup of hot tea
    75°C or 25°C

13. an icicle
    50°F or −10°F

Write the time for each. (Pages 240–243)

14. 25 minutes after 3:00

15. 15 minutes earlier than 4:20

Complete. (Pages 246–249, 254–257)

16. 3 ft = __?__ in.

17. 3 yd = __?__ ft

18. 4 pt = __?__ c

19. 5 gal = __?__ qt

20. 5 lb = __?__ oz

21. 5 T = __?__ lb

PROBLEM SOLVING • APPLICATIONS

22. Write the missing information. Huong is building a wooden raft. The length is 3 meters. What is the area? (Pages 234–235)

23. Susan is reading a book with 204 pages. She reads 24 pages in the morning and 46 pages in the afternoon. How many pages does she have left to read? (Pages 260–261)

Use the schedule to answer the question.

24. Alan arrives at Baton Rouge at 8:30 A.M. What time does the next riverboat leave to New Orleans? (Pages 244–245)

Riverboat Cruises	
Leaves Baton Rouge	**Arrives New Orleans**
8:10 A.M.	11:48 A.M.
10:20 A.M.	3:00 P.M.

COMPUTER APPLICATIONS

Flowcharts and Problem Solving

To solve a problem, it is important to do the steps in the correct order. A **flowchart** can help you do this.

PROBLEM: Write the steps in order for sending a letter. Make a flowchart to show this.

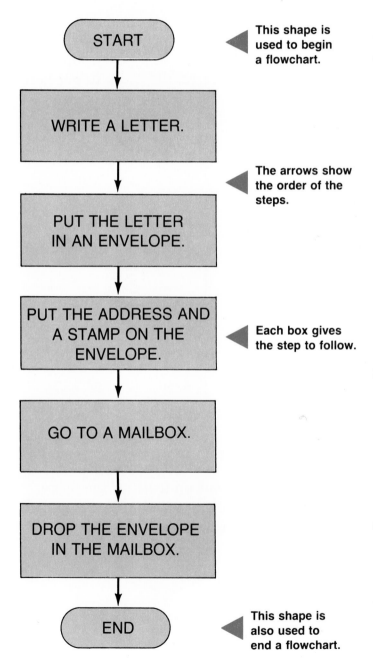

START
This shape is used to begin a flowchart.

WRITE A LETTER.

The arrows show the order of the steps.

PUT THE LETTER IN AN ENVELOPE.

PUT THE ADDRESS AND A STAMP ON THE ENVELOPE.
Each box gives the step to follow.

GO TO A MAILBOX.

DROP THE ENVELOPE IN THE MAILBOX.

END
This shape is also used to end a flowchart.

PROBLEMS

Write the steps in order. Then make a flowchart.

1. **Solving a mathematics problem**
   a. Read the problem.
   b. Check your answer.
   c. Find the answer.
   d. Make a plan.

2. **Making a phone call**
   a. Dial the number.
   b. Wait for the dial tone.
   c. Lift the receiver.
   d. Talk to the person.
   e. Hang up the receiver.

3. **Taking a field trip**
   a. Teacher assigns students to a group.
   b. Leave school.
   c. Return to school.
   d. Bring permission slip.
   e. Arrive at destination.

4. **Traveling to school**
   a. Board bus.
   b. Walk to bus stop.
   c. Enter school building.
   d. Ride to school.
   e. Get off at school.
   f. Wait for bus.

MAINTENANCE

Chapters 1 through 8

Mixed Practice • Choose the correct answers.

1. $21 \div 3 =$ ___?___

A. 8   B. 6
C. 7   D. not here

2. $49 \div 7 =$ ___?___

A. 8   B. 9
C. 6   D. not here

3. $\begin{array}{r} 8 \\ \times 6 \\ \hline \end{array}$

A. 42   B. 56
C. 48   D. not here

4. 121 ● 112

A. =   B. <
C. >   D. not here

5. 4,041 ● 4,014

A. >   B. =
C. <   D. not here

6. $24 \div$ ___?___ $= 4$

A. 4   B. 6
C. 7   D. not here

7. $63 \div$ ___?___ $= 7$

A. 9   B. 7
C. 8   D. not here

8. $5\overline{)23}$

A. 5 r1   B. 4 r3
C. 4 r2   D. not here

9. $33 \div 4 =$ ___?___

A. 9   B. 7 r5
C. 8 r1   D. not here

10. There are 20 girls helping at the party. There are 12 girls mixing punch and 5 girls setting the table. The other girls are making sandwiches. How many girls are making sandwiches?

A. 8   B. 3
C. 15   D. not here

11. Alex cut up fruit for the party. He cut up 12 oranges, 25 apples, and 22 bananas. About how many pieces of fruit did he cut in all?

A. 60   B. 50
B. 55   D. not here

268

CHAPTER 9

Fractions and Mixed Numbers

Ben Franklin ran a printing business in Philadelphia. During one part of his life, he lived in England for $17\frac{2}{8}$ years. He lived in France for $7\frac{1}{8}$ years.

● How many years was this in all?

James is an apprentice blacksmith. He works $5\frac{1}{4}$ hours in the morning and $3\frac{2}{3}$ hours in the afternoon.

● Estimate how much longer he works in the morning.

Fractions

Avis lived in early America. He made a toy spinner out of wood.

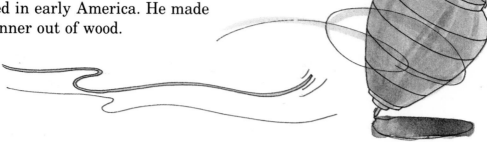

The top has 5 equal parts. Two of the parts are blue. You can use a **fraction** to tell what part of the top is blue.

● What fraction of the top is blue?

Think There are 2 blue parts.
There are 5 equal parts.

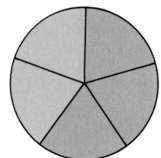

Number of blue parts ⟶ 2 ⟵ **numerator**
Total number of equal parts ⟶ 5 ⟵ **denominator**

Read $\frac{2}{5}$ as **two-fifths**.

So $\frac{2}{5}$ of the top is blue.

● What fraction of the top is green?

Think There are 5 green parts.
There are 5 equal parts.

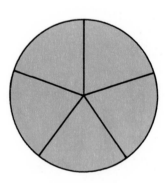

Number of green parts. ⟶ 5
Total number of equal parts ⟶ 5

$\frac{5}{5}$ is equal to one whole, or 1.

So $\frac{5}{5}$, or **all**, of the top is green.

PRACTICE • Write the fractions that tell what parts are blue.

1.

2.
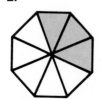

3.

4.
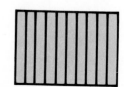

EXERCISES • Write the fractions that tell what parts are shaded.

5.

6.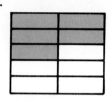

7.

8.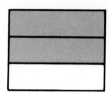

9.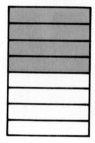

10.

11.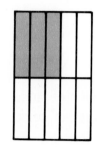

12.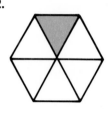

13.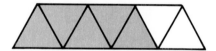

14.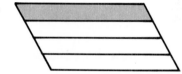

15.

16.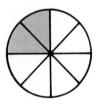

PROBLEM SOLVING • APPLICATIONS

17. A spinner has 6 equal parts. Six parts are blue. What fraction of the spinner is blue?

★**19.** A spinner has 8 equal parts. Three parts are red. What fraction of the spinner is *not* red?

18. Avis has 8 marbles. He brought 5 of them from England. What fraction of the marbles came from England?

PROJECT   International alphabet flags have a flag for each letter of the alphabet. Find the international alphabet flag for the letters E, G, J, K, and T. Write a fraction that tells what part of each flag is blue.

Fractions and Groups

Captain John Smith helped to settle the colony of Jamestown, Virginia. He saw animals and birds that he had never seen in England.

● What fraction of the group of wild turkeys are eating?

Think There are 2 turkeys eating. There are 3 turkeys in all.

$$\frac{2}{3} \longleftarrow \text{number of turkeys eating}$$
$$\phantom{\frac{2}{3}} \longleftarrow \text{number of turkeys in all}$$

So $\frac{2}{3}$ of the turkeys are eating.

PRACTICE • Write the fractions.

1.
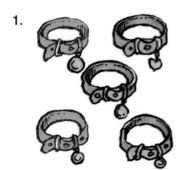

What part is brown?

2.

What part is on the rock?

3.

What part is brown?

4.

What part is flying?

5.

What part is red?

6.

What part is yellow?

EXERCISES • Write the fractions.

7.

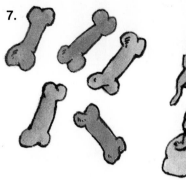

What part is red?

8.

What part is on the tree?

9.

What part is in the water?

10.

What part is yellow?

11.

What part is playing?

★ **12.**

What part is not on top?

PROBLEM SOLVING • APPLICATIONS

13. Captain John Smith saw 10 butterflies on a bush. There were 7 orange butterflies. What fraction of the group was orange?

14. Captain John Smith saw 5 red-headed woodpeckers. Two were flying. What fraction of the group was flying?

Captain John Smith also saw different types of birds. He noticed that $\frac{1}{4}$ of these birds are blue.

$\dfrac{1}{4}$ ⟵ pair of blue birds
⟵ total number of pairs

a. What fraction of these birds are brown?

b. What fraction have red wings?

c. What fraction have yellow beaks?

Fractions and Mixed Numbers • **273**

Finding Parts of a Group

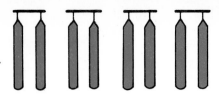

Hannah and her mother made 8 candles.
Hannah made $\frac{1}{4}$ of them.

● How many candles did Hannah make?

Think Divide the 8 candles into 4 equal groups.
There are 2 candles in each group. ⟶ $8 \div 4 = 2$

Hannah made $\frac{1}{4}$ of the candles. ⟶ $\frac{1}{4}$ of $8 = 2$

Hannah made **2 candles**.

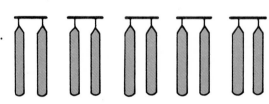

Beth and her mother made 10 candles.
Beth made $\frac{3}{5}$ of them.

● How many candles did Beth make?

Think Divide the 10 candles into 5 groups.
There are 2 candles in each group. ⟶ $10 \div 5 = 2$

Beth made 3 groups. ⟶ $3 \times 2 = 6$

Beth made **6 candles** in all. ⟶ $\frac{3}{5} \times 10 = 6$

PRACTICE • Complete.

1.

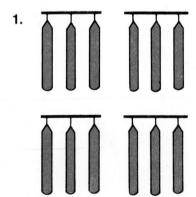

$\frac{1}{4}$ of 12 = ___?___

2.

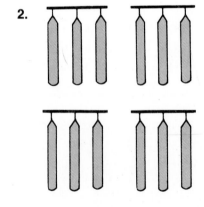

$\frac{3}{4}$ of 12 = ___?___

3. $\frac{1}{4}$ of 8 = ___?___

4. $\frac{2}{3}$ of 12 = ___?___

5. $\frac{2}{5}$ of 10 = ___?___

EXERCISES • Complete.

6. $\frac{1}{2}$ of 6 = __?__

7. $\frac{1}{8}$ of 16 = __?__

8. $\frac{1}{3}$ of 12 = __?__

9. $\frac{1}{5}$ of 15 = __?__

10. $\frac{2}{3}$ of 15 = __?__

11. $\frac{3}{4}$ of 12 = __?__

12. $\frac{3}{8}$ of 16 = __?__

13. $\frac{5}{6}$ of 48 = __?__

14. $\frac{4}{5}$ of 40 = __?__

15. $\frac{3}{5}$ of 45 = __?__

16. $\frac{1}{3}$ of 15 = __?__

17. $\frac{3}{4}$ of 16 = __?__

18. $\frac{1}{4}$ of 24 = __?__

19. $\frac{1}{6}$ of 30 = __?__

20. $\frac{2}{3}$ of 24 = __?__

21. $\frac{4}{5}$ of 10 = __?__

★ 22. $\frac{1}{10}$ of 100 = __?__

★ 23. $\frac{2}{10}$ of 200 = __?__

PROBLEM SOLVING • APPLICATIONS

24. Ann makes 9 candles. She gives $\frac{2}{3}$ of them to her sister. How many candles does Ann give to her sister?

25. Hannah makes 15 candles. She makes $\frac{3}{5}$ of them green. How many candles are green?

26. Ann makes 27 candles. She gives 3 of them to Mrs. Whitefield. How many candles does she have left?

★ 27. Hannah has 27 candles. She must dip $\frac{1}{3}$ of them again. How many candles are not dipped again?

CALCULATOR • Parts of a Group

Rebecca makes 36 candles. She keeps $\frac{2}{3}$ of them. How many does she keep?

Step 1 Divide the 36 candles into 3 equal groups.

Press ③ ⑥ ÷ ③ = ⟨ 12. ⟩

Step 2 To find how many candles in 2 groups, multiply 12 × 2.

Press ① ② × ② = ⟨ 24. ⟩

EXERCISES • Use a calculator to check your answers to Exercises **6–23.**

Equivalent Fractions

The colonists spun their own thread.

They wove it into cloth.

They used the cloth to make clothing.

Ruth is making dish towels. She has a large piece of cloth. How can she fold it into 8 equal parts?

Ruth folds the piece in half. There are 2 equal parts.

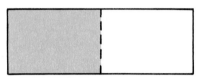

$\frac{1}{2}$ is shaded.

She folds the piece again. There are 4 equal parts.

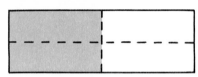

$\frac{1}{2} = \frac{2}{4}$

Ruth folds the piece once more. There are 8 equal parts.

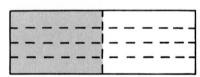

$\frac{1}{2} = \frac{2}{4} = \frac{4}{8}$

Ruth found that $\frac{1}{2}$, $\frac{2}{4}$, and $\frac{4}{8}$ all name the same part.

Since $\frac{1}{2} = \frac{2}{4} = \frac{4}{8}$, the three fractions are **equivalent.**

PRACTICE • Complete.

1.

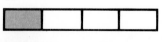

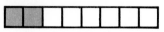

$\frac{1}{4} = \frac{?}{8}$

2.

$\frac{2}{3} = \frac{?}{6}$

3.

$\frac{4}{5} = \frac{?}{10}$

EXERCISES • Complete.

4.

$$\frac{1}{2} = \frac{?}{10}$$

5.

$$\frac{3}{4} = \frac{?}{8}$$

6.

$$\frac{6}{10} = \frac{?}{5}$$

7.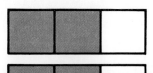

$$\frac{2}{3} = \frac{?}{9}$$

8.

$$\frac{10}{12} = \frac{?}{6}$$

9.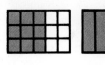

$$\frac{9}{15} = \frac{?}{5}$$

Write the equivalent fractions for the blue part of each figure.

10.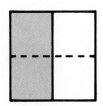

11.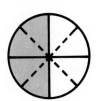

12.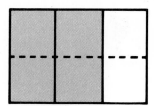

13.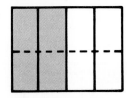

14.

★ **15.**

Complete. You may draw a picture to help you.

★ **16.** $\frac{1}{2} = \frac{?}{12}$

★ **17.** $\frac{1}{2} = \frac{?}{16}$

★ **18.** $\frac{1}{4} = \frac{?}{12}$

PROBLEM SOLVING • APPLICATIONS

19. Ruth has a piece of cloth that is $\frac{1}{2}$ of a yard long. How many sixths of a yard does she have?

20. A woolen thread is $\frac{2}{6}$ of a yard long. How many thirds of a yard is this?

Fractions and Mixed Numbers • **277**

Finding Equivalent Fractions by Multiplying

Each time Roger folds this paper, there are 2 times as many parts.

So each time there are 2 times as many shaded parts.

> To find an equivalent fraction, multiply the numerator and the denominator by the same number.

$$\frac{1}{2} = \frac{2 \times 1}{2 \times 2} = \frac{2}{4} \qquad\qquad \frac{1}{2} = \frac{4 \times 1}{4 \times 2} = \frac{4}{8}$$

$$\frac{1}{2} = \frac{2}{4} = \frac{4}{8}$$ ◀ Equivalent fractions

PRACTICE • Complete.

1.

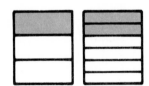

$$\frac{1}{3} = \frac{2 \times 1}{2 \times 3} = \frac{?}{6}$$

2.

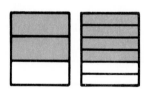

$$\frac{2}{3} = \frac{2 \times 2}{2 \times 3} = \frac{?}{6}$$

3.

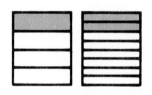

$$\frac{1}{4} = \frac{2 \times 1}{2 \times 4} = \frac{?}{8}$$

4.

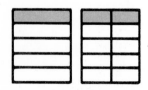

$$\frac{1}{5} = \frac{2 \times 1}{2 \times 5} = \frac{?}{10}$$

5.

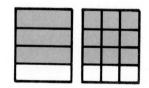

$$\frac{3}{4} = \frac{3 \times 3}{3 \times 4} = \frac{?}{12}$$

6.

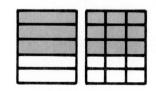

$$\frac{3}{5} = \frac{3 \times 3}{3 \times 5} = \frac{?}{15}$$

EXERCISES • Complete.

7.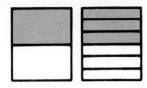

$$\frac{1}{2} = \frac{3 \times 1}{3 \times 2} = \frac{?}{6}$$

8.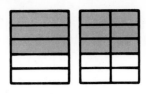

$$\frac{3}{5} = \frac{2 \times 3}{2 \times 5} = \frac{?}{10}$$

9.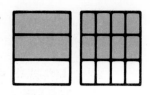

$$\frac{2}{3} = \frac{4 \times 2}{4 \times 3} = \frac{?}{12}$$

10. $\frac{1}{2} = \frac{5 \times 1}{5 \times 2} = \frac{?}{10}$

11. $\frac{1}{3} = \frac{4 \times 1}{4 \times 3} = \frac{?}{12}$

12. $\frac{4}{5} = \frac{2 \times 4}{2 \times 5} = \frac{?}{10}$

13. $\frac{3}{8} = \frac{2 \times 3}{2 \times 8} = \frac{6}{?}$

14. $\frac{1}{5} = \frac{3 \times 1}{3 \times 5} = \frac{3}{?}$

15. $\frac{5}{7} = \frac{2 \times 5}{2 \times 7} = \frac{10}{?}$

16. $\frac{1}{6} = \frac{2 \times 1}{2 \times 6} = \frac{?}{?}$

17. $\frac{3}{5} = \frac{5 \times 3}{5 \times 5} = \frac{?}{?}$

18. $\frac{5}{6} = \frac{4 \times 5}{4 \times 6} = \frac{?}{?}$

19. $\frac{3}{7} = \frac{? \times 3}{? \times 7} = \frac{?}{14}$

20. $\frac{5}{9} = \frac{? \times 5}{? \times 9} = \frac{?}{36}$

21. $\frac{3}{4} = \frac{? \times 3}{? \times 4} = \frac{?}{16}$

22. $\frac{4}{5} = \frac{? \times 4}{? \times 5} = \frac{?}{10}$

23. $\frac{2}{5} = \frac{? \times 2}{? \times 5} = \frac{?}{20}$

24. $\frac{4}{9} = \frac{? \times 4}{? \times 9} = \frac{?}{27}$

★ 25. $\frac{1}{2} = \frac{?}{8}$

★ 26. $\frac{2}{3} = \frac{?}{9}$

★ 27. $\frac{3}{5} = \frac{?}{20}$

★ 28. $\frac{1}{4} = \frac{?}{16}$

★ 29. $\frac{1}{4} = \frac{?}{12}$

★ 30. $\frac{1}{6} = \frac{?}{18}$

★ 31. $\frac{2}{5} = \frac{?}{15}$

★ 32. $\frac{3}{4} = \frac{?}{20}$

PROBLEM SOLVING • APPLICATIONS

33. Lori walks $\frac{2}{4}$ of a mile to school. Mary walks $\frac{1}{2}$ of a mile to school. How do you know that Lori and Mary walk the same distance?

34. David wants to draw a picture to go with a story he wrote. He has $\frac{1}{3}$ of a page left. His picture fills $\frac{5}{15}$ of the page. Will it fit in the space? Why?

35. Beth walks 4 miles to school. Richard walks 5 miles. David walks $\frac{2}{3}$ of a mile. How much farther does Richard walk than Beth?

★ 36. Joe walks 900 yards to go to school. He walked $\frac{3}{5}$ of the distance when he met Ben. How many yards were left to walk?

Comparing Fractions

Pohata shows Richard how to fasten birch bark to a wooden frame to make a canoe.

Richard covers $\frac{1}{4}$ of a frame.

Pohata covers $\frac{3}{4}$ of a frame.

● Which is less, $\frac{1}{4}$ or $\frac{3}{4}$?

> When the denominators are the same, compare the numerators.

Numerators: 1 and 3 ◀ **1 is less than 3.**

So $\frac{1}{4}$ is less than $\frac{3}{4}$. ⟶ $\frac{1}{4} < \frac{3}{4}$

● Which is greater, $\frac{2}{3}$ or $\frac{1}{4}$?

> When the denominators are different, write equivalent fractions with the same denominator.

Step 1

Make a list of equivalent fractions to find fractions with the same denominator.

$$\frac{2}{3} = \frac{4}{6} = \frac{6}{9} = \frac{8}{12}$$

$$\frac{1}{4} = \frac{2}{8} = \frac{3}{12} \longleftarrow \text{same denominator}$$

Step 2

Now the fractions have the same denominator.

Compare the numerators.

Since $8 > 3$, $\frac{8}{12} > \frac{3}{12}$.

So, $\frac{2}{3} > \frac{1}{4}$.

PRACTICE • Write > (is greater than) or < (is less than).

1. $\frac{1}{3}$ ● $\frac{2}{3}$ 2. $\frac{2}{6}$ ● $\frac{2}{3}$ 3. $\frac{3}{4}$ ● $\frac{2}{4}$ 4. $\frac{3}{5}$ ● $\frac{7}{10}$

5. $\frac{2}{4}$ ● $\frac{1}{4}$ 6. $\frac{3}{5}$ ● $\frac{2}{5}$ 7. $\frac{2}{4}$ ● $\frac{3}{8}$ 8. $\frac{2}{6}$ ● $\frac{1}{2}$

EXERCISES • Write > or <.

9. $\frac{3}{6}$ ⬤ $\frac{4}{6}$

10. $\frac{1}{4}$ ⬤ $\frac{4}{8}$

11. $\frac{1}{2}$ ⬤ $\frac{1}{3}$

12. $\frac{5}{6}$ ⬤ $\frac{6}{8}$

13. $\frac{2}{4}$ ⬤ $\frac{6}{8}$

14. $\frac{2}{5}$ ⬤ $\frac{3}{5}$

15. $\frac{2}{3}$ ⬤ $\frac{5}{6}$

16. $\frac{5}{10}$ ⬤ $\frac{3}{10}$

17. $\frac{1}{3}$ ⬤ $\frac{2}{5}$

18. $\frac{3}{6}$ ⬤ $\frac{4}{10}$

19. $\frac{3}{5}$ ⬤ $\frac{7}{8}$

20. $\frac{8}{10}$ ⬤ $\frac{2}{3}$

21. $\frac{3}{4}$ ⬤ $\frac{1}{2}$

22. $\frac{1}{5}$ ⬤ $\frac{2}{8}$

23. $\frac{1}{6}$ ⬤ $\frac{1}{3}$

24. $\frac{3}{8}$ ⬤ $\frac{2}{4}$

25. $\frac{7}{10}$ ⬤ $\frac{5}{6}$

26. $\frac{2}{3}$ ⬤ $\frac{5}{8}$

27. $\frac{4}{5}$ ⬤ $\frac{1}{2}$

28. $\frac{3}{10}$ ⬤ $\frac{3}{6}$

29. $\frac{3}{5}$ ⬤ $\frac{4}{6}$

30. $\frac{9}{10}$ ⬤ $\frac{3}{4}$

31. $\frac{5}{10}$ ⬤ $\frac{3}{5}$

32. $\frac{6}{8}$ ⬤ $\frac{7}{10}$

Write the fractions in order from least to greatest.

★ 33. $\frac{1}{8}, \frac{1}{2}, \frac{1}{4}$

★ 34. $\frac{3}{8}, \frac{2}{6}, \frac{5}{10}$

★ 35. $\frac{2}{3}, \frac{3}{5}, \frac{3}{8}$

★ 36. $\frac{5}{8}, \frac{1}{2}, \frac{4}{5}$

PROBLEM SOLVING • APPLICATIONS

37. John sewed strips of birch bark together for $\frac{1}{3}$ of an hour. Samuel sewed strips of birch bark for $\frac{1}{4}$ of an hour. Who sewed longer?

38. Pohata built two canoe frames that were the same size. He covered $\frac{3}{5}$ of one canoe with birch bark. James covered $\frac{2}{5}$ of the other frame with birch bark. Who covered more?

39. Richard paddled the canoe $\frac{3}{10}$ of a mile, Benjamin paddled $\frac{1}{4}$ of a mile, and Avis paddled $\frac{2}{5}$ of a mile. List the distances in order from least to greatest.

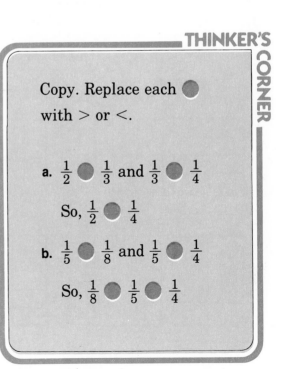

THINKER'S CORNER

Copy. Replace each ⬤ with > or <.

a. $\frac{1}{2}$ ⬤ $\frac{1}{3}$ and $\frac{1}{3}$ ⬤ $\frac{1}{4}$

So, $\frac{1}{2}$ ⬤ $\frac{1}{4}$

b. $\frac{1}{5}$ ⬤ $\frac{1}{8}$ and $\frac{1}{5}$ ⬤ $\frac{1}{4}$

So, $\frac{1}{8}$ ⬤ $\frac{1}{5}$ ⬤ $\frac{1}{4}$

Finding Equivalent Fractions by Dividing

> Divide the numerator and the denominator of a fraction by the same number to get an equivalent fraction.

  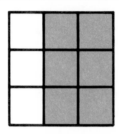 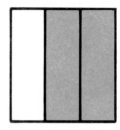

$\dfrac{2}{4} = \dfrac{2 \div 2}{4 \div 2} = \dfrac{1}{2}$

$\dfrac{2}{4}$ in **lowest terms** is $\dfrac{1}{2}$.

$\dfrac{6}{9} = \dfrac{6 \div 3}{9 \div 3} = \dfrac{2}{3}$

$\dfrac{6}{9}$ in **lowest terms** is $\dfrac{2}{3}$.

> A fraction is in lowest terms *when the only number that will divide both numerator and the denominator is 1.*

Abigail is making a patchwork quilt. She has sewn $\dfrac{8}{12}$ of the quilt.

● Write $\dfrac{8}{12}$ in lowest terms.

Think Divide 8 and 12 by 2.

$\dfrac{8}{12} = \dfrac{8 \div 2}{12 \div 2} = \dfrac{4}{6}$ ◄ You can divide 4 and 6 by 2.

$\dfrac{4}{6} = \dfrac{4 \div 2}{6 \div 2} = \dfrac{2}{3}$ ◄ You cannot divide again. So $\dfrac{8}{12} = \dfrac{2}{3}$. ◄ Lowest terms

PRACTICE • **Mental Math** Find the missing numerator.

1.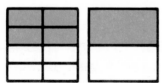

$\dfrac{4}{8} = \dfrac{4 \div 4}{8 \div 4} = \dfrac{?}{2}$

2.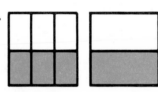

$\dfrac{3}{6} = \dfrac{3 \div 3}{6 \div 3} = \dfrac{?}{2}$

3.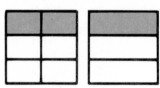

$\dfrac{2}{6} = \dfrac{2 \div 2}{6 \div 2} = \dfrac{?}{3}$

4.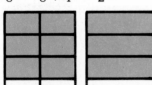

$\dfrac{6}{8} = \dfrac{6 \div 2}{8 \div 2} = \dfrac{?}{4}$

5.

$\dfrac{4}{10} = \dfrac{4 \div 2}{10 \div 2} = \dfrac{?}{5}$

6.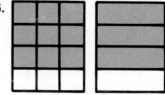

$\dfrac{9}{12} = \dfrac{9 \div 3}{12 \div 3} = \dfrac{?}{4}$

EXERCISES • Complete.

7.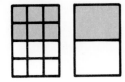

$$\frac{6}{12} = \frac{6 \div 6}{12 \div 6} = \frac{?}{2}$$

8.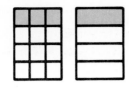

$$\frac{3}{12} = \frac{3 \div 3}{12 \div 3} = \frac{?}{4}$$

9.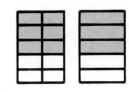

$$\frac{6}{10} = \frac{6 \div 2}{10 \div 2} = \frac{?}{5}$$

10. $\dfrac{5}{10} = \dfrac{5 \div 5}{10 \div 5} = \dfrac{?}{2}$ **11.** $\dfrac{3}{15} = \dfrac{3 \div 3}{15 \div 3} = \dfrac{?}{5}$ **12.** $\dfrac{7}{14} = \dfrac{7 \div 7}{14 \div 7} = \dfrac{?}{2}$

13. $\dfrac{4}{12} = \dfrac{4 \div 4}{12 \div 4} = \dfrac{1}{?}$ **14.** $\dfrac{4}{6} = \dfrac{4 \div 2}{6 \div 2} = \dfrac{2}{?}$ **15.** $\dfrac{8}{12} = \dfrac{8 \div 4}{12 \div 4} = \dfrac{?}{?}$

16. $\dfrac{12}{18} = \dfrac{12 \div 6}{18 \div 6} = \dfrac{?}{?}$ **17.** $\dfrac{8}{16} = \dfrac{8 \div ?}{16 \div ?} = \dfrac{?}{2}$ **18.** $\dfrac{10}{15} = \dfrac{10 \div ?}{15 \div ?} = \dfrac{?}{3}$

19. $\dfrac{12}{16} = \dfrac{12 \div ?}{16 \div ?} = \dfrac{?}{4}$ **20.** $\dfrac{9}{15} = \dfrac{?}{5}$ **21.** $\dfrac{12}{20} = \dfrac{?}{5}$ **22.** $\dfrac{16}{24} = \dfrac{2}{?}$

Write the fractions in lowest terms.

23. $\dfrac{6}{8}$ **24.** $\dfrac{6}{9}$ **25.** $\dfrac{12}{15}$ **26.** $\dfrac{20}{24}$ **27.** $\dfrac{16}{18}$ **28.** $\dfrac{8}{32}$

29. $\dfrac{6}{15}$ **30.** $\dfrac{4}{18}$ **31.** $\dfrac{12}{27}$ **32.** $\dfrac{18}{24}$ **33.** $\dfrac{7}{28}$ **34.** $\dfrac{5}{30}$

35. $\dfrac{8}{20}$ **36.** $\dfrac{9}{24}$ **37.** $\dfrac{10}{18}$ ★ **38.** $\dfrac{10}{40}$ ★ **39.** $\dfrac{20}{60}$ ★ **40.** $\dfrac{60}{90}$

PROBLEM SOLVING • APPLICATIONS

Solve. Write the fractions in lowest terms.

41. A quilt has 25 squares. Abigail makes 5 of them red. What fraction of the quilt is red?

42. A quilt has 32 squares. There are stars on 12 of the squares. What fraction of the quilt has stars?

43. There are 20 girls at a quilting bee. Of these 20 girls, 5 girls are cutting out squares and 10 girls are sewing squares together. What fraction of the girls are cutting out squares?

THINKER'S CORNER

The cotton backing for a quilt is folded in half many times. When opened up, it shows 16 squares. How many times was the backing folded?

Mixed Numbers

The colonial farmers raised apples in the Hudson River Valley. The grains and fruit were sold from wooden bins.

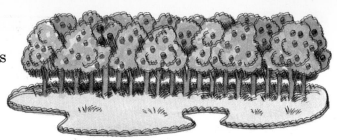

These bins are divided into two equal parts

These bins are divided into 3 equal parts.

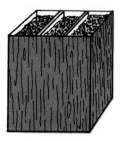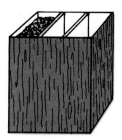

● How many halves are filled with apples?

Think   Count the halves.

$\frac{4}{2}$ are filled with apples.

$\frac{4}{2} = 2$ ◀ **Whole number**

There are **4 halves,** or **2 whole bins** filled with apples.

● How many thirds are filled with cornmeal?

Think   Count the thirds.

$\frac{4}{3}$ are filled with cornmeal.

$\frac{4}{3} = 1\frac{1}{3}$ ◀ **Mixed number**

There are $\frac{4}{3}$, or $1\frac{1}{3}$ **bins** filled with cornmeal.

PRACTICE • Write the whole number or the mixed number that tells how much is blue.

1.

2.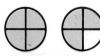

3.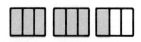

4.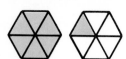

5.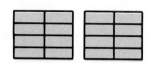

6.

7. **8.** 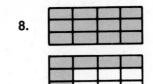 **9.**

EXERCISES • Write the whole number or the mixed number that tells how much is blue.

10. 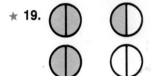 **11.** 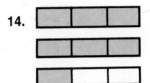 **12.**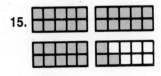

13. **14.** 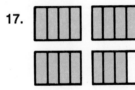 **15.**

16. **17.** 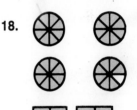 **18.**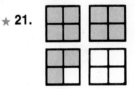

★ **19.** ★ **20.** ★ **21.**

PROBLEM SOLVING • APPLICATIONS

22. A traveler buys 3 apples and cuts them into fourths. How many fourths are there?

23. Tom bought 5 bags of flour. How many halves are there?

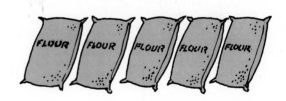

24. The cooper made 9 barrels. He sold 5 of them to farmers and 2 of them to merchants. He kept the rest for storage. What fraction of the barrels were used for storage?

NON-ROUTINE PROBLEM SOLVING

The Grade 4 students at Mercer School are learning about colonial times. Some of them spent a day at Plymouth Colonial Village during the summer vacation. During the day, they went to 3 craft exhibits.

BROOM MAKING

A.M.	P.M.
10:00–10:45	2:15–3:00
11:30–12:15	3:30–4:15

CANDLE MAKING

A.M.	P.M.
9:45–10:30	3:00–3:45
10:45–11:30	

SOAP MAKING

A.M.	P.M.
9:30–11:00	1:00–2:30

TANNING LEATHER

A.M.	P.M.
10:00–11:00	1:00–2:00
	3:00–4:00

NOTE: It takes 15 minutes to walk from one exhibit to the next or from an exhibit to the Village Cafeteria.

FINDING AND MAKING CHOICES

1. Alice and Stacy arrive at the village at 9:55. Which exhibits can they visit first?

2. Howard arrives at the village at 9:15. He wants to visit two exhibits before 12:30. What choices does he have?

3. Jim went to the Leather exhibit at 10 o'clock. He plans to meet a friend for lunch at 12:20 at the Village Cafeteria. Can he go to a second exhibit before lunch? Why or why not?

4. The Filmore twins made a list that showed which pairs of exhibits they could go to between 1:00 and 4:15. What choices were on their list?

5. Alice and Stacy take a half hour for lunch. They finish at 11:30. Which exhibit did they go to in the morning? (See Exercise 1)

6. Alice and Stacy want to go to 2 exhibits in the afternoon. Stacy will meet her parents at the Village entrance at 3:15. Which exhibits can they see?

7. Suppose you were visiting Plymouth Colonial Village. List 3 exhibits you would like to see and the times for each.

8. Suppose you were visiting Plymouth Colonial Village and you wanted to see <u>all</u> the exhibits in one day. List the choices and the times.

MID-CHAPTER REVIEW

Write the fraction. (Pages 270–273)

1.

What part is blue?

2. 3 green turtles
4 brown turtles

What part is green?

3. 5 black dogs
2 white dogs

What part is white?

Complete. (Pages 274–279)

4. $\frac{1}{5}$ of 15 = __?__

5. $\frac{1}{8}$ of 16 = __?__

6. $\frac{3}{4}$ of 12 = __?__

7. $\frac{2}{5} = \frac{?}{10}$

8. $\frac{5}{7} = \frac{?}{14}$

9. $\frac{2}{3} = \frac{?}{18}$

Use > or < to compare the fractions. (Pages 280–281)

10. $\frac{3}{5}$ ● $\frac{4}{5}$

11. $\frac{3}{6}$ ● $\frac{1}{3}$

12. $\frac{1}{4}$ ● $\frac{4}{8}$

Write the fraction in lowest terms. (Pages 282–283)

13. $\frac{6}{9}$

14. $\frac{5}{15}$

15. $\frac{8}{32}$

Write the whole number or the mixed number that tells how much is blue. (Pages 284–285)

16.

17.

MAINTENANCE • MIXED PRACTICE

Add or subtract Exercises 1–5.

1. $3.50
  + 4.21

2. $5.60
  + 1.73

3. $7.74
  − 0.95

4. $67.86
  − 19.97

5. $51.42
  − 7.56

6. 1 meter = __?__ centimeters

7. 1 kilometer = __?__ meters

8. 1 liter = __?__ milliliters

9. 1 kilogram = __?__ grams

10. How many minutes from 8:00 to 8:30?

11. How many minutes from 2:25 to 2:40?

12. A section on the river bank is 8 meters long and 4 meters wide. What is the area of that section?

13. The fence around the McAllister's pool is being installed. The width is 6 meters, and the length is 12 meters. How much fence is needed?

CONSUMER APPLICATIONS

Changing Units of Measure

These tables show how some units of measure are related.

12 inches (in.) = 1 foot (ft)	60 minutes (min) = 1 hour (hr)
3 feet (ft) = 1 yard (yd)	24 hours (hr) = 1 day (d)
36 inches (in) = 1 yard (yd)	7 days (d) = 1 week (wk)
16 ounces (oz) = 1 pound (lb)	52 weeks (wk) = 1 year (yr)

● How many inches are in 3 feet?

$$3 \text{ ft} = ? \text{ in.}$$

Multiply to change larger units of measure to smaller units.

Think 12 in. = 1 ft
$3 \times 12 = 36$

There are **36 inches** in 3 feet.

● How many days are in 72 hours?

$$72 \text{ h} = ? \text{ d}$$

Divide to change smaller units of measure to larger units.

Think 24 h = 1 d
$72 \div 24 = 3$

There are **3 days** in 72 hours.

EXERCISES • Use the tables to help you solve the exercises.

1. Avis bought 32 ounces of nails. How many pounds did he buy?

2. Avis wants to make shelves for the kitchen. He bought a board that is 5 feet long. Each shelf will be 30 inches long. How many shelves can he make?

3. Ruth and Avis measure the kitchen for a new rug. The length is 144 inches and the width is 108 inches. What is the length and the width in feet? What is the area of the rug in yards?

4. Each day for two weeks Ruth spent 90 minutes sewing curtains. How many hours did she spend in all?

PROJECT Find the area of a room in your home in feet and in yards.

Fractions and Mixed Numbers

John Jenney's gristmill in Plymouth, Massachusetts, is used to grind corn into cornmeal. John puts cornmeal in cloth bags.

● How much cornmeal is shown?

Think Count the number of thirds.

There are $\frac{4}{3}$, or $1\frac{1}{3}$ bags.

$$\frac{4}{3} = 1\frac{1}{3}$$

● You can change $\frac{4}{3}$ to a mixed number by dividing.

Step 1
Divide the numerator by the denominator.

$$\frac{4}{3} \longrightarrow \begin{array}{r} 1 \\ 3\overline{)4} \\ -3 \\ \hline 1 \end{array}$$

Step 2
Show the remainder as a fraction.

$$\begin{array}{r} 1\frac{1}{3} \\ 3\overline{)4} \\ -3 \\ \hline 1 \end{array}$$ ← remainder ← divisor

PRACTICE • Write the whole number or the mixed number that tells how much is blue.

I.

2.
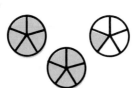

3.
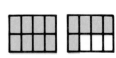

4.

5.
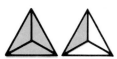

6.

Write each fraction as a whole number or as a mixed number.

7. $\frac{7}{5}$ **8.** $\frac{5}{4}$ **9.** $\frac{8}{4}$ **10.** $\frac{13}{6}$ **11.** $\frac{17}{7}$ **12.** $\frac{19}{8}$

EXERCISES • Write the fraction that tells how much is shaded.
Then write each fraction as a whole number or as a mixed number.

13.

14.

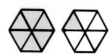

15.

16.

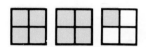

17.

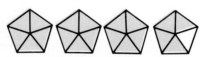

18.

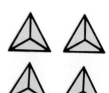

19.

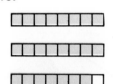

★ 20.

★ 21.

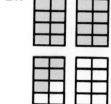

Write each fraction as a whole number or as a mixed number.

22. $\frac{9}{2}$ **23.** $\frac{7}{3}$ **24.** $\frac{13}{5}$ **25.** $\frac{9}{4}$ **26.** $\frac{14}{2}$ **27.** $\frac{11}{3}$

28. $\frac{23}{8}$ **29.** $\frac{24}{5}$ **30.** $\frac{23}{6}$ **31.** $\frac{25}{7}$ **32.** $\frac{37}{10}$ **33.** $\frac{15}{13}$

PROBLEM SOLVING • APPLICATIONS

34. John spends $\frac{10}{4}$ hours repairing the waterwheel on his mill. Write the fraction as a mixed number.

35. A farmer brings $\frac{4}{3}$ bags of corn to John's mill. Write the fraction as a mixed number.

36. John has 8 barrels. He fills 2 of them with wheat flour and 6 of them with cornmeal. What fraction of the barrels are filled with wheat flour?

★ 37. A piece of wood is 72 inches long. John cuts off $\frac{2}{3}$ of the piece to repair the bridge. How many inches long is the piece that is left?

Adding Fractions

Hans and his family were Swedish settlers who came to Delaware in 1840. They built a log cabin.

Hans notched $\frac{3}{8}$ of the logs.

Chris notched $\frac{2}{8}$ of the logs.

● What part of the logs are notched?

Think You know what part each person notched. Add to find the sum.

$$\frac{3}{8} + \frac{2}{8} = ?$$

$$\frac{3}{8} + \frac{2}{8} = \frac{5}{8} \quad \longleftarrow \text{ Add the numerators.}$$
$$\qquad\qquad\quad \longleftarrow \text{ Use the same denominator.}$$

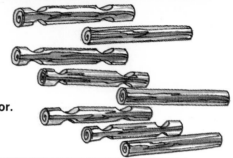

Hans and Chris notched $\frac{5}{8}$ of the logs.

> *To add fractions that have the same denominator, add the numerators. Use the same denominator.*

● $\dfrac{3}{10} + \dfrac{6}{10} = ?$

Think The denominators are the same. Add the numerators.

One Way: $\dfrac{3}{10} + \dfrac{6}{10} = \dfrac{3+6}{10}$

$\qquad\qquad\qquad = \dfrac{9}{10}$

Another Way:
$$\begin{array}{r} \frac{3}{10} \\ + \frac{6}{10} \\ \hline \frac{9}{10} \end{array}$$

PRACTICE • Add.

1.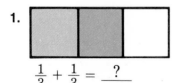

$\dfrac{1}{3} + \dfrac{1}{3} = \underline{\quad ? \quad}$

2.

$\dfrac{1}{5} + \dfrac{2}{5} = \underline{\quad ? \quad}$

3.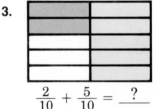

$\dfrac{2}{10} + \dfrac{5}{10} = \underline{\quad ? \quad}$

4. $\dfrac{1}{8} + \dfrac{4}{8} = \underline{\quad ? \quad}$

5. $\dfrac{3}{10} + \dfrac{4}{10} = \underline{\quad ? \quad}$

6. $\dfrac{2}{6} + \dfrac{3}{6} = \underline{\quad ? \quad}$

7. $\dfrac{1}{4} + \dfrac{2}{4} = \dfrac{?}{4}$

8. $\dfrac{1}{8} + \dfrac{2}{8} = \dfrac{?}{8}$

9. $\dfrac{2}{9} + \dfrac{3}{9} = \dfrac{?}{9}$

EXERCISES • Add.

10. $\frac{2}{5} + \frac{2}{5} = \frac{?}{5}$

11. $\frac{1}{10} + \frac{6}{10} = \frac{?}{10}$

12. $\frac{3}{8} + \frac{4}{8} = \frac{?}{8}$

13. $\frac{3}{7} + \frac{2}{7} = \underline{\ ?\ }$

14. $\frac{2}{10} + \frac{1}{10} = \underline{\ ?\ }$

15. $\frac{5}{9} + \frac{3}{9} = \underline{\ ?\ }$

16. $\frac{5}{8} + \frac{2}{8} = \underline{\ ?\ }$

17. $\frac{4}{8} + \frac{3}{8} = \underline{\ ?\ }$

18. $\frac{4}{10} + \frac{5}{10} = \underline{\ ?\ }$

19. $\begin{array}{r} \frac{2}{4} \\ + \frac{1}{4} \\ \hline \end{array}$

20. $\begin{array}{r} \frac{1}{5} \\ + \frac{3}{5} \\ \hline \end{array}$

21. $\begin{array}{r} \frac{4}{6} \\ + \frac{1}{6} \\ \hline \end{array}$

22. $\begin{array}{r} \frac{2}{7} \\ + \frac{4}{7} \\ \hline \end{array}$

23. $\begin{array}{r} \frac{6}{8} \\ + \frac{1}{8} \\ \hline \end{array}$

24. $\begin{array}{r} \frac{7}{9} \\ + \frac{1}{9} \\ \hline \end{array}$

25. $\begin{array}{r} \frac{3}{10} \\ + \frac{2}{10} \\ \hline \end{array}$

26. $\begin{array}{r} \frac{6}{8} \\ + \frac{1}{8} \\ \hline \end{array}$

27. $\begin{array}{r} \frac{5}{11} \\ + \frac{4}{11} \\ \hline \end{array}$

28. $\begin{array}{r} \frac{2}{9} \\ + \frac{5}{9} \\ \hline \end{array}$

29. $\begin{array}{r} \frac{1}{4} \\ + \frac{2}{4} \\ \hline \end{array}$

30. $\begin{array}{r} \frac{3}{6} \\ + \frac{2}{6} \\ \hline \end{array}$

31. $\begin{array}{r} \frac{5}{12} \\ + \frac{2}{12} \\ \hline \end{array}$

32. $\begin{array}{r} \frac{4}{13} \\ + \frac{7}{13} \\ \hline \end{array}$

33. $\begin{array}{r} \frac{5}{10} \\ + \frac{4}{10} \\ \hline \end{array}$

34. $\begin{array}{r} \frac{1}{7} \\ + \frac{3}{7} \\ \hline \end{array}$

35. $\begin{array}{r} \frac{6}{15} \\ + \frac{7}{15} \\ \hline \end{array}$

36. $\begin{array}{r} \frac{3}{11} \\ + \frac{5}{11} \\ \hline \end{array}$

Add. Write the answers in lowest terms.

★37. $\begin{array}{r} \frac{1}{4} \\ + \frac{1}{4} \\ \hline \frac{2}{4} = \frac{?}{2} \end{array}$

★38. $\begin{array}{r} \frac{2}{6} \\ + \frac{1}{6} \\ \hline \frac{3}{6} = \frac{?}{2} \end{array}$

★39. $\begin{array}{r} \frac{3}{6} \\ + \frac{1}{6} \\ \hline \frac{4}{6} = \frac{?}{3} \end{array}$

★40. $\begin{array}{r} \frac{1}{8} \\ + \frac{1}{8} \\ \hline \end{array}$

★41. $\begin{array}{r} \frac{2}{8} \\ + \frac{4}{8} \\ \hline \end{array}$

★42. $\begin{array}{r} \frac{3}{10} \\ + \frac{2}{10} \\ \hline \end{array}$

PROBLEM SOLVING • APPLICATIONS

43. Jules cleared $\frac{2}{4}$ of the lot. Hans cleared $\frac{1}{4}$ of the lot. How much of the lot has been cleared?

44. Hans placed $\frac{2}{8}$ of the logs on the roof. Chris placed $\frac{3}{8}$ of the logs on the roof. How many of the logs were in place on the roof?

45. How far is it from Han's house to school?

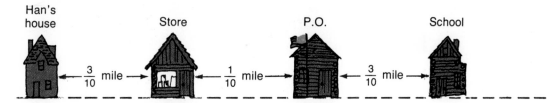

Han's house ←$\frac{3}{10}$ mile→ Store ←$\frac{1}{10}$ mile→ P.O. ←$\frac{3}{10}$ mile→ School

Sums of 1 and Greater Than 1

Mary Winslow cooks vegetables in an iron pot. She uses $\frac{1}{4}$ of a pot of squash for soup and $\frac{3}{4}$ of a pot of squash for bread. How much squash does she use in all?

Think You know how much squash she uses for each dish. Add to find the sum.

$$\frac{1}{4} + \frac{3}{4} = ?$$

$$\begin{array}{r} \frac{1}{4} \\ +\frac{3}{4} \\ \hline \frac{4}{4} \end{array}$$

NOTE: $\frac{4}{4}$ is the same as **1** whole.

Mary used **1 pot** of squash in all.

When the numerator is greater than the denominator write a mixed number.

● $\frac{4}{5} + \frac{3}{5} = ?$

Step 1
Add.

$$\begin{array}{r} \frac{4}{5} \\ +\frac{3}{5} \\ \hline \frac{7}{5} \end{array}$$ ◀ **7 > 5**

Step 2
Divide to get a mixed number.

$$5\overline{)7}\ \ 1\frac{2}{5}$$
$$\underline{-5}$$
$$2$$

Step 3
Write the sum as a mixed number.

$$\begin{array}{r} \frac{4}{5} \\ +\frac{3}{5} \\ \hline \frac{7}{5} \end{array} = 1\frac{2}{5}$$ ◀ **Answer**

PRACTICE • Add. Write the sums as whole numbers or as mixed numbers.

1. $\frac{2}{4}$
$+\frac{3}{4}$

2. $\frac{2}{3}$
$+\frac{2}{3}$

3. $\frac{3}{5}$
$+\frac{3}{5}$

4. $\frac{4}{6}$
$+\frac{2}{6}$

5. $\frac{4}{5}$
$+\frac{4}{5}$

6. $\frac{6}{10}$
$+\frac{4}{10}$

7. $\frac{6}{8}$
$+\frac{7}{8}$

8. $\frac{2}{5}$
$+\frac{3}{5}$

9. $\frac{9}{10}$
$+\frac{4}{10}$

10. $\frac{3}{8}$
$+\frac{6}{8}$

11. $\frac{3}{7}$
$+\frac{6}{7}$

12. $\frac{4}{9}$
$+\frac{7}{9}$

EXERCISES • Add. Write the answers as whole numbers or mixed numbers.

13. $\dfrac{7}{8}$
$+\dfrac{6}{8}$

14. $\dfrac{4}{5}$
$+\dfrac{3}{5}$

15. $\dfrac{4}{8}$
$+\dfrac{5}{8}$

16. $\dfrac{9}{10}$
$+\dfrac{8}{10}$

17. $\dfrac{8}{12}$
$+\dfrac{9}{12}$

18. $\dfrac{6}{5}$
$+\dfrac{3}{5}$

19. $\dfrac{4}{8}$
$+\dfrac{7}{8}$

20. $\dfrac{3}{7}$
$+\dfrac{5}{7}$

21. $\dfrac{2}{11}$
$+\dfrac{9}{11}$

22. $\dfrac{8}{9}$
$+\dfrac{8}{9}$

23. $\dfrac{2}{10}$
$+\dfrac{9}{10}$

24. $\dfrac{8}{9}$
$+\dfrac{6}{9}$

25. $\dfrac{6}{7}$
$+\dfrac{5}{7}$

26. $\dfrac{4}{12}$
$+\dfrac{8}{12}$

27. $\dfrac{6}{8}$
$+\dfrac{5}{8}$

28. $\dfrac{5}{9}$
$+\dfrac{8}{9}$

29. $\dfrac{4}{10}$
$+\dfrac{6}{10}$

30. $\dfrac{7}{11}$
$+\dfrac{8}{11}$

31. $\dfrac{7}{13}$
$+\dfrac{8}{13}$

32. $\dfrac{4}{8}$
$+\dfrac{9}{8}$

33. $\dfrac{5}{9}$
$+\dfrac{5}{9}$

34. $\dfrac{8}{12}$
$+\dfrac{5}{12}$

35. $\dfrac{9}{14}$
$+\dfrac{8}{14}$

36. $\dfrac{4}{7}$
$+\dfrac{5}{7}$

37. $\dfrac{7}{8} + \dfrac{6}{8} =$ _____?_____

38. $\dfrac{3}{7} + \dfrac{6}{7} =$ _____?_____

39. $\dfrac{9}{12} + \dfrac{8}{12} =$ _____?_____

★ 40. $\dfrac{4}{5} + \dfrac{1}{5} + \dfrac{3}{5} =$ _____?_____

★ 41. $\dfrac{2}{3} + \dfrac{2}{3} + \dfrac{2}{3} =$ _____?_____

★ 42. $\dfrac{4}{6} + \dfrac{5}{6} + \dfrac{2}{6} =$ _____?_____

PROBLEM SOLVING • APPLICATIONS

43. Mary uses $\dfrac{7}{8}$ of a cup of pumpkin to make bread. She uses $\dfrac{2}{8}$ of a cup of pumpkin in a stew. How many cups of pumpkin does she use in all? Write your answer as a mixed number.

★ 44. Mary makes a soup using $\dfrac{4}{8}$ of a cup of corn, $\dfrac{3}{8}$ of a cup of beans, and $\dfrac{7}{8}$ of a cup of carrots. How many cups of vegetables are in the soup? Write your answer as a mixed number.

Subtracting Fractions

The Indians showed the first settlers how to plant and harvest corn.

Jane mixed cornmeal, milk, and lard to bake cornbread. She cut the cornbread into eighths.

After dinner, $\frac{5}{8}$ of the cornbread was left.

Later, $\frac{2}{8}$ of the cornbread was eaten.

● How much of the cornbread is now left?

Think To find how much is left, subtract.

$$\frac{5}{8} - \frac{2}{8} = ?$$

$$\frac{5}{8} - \frac{2}{8} = \frac{3}{8} \longleftarrow \text{Subtract the numerators.}$$
$$\longleftarrow \text{Use the same denominator.}$$

There is $\frac{3}{8}$ of the cornbread left in the pan.

To subtract fractions that have the same denominator, subtract the numerators. Use the same denominator.

● You can show subtraction of fractions in two ways.

One Way: $\dfrac{7}{10} - \dfrac{4}{10} = \dfrac{3}{10}$

Another Way:
$$\begin{array}{r} \dfrac{7}{10} \\ -\dfrac{4}{10} \\ \hline \dfrac{3}{10} \end{array}$$

PRACTICE • Subtract.

1.

$\dfrac{4}{5} - \dfrac{1}{5} = \dfrac{?}{5}$

2.

$\dfrac{4}{4} - \dfrac{1}{4} = \dfrac{?}{4}$

3.

$\dfrac{6}{8} - \dfrac{3}{8} = \dfrac{?}{8}$

4. $\frac{9}{10} - \frac{6}{10} = \frac{?}{10}$

5. $\frac{7}{8} - \frac{4}{8} = \frac{?}{8}$

6. $\frac{6}{6} - \frac{5}{6} = \frac{?}{6}$

7. $\frac{6}{8} - \frac{1}{8} = \underline{\ ?\ }$

8. $\frac{8}{10} - \frac{1}{10} = \underline{\ ?\ }$

9. $\frac{3}{4} - \frac{2}{4} = \underline{\ ?\ }$

EXERCISES • Subtract.

10. $\frac{4}{8} - \frac{3}{8} = \frac{?}{8}$

11. $\frac{10}{10} - \frac{1}{10} = \frac{?}{10}$

12. $\frac{5}{6} - \frac{4}{6} = \frac{?}{6}$

13. $\frac{3}{4} - \frac{2}{4} = \underline{\ ?\ }$

14. $\frac{8}{8} - \frac{3}{8} = \underline{\ ?\ }$

15. $\frac{4}{5} - \frac{3}{5} = \underline{\ ?\ }$

16. $\frac{7}{8}$
$-\frac{2}{8}$

17. $\frac{9}{10}$
$-\frac{2}{10}$

18. $\frac{4}{5}$
$-\frac{1}{5}$

19. $\frac{4}{6}$
$-\frac{3}{6}$

20. $\frac{6}{9}$
$-\frac{2}{9}$

21. $\frac{5}{7}$
$-\frac{2}{7}$

22. $\frac{5}{9}$
$-\frac{3}{9}$

23. $\frac{6}{7}$
$-\frac{3}{7}$

24. $\frac{8}{8}$
$-\frac{5}{8}$

25. $\frac{10}{10}$
$-\frac{3}{10}$

26. $\frac{7}{8}$
$-\frac{6}{8}$

27. $\frac{8}{9}$
$-\frac{3}{9}$

Subtract. Write the answers in lowest terms.

★ **28.** $\frac{5}{6}$
$-\frac{3}{6}$
$\frac{2}{6} = \frac{?}{3}$

★ **29.** $\frac{3}{4}$
$-\frac{1}{4}$
$\frac{2}{4} = \frac{?}{2}$

★ **30.** $\frac{5}{8}$
$-\frac{1}{8}$

★ **31.** $\frac{7}{10}$
$-\frac{3}{10}$

★ **32.** $\frac{7}{8}$
$-\frac{3}{8}$

PROBLEM SOLVING • APPLICATIONS

33. June has $\frac{7}{8}$ of a cup of cornmeal. She uses $\frac{5}{8}$ of a cup in cooking. How much cornmeal does she have left?

34. Alice has $\frac{1}{8}$ of a cup of cornmeal. She needs $\frac{6}{8}$ of a cup to make cornbread. How much more does she need?

Write the information that is missing in Problem 35.

★ **35.** Anna has $\frac{3}{4}$ of a pan of cornbread. She gives some to Martha. How much cornbread does Anna have left?

★ **36.** Ellen had 16 ears of corn. She gave $\frac{3}{8}$ of them to her friend. How many did she have left?

Adding and Subtracting Mixed Numbers

Benjamin Franklin spent many hours
each day working in his print shop
on Market Street in Philadelphia.

Suppose that he spent $4\frac{3}{5}$ hours in writing
for his almanac and $3\frac{1}{5}$ hours in printing
newspaper articles.

● How long did he work?

Think You know how long he worked on
each job. Add to find the sum.

$$4\frac{3}{5} + 3\frac{1}{5} = ?$$

Step 1
Add the
fractions.

$$\begin{array}{r} 4\frac{3}{5} \\ +3\frac{1}{5} \\ \hline \frac{4}{5} \end{array}$$

Step 2
Add the
whole
numbers.

$$\begin{array}{r} 4\frac{3}{5} \\ +3\frac{1}{5} \\ \hline 7\frac{4}{5} \end{array}$$

He worked $7\frac{4}{5}$ **hours.**

● How much longer did Ben Franklin spend
in writing for his almanac than he spent
in printing newspaper articles?

Step 1
Subtract
the
fractions.

$$\begin{array}{r} 4\frac{3}{5} \\ -3\frac{1}{5} \\ \hline \frac{2}{5} \end{array}$$

Step 2
Subtract
the whole
numbers.

$$\begin{array}{r} 4\frac{3}{5} \\ -3\frac{1}{5} \\ \hline 1\frac{2}{5} \end{array}$$

He spent $1\frac{2}{5}$ **hours** longer writing for his
almanac.

PRACTICE • Add.

1. $\begin{array}{r} 3\frac{1}{3} \\ +4\frac{1}{3} \\ \hline \end{array}$

2. $\begin{array}{r} 2\frac{1}{5} \\ +1\frac{3}{5} \\ \hline \end{array}$

3. $\begin{array}{r} 4\frac{2}{4} \\ +2\frac{1}{4} \\ \hline \end{array}$

4. $\begin{array}{r} 3\frac{2}{8} \\ +3\frac{3}{8} \\ \hline \end{array}$

5. $\begin{array}{r} 2\frac{4}{6} \\ +5\frac{1}{6} \\ \hline \end{array}$

Subtract.

6. $8\frac{3}{5}$
$-2\frac{1}{5}$

7. $7\frac{5}{6}$
$-5\frac{4}{6}$

8. $9\frac{5}{8}$
$-4\frac{4}{8}$

9. $6\frac{2}{4}$
$-4\frac{1}{4}$

10. $5\frac{2}{3}$
$-4\frac{1}{3}$

EXERCISES • Add or subtract. Write the answers in lowest terms.

11. $2\frac{1}{8}$
$+3\frac{4}{8}$

12. $4\frac{4}{10}$
$+4\frac{3}{10}$

13. $2\frac{2}{6}$
$+4\frac{3}{6}$

14. $3\frac{2}{8}$
$+4\frac{5}{8}$

15. $3\frac{2}{6}$
$+5\frac{3}{6}$

16. $2\frac{1}{6}$
$+3\frac{4}{6}$

17. $7\frac{2}{10}$
$+\ \ \frac{5}{10}$

18. $5\frac{2}{4}$
$+1\frac{1}{4}$

19. $9\frac{5}{8}$
$+\ \ \frac{2}{8}$

20. $4\frac{2}{5}$
$+4\frac{1}{5}$

21. $6\frac{1}{3}$
$+2\frac{1}{3}$

22. $1\frac{3}{9}$
$+3\frac{2}{9}$

23. $2\frac{3}{8}$
$+3\frac{2}{8}$

24. $4\frac{2}{5}$
$+3\frac{2}{5}$

25. $6\frac{1}{7}$
$+3\frac{3}{7}$

26. $6\frac{4}{5}$
$-3\frac{2}{5}$

27. $9\frac{7}{8}$
$-4\frac{4}{8}$

28. $7\frac{3}{6}$
$-5\frac{2}{6}$

29. $8\frac{5}{8}$
$-5\frac{2}{8}$

30. $5\frac{3}{10}$
$-2\frac{2}{10}$

31. $8\frac{4}{6}$
$-8\frac{3}{6}$

32. $9\frac{8}{10}$
$-\ \ \frac{5}{10}$

33. $5\frac{7}{8}$
$-\ \ \frac{2}{8}$

34. $7\frac{3}{6}$
-3

35. $5\frac{7}{8}$
$-\ \ \frac{4}{8}$

PROBLEM SOLVING • APPLICATIONS

36. Suppose that Ben Franklin spent $6\frac{3}{4}$ hours writing newspaper articles and $2\frac{2}{4}$ hours working the hand press. How much longer did he spend writing?

37. Ben Franklin lived in England for about $17\frac{2}{8}$ years. He lived in France for about $7\frac{1}{8}$ years. How many years is this in all?

THINKER'S CORNER

Write + or − to make true sentences.

a. $2\frac{1}{3}$ ⬤ $3\frac{1}{3}$ ⬤ $1\frac{2}{3} = 4$

b. $3\frac{5}{8}$ ⬤ $2\frac{1}{8}$ ⬤ $1\frac{1}{8} = 2\frac{5}{8}$

Adding Fractions with Unlike Denominators

Walter Eaton runs a ferryboat service near
Baltimore on the Patapsco River. He travels
$\frac{1}{2}$ of a mile to the first stop. Then he
travels $\frac{2}{5}$ of a mile to the second stop.

● How far does he travel?

| **Think** | You know how far he travels between each stop. Add to find the total distance. |

$$\frac{1}{2} + \frac{2}{5} = ?$$

To add fractions with unlike denominators, first write equivalent
fractions so that both fractions have the same denominator.

Step 1
Find equivalent
fractions for $\frac{1}{2}$
and $\frac{2}{5}$ that have
the same denominator.

$$\frac{1}{2} = \frac{5 \times 1}{5 \times 2} = \frac{5}{10}$$

$$\frac{2}{5} = \frac{2 \times 2}{2 \times 5} = \frac{4}{10}$$

Step 2
Add.

$$\begin{array}{r} \frac{1}{2} = \frac{5}{10} \\ +\frac{2}{5} = +\frac{4}{10} \\ \hline \frac{9}{10} \end{array}$$

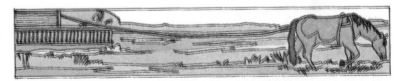

He travels $\frac{9}{10}$ of a mile.

PRACTICE • Complete.

1.
$$\begin{array}{r} \frac{1}{3} = \frac{?}{6} \\ +\frac{1}{6} = \frac{1}{6} \\ \hline \frac{?}{6} \end{array}$$

2.
$$\begin{array}{r} \frac{1}{4} = \frac{?}{8} \\ +\frac{3}{8} = \frac{3}{8} \\ \hline \frac{?}{8} \end{array}$$

3.
$$\begin{array}{r} \frac{1}{2} = \frac{?}{10} \\ +\frac{1}{5} = \frac{2}{10} \\ \hline \frac{?}{10} \end{array}$$

4.
$$\begin{array}{r} \frac{1}{5} = \frac{?}{10} \\ +\frac{7}{10} = \frac{7}{10} \\ \hline \frac{?}{10} \end{array}$$

5.
$$\begin{array}{r} \frac{1}{3} = \frac{?}{24} \\ +\frac{3}{8} = \frac{9}{24} \\ \hline \frac{?}{24} \end{array}$$

6.
$$\begin{array}{r} \frac{5}{12} = \frac{5}{12} \\ +\frac{1}{4} = \frac{?}{12} \\ \hline \frac{?}{12} \end{array}$$

7.
$$\begin{array}{r} \frac{3}{7} = \frac{6}{14} \\ +\frac{1}{2} = \frac{?}{14} \\ \hline \frac{?}{14} \end{array}$$

8.
$$\begin{array}{r} \frac{5}{12} = \frac{5}{12} \\ +\frac{1}{2} = \frac{?}{12} \\ \hline \frac{?}{12} \end{array}$$

EXERCISES • Complete.

9. $\dfrac{1}{2} = \dfrac{?}{8}$
   $+\dfrac{3}{8} = \dfrac{3}{8}$
   _____
   $\dfrac{?}{8}$

10. $\dfrac{1}{8} = \dfrac{?}{16}$
    $+\dfrac{1}{16} = \dfrac{1}{16}$
    _____
    $\dfrac{?}{16}$

11. $\dfrac{1}{6} = \dfrac{2}{12}$
    $+\dfrac{2}{4} = \dfrac{?}{12}$
    _____
    $\dfrac{?}{12}$

12. $\dfrac{4}{15} = \dfrac{4}{15}$
    $+\dfrac{2}{5} = \dfrac{?}{15}$
    _____
    $\dfrac{?}{15}$

Add. Write the answers in lowest terms.

13. $\dfrac{1}{4}$
    $+\dfrac{3}{5}$

14. $\dfrac{3}{4}$
    $+\dfrac{1}{8}$

15. $\dfrac{1}{3}$
    $+\dfrac{5}{9}$

16. $\dfrac{5}{6}$
    $+\dfrac{1}{9}$

17. $\dfrac{2}{5}$
    $+\dfrac{5}{10}$

18. $\dfrac{2}{3}$
    $+\dfrac{2}{9}$

19. $\dfrac{2}{5}$
    $+\dfrac{1}{4}$

20. $\dfrac{5}{8}$
    $+\dfrac{1}{3}$

21. $\dfrac{8}{12}$
    $+\dfrac{1}{8}$

22. $\dfrac{1}{3}$
    $+\dfrac{2}{9}$

23. $\dfrac{2}{6}$
    $+\dfrac{1}{6}$

24. $\dfrac{3}{5}$
    $+\dfrac{1}{10}$

25. $\dfrac{2}{3}$
    $+\dfrac{2}{7}$

26. $\dfrac{1}{4}$
    $+\dfrac{9}{16}$

27. $\dfrac{1}{3}$
    $+\dfrac{1}{3}$

28. $\dfrac{3}{8}$
    $+\dfrac{1}{16}$

29. $\dfrac{5}{12}$
    $+\dfrac{1}{6}$

30. $\dfrac{2}{3}$
    $+\dfrac{3}{15}$

Add. Write the answers as mixed numbers.

★ 31. $\dfrac{1}{2}$
      $+\dfrac{3}{4}$

★ 32. $\dfrac{5}{6}$
      $+\dfrac{1}{3}$

★ 33. $\dfrac{2}{3}$
      $+\dfrac{4}{9}$

★ 34. $\dfrac{3}{8}$
      $+\dfrac{3}{4}$

★ 35. $\dfrac{3}{4}$
      $+\dfrac{5}{8}$

★ 36. $\dfrac{7}{9}$
      $+\dfrac{2}{3}$

PROBLEM SOLVING • APPLICATIONS

37. A ferryboat travels $\dfrac{1}{4}$ of a mile to the first stop. Then it travels $\dfrac{1}{2}$ of a mile to the next stop. How far does the ferryboat travel?

38. Mr. Dunn rides with Walter for $\dfrac{1}{3}$ of an hour in the morning and $\dfrac{1}{2}$ of an hour in the afternoon. How many hours does Mr. Dunn spend riding with Walter?

★ 39. How far does Walter travel from the first stop to the fourth stop?

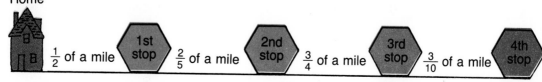

Home | $\frac{1}{2}$ of a mile | 1st stop | $\frac{2}{5}$ of a mile | 2nd stop | $\frac{3}{4}$ of a mile | 3rd stop | $\frac{3}{10}$ of a mile | 4th stop

Subtracting Fractions with Unlike Denominators

John and Dale lived in the Bay Colony. They caught fish in the Charles River.

John rowed his boat $\frac{1}{2}$ of a mile from the shore. Dale rowed his boat $\frac{2}{5}$ of a mile from the shore.

● How much farther from shore was John than Dale?

Think You know how far each person travels. Subtract to compare.

$$\frac{1}{2} - \frac{2}{5} = ?$$

> To subtract fractions with unlike denominators, first find equivalent fractions so that both fractions have the same denominator.

Step 1
Find equivalent fractions.

$$\frac{1}{2} = \frac{5 \times 1}{5 \times 2} = \frac{5}{10}$$

$$\frac{2}{5} = \frac{2 \times 2}{2 \times 5} = \frac{4}{10}$$

Step 2
Subtract.

$$\begin{array}{r} \frac{1}{2} = \frac{5}{10} \\ -\frac{2}{5} = -\frac{4}{10} \\ \hline \frac{1}{10} \end{array}$$

John was $\frac{1}{10}$ **of a mile** farther from shore than Dale.

More Examples

$$\begin{array}{r} \frac{1}{2} = \frac{2}{4} \\ -\frac{1}{4} = -\frac{1}{4} \\ \hline \frac{1}{4} \end{array}$$ ◀ $\frac{2 \times 1}{2 \times 2}$

$$\begin{array}{r} \frac{7}{10} = \frac{7}{10} \\ -\frac{2}{5} = -\frac{4}{10} \\ \hline \frac{3}{10} \end{array}$$ ◀ $\frac{2 \times 2}{2 \times 5}$

PRACTICE • Complete.

1.
$$\begin{array}{r} \frac{1}{2} = \frac{?}{8} \\ -\frac{1}{8} = \frac{1}{8} \\ \hline \frac{?}{8} \end{array}$$

2.
$$\begin{array}{r} \frac{1}{4} = \frac{?}{24} \\ -\frac{1}{6} = \frac{4}{24} \\ \hline \frac{?}{24} \end{array}$$

3.
$$\begin{array}{r} \frac{1}{2} = \frac{?}{6} \\ -\frac{1}{6} = \frac{1}{6} \\ \hline \frac{?}{6} \end{array}$$

4.
$$\begin{array}{r} \frac{1}{4} = \frac{?}{20} \\ -\frac{1}{5} = \frac{4}{20} \\ \hline \frac{?}{20} \end{array}$$

5.
$$\begin{array}{r} \frac{5}{8} = \frac{5}{8} \\ -\frac{1}{4} = \frac{?}{8} \\ \hline \frac{?}{8} \end{array}$$

6.
$$\begin{array}{r} \frac{5}{6} = \frac{15}{18} \\ -\frac{1}{9} = \frac{?}{18} \\ \hline \frac{?}{18} \end{array}$$

7.
$$\begin{array}{r} \frac{3}{4} = \frac{?}{8} \\ -\frac{1}{8} = \frac{1}{8} \\ \hline \frac{?}{8} \end{array}$$

8.
$$\begin{array}{r} \frac{7}{8} = \frac{7}{8} \\ -\frac{1}{2} = \frac{?}{8} \\ \hline \frac{?}{8} \end{array}$$

9. $\dfrac{5}{8} = \dfrac{5}{8}$
$-\dfrac{1}{2} = \dfrac{?}{8}$
$\overline{\dfrac{?}{8}}$

10. $\dfrac{5}{6} = \dfrac{5}{6}$
$-\dfrac{1}{3} = \dfrac{?}{6}$
$\overline{\dfrac{?}{6}}$

11. $\dfrac{4}{5} = \dfrac{16}{20}$
$-\dfrac{3}{4} = \dfrac{?}{20}$
$\overline{\dfrac{?}{20}}$

12. $\dfrac{1}{3} = \dfrac{?}{9}$
$-\dfrac{1}{9} = \dfrac{1}{9}$
$\overline{\dfrac{?}{9}}$

EXERCISES • Subtract.

13. $\dfrac{2}{3}$ $-\dfrac{1}{9}$

14. $\dfrac{1}{2}$ $-\dfrac{4}{10}$

15. $\dfrac{4}{5}$ $-\dfrac{1}{3}$

16. $\dfrac{9}{10}$ $-\dfrac{1}{5}$

17. $\dfrac{5}{6}$ $-\dfrac{3}{4}$

18. $\dfrac{5}{6}$ $-\dfrac{5}{12}$

19. $\dfrac{3}{4}$ $-\dfrac{5}{8}$

20. $\dfrac{11}{12}$ $-\dfrac{3}{6}$

21. $\dfrac{7}{9}$ $-\dfrac{1}{6}$

22. $\dfrac{7}{8}$ $-\dfrac{4}{8}$

23. $\dfrac{5}{7}$ $-\dfrac{2}{3}$

24. $\dfrac{4}{5}$ $-\dfrac{1}{10}$

25. $\dfrac{2}{3}$ $-\dfrac{1}{12}$

26. $\dfrac{7}{12}$ $-\dfrac{2}{12}$

27. $\dfrac{10}{12}$ $-\dfrac{3}{8}$

28. $\dfrac{3}{5}$ $-\dfrac{3}{10}$

29. $\dfrac{3}{4}$ $-\dfrac{4}{12}$

30. $\dfrac{9}{10}$ $-\dfrac{3}{5}$

Subtract. Write the answers in lowest terms.

★31. $\dfrac{2}{3}$ $-\dfrac{2}{12}$ $\overline{\dfrac{?}{12}} = \dfrac{?}{2}$

★32. $\dfrac{3}{5}$ $-\dfrac{1}{10}$ $\overline{\dfrac{?}{10}} = \dfrac{?}{2}$

★33. $\dfrac{9}{10}$ $-\dfrac{2}{5}$ $\overline{\dfrac{?}{10}} = ?$

★34. $\dfrac{11}{12}$ $-\dfrac{1}{6}$ $\overline{\dfrac{?}{12}} = ?$

★35. $\dfrac{1}{4}$ $-\dfrac{2}{16}$

★36. $\dfrac{11}{12}$ $-\dfrac{2}{3}$

PROBLEM SOLVING • APPLICATIONS

37. It took John $\dfrac{3}{4}$ of an hour to catch his first halibut. It took Dale $\dfrac{1}{3}$ of an hour to catch his first halibut. How much longer did it take John?

38. John caught $\dfrac{3}{4}$ of a basket of herring in the morning and $\dfrac{1}{2}$ of a basket in the afternoon. How much more did he catch in the morning?

★39. Dale caught 23 fish. He divided them equally among his 5 friends and kept the fish left over. How many did he keep?

★40. John caught 18 cod. He gave $\dfrac{1}{3}$ of them to his friend. How many did he keep?

PROBLEM SOLVING • STRATEGIES

Using Estimation with Mixed Numbers

You can estimate answers to problems involving fractions by first rounding each fraction to the nearest whole number.

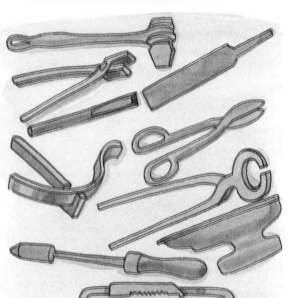

> **If the fractional part of a mixed number is less than $\frac{1}{2}$, round down.**

James is an apprentice blacksmith. He works $3\frac{1}{4}$ hours in the morning.

● What is $3\frac{1}{4}$ rounded to the nearest whole number?

Think $\frac{1}{4}$ is less than $\frac{1}{2}$.

So $3\frac{1}{4}$ rounded to the nearest whole number is **3**.

> **If the fractional part of a mixed number is $\frac{1}{2}$ or more, round up.**

James works $5\frac{3}{4}$ hours in the afternoon.

● What is $5\frac{3}{4}$ rounded to the nearest whole number?

Think $\frac{3}{4}$ is more than $\frac{1}{2}$.

So $5\frac{3}{4}$ rounded to the nearest whole number is **6**.

E PROBLEMS • Round to the nearest whole number.

1. $1\frac{5}{6}$
2. $7\frac{2}{7}$
3. $10\frac{3}{5}$
4. $18\frac{2}{6}$
5. $36\frac{1}{7}$

Choose the best estimate. The answer is between:

6. $1\frac{7}{8} + 4\frac{2}{16}$ **a.** 2 and 4   **b.** 5 and 7   **c.** 8 and 10

7. $8\frac{9}{10} - 1\frac{4}{5}$ **a.** 9 and 12   **b.** 1 and 4   **c.** 5 and 8

8. $12\frac{6}{12} + 8\frac{1}{9}$ **a.** 20 and 25   **b.** 15 and 19   **c.** 26 and 30

Choose the best estimate. Choose **a**, **b**, or **c**.

9. Benjamin is an apprentice printer. He spends $5\frac{5}{6}$ hours in the morning learning his craft, and $4\frac{1}{6}$ hours in the afternoon. How many more hours does he work in the morning than in the afternoon?

   a. $5 - 4$ **b.** $6 - 4$ **c.** $6 - 5$

10. Annabell is an apprentice cook. She uses $2\frac{3}{4}$ cups of water to make the soup. Later, she adds $1\frac{7}{8}$ cups of water. How many cups of water does she use in all?

    a. $2 + 1$ **b.** $2 + 2$ **c.** $3 + 2$

11. Jeremiah is a shoemaker. He uses $7\frac{2}{3}$ yards of leather to make shoes and $9\frac{1}{6}$ yards of leather to make boots. How many more yards of leather does he use for the boots than the shoes?

    a. $9 - 7$ **b.** $9 - 8$ **c.** $10 - 8$

12. Matthew works for $6\frac{7}{12}$ years as an apprentice and $4\frac{1}{12}$ years as a journeyman. Then he becomes a master. How many years does he work before he becomes a master?

    a. $7 + 4$ **b.** $7 + 5$ **c.** $8 + 5$

13. Abigail is a housekeeper. She spends $11\frac{2}{3}$ hours cleaning rooms in the mansion each day and $2\frac{2}{3}$ hours polishing the silver. How many hours does she spend working each day?

    a. 13   **b.** 14   **c.** 15

14. Luke is an apprentice blacksmith. He walks $1\frac{3}{4}$ miles to work each day. How many miles does he walk to and from work?

    a. 2   **b.** 3   **c.** 4

15. Martha is a needleworker. She has $2\frac{7}{12}$ yards of braid. She uses $1\frac{1}{12}$ yards to trim a dress. How many yards does she have left?

    a. 1   **b.** 2   **c.** 3

16. Alexander became a master craftsman in $12\frac{3}{4}$ years. During this time, he spent $7\frac{1}{2}$ years as an apprentice and the other years as a journeyman. How many years did he spend working as a journeyman?

    a. 5   **b.** 6   **c.** 7

CHAPTER REVIEW

Part 1: VOCABULARY

For Exercises 1–7, choose the word(s) from the box at the right that completes each statement.

1. To name a part of something you would use a __?__ .
   (Page 270)

2. In a fraction, the number which tells how many equal parts there are is the __?__ . (Page 270)

3. Fractions are __?__ if they name the same part.
   (Page 276)

4. To find an equivalent fraction, multiply the __?__ and the denominator by the same number.
   (Page 278)

5. A fraction is in __?__ when the only number that will divide both the numerator and the denominator is 1. (Page 282)

6. A fraction greater than one can be changed to a __?__ by dividing the numerator by the denominator. (Page 290)

7. To add fractions with __?__ denominators, first write equivalent fractions so that both fractions have the same denominator. (Page 300)

> denominator
> equivalent
> fraction
> lowest terms
> mixed number
> numerator
> unlike

Part 2: SKILLS

Write the fractions that tell what parts are blue. (Pages 270–271)

8.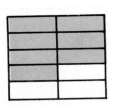

9.

10.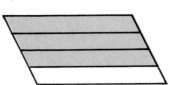

11.

Complete. (Pages 274–275)

12. $\frac{1}{2}$ of 6 = __?__

13. $\frac{1}{5}$ of 15 = __?__

14. $\frac{3}{4}$ of 8 = __?__

15. $\frac{5}{6}$ of 12 = __?__

(Pages 276–279)

16. $\frac{3}{5} = \frac{2 \times 3}{2 \times 5} = \frac{?}{10}$

17. $\frac{3}{4} = \frac{3 \times 3}{3 \times 4} = \frac{?}{?}$

18. $\frac{3}{7} = \frac{? \times 3}{? \times 7} = \frac{?}{21}$

Write > or <. (Pages 280–281)

19. $\frac{3}{6}$ ⬤ $\frac{5}{6}$ **20.** $\frac{1}{2}$ ⬤ $\frac{3}{8}$

Complete. (Pages 282–283)

21. $\frac{12}{16} = \frac{?}{4}$ **22.** $\frac{10}{25} = \frac{?}{5}$

Write each fraction as a whole number or as a mixed number. (Pages 290–291)

23. $\frac{21}{3}$ **24.** $\frac{11}{3}$ **25.** $\frac{32}{8}$ **26.** $\frac{16}{3}$

Add. (Pages 292–293)

27. $\frac{1}{4} + \frac{2}{4} = \underline{\ ?\ }$ **28.** $\frac{3}{8} + \frac{4}{8} = \underline{\ ?\ }$ **29.** $\frac{5}{8} + \frac{2}{8} = \underline{\ ?\ }$ **30.** $\frac{8}{16} + \frac{5}{16} = \underline{\ ?\ }$

Subtract. Write the answers in lowest terms. (Pages 296–297)

31. $\frac{5}{8} - \frac{2}{8} = \underline{\ ?\ }$ **32.** $\frac{4}{5} - \frac{1}{5} = \underline{\ ?\ }$ **33.** $\frac{8}{10} - \frac{3}{10} = \underline{\ ?\ }$ **34.** $\frac{6}{6} - \frac{3}{6} = \underline{\ ?\ }$

Add or subtract. Write the answers in lowest terms. (Pages 298–299)

35. $2\frac{2}{8}$
$+3\frac{4}{8}$

36. $3\frac{3}{9}$
$+4\frac{5}{9}$

37. $7\frac{5}{6}$
$-2\frac{3}{6}$

38. $9\frac{6}{10}$
$-\ \ \frac{4}{10}$

Add or subtract. (Pages 300–303)

39. $\frac{2}{3}$
$+\frac{1}{9}$

40. $\frac{2}{4}$
$+\frac{3}{8}$

41. $\frac{3}{5}$
$-\frac{1}{4}$

42. $\frac{9}{10}$
$-\frac{3}{5}$

Part 3: *PROBLEM SOLVING* • *APPLICATIONS*

Choose the best estimate. Choose **a, b,** or **c.** (Pages 304–305)

43. John rode his horse $12\frac{3}{5}$ miles on Monday, and $6\frac{1}{5}$ miles on Tuesday. How many miles did he ride in all?

a. $13 + 6$ **b.** $13 + 7$ **c.** $12 + 7$

44. Anna has $3\frac{3}{4}$ bags of marbles. She gives $1\frac{1}{3}$ bags to Mary. How many bags does she have left?

a. 2   **b.** 3   **c.** 4

Fractions and Mixed Numbers • **307**

CHAPTER TEST

Write the fractions.

1.

What part is blue?

2.

3. 4 blue marbles
7 red marbles

What part is red?

4. 3 black cats
5 white cats

What part is black?

Complete

5. $\frac{1}{2}$ of 12 = _?_   **6.** $\frac{3}{5}$ of 10 = _?_   **7.** $\frac{3}{5} = \frac{?}{15}$ **8.** $\frac{2}{3} = \frac{?}{9}$

Use > ● < to compare the fractions.

9. $\frac{2}{6}$ ● $\frac{1}{2}$ **10.** $\frac{3}{6}$ ● $\frac{2}{3}$

Write each fraction as a whole number or as a mixed number.

11. $\frac{21}{7}$ = _?_   **12.** $\frac{17}{4}$ = _?_

Add.

13. $\frac{2}{6} + \frac{3}{6}$ = _?_   **14.** $\begin{array}{r} \frac{5}{11} \\ + \frac{4}{11} \\ \hline \end{array}$

Subtract.

15. $\frac{7}{8} - \frac{4}{8}$ = _?_   **16.** $\begin{array}{r} \frac{15}{18} \\ - \frac{7}{18} \\ \hline \end{array}$

Add or subtract. Write the answers as whole numbers or as mixed numbers.

17. $\begin{array}{r} \frac{7}{10} \\ + \frac{3}{10} \\ \hline \end{array}$ **18.** $\begin{array}{r} \frac{29}{18} \\ - \frac{6}{18} \\ \hline \end{array}$ **19.** $\frac{9}{11} + \frac{8}{11}$ = _?_   **20.** $\frac{4}{7} + \frac{5}{7}$ = _?_

Add or subtract. Write the answers in lowest terms.

21. $\begin{array}{r} \frac{1}{5} \\ + \frac{3}{10} \\ \hline \end{array}$ **22.** $\begin{array}{r} \frac{6}{8} \\ - \frac{1}{2} \\ \hline \end{array}$ **23.** $\begin{array}{r} \frac{5}{6} \\ - \frac{1}{12} \\ \hline \end{array}$

Choose the best estimate. Choose **a, b,** or **c.**

24. Amy is a seamstress. She used $6\frac{5}{8}$ yards of ribbon to trim a dress. She used $2\frac{3}{4}$ yards of ribbon to trim a hat. How much more ribbon did she use to trim the dress than the hat?

a. 6 − 3   **b.** 7 − 3   **c.** 6 − 2

25. Jeremy is an apprentice carpenter. He cut wood for $3\frac{3}{4}$ hours in the morning. He spent $1\frac{1}{2}$ hours sanding the wood in the afternoon. How much longer did it take him to cut the wood than to sand the wood?

a. 1   **b.** 2   **c.** 3

ENRICHMENT

Probability as a Fraction

You can use a fraction to predict the results of an experiment.

$\frac{1}{2}$ of this spinner is blue.

$\frac{1}{4}$ of this spinner is yellow.

$\frac{1}{4}$ of this spinner is red.

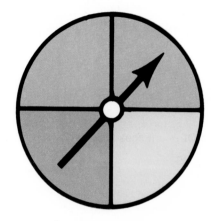

Since $\frac{1}{2}$ of the spinner is blue, the **probability**, or chance, that the pointer will stop on blue is $\frac{1}{2}$. Since $\frac{1}{4}$ of the spinner is red, the probability that the pointer will stop on red is $\frac{1}{4}$.

What is the probability that the pointer will stop on yellow?

EXERCISES • Use this spinner. Find the probability that the pointer will stop on

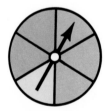

1. red.   **2.** blue.   **3.** yellow.

Use the dish of marbles. If you pick a marble without looking, what is the probability of picking a

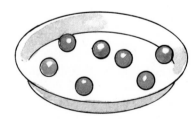

4. blue marble?   **5.** red marble?

6. green marble?

7. Find a dish and use the same color marbles as above. Without looking, pick a marble. Record the color and replace the marble. Do this 70 times. Compare your results with your answers for Exercises 4–6.

ADDITIONAL PRACTICE

SKILLS

Complete. (Pages 274–275, 278–279)

1. $\frac{1}{3}$ of $18 = $ ___?___ **2.** $\frac{2}{5}$ of $20 = $ ___?___ **3.** $\frac{3}{4}$ of $28 = $ ___?___ **4.** $\frac{5}{8}$ of $32 = $ ___?___

5. $\frac{2}{5} = \frac{3 \times 2}{3 \times 5} = \frac{?}{15}$ **6.** $\frac{1}{8} = \frac{4 \times 1}{4 \times 8} = \frac{?}{?}$ **7.** $\frac{3}{7} = \frac{? \times 3}{? \times 7} = \frac{15}{35}$ **8.** $\frac{4}{9} = \frac{? \times 4}{? \times 9} = \frac{24}{?}$

Write $>$ or $<$. (Pages 280–281)

9. $\frac{3}{5}$ ⬤ $\frac{2}{5}$ **10.** $\frac{1}{3}$ ⬤ $\frac{4}{9}$ **11.** $\frac{5}{6}$ ⬤ $\frac{3}{4}$ **12.** $\frac{7}{8}$ ⬤ $\frac{9}{10}$

Complete. (Pages 282–283)

13. $\frac{9}{12} = \frac{9 \div 3}{12 \div 3} = \frac{?}{4}$ **14.** $\frac{25}{45} = \frac{25 \div ?}{45 \div ?} = \frac{5}{9}$ **15.** $\frac{36}{63} = \frac{36 \div ?}{63 \div ?} = \frac{?}{7}$

Write each fraction as a whole number or as a mixed number.
(Pages 290–291)

16. $\frac{9}{5}$ **17.** $\frac{19}{8}$ **18.** $\frac{24}{4}$ **19.** $\frac{13}{3}$ **20.** $\frac{22}{7}$

Add or subtract. (Pages 292–303)

21. $\frac{3}{7} + \frac{1}{7} = $ ___?___ **22.** $\frac{1}{2} + \frac{1}{8} = $ ___?___ **23.** $\frac{1}{3} + \frac{2}{9} = $ ___?___

24. $\frac{5}{8} - \frac{2}{8} = $ ___?___ **25.** $\frac{8}{9} - \frac{2}{3} = $ ___?___ **26.** $\frac{5}{8} + \frac{6}{8} = $ ___?___

27. $\begin{array}{r} 4\frac{1}{6} \\ +2\frac{4}{6} \\ \hline \end{array}$ **28.** $\begin{array}{r} \frac{3}{10} \\ +\frac{3}{5} \\ \hline \end{array}$ **29.** $\begin{array}{r} 7\frac{6}{7} \\ -5\frac{1}{7} \\ \hline \end{array}$ **30.** $\begin{array}{r} \frac{4}{6} \\ -\frac{3}{8} \\ \hline \end{array}$ **31.** $\begin{array}{r} \frac{11}{12} \\ -\frac{3}{5} \\ \hline \end{array}$

PROBLEM SOLVING • APPLICATIONS

Choose the best estimate. Choose **a**, **b**, or **c**. (Pages 304–305)

32. Abigail spends $1\frac{1}{2}$ hours ironing in the morning and $\frac{3}{4}$ hour ironing in the afternoon. How many hours does she spend ironing in all?

    a. $2 + 1$ **b.** $1 + 1$ **c.** $3 + 2$

33. Matthew walks $2\frac{6}{10}$ miles to town. Then he walks $1\frac{4}{10}$ miles more. How many miles does he walk in all?

    a. 2 **b.** 4 **c.** 3

COMMON ERRORS

Each of these problems contains a common error.

a. Find the correct answer.

b. Find the error.

1. Measure to the nearest centimeter.

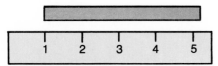

Length: **5 cm**

2. Find the area.

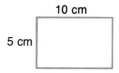

10 cm

5 cm

Area $= 5 + 10 + 5 + 10 = $ **30 cm**

3. Find the volume.

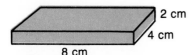

2 cm

4 cm

8 cm

Volume $= 8 + 4 + 2 = $ **14 cm**

4. Write the time.

It is **5:10.**

5. 300 cm $= \underline{}$ m

100 cm $= 1$ m

$300 \times 100 = $ **30,000 m**

6. 4 qt $= \underline{}$ pt

2 pt $= 1$ qt

$4 \div 2 = $ **2 pt**

7. Write the fraction that tells what part is blue.

$\dfrac{1}{3}$

8. Complete.

$\dfrac{3}{4}$ of 24 $= \underline{}$

$\dfrac{3}{4}$ of 24 $=$ **6**

9. Write the mixed number that tells how much is blue.

$\dfrac{11}{12}$

10. Write $>$ or $<$.

$\dfrac{2}{3} \bullet \dfrac{5}{12}$

$\dfrac{2}{3} < \dfrac{5}{12}$

11.
$$\begin{array}{r} \frac{2}{3} \\ +\frac{1}{3} \\ \hline \frac{3}{6} \end{array}$$

12.
$$\begin{array}{r} 2\frac{1}{5} \\ +4\frac{2}{5} \\ \hline 6\frac{3}{10} \end{array}$$

13.
$$\begin{array}{r} \frac{2}{5} = \frac{4 \times 2}{4 \times 5} = \frac{8}{20} \\ -\frac{1}{4} = \frac{4 \times 1}{4 \times 4} = \frac{4}{16} \\ \hline \frac{4}{4}, \text{ or } 1 \end{array}$$

CUMULATIVE REVIEW

Chapters 1 through 9

Choose the correct answers.

1. What is 706 rounded to the nearest ten?

A. 700   **B.** 705
C. 710   **D.** not here

2. $878 + 7 + 1,614 = \underline{\quad ? \quad}$

A. 2,499   **B.** 2,507
C. 2,599   **D.** not here

3. $6,874$
$-4,985$

A. 1,881   **B.** 1,889
C. 1,989   **D.** not here

4. $8,000$
$-6,432$

A. 2,672   **B.** 1,578
C. 1,468   **D.** not here

5. $12 \times 3 =$
$(6 \times \underline{\quad ? \quad}) \times 3$

A. 3   **B.** 4
C. 2   **D.** not here

6. $56 \div \underline{\quad ? \quad} = 7$

A. 6   **B.** 7
C. 8   **D.** not here

7. 846
$\times \quad 6$

A. 5,076   **B.** 5,166
C. 5,176   **D.** not here

8. $4,007$
$\times \quad 9$

A. 36,068   **B.** 36,003
C. 36,963   **D.** not here

9. $59 \div 7 = \underline{\quad ? \quad}$

A. 7 r9   **B.** 8 r3
C. 8 r4   **D.** not here

10. Choose the information you need to solve the problem. Then solve the problem.

Mai Lai bought a flower for each of her friends. Each flower costs the same amount. She spent $3.00 in all. How much did each flower cost?

A. She bought 4 vases; $0.75
B. She had 6 friends; $0.50
C. She spent $2.00; $5.00
D. She received change; $2.00

11. Use the schedule to answer the question.

Leaves Miami	Arrives Atlanta
8:40 A.M.	11:20 A.M.
9:30 A.M.	12:10 P.M.
1:40 P.M.	3:20 P.M.

Walter needs to leave Miami after 9:00 A.M. but before 1:30 P.M. What time will he arrive in Atlanta?

A. 3:20 P.M.   **B.** 11:20 A.M.
C. 1:40 P.M.   **D.** 12:10 P.M.

12. $6\overline{)278}$

A. 46 r2
B. 47 r1
C. 45 r2
D. not here

13. $4\overline{)7,468}$

A. 1,483 r3
B. 1,493 r3
C. 1,583 r3
D. not here

14. 6 m = _?_ cm

A. 60
B. 6,000
C. 600
D. not here

---

15. Choose the correct measure for a glass of milk.

A. 150 L
B. 150 g
C. 150 ml
D. not here

16. Find the area.

3 cm
9 cm

A. 27 sq cm
B. 24 sq cm
C. 12 sq cm
D. not here

17. Find the volume.

2 cm   2 cm
2 cm

A. 11 cubic cm
B. 4 cubic cm
C. 8 cubic cm
D. not here

---

18. Choose the time for fifteen minutes to ten.

A. 9:45
B. 10:15
C. 9:15
D. not here

19. $\frac{2}{3}$ of 6 = _?_

A. 2
B. 5
C. 4
D. not here

20. $\frac{2}{8}$ ● $\frac{1}{2}$

A. =
B. <
C. >
D. not here

---

21. $\frac{4}{5} = \frac{?}{15}$

A. 3   B. 7

C. 12   D. not here

22. $\frac{5}{12}$ $+ \frac{2}{12}$

A. $\frac{7}{12}$ B. $\frac{3}{12}$

C. $\frac{7}{24}$ D. not here

23. $\frac{8}{7} + \frac{9}{7} =$ _?_

A. $2\frac{2}{7}$ B. $2\frac{3}{7}$

C. $2\frac{4}{7}$ D. not here

---

24. Annette is reading a 328 page book. She read 56 pages on Friday and 75 pages on Saturday. How many pages does she have left to read?

A. 272   B. 253
C. 197   D. 131

25. Alex spent $3\frac{1}{2}$ hours building a model and $2\frac{1}{4}$ hours reading a book. How many hours did he spend in all? Estimate your answer.

A. 6   B. 5
C. 4   D. 7

Mixed Practice • Choose the correct answers.

1. 9
    ×4

    A. 35   **B.** 36
    C. 32   **D.** not here

2. 23
    × 2

    A. 46   **B.** 41
    C. 45   **D.** not here

3. $0.17
    ×   4

    A. $0.64   **B.** $0.61
    C. $0.68   **D.** not here

4. 316
    ×   3

    A. 933   **B.** 938
    C. 949   **D.** not here

5. $4.08
    ×   6

    A. $24.48   **B.** $24.08
    C. $24.56   **D.** not here

6. 3,460
    +18,972

    A. 22,332   **B.** 22,432
    C. 21,432   **D.** not here

7. 7,618
    +38,948

    A. 46,556   **B.** 45,566
    C. 46,566   **D.** not here

8. Estimate the sum.

    87
    +32

    A. 110   **B.** 120
    C. 130   **D.** not here

9. Estimate the sum.

    109
    +274

    A. 400   **B.** 300
    C. 350   **D.** not here

10. Manuel has 168 tulip bulbs to plant in his flower garden. He planted 37 on Monday and 52 on Tuesday. How many more does he have to plant?

    A. 79   **B.** 78
    C. 91   **D.** not here

11. Manuel planted the tulip bulbs in rows of 26 bulbs. He planted 7 rows. How many tulip bulbs did he plant in all?

    A. 146   **B.** 142
    C. 172   **D.** not here

Multiplying by Two-Digit Numbers

Mrs. Tucker owns Tucker's Nursery. She uses small plastic tags to label and price each plant. She orders 24 boxes of tags. There are 168 tags in each box.

● How many tags is this in all?

Mrs. Tucker sells mulch in 30-pound bags. She sold 13 bags on Tuesday, 5 bags on Thursday, and 9 bags on Friday.

● How many pounds of mulch was this in all?

Multiplying by 10 • Mental Math

Look for a pattern.

$$10 \times 3 = 30$$
$$10 \times 46 = 460$$
$$10 \times 785 = 7{,}850$$

	3	46	785
	$\times 10$	$\times 10$	$\times\ \ 10$
	30	460	7,850

The blue digits in the product are the same as the blue digits in the factor.
There is always a 0 in the ones place of the product.

Mrs. Tucker buys plants in flats. She buys 42 flats. Each flat holds 10 plants.

● How many plants are there in all?

Think | You know how many plants there are in 1 flat. Multiply to find how many there are in 42 flats.

$$10 \times 42 = ?$$

Step 1
Write a 0 in the ones place.

42
$\times 10$
———
0

Step 2
Multiply by the 1.

42
$\times 10$
———
420 ◀ **There are 420 plants.**

PRACTICE • Multiply.

1. 38 $\times 10$	**2.** 6 $\times 10$	**3.** 57 $\times 10$	**4.** 92 $\times 10$	**5.** 76 $\times 10$	**6.** 40 $\times 10$
7. 124 $\times\ 10$	**8.** 415 $\times\ 10$	**9.** 241 $\times\ 10$	**10.** 453 $\times\ 10$	**11.** 619 $\times\ 10$	**12.** 411 $\times\ 10$

EXERCISES • Multiply.

13. 59 $\times 10$	**14.** 63 $\times 10$	**15.** 89 $\times 10$	**16.** 7 $\times 10$	**17.** 45 $\times 10$	**18.** 32 $\times 10$
19. 27 $\times 10$	**20.** 48 $\times 10$	**21.** 73 $\times 10$	**22.** 60 $\times 10$	**23.** 19 $\times 10$	**24.** 4 $\times 10$

25. 168 × 10	**26.** 405 × 10	**27.** 752 × 10	**28.** 800 × 10	**29.** 537 × 10	**30.** 328 × 10
31. 732 × 10	**32.** 176 × 10	**33.** 219 × 10	**34.** 454 × 10	**35.** 998 × 10	**36.** 392 × 10
37. 530 × 10	**38.** 813 × 10	**39.** 409 × 10	**40.** 518 × 10	**41.** 601 × 10	**42.** 300 × 10

43. $10 \times 87 =$ __?__   **44.** $10 \times 9 =$ __?__   **45.** $10 \times 44 =$ __?__

46. $10 \times 240 =$ __?__   **47.** $10 \times 313 =$ __?__   **48.** $10 \times 600 =$ __?__

⋆**49.** $100 \times 537 =$ __?__   ⋆**50.** $100 \times 92 =$ __?__   ⋆**51.** $100 \times 637 =$ __?__

PROBLEM SOLVING • APPLICATIONS   CHOOSE   • mental math   • pencil and paper   • calculator   SOLVE

52. Mrs. Tucker asks her son, Tim, to water the rose bushes. There are 37 rows of bushes. Each row has 10 bushes. How many bushes will he water?

53. Mrs. Tucker uses clay pots for starting new plants. She orders 45 boxes of pots. Each box holds 10 pots. How many pots does she order?

54. Mr. Davis is a builder. He needs plants to landscape a new apartment building. He buys 116 plants one week and 74 more plants the next week. How many plants does he buy in all?

⋆**55.** Mrs. Tucker owns 12 garden hoses. Each hose is 100 feet long. She connects all the hoses. About how far will they reach?

Multiplying by Tens

Old railroad ties are often used around flower beds and trees. Mrs. Tucker orders a load of 30 railroad ties. Each tie weighs about 128 pounds.

● How much will the load of railroad ties weigh?

Think You know the weight of one tie. Multiply to find the weight of 30 ties.

$$30 \times 128 = ?$$

Step 1
Write 0 in the ones place.

$$
\begin{array}{r}
128 \\
\times\ 30 \\
\hline
0
\end{array}
$$

Step 2
Multiply by the 3.

$$
\begin{array}{r}
\overset{2}{1}28 \\
\times\ \ 30 \\
\hline
3{,}840
\end{array}
$$

The load of railroad ties weighs about **3,840 pounds**.

PRACTICE • Multiply.

1. 17 ×20	2. 43 ×20	3. 70 ×40	4. 583 × 20	5. 189 × 60	6. 245 × 30
7. 126 × 30	8. 84 ×20	9. 75 ×40	10. 114 × 70	11. 289 × 30	12. 724 × 50

EXERCISES • Multiply.

13. 7 ×90	14. 2 ×30	15. 53 ×20	16. 38 ×40	17. 16 ×20	18. 27 ×80
19. 60 ×50	20. 71 ×40	21. 49 ×30	22. 66 ×40	23. 50 ×90	24. 72 ×50
25. 324 × 10	26. 156 × 20	27. 310 × 70	28. 207 × 50	29. 621 × 10	30. 538 × 20

31. 409	32. 274	33. 382	34. 903	35. 320	36. 756
× 60	× 40	× 10	× 80	× 90	× 50

37. 482	38. 678	39. 423	40. 951	41. 145	42. 658
× 30	× 50	× 80	× 40	× 30	× 70

43. 50 × 130 = ___?___   **44.** 70 × 245 = ___?___   **45.** 20 × 800 = ___?___

Mental Math   Multiply each number by 10.

46. 87   **47.** 46   **48.** 23   **49.** 91   **50.** 64   **51.** 57

52. 518   **53.** 364   **54.** 273   **55.** 821   **56.** 436   **57.** 615

PROBLEM SOLVING • APPLICATIONS

58. Mulch for planters can be bought in 30-pound bags. Mrs. Tucker has 289 bags. How much do the bags weigh in all?

59. Aluminum edging for flower beds can be bought in sections that are 20 feet long. Mrs. Tucker has 319 of these sections. How many feet of edging does she have?

60. Tucker's nursery had a sale last week on rose bushes. Here are the number of bushes sold each day: Monday–13; Tuesday–17; Wednesday–20; Thursday–11; Friday–15. Make a bar graph to show this information.

61. A customer bought a plant for $19.57. He paid with a 20-dollar bill. What 6 coins did he receive as change?

THINKER'S CORNER

One of the greenhouses has some tables that hold small potted plants. Some of the tables have 3 legs and some have 4 legs. There are 31 table legs in all.

How many tables have 3 legs? How many have 4 legs? (Hint: More than one answer is possible.)

Multiplying Two-Digit Numbers

Mr. Martinez buys 36 trays of grass plugs from
Mrs. Tucker's nursery. There are 32 grass
plugs in each tray.

● **Estimate** how many plugs there
are in 36 trays.

> **Think**   There are 36 groups of 32.

$$36 \times 32 = ?$$

Round 32 to 30.	$32 \longrightarrow 30$
Round 36 to 40.	$\times 36 \longrightarrow \times 40$
Multiply.	$1{,}200$ ◀ **Estimate**

● Find the exact product.
Compare with the estimate.

Step 1
Think of 36 as 30 + 6.
Multiply by 6.

```
  1
  3 2
× 3 6
─────
  1 9 2 ← 6 × 32
```

Step 2
Multiply by 30.

```
  1
  3 2
× 3 6
─────
  1 9 2
  9 6 0 ← 30 × 32
```

Step 3
Add the products.

```
  1
  3 2
× 3 6
─────
  1 9 2
  9 6 0
─────
1,1 5 2
```

The estimate is 1,200. So **1,152 plugs** is a reasonable answer.

Ⓔ PRACTICE • Estimate each product. Find the exact product. Compare.

1. 73	2. 29	3. 58	4. 86	5. 78	6. 67
×48	×18	×47	×54	×42	×33

7. 37	8. 21	9. 89	10. 39	11. 94	12. 49
×42	×76	×61	×19	×37	×43

Ⓔ EXERCISES • Estimate each product. Find the exact product. Compare.

13. 82	14. 64	15. 73	16. 46	17. 91	18. 83
×47	×28	×39	×71	×17	×24

19. 25	20. 57	21. 28	22. 39	23. 94	24. 43
×94	×63	×46	×82	×57	×33

25. 85	26. 47	27. 29	28. 17	29. 48	30. 77
×36	×73	×60	×92	×50	×70

31. 63	32. 94	33. 82	34. 29	35. 71	36. 50
×60	×30	×25	×48	×39	×75

37. $71 \times 42 =$ __?__   **38.** $18 \times 55 =$ __?__   **39.** $60 \times 34 =$ __?__

40. $35 \times 23 =$ __?__   **41.** $54 \times 49 =$ __?__   **42.** $27 \times 36 =$ __?__

PROBLEM SOLVING • APPLICATIONS

The Watertown Garden Club has decided to landscape 18 parks in the city. Mrs. Tucker's nursery will supply the needed plants and materials.

43. The wild flower garden in each park will need 36 yards of aluminum edging. How many yards are needed for all the parks?

44. The club orders 8 large trees, 32 bushes, and 38 azalea plants for each park. How many plants do they order in all?

CALCULATOR • Guess and Check

Find the missing digits.

Think   The missing digit in ▢7 is one of the digits 1–9.

$$\begin{array}{r} ▢\,7 \\ \times\ 3\ 9 \\ \hline 2\,2\ ▢\ ▢ \end{array}$$

Guesses: Try 1. ① ⑦ ✕ ③ ⑨ = (663) ← Much too small.

Try 4. ④ ⑦ ✕ ③ ⑨ = (1833) ← Close

Try 5. ⑤ ⑦ ✕ ③ ⑨ = (2223) ← That's it!

$57 \times 39 = 2,223$

EXERCISES • Find the missing digits.

1. ▢9	2. ▢7	3. 4 6	4. 9 3
× 5 8	× 4 6	× ▢8	× ▢5
5,1 ▢▢	1,2 ▢▢	1,2 ▢▢	2,3 ▢▢

PROBLEM SOLVING • STRATEGIES

Guess and Check

Sometimes you can solve a problem by finding two clues.

Example

Mr. Davis planted rows of bushes in front of his house. The number of rows times the number of bushes in each row is 24. The difference between the number of rows and the number of bushes in each row is 5.

● How many rows of bushes did Mr. Davis plant?
● How many bushes did he plant in each row?

Think   Clue 1: **Number of rows × number of bushes in each row = 24**
Clue 2: **Number of rows − number of bushes in each row = 5**

Use Clue 1 for the first guess.
Use Clue 2 to check the guess.

Guess 1: Use Clue 1

$$\begin{array}{r} \text{Number of rows} \quad 12 \\ \text{Number of plants} \quad \underline{\times\ 2} \\ 24 \end{array}$$

Check: Use Clue 2

Does $12 - 2 = 5$? No

◀ Since $12 - 2 = 10$, this is too large.

Guess 2: Use Clue 1

$$\begin{array}{r} \text{Number of rows} \quad 6 \\ \text{Number of bushes} \quad \underline{\times 4} \\ 24 \end{array}$$

Check: Use Clue 2

Does $6 - 4 = 5$? No

◀ Since $6 - 4 = 2$, this is too small.

Guess 3: Use Clue 1

$$\begin{array}{r} \text{Number of rows} \quad 8 \\ \text{Number of bushes} \quad \underline{\times 3} \\ 24 \end{array}$$

Check: Use Clue 2

Does $8 - 3 = 5$? Yes!

◀ The third guess is correct.

Mr. Davis planted **8 rows of bushes.**
He planted **3 bushes in each row.**

PROBLEMS • Use the two clues to select the correct choice.

1. Product of two numbers: 56
   Sum of the numbers: 15

   a. 14, 4   **b.** 9, 6   **c.** 8, 7

2. Product of two numbers: 12
   Difference between the numbers: 1

   a. 6, 5   **b.** 4, 3   **c.** 6, 2

3. Sum of two numbers: 14
   Product of the numbers: 48

   a. 8, 6   **b.** 7, 7   **c.** 16, 3

4. Sum of two numbers: 17
   Difference between the numbers: 1

   a. 10, 7   **b.** 9, 8   **c.** 10, 9

5. Mrs. Tucker has 47 flowers for sale. There are 15 more roses than tulips. How many roses and how many tulips does she have?

   a. 32 roses and 15 tulips

   b. 27 roses and 20 tulips

   c. 31 roses and 16 tulips

6. Steve buys a sprinkler and a rake for $9.00. The rake costs two times as much as the sprinkler. How much does the rake and the sprinkler cost?

   a. the rake costs $6.00
   the sprinkler costs $3.00

   b. the rake costs $5.00
   the sprinkler costs $4.00

   c. the rake costs $8.00
   the sprinkler costs $4.00

7. Marcia worked 7 hours in her garden. She worked 1 more hour in the morning than in the afternoon. How long did she work in the morning and in the afternoon?

   a. 7 hours in the morning
   1 hour in the afternoon

   b. 6 hours in the morning
   1 hour in the afternoon

   c. 4 hours in the morning
   3 hours in the afternoon

Solve.

8. Angela is putting 45 tomato plants on shelves in the nursery. The difference between the number of shelves and the number of plants on each shelf is 4. How many shelves did Angela use, and how many plants did she put on each shelf?

First find the two clues.

---

9. There are 25 workers at the Watertown Garden Club Fair. There are 4 times as many men working as women. How many men and women are working at the fair?

10. Juliet bought two plants at the fair for $20.00. One of the plants cost $10.00 more than the other plant. How much did each plant cost?

Multiplying by Two-Digit Numbers • **323**

MID-CHAPTER REVIEW

Multiply. (Pages 316–317)

1. 34 ×10	2. 692 × 10	3. 79 ×10	4. 57 ×10	5. 845 × 10

(Pages 318–319)

6. 48 ×20	7. 36 ×20	8. 63 ×70	9. 19 ×50	10. 98 ×60

Estimate each product. Find the exact product. Compare.

(Pages 320–321)

11. 79 ×32	12. 39 ×31	13. 66 ×41	14. 84 ×15	15. 25 ×56
16. 63 ×38	17. 22 ×26	18. 38 ×50	19. 61 ×29	20. 43 ×40

Solve.

Use the two clues to select the correct choice.

21. Product of two numbers: 72
    Sum of the numbers: 17
    (Pages 322–323)
    a. 9,8   b. 12,6   c. 10,7

22. Michael has two large plants. One of the plants is 3 times as tall as the other plant. The sum of the heights is 8 feet. How tall are both of the plants?
    (Pages 322–323)

MAINTENANCE • MIXED PRACTICE

In the number 3,457, what number is in the

1. hundreds place?   2. tens place?   3. thousands place?

Use > or < to compare the numbers.

4. 44 ● 41   5. 382 ● 394   6. 515 ● 212   7. 5,120 ● 6,420

Write in order from least to greatest.

8. 5,305; 5,350; 5,310; 5,301   9. 2,115; 528; 56; 398

10. Ted has a box for his camera. The box is 5 inches high, 6 inches wide, and 8 inches long. What is the volume?

11. Roberto makes an area rug for his model home. The rug is 6 inches long, and 5 inches wide. What is the area of the rug?

Mail-Order Buying

This is a page from a mail-order catalog.

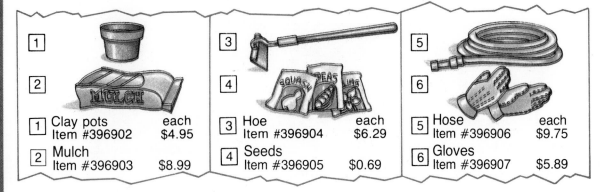

1	Clay pots	each
1	Item #396902	$4.95
2	Mulch	
2	Item #396903	$8.99
3	Hoe	each
3	Item #396904	$6.29
4	Seeds	
4	Item #396905	$0.69
5	Hose	each
5	Item #396906	$9.75
6	Gloves	
6	Item #396907	$5.89

EXERCISES • Copy the order form shown below.

1. Use the catalog page to find the price of each item listed on the order form. Write the prices in the Price for Each column.

2. Multiply to find the total price for each item. Complete the Total Price column.

3. Add to find the Total Amount Enclosed. Write the sum at the bottom of the Total Price column.

Item Number	Quantity	Price for Each	Total Price
396903	6		
396905	15		
396906	6		
396907	7		
Total Amount Enclosed			

CALCULATOR • Use your calculator to check your Total Prices.

PROJECT   Make a blank order form. Write an order so that
a. each member of your family gets a pair of gloves.
b. each girl in your class gets a clay pot.
c. each boy in your class gets a package of seeds.

Multiplying Three-Digit Numbers

Mrs. Tucker uses small plastic tags to label and price each plant. She orders 24 boxes of tags. There are 168 tags in each box.

● How many tags will she receive?

Think   There are 24 groups of 168. Multiply.

$$24 \times 168 = ?$$

Step 1
Multiply by 4.

```
  2 3
  1 6 8
×   2 4
  6 7 2  ←— 4 × 168
```

Step 2
Multiply by 20.

```
  1 1
  2 3
  1 6 8
×   2 4
  6 7 2
3 3 6 0  ←— 20 × 168
```

Step 3
Add.

```
  1 1
  2 3
  1 6 8
×   2 4
  6 7 2
3 3 6 0
4,0 3 2  ←— 672 + 3,360
```

Mrs. Tucker will receive **4,032 plastic tags.**

More Examples

```
    201          7 5          2 4
  × 63          4 9 7         2 5
  -----       ×   1 8         5 4 9
    603        3 9 7 6      ×   5 6
  12060        4 9 7 0      3 2 9 4
  ------       -------     2 7 4 5 0
  12,663       8,9 4 6     3 0,7 4 4
```

PRACTICE • Multiply.

1. 107
   × 38

2. 436
   × 29

3. 238
   × 49

4. 395
   × 45

5. 627
   × 58

6. 459
   × 15

7. 345
   × 63

8. 792
   × 72

9. 655
   × 27

10. 209
    × 35

11. 784
    × 67

12. 514
    × 46

EXERCISES • Multiply.

13. 304 × 94	**14.** 273 × 28	**15.** 294 × 93	**16.** 493 × 43	**17.** 329 × 67	**18.** 429 × 84
19. 406 × 67	**20.** 639 × 28	**21.** 247 × 67	**22.** 539 × 47	**23.** 728 × 64	**24.** 426 × 53
25. 536 × 60	**26.** 294 × 57	**27.** 225 × 26	**28.** 146 × 70	**29.** 271 × 98	**30.** 465 × 29
31. 418 × 24	**32.** 397 × 52	**33.** 511 × 40	**34.** 287 × 48	**35.** 539 × 65	**36.** 892 × 38

37. 69 × 846 = ___?___   **38.** 82 × 846 = ___?___   **39.** 56 × 428 = ___?___

40. 46 × 375 = ___?___   ★**41.** 39 × 1,479 = ___?___   ★**42.** 95 × 2,968 = ___?___

PROBLEM SOLVING • APPLICATIONS

43. Some plants are fertilized with small fertilizer sticks. These sticks come in boxes of 24. Mrs. Tucker orders 212 boxes. How many sticks will she receive?

44. Potting soil can be bought in 15-pound bags. The nursery has 173 bags of potting soil. How many pounds of soil is this in all?

45. Mrs. Tucker sells about 115 plants each day. The average price for each plant is $8.50. How many plants are sold in 30 days?

46. Mrs. Tucker needs to mark off 2 new rows of plants. She will need 48 feet of string for each row. She has 120 feet of string. How much string will she have left?

THINKER'S CORNER

In a contest sponsored by the nursery, students sold packages of seeds. Tyrone sold four times as many as Kevin. Joseph sold twice as many as Tyrone. Joseph said that the number of packages he sold, rounded to the nearest 10, was 30.

Exactly how many packages did each boy sell?

Multiplying Money

A restaurant buys 24 ferns to hang in its dining rooms. Each fern costs $3.98.

● How much does the restaurant spend on ferns?

Think You know the cost of one fern.
Multiply to find the cost of 24 ferns.

24 × $3.98 = ?

Multiply amounts of money as if you were multiplying whole numbers. Remember to write the dollar sign and the cents point in the answer.

Think:	Write:
1 1	1 1
3 3	3 3
398	$3.98
× 24	× 24
1592	1592
7960	7960
9552	$95.52

The restaurant spends **$95.52** on ferns.

More Examples

56 × $7.73 = ?

Think:	Write:
3 1	3 1
4 1	4 1
773	$7.73
× 56	× 56
4638	4638
38650	38650
43288	$432.88

94 × $10.35 = ?

Think:	Write:
3 4	3 4
1 2	1 2
1035	$10.35
× 94	× 94
4140	4140
93150	93150
97290	$972.90

PRACTICE • Multiply.

1. $1.75
× 36

2. $3.42
× 14

3. $4.18
× 23

4. $8.42
× 31

5. $6.72
× 47

6. $8.95
× 12

7. $5.83
× 48

8. $5.79
× 24

9. $2.89
× 57

10. $7.04
× 63

11. $9.19
× 37

12. $4.83
× 27

EXERCISES • Multiply.

13. $1.89
× 34

14. $2.79
× 45

15. $6.92
× 71

16. $4.52
× 33

17. $3.76
× 53

18. $4.85
× 31

19. $7.29
× 54

20. $7.38
× 72

21. $8.04
× 52

22. $4.15
× 46

23. $3.68
× 92

24. $5.19
× 73

25. $6.82
× 19

26. $4.69
× 41

27. $7.83
× 68

28. $5.34
× 27

29. $3.95
× 57

30. $8.15
× 96

31. $2.48
× 55

32. $1.98
× 99

33. $4.09
× 76

34. $5.87
× 48

35. $6.06
× 37

36. $7.21
× 54

37. $4.93
× 69

38. $3.64
× 72

39. $1.49
× 78

40. $3.43
× 51

41. $7.08
× 42

42. $8.51
× 60

43. $15 \times \$2.65 = $ ___?___

44. $82 \times \$2.08 = $ ___?___

45. $69 \times \$3.17 = $ ___?___

46. $43 \times \$4.18 = $ ___?___

★ 47. $53 \times \$16.05 = $ ___?___

★ 48. $70 \times \$35.74 = $ ___?___

PROBLEM SOLVING • APPLICATIONS

49. The table shows that 27 tulips are sold on Friday. How much money is collected for tulips?

50. On Saturday, 64 marigolds are sold. How much money is collected for marigolds?

51. Tim sells one customer 14 geraniums and 18 daffodils. How much money does the customer spend?

Tucker's Nursery Price List	
Flower	Cost
Geranium	$2.49
Daffodil	$1.63
Marigold	$1.87
Tulip	$2.65

Write Your Own Problem

Use the table to write a story problem about buying flowers. Have the problem use multiplication and addition to find the answer.

Multiplying by Two-Digit Numbers • **329**

PROBLEM SOLVING • STRATEGIES

More Than One Step

Example

Keith buys 2 pairs of clippers at $4.35 each. He gives the clerk $10.00.

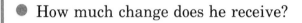

● How much change does he receive?

Think To find how much change Keith receives, you must first answer this question.

How much did the clippers cost?

This is the **hidden question** in the problem.

Step 1

Find the cost of
2 pairs of clippers.

$$\begin{array}{r} \$4.35 \\ \times\ \ \ 2 \\ \hline \$8.70 \end{array}$$

Step 2

Find how much change
Keith will receive.

$$\begin{array}{r} \$10.00 \\ -\ \ 8.70 \\ \hline \$\ 1.30 \end{array}$$

Keith will receive **$1.30** in change.

PROBLEMS • Answer the hidden question first.
Then solve the problem.

1. On Monday, the nursery had 73 ferns. Mrs. Tucker sold 40 ferns on Tuesday. She sold 31 ferns on Wednesday. How many ferns does she have left?

   Hidden question: How many ferns did Mrs. Tucker sell on Tuesday and Wednesday?

2. Mr. Jacob needs some new tools for gardening. He buys a spade for $2.69 and a hoe for $5.19. He gives the store owner $20.00. How much change does he receive?

   Hidden question: How much do the spade and hoe cost together?

3. John, Amy and Michael are each going to plant the same number of trees. There are 13 oak trees and 23 maple trees. How many trees will each person plant?

Hidden question: How many trees are there to be planted?

4. Jason has 6 cups of juice. He pours 2 cups of juice for Alice and 1 cup for himself. How much juice does he have left?

Hidden question: How much juice did John pour for Alice and himself?

Find the hidden question. Answer the hidden question first. Then solve.

5. Robert waters the rose bushes for the nursery each week. There are 15 rows of rose bushes in front of the nursery, and 37 rows of rose bushes behind the nursery. On Monday, Robert watered 33 rows. How many more rows of rose bushes does he have left to water?

6. Mrs. Tucker buys mulch in 30-pound bags. She sold 13 bags on Tuesday, 5 bags on Thursday, and 9 bags on Friday. How many pounds of mulch did Mrs. Tucker sell in all?

★ 7. Mark buys two pair of gloves for $5.75 each. Janet buys a rake for $6.75 and a sprinkler for $3.50. They each give the clerk $15.00. Who receives more change?

Write Your Own Problem

Write two story problems like Problem 2 on page 330. Have a hidden question in each problem.

Exchange problems with a friend. Find the hidden questions and solve the problems.

CHAPTER REVIEW

Part 1: VOCABULARY

For Exercises 1–7, choose the word from the box at the right that completes each statement.

estimate
hundreds
multiply
product
round
ones
tens

1. To find the answer that is close to the exact answer, you __?__. (Page 320)

2. To estimate the product, first you __?__ the numbers and then multiply. (Page 320)

3. The answer in a multiplication problem is called the __?__. (Page 316)

4. When you multiply by ten, there is always a zero in the __?__ place of the product. (Page 316)

5. To find the product, you __?__. (Page 316)

6. In the number 420, the 4 is in the __?__ place. (Page 320)

7. In the number 785, the 8 is in the __?__ place. (Page 320)

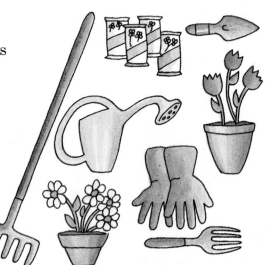

Part 2: SKILLS

Multiply. (Pages 316–319)

8. 48 ×10	9. 72 ×10	10. 36 ×10	11. 68 ×10	12. 25 ×10
13. 39 ×10	14. 129 × 10	15. 516 × 10	16. 171 × 10	17. 632 × 10
18. 81 70	19. 93 ×30	20. 49 ×30	21. 72 ×80	22. 272 × 40
23. 355 × 50	24. 473 × 80	25. 485 × 40	26. 239 × 70	27. 305 × 50

Estimate each product. Find the exact product. Compare. (Pages 320–321)

28. 77
  ×26

29. 93
  ×41

30. 52
  ×36

31. 84
  ×57

32. 38
  ×44

33. 18
  ×83

34. 24
  ×61

35. 32
  ×76

36. 29
  ×15

37. 62
  ×25

Multiply. (Pages 326–329)

38. 215
  × 34

39. 179
  × 62

40. 408
  × 51

41. 926
  × 45

42. 833
  × 79

43. 621
  × 52

44. 457
  × 29

45. 937
  × 14

46. 518
  × 73

47. 784
  × 39

48. $1.70
  × 69

49. $2.76
  × 25

50. $5.39
  × 48

51. $6.65
  × 87

52. $5.09
  × 64

Part 3: PROBLEM SOLVING • APPLICATIONS

Use the two clues to select the correct choice.

53. Product of two numbers: 64
Difference of the two numbers: 0
(Pages 322–323)

  a. 32, 2   **b.** 8, 8   **c.** 6, 6

54. There are 24 workers at the nursery. There are 2 times as many girls as there are boys. How many girls and boys work at the nursery? (Pages 322–323)

Answer the hidden question first.
Then solve the problem.

55. Mrs. Tucker had 397 plants. She sold 46 plants on Monday, and 184 plants on Tuesday. How many plants does she have left?

Hidden question: How many plants did she sell on Monday and Tuesday? (Pages 330–331)

56. Barbara buys a spade for $2.09 and a rake for $6.75. She has $10.00. How much change will she receive? (Pages 330–331)

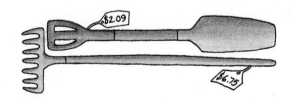

Multiplying by Two-Digit Numbers • **333**

CHAPTER TEST

Multiply.

1. 93 ×10	**2.** 19 ×10	**3.** 175 × 10	**4.** 508 × 10
5. 55 ×60	**6.** 60 ×30	**7.** 311 × 20	**8.** 952 × 50
9. 435 × 74	**10.** 307 × 48	**11.** 225 × 58	**12.** 397 × 95
13. $6.48 × 56	**14.** $6.94 × 85	**15.** $8.53 × 67	**16.** $7.30 × 78

Estimate each product. Find the exact product. Compare.

17. 47 ×56	**18.** 82 ×32	**19.** 57 ×91	**20.** 44 ×88

Solve.

Use the two clues to select the correct choice.

21. Product of two numbers: 20
Sum of the numbers: 9

   a. 5, 4   **b.** 10, 2   **c.** 6, 3

Answer the hidden question first.
Then solve the problem.

23. Angela buys 2 pairs of gloves for $1.59 each. She gives the clerk $5.00. How much change does she receive?

Hidden question: How much do the 2 pairs of gloves cost?

22. Patsy has 30 packages of seeds to plant. There are 4 times as many carrot seeds as there are radish seeds. How many packages of carrot seeds and radish seeds does Patsy have?

24. Steve wants to buy a rake for $3.25 and a hoe for $6.50. He has $10.00. Does he have enough money?

25. Mr. Davis needs 97 flowers. He buys 58 on Monday and 23 on Wednesday. How many more flowers does Mr. Davis need?

ENRICHMENT

The Lattice Method of Multiplying

You can use the **lattice method** of multiplying to help you solve multiplication problems.

Example **A** shows two **partial products,** 12 and 140.

In the lattice method, 2×6 is shown this way.

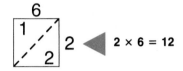

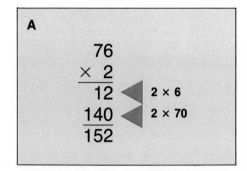

- To find 76×2, draw two squares, one for each digit in the numeral 76. The 2 is written at the right.

- Find 2×6 and 2×7. Write each product as shown. Then add along the diagonals. Compare the answers in Examples **A** and **B**.

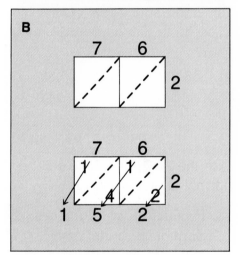

EXERCISES • Use the lattice method of multiplying.

1.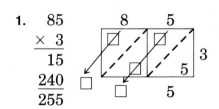

2.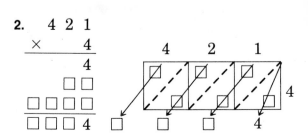

ADDITIONAL PRACTICE

SKILLS

Multiply. (Pages 316–319)

1. 63 ×10	**2.** 47 ×10	**3.** 526 × 10	**4.** 203 × 10	**5.** 135 × 10
6. 42 ×30	**7.** 78 ×20	**8.** 324 × 70	**9.** 276 × 50	**10.** 306 × 40

Estimate each product. Find the exact product. Compare. (Pages 320–321)

11. 67 ×16	**12.** 28 ×73	**13.** 34 ×27	**14.** 44 ×38	**15.** 81 ×34

Multiply. (Pages 326–329)

16. 215 × 43	**17.** 139 × 58	**18.** 306 × 31	**19.** 916 × 25	**20.** 830 × 74
21. $8.31 × 14	**22.** $5.83 × 47	**23.** $3.95 × 81	**24.** $7.40 × 69	**25.** $1.79 × 73

PROBLEM SOLVING • APPLICATIONS

Use the two clues to select the correct choice.

26. Product of two numbers: 24
Sum of the numbers: 11
(Pages 322–323)

   a. 12,2   **b.** 6,5   **c.** 8,3

Answer the hidden question first. Then solve the problem.

28. Stuart wants to buy a rake for $6.75 and a hoe for $5.18. He has $9.00. How much more money does he need?

   Hidden question: How much do the rake and the hoe cost together? (Pages 330–331)

27. The nursery has 350 trees. There are 4 times as many oak trees as there are maple trees. How many oak trees and maple trees does the nursery have?
(Pages 322–323)

29. Jake buys 2 clippers at $4.35 each. He has $10.00. How much change does he receive? (Pages 330–331)

30. There are 42 plants to be planted. Joan plants 24 plants in the morning and 16 plants in the afternoon. How many plants does she have left to plant?
(Pages 330–331)

PROBLEM SOLVING MAINTENANCE

Chapters 1 through 10

Solve.

1. Mrs. Amos had a place to put 34 rose bushes. She bought 16 red rose bushes and 9 yellow rose bushes. How many more rose bushes does she need to buy? (Page 16)

2. John planted a row of trees. He planted a dogwood directly in front of a maple. He planted an oak between the maple and a redbud tree. He planted a poplar tree between the oak and the redbud. Draw a picture to show the order of the trees. (Page 34)

3. There were 8 shelves of tulip bulbs at the nursery. Each shelf held 145 bulbs. How many bulbs were there in all? (Page 126)

4. Samuel spent $3.50 for 7 begonia plants. He received $1.50 change. How much did each begonia plant cost? (Page 174)

5. Jessica planted about 85 tulip bulbs. In the spring 67 bulbs came up and bloomed. About how many bulbs did not come up? (Page 204)

Tell what other information you need to solve Problem 6.

6. The tulip bulbs are shipped in a box 12 centimeters long and 8 centimeters high. What is the volume of the box? (Page 234)

Use the schedule to answer the question.

Hours of Flower Market		
Day	**Open**	**Close**
Monday	8:30 AM	5:00 PM
Tuesday	8:30 AM	6:00 PM
Wednesday	8:00 AM	4:30 PM
Thursday	8:00 AM	9:00 PM
Friday	7:30 AM	6:30 PM

7. Martin arrived at the nursery at 7:12 A.M. on Friday morning. How many minutes did he have to wait for the nursery to open? (Page 244)

8. Jack bought 64 feet of wood to put around his row of rose bushes. He used 18 feet for one side and 14 feet for another side. How much wood does he have left? (Page 260)

9. Elaine dug a $7\frac{1}{4}$ foot flower bed along one side of the fence, and an $8\frac{1}{2}$ foot one along the other side of the fence. About how many feet did she dig in all? Estimate your answer. (Page 304)

10. Julia bought two trees at the nursery for $20.00. One of the trees cost $8.00 more than the other. How much did each tree cost? (Page 322)

MAINTENANCE

Mixed Practice • Choose the correct answers.

1. $27 \div 3 = \underline{\ ?\ }$

A. 8   **B.** 9
C. 7   **D.** not here

2. $3\overline{)210}$

A. 70   **B.** 7
C. 80   **D.** not here

3. $3\overline{)3,000}$

A. 50   **B.** 600
C. 500   **D.** not here

4. $88 \div 4 = \underline{\ ?\ }$

A. 21   **B.** 24
C. 22   **D.** not here

5. $5\overline{)\$2.50}$

A. $0.05   **B.** $0.50
C. $5.00   **D.** not here

6. Round 156 to the nearest ten.

A. 150   **B.** 160
C. 200   **D.** not here

7. Round 195 to the nearest ten.

A. 200   **B.** 190
C. 150   **D.** not here

8.
$$\begin{array}{r} 24 \\ \times 15 \\ \hline \end{array}$$

A. 144   **B.** 350
C. 260   **D.** not here

9.
$$\begin{array}{r} 36 \\ \times 24 \\ \hline \end{array}$$

A. 861   **B.** 216
C. 864   **D.** not here

10. Dana put 164 wrenches on 8 shelves. How many wrenches did she put on each shelf? How many wrenches were left over?

   A. 20, 0 left over
   B. 21, 4 left over
   C. 22, 0 left over
   D. not here

11. Kay sold screwdrivers to 24 customers. Each customer bought a set of 8 screwdrivers. How many screwdrivers did Kay sell?

   A. 16
   B. 192
   C. 3
   D. not here

Dividing by Two-Digit Numbers

Susan is a warehouse supervisor. She fills an order for 195 flashlights on Monday and an order for 243 flashlights on Friday.

● How many flashlights was this in all?

Brad and Tom are checking an order of 564 calculators. The calculators are packed in cartons. Each carton holds 74 calculators.

● How many cartons are full?

● How many calculators are left over?

339

Dividing by Tens

You can use a basic fact to help you divide by tens.

$$\begin{array}{r} 7 \\ 1\overline{)7} \end{array} \qquad \begin{array}{r} 7 \\ 10\overline{)70} \end{array} \qquad \begin{array}{r} 6 \\ 3\overline{)18} \end{array} \qquad \begin{array}{r} 6 \\ 30\overline{)180} \end{array}$$

$$\begin{array}{r} 2 \\ 4\overline{)8} \end{array} \qquad \begin{array}{r} 2 \\ 40\overline{)80} \end{array} \qquad \begin{array}{r} 8 \\ 5\overline{)40} \end{array} \qquad \begin{array}{r} 8 \\ 50\overline{)400} \end{array}$$

Handy Mart received an order of 215 wrenches. Greg is sorting them into bins. Each bin holds 40 wrenches.

 How many bins does he fill?
How many wrenches are left over?

Think To separate 215 wrenches into groups of 40, divide.

$$215 \div 40 = ?$$

The remainder will show how many are left.

You can use a basic fact to find the quotient.

Step 1

Think: $\begin{array}{r} 5 \\ 4\overline{)21} \end{array}$

Try: $\begin{array}{r} 5 \\ 40\overline{)215} \end{array}$

Step 2
Multiply.

$$\begin{array}{r} 5 \\ 40\overline{)215} \\ 200 \end{array} \longrightarrow 5 \times 40$$

Step 3
Subtract.

$$\begin{array}{r} 5\,\text{r}15 \\ 40\overline{)215} \\ -200 \\ \hline 15 \end{array}$$
$\uparrow$ remainder

Check.

$$\begin{array}{r} 40 \\ \times\ 5 \\ \hline 200 \\ +\ 15 \\ \hline 215 \end{array}$$
$\longleftarrow$ divisor
$\longleftarrow$ quotient
$\longleftarrow$ remainder
$\longleftarrow$ dividend

Greg fills 5 **bins.** He has **15 wrenches** left over.

PRACTICE • Divide.

1. $10\overline{)90}$ 2. $30\overline{)60}$ 3. $40\overline{)240}$ 4. $80\overline{)480}$ 5. $60\overline{)300}$

6. $50\overline{)278}$ 7. $40\overline{)347}$ 8. $70\overline{)509}$ 9. $90\overline{)575}$ 10. $80\overline{)519}$

EXERCISES • Find the quotients.

11. $10\overline{)40}$ 12. $20\overline{)80}$ 13. $40\overline{)320}$ 14. $60\overline{)360}$ 15. $50\overline{)400}$

16. $60\overline{)475}$ 17. $20\overline{)105}$ 18. $80\overline{)267}$ 19. $90\overline{)210}$ 20. $30\overline{)214}$

21. $50\overline{)307}$ 22. $20\overline{)180}$ 23. $40\overline{)276}$ 24. $80\overline{)477}$ 25. $60\overline{)420}$

26. $40\overline{)240}$ 27. $50\overline{)450}$ 28. $70\overline{)576}$ 29. $70\overline{)319}$ 30. $80\overline{)495}$

31. $60\overline{)375}$ 32. $90\overline{)381}$ 33. $50\overline{)447}$ 34. $90\overline{)540}$ 35. $30\overline{)294}$

36. $60 \div 10 = \underline{\quad?\quad}$ 37. $240 \div 60 = \underline{\quad?\quad}$ 38. $177 \div 40 = \underline{\quad?\quad}$

39. $261 \div 30 = \underline{\quad?\quad}$ 40. $788 \div 90 = \underline{\quad?\quad}$ 41. $630 \div 70 = \underline{\quad?\quad}$

42. $392 \div 50 = \underline{\quad?\quad}$ 43. $399 \div 80 = \underline{\quad?\quad}$ 44. $190 \div 60 = \underline{\quad?\quad}$

★ 45. $6,400 \div 80 = \underline{\quad?\quad}$ ★ 46. $4,200 \div 70 = \underline{\quad?\quad}$

PROBLEM SOLVING • APPLICATIONS

Complete the table.

	Type of Wrench	Number of Wrenches	Number of Wrenches in a Bin	Number of Full Bins	Number of Wrenches Left Over
47.	Allen	245	50	?	?
48.	Adjustable	380	40	?	?
49.	Pipe	188	20	?	?

★ 50. The manager of Handy-Mart buys wrenches packaged in boxes of 20. In 1986, Tom sold 130 wrenches and Debbie sold 250 wrenches. How many boxes were sold in 1986?

Rounding Divisors Down

Debbie is unpacking a new shipment of flashlights. She unpacks 168 flashlights. Each shelf holds 32 flashlights.

● How many shelves does she fill? How many flashlights are left over?

Think You need to separate the 168 flashlights into groups of 32. Divide.

$$168 \div 32 = ?$$

The remainder will tell how many are left.

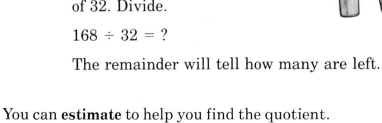

You can **estimate** to help you find the quotient.

Step 1 Round 32 to 30. **Think:** $30\overline{)168}$	**Step 2** Multiply.	**Step 3** Subtract. Show the remainder.	**Check.**
$\begin{array}{r} 5 \\ \textbf{Try: } 32\overline{)168} \end{array}$	$\begin{array}{r} 5 \\ 32\overline{)168} \\ 160 \leftarrow 5 \times 32 \end{array}$	$\begin{array}{r} 5\,r\,8 \\ 32\overline{)168} \\ \underline{160} \\ 8 \leftarrow 168-160 \end{array}$	$\begin{array}{rl} 32 & \leftarrow \text{divisor} \\ \times\ 5 & \leftarrow \text{quotient} \\ \hline 160 & \\ +\ \ 8 & \leftarrow \text{remainder} \\ \hline 168 & \leftarrow \text{dividend} \end{array}$

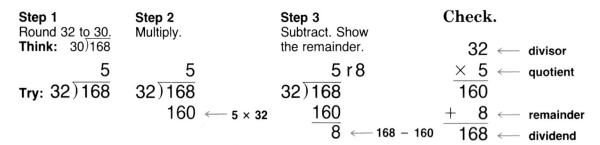

Debbie filled **5 shelves.** There are **8 flashlights** left over.

Another Method: $89 \div 43 = ?$

Think Find **convenient (compatible)** numbers that are easy to divide.

$\begin{array}{r} 2 \\ 40\overline{)80} \end{array}$ ◀ **Try 2 in the quotient.**

$\begin{array}{r} 2\,r\,3 \\ 43\overline{)89} \\ -86 \\ \hline 3 \end{array}$

PRACTICE • Divide. Check your answers.

1. $22\overline{)96}$
2. $41\overline{)56}$
3. $23\overline{)95}$
4. $31\overline{)65}$
5. $62\overline{)86}$

6. $82\overline{)740}$
7. $63\overline{)221}$
8. $51\overline{)324}$
9. $42\overline{)264}$
10. $91\overline{)289}$

EXERCISES • Divide.

11. $34\overline{)78}$ 12. $23\overline{)97}$ 13. $41\overline{)96}$ 14. $22\overline{)56}$ 15. $32\overline{)64}$

16. $42\overline{)281}$ 17. $61\overline{)211}$ 18. $82\overline{)495}$ 19. $31\overline{)265}$ 20. $83\overline{)352}$

21. $73\overline{)523}$ 22. $50\overline{)323}$ 23. $94\overline{)659}$ 24. $54\overline{)384}$ 25. $54\overline{)444}$

26. $60\overline{)445}$ 27. $81\overline{)435}$ 28. $73\overline{)596}$ 29. $83\overline{)593}$ 30. $62\overline{)350}$

31. $71\overline{)200}$ 32. $72\overline{)224}$ 33. $60\overline{)505}$ 34. $72\overline{)235}$ 35. $43\overline{)322}$

36. $92 \div 44 =$ __?__

37. $89 \div 32 =$ __?__

38. $243 \div 54 =$ __?__

39. $257 \div 61 =$ __?__

40. $394 \div 40 =$ __?__

41. $747 \div 92 =$ __?__

Find the missing dividend.

★ 42. $52\overline{)}\ ^{9\ r9}$ ★ 43. $83\overline{)}\ ^{3\ r12}$ ★ 44. $41\overline{)}\ ^{8\ r19}$ ★ 45. $91\overline{)}\ ^{8\ r18}$

PROBLEM SOLVING • APPLICATIONS

46. Robert unpacks 200 screwdrivers. He puts 24 screwdrivers in each compartment. How many compartments does he fill? How many screwdrivers are left over?

47. Gayle is setting up a display of 258 tape measures. She puts 32 tape measures in each stack. How many stacks does she make? How many tape measures are left over?

THINKER'S CORNER

Brad needs to package 10 ceiling fan motors and the blades for the fans in boxes to be sold. There are 47 fan blades in all. How many fans have 4 blades? How many fans have 5 blades?

Correcting Overestimates

Brad and Tom are checking an order of 564 calculators. The calculators are packed in cartons. Each carton can hold 74 calculators.

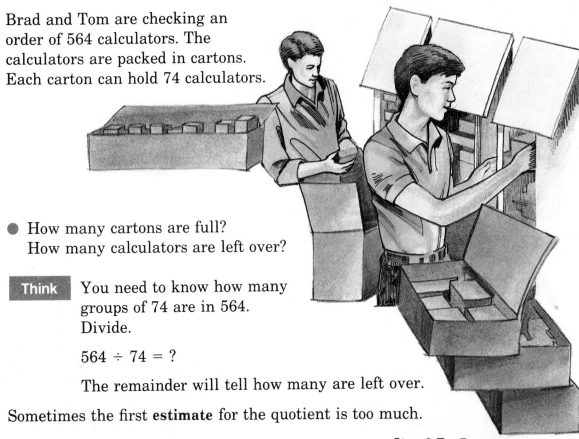

● How many cartons are full?
  How many calculators are left over?

Think You need to know how many groups of 74 are in 564. Divide.

$564 \div 74 = ?$

The remainder will tell how many are left over.

Sometimes the first **estimate** for the quotient is too much.

Step 1 Round 74 to 70

Think: $70\overline{)564}$

Try 8. $74\overline{)564}$

Basic fact: $7\overline{)56}$ → 8

Step 2 Multiply.

$$\begin{array}{r} 8 \\ 74\overline{)564} \\ -592 \end{array}$$

◄ **592 > 564**

Since 592 > 564, 8 is too much.

Step 3 Try 7.

$$\begin{array}{r} 7 \text{ r}46 \\ 74\overline{)564} \\ -518 \\ \hline 46 \end{array}$$

← 74×7

← Remainder

There are **7 full cartons.** There are **46 calculators** left over.

E PRACTICE • Is the first estimate too much? Write YES or NO.

1. $43\overline{)82}^{\,2}$

2. $34\overline{)65}^{\,2}$

3. $22\overline{)69}^{\,3}$

4. $74\overline{)675}^{\,9}$

5. $93\overline{)325}^{\,9}$

Divide. Check your answers.

6. $24\overline{)71}$

7. $41\overline{)87}$

8. $94\overline{)747}$

9. $63\overline{)503}$

10. $84\overline{)435}$

EXERCISES • Divide.

11. $23\overline{)82}$ 12. $33\overline{)61}$ 13. $42\overline{)83}$ 14. $24\overline{)91}$ 15. $34\overline{)63}$

16. $63\overline{)187}$ 17. $84\overline{)413}$ 18. $93\overline{)649}$ 19. $84\overline{)495}$ 20. $72\overline{)141}$

21. $94\overline{)654}$ 22. $63\overline{)430}$ 23. $73\overline{)535}$ 24. $54\overline{)423}$ 25. $74\overline{)219}$

26. $83\overline{)579}$ 27. $74\overline{)179}$ 28. $64\overline{)503}$ 29. $83\overline{)324}$ 30. $52\overline{)152}$

31. $72\overline{)286}$ 32. $63\overline{)370}$ 33. $40\overline{)385}$ 34. $62\overline{)336}$ 35. $72\overline{)637}$

36. $44\overline{)295}$ 37. $83\overline{)267}$ 38. $64\overline{)238}$ 39. $73\overline{)352}$ 40. $54\overline{)475}$

41. $82 \div 44 =$ ___?___

42. $283 \div 32 =$ ___?___

43. $238 \div 44 =$ ___?___

PROBLEM SOLVING • APPLICATIONS

CHOOSE • mental math • pencil and paper • calculator SOLVE

44. There are 92 solar-powered calculators. Brad puts these into display boxes. Each box holds 24 calculators. How many boxes does he fill? How many calculators are left over?

45. Tom is putting price tag labels on 212 calculators. There are 43 price tags on each sheet of labels. How many full sheets does he use? How many more price tags does he need?

46. Jane bought a calculator for $17.95 and a battery for $1.75. She gave the clerk $20.00. How much change did she receive?

47. On Monday, Betty sold 6 calculators. She sold 12 on Tuesday and 9 calculators on Wednesday. How many calculators did she sell in all?

THINKER'S CORNER

Find the missing digits.

a. $7\ r16$
$35\overline{)2\blacksquare\blacksquare}$

b. $5\ r2$
$4\blacksquare\overline{)217}$

c. $\blacksquare\ r2$
$25\overline{)15\blacksquare}$

PROBLEM SOLVING · STRATEGIES

Interpreting the Remainder

When you divide, there is often
a remainder in your answer.

Sometimes the answer to the problem
is the next greater whole number.
Sometimes the answer is the quotient.
Sometimes the answer is the remainder.

Example   Mrs. Davis needs 162 drapery hooks
to hang drapes. The hooks are
sold in packages of 12.

● How many packages does Mrs. Davis
need to buy?

First you must divide to find how
many groups of 12 are in 162.

Think   There are 13 groups of 12 in 162.
There are 6 extra hooks which can
only be bought in another package.

$$\begin{array}{r} 13\ \text{r}6 \\ 12\overline{)162} \\ -12 \\ \hline 42 \\ -36 \\ \hline 6 \end{array}$$

The answer is the next greater
whole number.

Mrs. Davis needs to buy **14 packages** of hooks.

● How many full packages of hooks
will Mrs. Davis use?

Think   She will only use 6 hooks
out of one package. She
will use the full amount
from 13 packages. The
answer is the quotient.

Mrs. Davis will use **13 full
packages** of hooks.

● How many hooks will be used
from the last package?

Think   When you divided there were
6 extra hooks. The answer
is the remainder.

Mrs. Davis will use **6 hooks**
from the last package.

PROBLEMS

1. Mr. Crane needs to replace 13 light bulbs that have burned out. The light bulbs are sold in packages of 4. How many packages does he need to buy?

2. Mr. Martinez wants to buy 363 feet of string. The string comes in rolls of 50 feet. How many rolls will he need to buy?

3. Sharon bought enough paint to paint 286 square feet of fence. Each can of paint will cover about 45 square feet. How many full cans of paint will she use?

4. Karen needs to buy 432 tiles for her bathroom walls. The tiles are sold in boxes of 50. How many boxes does she need to buy?

5. Wesley has 178 nails to put in packages. Each full package will have 24 nails. How many full packages will he have?

6. The hammer display racks are empty. Each rack will hold 8 hammers. Dave puts 66 hammers in the racks. How many racks are full?

7. Greg is packing 206 cans of oil into boxes. Each box holds 24 cans. How many cans will be left over?

8. The warehouse has 342 shovels. Each of the 43 stores in this area are to get the same number of shovels. How many shovels will be left in the warehouse?

Write Your Own Problem

Mark is a carpenter. He is cutting wood into pieces 12 inches long.

Write a story problem about Mark and his work. Write the problem so that the answer is the remainder.

MID-CHAPTER REVIEW

Divide. (Pages 340–341)

1. $30\overline{)150}$ **2.** $50\overline{)252}$ **3.** $40\overline{)355}$ **4.** $10\overline{)40}$ **5.** $70\overline{)576}$

(Pages 342–343)

6. $11\overline{)63}$ **7.** $14\overline{)86}$ **8.** $81\overline{)275}$ **9.** $63\overline{)507}$ **10.** $22\overline{)192}$

(Pages 344–345)

11. $23\overline{)82}$ **12.** $84\overline{)413}$ **13.** $73\overline{)535}$ **14.** $83\overline{)324}$ **15.** $64\overline{)238}$

Solve.

16. Martha wants to buy 396 feet of macrame yarn. The yarn comes in rolls of 45 feet. How many rolls does she need to buy? (Pages 346–347)

17. Nicky is packing 584 boxes of nails into cartons. Each carton will hold 75 boxes of nails. How many boxes will he have left over? (Pages 346–347)

MAINTENANCE • MIXED PRACTICE

Add or subtract.

1. $\begin{array}{r} \frac{2}{6} \\ +\frac{3}{6} \\ \hline \end{array}$ **2.** $\begin{array}{r} \frac{8}{9} \\ -\frac{1}{9} \\ \hline \end{array}$ **3.** $\begin{array}{r} \frac{7}{8} \\ -\frac{4}{8} \\ \hline \end{array}$ **4.** $\begin{array}{r} \frac{1}{3} \\ -\frac{2}{9} \\ \hline \end{array}$ **5.** $\begin{array}{r} \frac{1}{10} \\ +\frac{3}{5} \\ \hline \end{array}$ **6.** $\begin{array}{r} \frac{5}{8} \\ -\frac{1}{2} \\ \hline \end{array}$

Complete.

7. 3 m = __?__ cm   **8.** 2 km = __?__ m   **9.** __?__ g = 7 kg

10. Find the perimeter.   **11.** Find the area in square centimeters.   **12.** Find the volume in cubic centimeters.

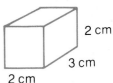

13. School begins at 8:15 A.M. Math class starts 30 minutes later. What time does math begin?

14. Joan's lunch time begins at 12:15 and ends at 12:35. How much time does she have for lunch?

CAREER APPLICATIONS

Carpet Installers

Carpet installers use a table like the one below to estimate the number of packages of carpet squares needed to cover a floor. A package of 10 carpet squares costs $12.50.

Room Length (feet)	Room Width (feet)									
	4	6	8	9	10	12	14	16	18	20
4	2	3	4	4	4	5	6	7	8	8
6	3	4	5	6	6	8	9	10	11	12
8	4	5	7	8	8	10	12	13	15	16
9	4	6	8	9	9	11	13	15	17	18
10	4	6	8	9	10	12	14	16	18	20
12	5	8	10	11	12	15	17	20	22	24

● How much will the carpet cost for a room that is 12 feet long and 9 feet wide?

Think You must first answer the **hidden question**.

How many packages are needed?

[1] Find the 12 in the 'Room Length' column.
Move right. Stop when you reach the "9" column.
Read the number: **11** This is the number of packages.

[2] Since the cost of 1 package is $12.50, multiply 11 times $12.50.

Press: ① ① ✕ ① ② • ⑤ ⓪ ＝ [137.50] ◀ The carpet cost $137.50

EXERCISES • Use paper and pencil or a calculator.
How many packages of carpet are needed for a room that is

1. 9 feet long,
6 feet wide?

2. 10 feet long,
8 feet wide?

3. 8 feet long,
6 feet wide?

4. Use your calculator to find the cost for the carpet in Exercises 1–3.

PROJECT Find the cost for carpet squares for a room in your house.

Rounding Divisors Up

This week, the employees at Handy Mart will count all of the stock. The manager and employees will work a total of 247 extra hours. Each of the 28 employees will work the same number of hours. The manager will work the remaining hours.

● How many extra hours will each employee work?
How many extra hours of work are left for the manager?

Think You need to separate the 247 hours into 28 equal groups. Divide.

$247 \div 28 = ?$

The remainder will tell the extra hours that are left.

Step 1
Round 28 to 30.
Think: $30\overline{)247}$

Try 8. $28\overline{)247}$

Step 2
Multiply.

$\begin{array}{r} 8 \\ 28\overline{)247} \\ 224 \end{array}$ ← 8 × 28

Step 3
Subtract.

$\begin{array}{r} 8\ r23 \\ 28\overline{)247} \\ -224 \\ \hline 23 \end{array}$ ← 247 − 224

Check.

$\begin{array}{r} 28 \\ \times\ 8 \\ \hline 224 \\ +\ 23 \\ \hline 247 \end{array}$ ← divisor
← quotient

← remainder
← dividend

Each employer will work **8 extra hours**. The manager will work **23 extra hours**.

PRACTICE • Divide. Check your answers.

1. $27\overline{)62}$ 2. $18\overline{)68}$ 3. $36\overline{)83}$ 4. $19\overline{)80}$ 5. $29\overline{)67}$

6. $46\overline{)352}$ 7. $75\overline{)568}$ 8. $67\overline{)569}$ 9. $78\overline{)489}$ 10. $59\overline{)434}$

EXERCISES • Divide.

11. $28\overline{)94}$　　　12. $17\overline{)63}$　　　13. $35\overline{)92}$　　　14. $18\overline{)86}$　　　15. $27\overline{)75}$

16. $47\overline{)305}$　　17. $68\overline{)494}$　　18. $86\overline{)275}$　　19. $27\overline{)256}$　　20. $56\overline{)558}$

21. $85\overline{)740}$　　22. $57\overline{)372}$　　23. $68\overline{)532}$　　24. $46\overline{)219}$　　25. $69\overline{)507}$

26. $49\overline{)327}$　　27. $67\overline{)459}$　　28. $98\overline{)804}$　　29. $27\overline{)192}$　　30. $57\overline{)348}$

31. $90 \div 36 = \underline{\ ?\ }$　　　　32. $457 \div 86 = \underline{\ ?\ }$　　　　33. $368 \div 74 = \underline{\ ?\ }$

34. $504 \div 58 = \underline{\ ?\ }$　　　　35. $240 \div 34 = \underline{\ ?\ }$　　　　36. $663 \div 74 = \underline{\ ?\ }$

37. $728 \div 79 = \underline{\ ?\ }$　　　　38. $581 \div 67 = \underline{\ ?\ }$　　　　39. $387 \div 95 = \underline{\ ?\ }$

PROBLEM SOLVING • APPLICATIONS

40. Brad counted 127 lawn sprinklers. Each full box had 28 sprinklers. How many full boxes were there? How many sprinklers were left in the open box?

41. Debbie counted 140 extension cords. The cords were tied together in bundles of 19. How many bundles were there? How many loose cords were there?

Mon.	Tues.	Wed.	Thur.	Fri.
10	13	11	16	15

42. This table shows the number of hours that the store manager worked each day this week. What is the average number of hours he worked each day?

Correcting Underestimates

Dave, the store manager, made a computer printout of the store's inventory. The printout listed 192 items. Each sheet of printout paper listed 25 items.

● How many sheets of paper were filled?
How many items were left for another sheet?

Think You need to separate the 192 items into groups of 25. Divide.

$$192 \div 25 = ?$$

The remainder will tell the number of items left for another sheet.

Sometimes the first **estimate** is too small.

Step 1
Round 25 to 30.
Think: $30\overline{)192}$

Try 6. $25\overline{)192}^{6}$

Step 2
Multiply.

$$25\overline{)192}^{6}$$
$$-150 \leftarrow 6 \times 25$$
$$\overline{42} \leftarrow 192 - 150$$

Since 42 > 25,
6 is too small.

Step 3
Try 7.

$$25\overline{)192}^{7\,r17}$$
$$-175 \leftarrow 7 \times 25$$
$$\overline{17} \leftarrow 192 - 175$$

There are **7 sheets** that are full. There are **17 items** left over.

 PRACTICE • Is the first estimate enough? Write YES or NO.

1. $28\overline{)86}^{3}$
2. $47\overline{)98}^{2}$
3. $75\overline{)600}^{7}$
4. $86\overline{)672}^{7}$
5. $55\overline{)427}^{6}$

Divide. Check your answers.

6. $19\overline{)79}$
7. $36\overline{)74}$
8. $55\overline{)495}$
9. $85\overline{)356}$
10. $77\overline{)475}$

EXERCISES • Divide.

11. $16\overline{)51}$ 12. $25\overline{)78}$ 13. $46\overline{)93}$ 14. $37\overline{)74}$ 15. $29\overline{)89}$

16. $46\overline{)276}$ 17. $69\overline{)208}$ 18. $25\overline{)191}$ 19. $47\overline{)290}$ 20. $68\overline{)343}$

21. $78\overline{)473}$ 22. $56\overline{)463}$ 23. $39\overline{)245}$ 24. $75\overline{)153}$ 25. $68\overline{)206}$

26. $29\overline{)147}$ 27. $60\overline{)405}$ 28. $45\overline{)185}$ 29. $39\overline{)159}$ 30. $23\overline{)119}$

31. $57\overline{)297}$ 32. $47\overline{)406}$ 33. $77\overline{)385}$ 34. $82\overline{)652}$ 35. $48\overline{)344}$

36. $76 \div 36 =$ ____?____   37. $84 \div 27 =$ ____?____   38. $246 \div 35 =$ ____?____

39. $325 \div 65 =$ ____?____   40. $559 \div 69 =$ ____?____   41. $374 \div 58 =$ ____?____

Find the missing divisor.

★ 42. $280 \div$ ____?____ $= 7\,r14$ ★ 43. $163 \div$ ____?____ $= 6\,r19$ ★ 44. $482 \div$ ____?____ $= 8\,r26$

PROBLEM SOLVING • APPLICATIONS

45. As items are purchased they are logged in an inventory book. There is room to log 28 items on each page. If 168 items are logged, how many full pages are used?

46. Debbie changes the 9 rolls of wallpaper in the store's display each month. There are 70 different patterns she can display. How many months will it take to show all the patterns?

CALCULATOR • Using a Formula

Use **quotient × divisor + remainder = dividend** to find the missing digits.

$$25\overline{)\square\square\square}\ ^{7\,r17}$$

Press ② ⑤ ✕ ⑦ ＋ ① ⑦ ＝ 〔 *192* 〕

EXERCISES   Use the formula to find the missing digits.

1. $9\overline{)\blacksquare\blacksquare}$ ^{2 r6}   2. $9\overline{)\blacksquare\blacksquare}$ ^{9 r6}   3. $87\overline{)\blacksquare\blacksquare\blacksquare}$ ^{8 r1}   4. $25\overline{)\blacksquare\blacksquare\blacksquare}$ ^{4 r5}   5. $31\overline{)\blacksquare\blacksquare\blacksquare}$ ^{5 r4}

Two-Digit Quotients

The paint section of the store is being moved to a new area. All 750 cans must be packed in boxes and moved. Each box holds 24 cans.

● How many boxes will be filled? How many cans will be left over?

Think To separate the 750 cans into groups of 24, divide.

$$750 \div 24 = \,?$$

The remainder will tell the number of cans left over.

Step 1 There are two digits in the divisor.
Draw a line after the second digit in the dividend.

$$\begin{array}{r} X \\ 24\overline{)75\,|\,0} \end{array}$$ Since 75 > 24, the first digit goes over the 5.

Step 2 Round 24 to 20.
Divide the tens.

Think: $20\overline{)75}$ Try 3.

$$\begin{array}{r} 3 \\ 24\overline{)750} \\ -72 \\ \hline 3 \end{array}$$

Step 3 Bring down the 0.

Think: $24\overline{)30}^{\,1}$

$$\begin{array}{r} 31\ \text{r}6 \\ 24\overline{)750} \\ -72\downarrow \\ \hline 30 \\ -24 \\ \hline 6 \end{array}$$

Check the answer.

$$\begin{array}{r} 31 \leftarrow \text{quotient} \\ \times 24 \leftarrow \text{divisor} \\ \hline 124 \\ 620 \\ \hline 744 \\ +\quad 6 \leftarrow \text{remainder} \\ \hline 750 \leftarrow \text{dividend} \end{array}$$

There will be **31 full boxes** and **6 cans left over.**

PRACTICE • Divide. Check your answers.

1. $41\overline{)861}$ 2. $23\overline{)486}$ 3. $24\overline{)746}$ 4. $33\overline{)382}$ 5. $23\overline{)305}$

6. $32\overline{)736}$ 7. $34\overline{)821}$ 8. $45\overline{)851}$ 9. $57\overline{)843}$ 10. $36\overline{)852}$

EXERCISES • Divide. Check your answers.

11. $21\overline{)672}$ 12. $14\overline{)291}$ 13. $30\overline{)957}$ 14. $71\overline{)900}$ 15. $48\overline{)575}$

16. $39\overline{)526}$ 17. $70\overline{)786}$ 18. $51\overline{)969}$ 19. $42\overline{)893}$ 20. $66\overline{)873}$

21. $43\overline{)994}$ **22.** $29\overline{)795}$ **23.** $38\overline{)808}$ **24.** $20\overline{)516}$ **25.** $23\overline{)498}$

26. $28\overline{)682}$ **27.** $52\overline{)647}$ **28.** $31\overline{)456}$ **29.** $19\overline{)674}$ **30.** $62\overline{)746}$

31. $40\overline{)872}$ **32.** $24\overline{)504}$ **33.** $78\overline{)943}$ **34.** $57\overline{)768}$ **35.** $34\overline{)889}$

36. $625 \div 50 = \underline{\quad?\quad}$ **37.** $614 \div 46 = \underline{\quad?\quad}$ **38.** $402 \div 17 = \underline{\quad?\quad}$

39. $618 \div 32 = \underline{\quad?\quad}$ **40.** $870 \div 26 = \underline{\quad?\quad}$ **41.** $716 \div 67 = \underline{\quad?\quad}$

PROBLEM SOLVING • APPLICATIONS

42. Tom counted 264 receipt booklets in the store's inventory. There are 38 booklets in each box.
   a. How many full boxes are there?
   b. How many booklets are left over?

43. Brad counted 63 aluminum towel racks and 38 wooden towel racks. How many towel racks were there in the Handy-Mart inventory?

44. Jill sold 4 cans of soup for $0.82 each. The customer gave her $5.00. How much change did Jill give to the customer?

★ **45.** There are 438 cans of soup that need to be packed into cartons. Each carton holds 28 cans. What is the least number of cartons needed?

THINKER'S CORNER

Find the missing digits.

a.
```
        1 6 r1
 2 4 )3 □ 5
    - 2 4
      □ 4 5
    - 1 4 4
          1
```

b.
```
        □ 4 r11
 1 □ )6 5 7
   - 5 □
     8 □
   - 7 6
     1 1
```

c.
```
        1 7 r2□
 2 8 )□ □ 1
    - 2 8
      2 2 1
    - 1 □ 6
        2 □
```

d.
```
        3 7 r17
 □ 4 )9 □ 5
   - □ 2
     1 8 □
   - 1 6 8
       1 7
```

e.
```
        5 7 r□
 □ 3 )7 □ 5
   - 6 5
     □ 5
   - □ □
       □
```

f.
```
        2 □ r4
 1 □ )□ 3 6
   - 3 6
     □ 6
   - □ □
       4
```

Dividing Money

Mr. Quiñones is building an addition to his home. He shopped at Handy-Mart and bought 12 packages of nails for $9.84.

● How much did each package cost?

Think   To separate $9.84 into 12 equal groups, divide.

$$\$9.84 \div 12 = ?$$

Divide amounts of money as if you were dividing whole numbers.

Remember to write the dollar sign and the cents point in the answer.

```
                82
Think:   12)984
           -96
            24
           -24
             0
```

```
                $0.82      Use a 0 to show
Write:   12)$9.84          there are no
            -9 6↓          dollars.
             24
            -24
              0
```

Each package of nails costs **$0.82**.

More Examples

```
   $0.44
6)$2.64
 -2 4
   24
  -24
    0
```

```
   $1.70 ←
5)$8.50
 -5        |
  3 5      |
 -3 5↓     |
   00 ← 0 ÷ 5 = 0
  -0  ← 0 × 5 = 0
    0
```

```
   $2.07
3)$6.21
 -6
   2       Since 2 < 3,
  -0       write a 0
  21       over the 2.
 -21
   0
```

PRACTICE • Divide.

1. 13)$9.62   2. 23)$8.05   3. 64)$7.68   4. 32)$9.28   5. 15)$9.75

6. 21)$7.98   7. 38)$6.08   8. 42)$8.82   9. 57)$9.12   10. 12)$2.16

EXERCISES • Divide.

11. $21\overline{)\$7.35}$ **12.** $49\overline{)\$9.80}$ **13.** $19\overline{)\$5.13}$ **14.** $72\overline{)\$6.48}$ **15.** $25\overline{)\$8.00}$

16. $13\overline{)\$6.37}$ **17.** $31\overline{)\$7.44}$ **18.** $27\overline{)\$8.91}$ **19.** $32\overline{)\$7.68}$ **20.** $58\overline{)\$8.70}$

21. $80\overline{)\$4.80}$ **22.** $16\overline{)\$1.60}$ **23.** $18\overline{)\$2.34}$ **24.** $20\overline{)\$1.80}$ **25.** $63\overline{)\$3.78}$

26. $24\overline{)\$9.84}$ **27.** $40\overline{)\$7.20}$ **28.** $45\overline{)\$6.75}$ **29.** $22\overline{)\$8.36}$ **30.** $21\overline{)\$9.03}$

31. $\$6.49 \div 11 = \underline{\quad?\quad}$ **32.** $\$7.28 \div 52 = \underline{\quad?\quad}$ **33.** $\$5.46 \div 13 = \underline{\quad?\quad}$

34. $\$7.68 \div 16 = \underline{\quad?\quad}$ **35.** $\$7.02 \div 27 = \underline{\quad?\quad}$ **36.** $\$9.45 \div 27 = \underline{\quad?\quad}$

★ **37.** $\$27.36 \div 57 = \underline{\quad?\quad}$ ★ **38.** $\$59.52 \div 24 = \underline{\quad?\quad}$ ★ **39.** $\$61.56 \div 18 = \underline{\quad?\quad}$

PROBLEM SOLVING • APPLICATIONS

40. Ling spends $8.28 for tubes of caulking. She buys 12 tubes. How much does each tube of caulking cost?

41. Adam bought a 50-foot extension cord for $12.45. He also bought a 20-foot extension cord for $6.99. How much more was the 50-foot cord?

42. Mrs. Lawrence bought 11 cans of spray paint. Her total bill was $9.79. How much did each can of paint cost?

★ **43.** Jan had $10.00. She spent $3.49 for a hose nozzle. She divided the change she received equally among her three children. How much money did each child receive?

44. Alfonzo wants to buy a quart of paint for $5.89 and a paint brush for $1.97. He has $9.00. Does he have enough money?

★ **45.** The wholesale price of a box of 48 faucet screens is $5.76. The store wants to make a profit of $0.03 on each screen. What will be the selling price of each faucet screen?

PROBLEM SOLVING · STRATEGIES

Choosing the Operation · Using Number Sentences

Sometimes writing a number sentence for a problem makes it easier to solve.

Example

Susan is a warehouse supervisor. She fills two orders of flashlights for the Handy Mart. Susan sends out 195 flashlights on Monday and 243 flashlights on Friday. How many flashlights does she send out all together?

Which number sentence will help you solve the problem?

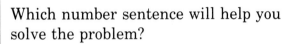

a. 195 + 243 = ?   **b.** 243 − 195 = ?   **c.** 195 × 243 = ?   **d.** 243 ÷ 195 = ?

Think   You want to know how many flashlights she sent out all together. Add.

195 + 243 = 438

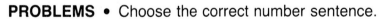

Susan sent out **438 flashlights**.

PROBLEMS • Choose the correct number sentence.

1. Mark puts batteries in the calculators that are on sale. He has 242 batteries. Each calculator needs 2 batteries. How many calculators can he sell with batteries?

   a. 242 + 2 = ?
   b. 242 − 2 = ?
   c. 242 × 2 = ?
   d. 242 ÷ 2 = ?

2. Kim sells plants to 16 customers. Each customer buys 7 plants. How many plants does Kim sell all together?

   a. 16 + 7 = ?
   b. 16 − 7 = ?
   c. 16 × 7 = ?
   d. 16 ÷ 7 = ?

3. Handy Mart had a 2-day sale on lawnmowers. The first day they sold 43 lawnmowers. The second day of the sale they sold 21 lawnmowers. How many more lawnmowers did they sell on the first day than on the second day?

   a. 43 + 21 = ?

   b. 43 − 21 = ?

   c. 43 × 21 = ?

   d. 43 ÷ 21 = ?

4. Leann spends $18.56 for a sprinkler and $5.43 for a hose. How much does she spend all together?

   a. $18.56 + $5.43 = ?

   b. $18.56 − $5.43 = ?

   c. $18.56 × $5.43 = ?

   d. $18.56 ÷ $5.43 = ?

Write the number sentence.
Then solve.

5. Amy bought 15 boxes of tiles for her kitchen counter. Each box holds 20 tiles. How many tiles did Amy buy all together?

6. Tom, the store manager, needed to work 23 extra hours to finish a new display for the paint department. He worked 8 extra hours on Monday. How many more hours does he need to work on the display?

7. Nancy ran the store computer. The printout listed new items received in the warehouse. The first printout listed 173 new items. The second printout listed 92 items. How many new items were listed on the printout all together?

Read the problem. Then choose the correct operation.

---

8. James has 296 boxes of door knobs to put on the shelves. Each shelf will hold 74 boxes. How many shelves will James fill?

9. Bill counted 297 receipt booklets for the store inventory in January. He had 305 booklets in February. How many receipt booklets did Bill count in the two months all together?

Write Your Own Problem

Write a story problem that uses money and division. Write a number sentence for your problem.

CHAPTER REVIEW

Part 1: VOCABULARY

For Exercises 1–5, choose from the box at the right the word that completes each statement.

1. The answer to a division problem is called the __?__ (Page 340)

2. To find the quotient, first round the __?__ to the nearest ten. (Page 342)

3. When you divide and the number does not divide evenly, the number left over is called a __?__ (Page 340)

4. Divide money as if you were dividing __?__ numbers. (Page 356)

5. When dividing money, you must write the __?__ sign and the cents point (Page 356)

dividend
divisor
dollar
product
quotient
remainder
whole

Part 2: SKILLS

Divide. (Pages 340–345)

6. $30\overline{)90}$ 7. $50\overline{)250}$ 8. $60\overline{)430}$ 9. $20\overline{)187}$ 10. $70\overline{)500}$

11. $21\overline{)84}$ 12. $43\overline{)258}$ 13. $42\overline{)370}$ 14. $33\overline{)235}$ 15. $64\overline{)532}$

16. $34\overline{)196}$ 17. $51\overline{)252}$ 18. $62\overline{)241}$ 19. $43\overline{)330}$ 20. $72\overline{)645}$

Divide. (Pages 350–353)

21. $57\overline{)248}$ 22. $38\overline{)326}$ 23. $49\overline{)253}$ 24. $86\overline{)275}$ 25. $75\overline{)404}$

26. $45\overline{)93}$ 27. $36\overline{)216}$ 28. $87\overline{)351}$ 29. $59\overline{)414}$ 30. $67\overline{)547}$

Divide. (Pages 354–357)

31. $24\overline{)792}$ 32. $48\overline{)864}$ 33. $65\overline{)980}$ 34. $81\overline{)935}$ 35. $39\overline{)963}$

36. $52\overline{)676}$ 37. $31\overline{)598}$ 38. $27\overline{)837}$ 39. $46\overline{)758}$ 40. $17\overline{)986}$

41. $14\overline{)\$3.22}$ 42. $26\overline{)\$8.32}$ 43. $46\overline{)\$9.66}$ 44. $19\overline{)\$7.03}$ 45. $22\overline{)\$7.70}$

Part 3: PROBLEM SOLVING • APPLICATIONS

Solve. (Pages 346–347)

46. Mei needs 95 drapery hooks to hang the new drapes. The hooks are sold in packages of 6. How many packages does Mei need to buy?

47. Dac is putting cans of oil on the shelf. Each shelf holds 24 cans. There are 90 cans in all. How many cans will be left over?

Choose the correct number sentence. (Pages 358–359)

48. Handy Mart is having a sale on locks. Each lock costs $3.49. How much will 3 locks cost?

   a. $3.49 + 3 = ?

   b. $3.49 − 3 = ?

   c. $3.49 × 3 = ?

   d. $3.49 ÷ 3 = ?

49. Ty works 32 hours each week. Salena works 40 hours each week. How many more hours does Salena work than Ty?

   a. 32 + 40 = ?

   b. 40 − 32 = ?

   c. 32 × 40 = ?

   d. 40 ÷ 32 = ?

Write the number sentence. Then solve. (Pages 358–359)

50. Lucy needs 21 light bulbs. There are 3 light bulbs in one package. How many packages does Lucy buy?

51. Handy Mart sold 58 ceiling fans this week. Last week they sold 43 ceiling fans. How many ceiling fans did Handy Mart sell in all?

CHAPTER TEST

Divide.

1. $20\overline{)80}$

2. $50\overline{)382}$

3. $60\overline{)446}$

4. $32\overline{)96}$

5. $43\overline{)189}$

6. $72\overline{)632}$

7. $62\overline{)238}$

8. $51\overline{)452}$

9. $34\overline{)296}$

10. $47\overline{)339}$

11. $29\overline{)244}$

12. $85\overline{)971}$

13. $79\overline{)486}$

14. $46\overline{)950}$

15. $55\overline{)832}$

16. $39\overline{)527}$

17. $24\overline{)505}$

18. $39\overline{)808}$

19. $42\overline{)\$9.24}$

20. $63\overline{)\$4.41}$

21. $27\overline{)\$7.56}$

Solve.

22. The film developer packs 135 rolls of film into boxes that will hold 18 rolls each. How many boxes does he fill completely?

23. Ben stacks 334 cans of paint on the shelves. Each shelf will hold 27 cans. How many cans of paint does he have left over?

Choose the correct number sentence. Then solve.

24. Janelle bought a case of glue for $9.84. There are 24 bottles in the case. How much does each bottle cost?

    a. $9.84 + 24 = ?

    b. $9.84 − 24 = ?

    c. $9.84 × 24 = ?

    d. $9.84 ÷ 24 = ?

Write the number sentence. Then solve.

25. The Handy Mart store is having a special sale on their laundry soap. They are selling 12 boxes for $8.16. How much does one box of laundry soap cost?

Prime-Number Sieves

A **prime number** is a whole number greater than 1 that is only divisible by itself and 1.

Examples

2, 3, 5, 7, 11

The **prime-number sieve** is a method for finding all the prime numbers that are less than a given number.

Example Use the prime-number sieve to write all the prime numbers less than 50.

1 Arrange the numerals from 2 to 50.

2 Cross out numerals after **2** for numbers divisible by 2. (4, 6, 8, 10, · · ·)

3 Cross out numerals after **3**, the next prime, for numbers divisible by 3. (6, 9, 12, 15, · · ·)

4 Cross out numerals after **5** for numbers divisible by 5. (10, 15, 20, 25, · · ·)

5 Cross out numerals after **7** for numbers divisible by 7. (14, 21, 28, 35, · · ·)

6 Look for numerals after **11** for numbers divisible by 11. Since there are none, you are finished. The numerals not crossed out represent the prime numbers less than 50.

		[2]		[2]		[2]	[3]	[2]	
2	3	4	5	6	7	8	9	10	
	[2]		[2]	[3]	[2]		[2]		[2]
11	12	13	14	15	16	17	18	19	20
[3]	[2]		[2]	[4]	[2]	[3]	[2]		[2]
21	22	23	24	25	26	27	28	29	30
	[2]	[3]	[2]	[4]	[2]		[2]	[3]	[2]
31	32	33	34	35	36	37	38	39	40
	[2]		[2]	[3]	[2]		[2]	[5]	[2]
41	42	43	44	45	46	47	48	49	50

EXERCISES

1. Write the prime numbers from 50 to 75.
2. Write the prime numbers from 75 to 100.
⭐ 3. What are the next two prime numbers greater than 100?

ADDITIONAL PRACTICE

SKILLS

Divide. (Pages 340–345)

1. $70 \div 10 = \underline{\quad?\quad}$

2. $320 \div 40 = \underline{\quad?\quad}$

3. $210 \div 70 = \underline{\quad?\quad}$

4. $115 \div 20 = \underline{\quad?\quad}$

5. $504 \div 60 = \underline{\quad?\quad}$

6. $421 \div 90 = \underline{\quad?\quad}$

7. $50\overline{)182}$ **8.** $90\overline{)667}$ **9.** $60\overline{)226}$ **10.** $43\overline{)91}$ **11.** $24\overline{)85}$

12. $13\overline{)77}$ **13.** $31\overline{)162}$ **14.** $52\overline{)344}$ **15.** $71\overline{)201}$ **16.** $63\overline{)520}$

17. $84\overline{)459}$ **18.** $93\overline{)600}$ **19.** $41\overline{)235}$ **20.** $22\overline{)173}$ **21.** $53\overline{)389}$

Divide. (Pages 350–357)

22. $251 \div 66 = \underline{\quad?\quad}$

23. $410 \div 88 = \underline{\quad?\quad}$

24. $528 \div 76 = \underline{\quad?\quad}$

25. $473 \div 48 = \underline{\quad?\quad}$

26. $929 \div 28 = \underline{\quad?\quad}$

27. $855 \div 38 = \underline{\quad?\quad}$

28. $38\overline{)725}$ **29.** $48\overline{)697}$ **30.** $27\overline{)987}$ **31.** $19\overline{)560}$ **32.** $39\overline{)481}$

33. $45\overline{)824}$ **34.** $18\overline{)936}$ **35.** $37\overline{)\$8.51}$ **36.** $57\overline{)\$7.98}$ **37.** $46\overline{)\$9.66}$

PROBLEM SOLVING • APPLICATIONS

Solve. (Pages 346–347)

38. Mrs. Stein has 432 batteries. She puts 24 batteries in each bin. How many bins does she fill with batteries?

39. Mr. Davis packs 125 boxes of nails into cartons for a builder. Each carton will hold 30 boxes. How many boxes of nails does Mr. Davis put into the last carton?

40. Janet bought 4 plants for $2.53 each. Choose the number sentence that shows how much the plants cost. (Pages 358–359)

   a. $\$2.53 + 4 = ?$

   b. $\$2.53 - 4 = ?$

   c. $\$2.53 \times 4 = ?$

   d. $\$2.53 \div 4 = ?$

41. Betty sold 14 cans of paint. Allen sold 28 cans of paint. How many more cans of paint did Allen sell than Betty? (Pages 358–359)

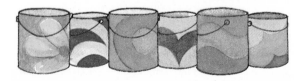

Each of these problems contains a common error.

a. Find the correct answer.

b. Find the error.

1. 235
   × 40
   ━━━
   940

2.   ²
    428
   × 30
   ━━━━
   14,640

3.   98
   ×63
   ━━━
    24
   540
   ━━━
   564

4.   37
   ×54
   ━━━
   148
   185
   ━━━
   333

5. 2 4
    1 2
    2 3 7
   ×   6 4
   ━━━━━━
     9 4 8
   1 3 0 2 0
   ━━━━━━
   1 3,9 6 8

6. $2.58
   ×   26
   ━━━━━
   2148
   5160
   ━━━━━
   7,308

7.   **60**
    70)420

8.   **3 r11**
    42)131
       120
       ━━━
        11

9.   **6 r47**
    35)257
       210
       ━━━
        47

10.   **18 r7**
    27)491
       27
       ━━━
       221
       214
       ━━━
         7

11.   **219 r23**
    31)674
        62
       ━━━
       612
       589
       ━━━
        23

12.   **28**
    28)$7.84
        5 6
       ━━━
       2 24
       2 24
       ━━━
          0

CUMULATIVE REVIEW
Chapters 1 through 11

Choose the correct answers.

1. In 38,654 what digit is in the ten thousands place?

A. 8　　　**B.** 3
C. 6　　　**D.** not here

2.
$$\begin{array}{r} 838 \\ 1,689 \\ 18 \\ +\quad 8 \end{array}$$

A. 2,453　　**B.** 2,553
C. 2,562　　**D.** not here

3.
$$\begin{array}{r} \$12.00 \\ -\quad 6.89 \end{array}$$

A. $5.11　　**B.** $6.11
C. $6.89　　**D.** not here

4.
$$\begin{array}{r} 347 \\ \times\quad 6 \end{array}$$

A. 2,072　　**B.** 2,082
C. 2,086　　**D.** not here

5. $4\overline{)7,649}$

A. 1,902 r1　**B.** 1,912 r1
C. 1,112 r1　**D.** not here

6. Choose the correct measure for a tennis ball.

A. 5 kg　　**B.** 5 m
C. 5 g　　　**D.** not here

7. Find the area.

3 cm

12 cm

A. 30 sq cm　**B.** 15 sq cm
C. 36 sq cm　**D.** not here

8. Choose the time for seventeen minutes before four.

A. 3:37　　**B.** 4:17
C. 3:43　　**D.** not here

9. $\frac{4}{5}$ of 15 = _____?_____

A. 12　　**B.** 7
C. 8　　　**D.** not here

10. Larry bought a package of sandpaper at the hardware store for $1.57. He gave the clerk $5.00. He received 3 dollars, 3 pennies and some dimes in change. How many dimes did he receive?

A. 5

B. 6

C. 4

D. 3

11. Scott worked 8 hours at the hardware store. He worked 2 more hours in the morning than in the afternoon. How long did he work in the morning and in the afternoon?

A. 5 hours in morning
　　3 hours in afternoon

B. 6 hours in morning
　　2 hours in afternoon

C. 4 hours in morning
　　4 hours in afternoon

D. 3 hours in morning
　　5 hours in afternoon

12. $\frac{2}{3}$ ⬤ $\frac{4}{6}$

A. > B. <

C. = D. not here

13. $\frac{13}{15}$
$-\frac{9}{15}$

A. $\frac{22}{15}$ B. $\frac{4}{15}$

C. $\frac{5}{15}$ D. not here

14. 87
$\times 10$

A. 87 B. 870

C. 807 D. not here

15. 852
$\times\ 40$

A. 34,080
B. 32,080
C. 34,020
D. not here

16. 326
$\times\ 62$

A. 21,212
B. 20,202
C. 21,122
D. not here

17. $7.19
$\times\ \ \ 46$

A. $340.74
B. $330.84
C. $330.74
D. not here

18. 48
$\times 57$

A. 2,746
B. 2,736
C. 2,636
D. not here

19. 90 ÷ 30 = ___?___

A. 3
B. 30
C. 60
D. not here

20. 70$\overline{)578}$

A. 80 r18
B. 8 r28
C. 8 r18
D. not here

21. 92$\overline{)389}$

A. 4 r21
B. 40 r21
C. 4 r31
D. not here

22. 23$\overline{)746}$

A. 29 r76
B. 32 r9
C. 31 r33
D. not here

23. 64$\overline{)\$7.68}$

A. $0.12
B. $1.12
C. $0.11
D. not here

24. Maria bought 3 cans of oil at $0.69 each. She gave the clerk $10.00. How much change will she receive?

A. $7.83 B. $2.07
C. $9.31 D. $7.93

25. Shannon needs 147 nails for her math project. The nails are sold in packages of 12. How many packages will Shannon need to buy?

A. 12 B. 13
C. 9 D. 11

Mixed Practice • Choose the correct answers.

1. Which fraction tells what part of the square is blue?

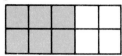

A. $\frac{4}{10}$ B. $\frac{6}{10}$

C. $\frac{8}{10}$ D. not here

2. Which fraction tells how much is blue?

A. $1\frac{4}{10}$ B. $1\frac{6}{10}$

C. $1\frac{6}{9}$ D. not here

3. In the numeral 687, which digit is in the tens place?

A. 8   B. 6

C. 7   D. not here

4. In the numeral 1,067, which digit is in the hundreds place?

A. 1   B. 6
C. 0   C. not here

5. Choose the correct sign.

6011 ● 6101

A. =   B. >
C. <   D. not here

6. Choose the correct sign.

828 ● 818

A. >   B. =
C. <   D. not here

7.   876
   +489

A. 1,355   B. 1,365
C. 1,265   D. not here

8.   806
   −398

A. 508   B. 412
C. 418   D. not here

9.   1,700
   − 986

A. 824   B. 724
C. 714   D. not here

10. Shawn waxed $\frac{5}{10}$ of the floor. Billy waxed $\frac{3}{10}$ of the floor. How much of the floor was waxed?

A. $\frac{2}{10}$ B. $\frac{8}{20}$

C. $\frac{8}{10}$ D. not here

11. Bonnie is cooking soup. She had $\frac{7}{10}$ of a cup of chopped celery. She put $\frac{3}{10}$ of a cup of the celery into the soup. How much of the celery does she have left?

A. $\frac{13}{10}$ B. $\frac{13}{20}$

C. $\frac{4}{10}$ D. not here

Decimals

In a 400-meter Olympics race, one runner's time was 51.74 seconds. Another runner's time was 51.47 seconds.

● Which time was less?

In a Special Olympics race, Sharon completed the first lap in 29.3 seconds.

● Round 29.3 to the nearest whole number.

Tenths

A running track has been divided into 10 equal lanes.

One tenth is blue.

fraction   decimal

$$\frac{1}{10} = 0.1$$

decimal point

Each lane is **one tenth** of the track.

You can write decimals to name numbers greater than one.

● Write a decimal and a mixed number
  to show how much is blue.

Think Count the number of wholes.
  Count the number of tenths.

There are **two wholes and six tenths**.

mixed number   decimal

Write: $2\frac{6}{10}$ =   **2.6**

Place-value chart ▶

ones	tenths
2 ●	6

Read: **two and six tenths**

PRACTICE • Write the decimal that tells how much is blue.

1.   2.   3.

Write each decimal.

4.
tens	ones	tenths
2	4 ●	3

5.
tens	ones	tenths
	0 ●	8

6. $6\frac{5}{10}$ 7. $3\frac{3}{10}$ 8. $19\frac{7}{10}$ 9. $\frac{5}{10}$ 10. $\frac{9}{10}$ 11. $\frac{8}{10}$

12. three and seven tenths   13. twenty and five tenths

EXERCISES • Write the decimal that tells how much is blue.

14. 15. 16.

Write each decimal.

17.

tens	ones	tenths
2	8	9

18.

tens	ones	tenths
7	6	4

19.

tens	ones	tenths
	0	6

20.

tens	ones	tenths
9	8	8

21. $5\frac{3}{10}$ 22. $6\frac{1}{10}$ 23. $9\frac{2}{10}$ 24. $8\frac{1}{10}$ 25. $1\frac{4}{10}$ 26. $2\frac{7}{10}$

27. $18\frac{6}{10}$ 28. $35\frac{9}{10}$ 29. $\frac{7}{10}$ 30. $\frac{8}{10}$ 31. $30\frac{3}{10}$ 32. $14\frac{5}{10}$

33. nine and six tenths

34. seven and seven tenths

35. thirteen and three tenths

36. one tenth

37. eight tenths

38. eight and seven tenths

39. twenty-five and nine tenths

40. four tenths

Write each decimal in words.

★ 41. 8.8   ★ 42. 7.2   ★ 43. 0.3   ★ 44. 0.6   ★ 45. 10.2   ★ 46. 35.7

PROBLEM SOLVING • APPLICATIONS

Write a decimal for the underlined words.

47. In 1968, James Hines set an Olympic record for the 100-meter run. His time was <u>nine and nine tenths</u> seconds.

48. In 1984, Roger Kingdom set an Olympic record in the 100-meter hurdles. His time was <u>thirteen and two tenths</u> seconds.

Hundredths

One large tile in a swimming pool is divided into 100 equal parts. Each part is **one hundredth** of the whole.

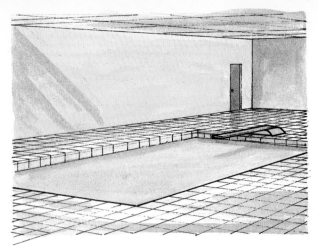

  One hundredth is blue.

fraction   **decimal**

$$\frac{1}{100} = 0.01$$

decimal point

● Write a decimal and a mixed number to show how much is blue.

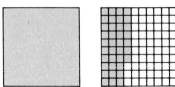

Think Count the number of wholes.
Count the number of hundredths.

mixed number   **decimal**

Write: $1\frac{37}{100}$ = **1.37**

● You can use a place-value chart to show tenths and hundredths.

tens	ones	tenths	hundredths
4	6	7	5

Read: **forty-six <u>and</u> seventy-five hundredths**   Write: **46.75**

PRACTICE • Write the decimal that tells how much is blue.

1.    2.    3.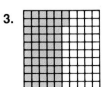

Write each decimal.

4. hundreds	tens	ones	tenths	hundredths
3	8	5	3	6

5. $1\frac{42}{100}$ 6. $3\frac{38}{100}$ 7. $7\frac{45}{100}$ 8. $5\frac{36}{100}$ 9. $\frac{65}{100}$ 10. $\frac{27}{100}$

11. seventy-two hundredths   12. sixteen and sixty-one hundredths

EXERCISES • Write each decimal.

13. $4\frac{85}{100}$ 14. $5\frac{38}{100}$ 15. $7\frac{16}{100}$ 16. $12\frac{47}{100}$ 17. $\frac{8}{100}$ 18. $\frac{3}{100}$

19. thirteen hundredths

20. twenty-nine hundredths

21. fifteen and thirty-seven hundredths

22. one hundred twenty-eight and forty-five hundredths

23. eight and nine hundredths

24. fourteen and sixty-seven hundredths

25. one hundred seven and four hundredths

Mental Math   In what place is the 6?

26. 15.67   27. 6.95   28. 0.76   29. 605.42

Mental Math   Name 1 more hundredth for each.

⭐ **30.** 0.18   ⭐ **31.** 5.35   ⭐ **32.** 3.47   ⭐ **33.** 6.89

PROBLEM SOLVING • APPLICATIONS

Write a decimal for the underlined words.

34. In the 1976 Olympics, the 100-meter freestyle swim race was won by Kornelia Ender with a time of <u>fifty-five and sixty-five hundredths</u> seconds.

35. In the 1980 Olympics, Par Arvidsson won the gold medal in the men's 100-meter butterfly with a time of <u>fifty-four and ninety-two hundredths</u> seconds.

THINKER'S CORNER

There are 4 digits in my number. There is a decimal point after the first 2 digits. The tenths digit is 9 times the tens digit. The hundredths digit is 3 more than the tens digit. The ones digit is 2 times the hundredths digit. What is the number?

Comparing Decimals

The table shows Olympic records set for the women's 400-meter race by each runner.

Runner	Time (in seconds)
Seidler	51.68
Rendina	51.94
Szewinska	50.48
Balogh	51.74
Zehrt	51.47

● Which runner's time was less, Seidler's or Balogh's?

Think Use >, <, or = to compare the decimals.

Same number of tens. $\longrightarrow$ **5**1.68   **5**1.74
Same number of ones. $\longrightarrow$ 5**1**.68   5**1**.74
Compare the tenths. $\longrightarrow$ 51.**6**8   51.**7**4
                              6 < 7

Since 6 < 7, **51.68 < 51.74.** ◀ **Seidler's time is less.**

● Which is greater, 6.93 or 6.91?

Think Compare the decimals.

Same number of ones. $\longrightarrow$ **6**.93   **6**.91
Same number of tenths. $\longrightarrow$ 6.**9**3   6.**9**1
Compare the hundredths. $\longrightarrow$ 6.9**3**   6.9**1**
                              3 > 1

Since 3 > 1, **6.93 > 6.91.**

● Which is greater, 0.3 or 0.30?

Think Draw a figure to compare the decimals.

0.3 and 0.30 are names for the same number.

So, **0.3 = 0.30.**

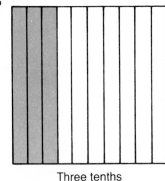

Three tenths

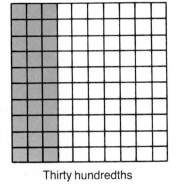

Thirty hundredths

PRACTICE • Write >, <, or =.

1. 0.9 ● 0.5

2. 0.75 ● 0.79

3. 13.46 ● 13.52

4. 5.4 ● 5.1

5. 28.15 ● 28.13

6. 4.2 ● 4.20

EXERCISES • Write >, <, =.

7. 0.89 ● 0.86   8. 1.78 ● 1.75   9. 1.31 ● 1.33

10. 7.4 ● 7.40   11. 6.4 ● 6.9   12. 0.47 ● 0.58

13. 12.27 ● 12.17   14. 56.43 ● 56.51   15. 18.50 ● 18.5

16. 0.64 ● 0.75   17. 20.19 ● 20.19   18. 19.41 ● 19.14

19. 7.06 ● 7.60   20. 0.67 ● 0.73   21. 52.39 ● 52.35

22. 6.34 ● 6.3   23. 15.49 ● 15.5   24. 27.6 ● 27.75

Compare the decimals, two at a time. Then write in order from least to greatest.

25. 4.06, 6.40, 0.46, 0.64

26. 27.80, 24.08, 27.84, 25.48

27. 0.53, 0.43, 0.57, 0.35

28. 48.09, 49.80, 47.09, 47.08

★ 29. 1.342, 1.437, 1.324, 1.473

★ 30. 24.095, 24.509, 24.590, 24.495

PROBLEM SOLVING • APPLICATIONS

Use the table on page 374 for Exercises 31–34.

31. Which runner's time was less, Zehrt's or Rendina's?

32. Which runner's time was greater, Balogh's or Zehrt's?

33. Which runner had the least time?

34. Which runner had the greatest time?

CALCULATOR • Decimals and Fractions

You can use a calculator to write a decimal for a fraction.

EXAMPLE Write a decimal for $\frac{3}{4}$.

$\frac{3}{4}$ means $3 \div 4$. **Press** ③ ÷ ④ ＝ ⎡0.75⎤ ◀ $\frac{3}{4} = 0.75$.

EXERCISES • Write a decimal for each fraction. Use a calculator.

1. $\frac{1}{2}$ 2. $\frac{4}{5}$ 3. $\frac{3}{10}$ 4. $\frac{7}{25}$ 5. $\frac{3}{5}$

PROBLEM SOLVING · STRATEGIES

Working Backwards

Sometimes you can solve a problem by working backwards.

To work backwards, you use **opposite** operations.

Addition and subtraction are opposite operations.

Multiplication and division are opposite operations.

$$9 + 6 = 15 \qquad 15 - 6 = 9$$

$$8 \times 3 = 24 \qquad 24 \div 3 = 8$$

Example

In the 1984 Summer Olympics, the United States won more gold medals than any other country. If you take the number of gold medals won, add 5, and subtract 13, the result is 75.

● How many gold medals did the United States win?

Think Draw a flowchart to show the operations.

Step 1 Show the steps of the problem. Follow the order given.

| Medals | ⟶ | Add 5 | ⟶ | Subtract 13 | ⟶ | 75 |

Step 2 Use the opposite operations to work backwards.

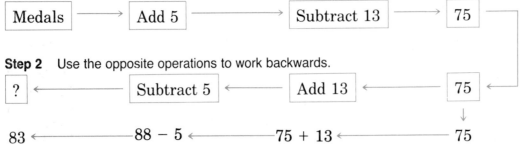

The United States won **83 gold medals** in the 1984 Summer Olympics.

PROBLEMS • Work backwards to find the amount of money.
Use opposite operations.

1. | Amount of money | → | Add $5.00 | → | Subtract $1.75 | → | $10.00 |

2. | Amount of money | → | Divide by 5 | → | Add $0.75 | → | $4.75 |

3. | Amount of money | → | Multiply by 2 | → | Subtract $3.50 | → | $8.50 |

Work backwards to solve. Use opposite operations.

4. Canada entered the 1984 Summer Olympics and was one of the four top countries winning the most medals. If you take the number of medals won, add 25, and divide by 3, the result is 23. How many medals did Canada win in the 1984 Summer Olympics?

6. The first Summer Games were played in Athens, Greece. If you take the year these games were played, add 497, and subtract 21, the result is 2,372. In what year were the first Summer Games played in Greece?

5. In 1896, James Connolly from the United States won the triple jump. If you take the amount of feet he jumped, multiply by 20, and subtract 50, the result is 850. How many feet did James Connolly jump?

★ 7. Betty Cuthbert from Australia won the 400-meter run. Her time was 52 seconds. If you take the year that Betty won the medal, add 68, divide by 4, and multiply by 15, the result is 7,620. In what year did Betty Cuthbert win the 400-meter run?

MID-CHAPTER REVIEW

Write the decimal that tells how much is blue. (Pages 370–373)

1.

2.

3.

Write each decimal. (Pages 370–373)

4. $\frac{9}{10}$

5. $2\frac{23}{100}$

6. two hundredths

7. eleven and fifteen hundredths

Write $>$, $<$, or $=$. (Pages 374–375)

8. 11.76 ● 11.67

9. 3.4 ● 3.40

10. 8.59 ● 8.6

Work backward to solve. Use opposite operations. (Pages 376–377)

11. Jean Claude Killy won the World Cup Alpine Championship two years in a row. If you take the first year that he won the title, add 456, and subtract 38, the result is 2,385. In what year did Jean Claude Killy win his first title?

12. Gertrude Gabl also won the World Cup Alpine Championship. If you take the year that she won, add 87, and divide by 4, the result is 514. In what year did Gertrude Gabl win the Championship?

MAINTENANCE • MIXED PRACTICE

Multiply or divide.

1. 156×30

2. 52×37

3. 374×45

4. $\$3.27 \times 81$

5. 83×14

6. $60\overline{)430}$

7. $64\overline{)532}$

8. $75\overline{)330}$

9. $75\overline{)404}$

10. $26\overline{)\$8.32}$

Add.

11. $\frac{5}{8} + \frac{2}{8}$

12. $\frac{3}{7} + \frac{2}{7}$

13. $\frac{3}{4} + \frac{2}{4}$

14. $\frac{5}{6} + \frac{2}{6}$

15. $\frac{4}{9} + \frac{7}{9}$

16. There are 76 swimmers going to the swim meet in a minibus. Each minibus holds 6 swimmers. How many minibuses do they need?

17. The 100-meter freestyle relay has 4 swimmers on each team. There are 8 teams. How many swimmers are there in all?

CONSUMER APPLICATIONS

Choosing the Better Buy

A good shopper finds the better buy by calculating the price of one item.

Example

The sports store sells 3 pairs of socks for $3.00. The department store has socks on sale for $1.25 per pair. Which is the better buy?

Divide to find the cost for 1 pair of socks at the sports store.

$$\$3.00 \div 3 = \$1.00$$

Compare the two prices.

At the sports store, 1 pair of socks is $1.00. The department store sells 1 pair of socks for $1.25.

$$\$1.00 < \$1.25$$

The better buy is **3 pairs of socks for $3.00.**

EXERCISES • Use paper and pencil or your calculator to solve each exercise.

What is the price for one item?

1. 12 balls for $48.00

2. 2 swimming caps for $5.00

Which is the better buy?

3. Letters for T-shirts are $0.25 each or 5 letters for $1.00.

4. Numbers for T-shirts are $0.50 each or 2 numbers for $1.10.

PROJECT Check the prices for different brands of sport socks at the sports store. Choose the better buy.

Adding Decimals

Roger Bannister was the first person to
run a mile in less than four minutes. He
ran the first half-mile in 118.2 seconds.
He ran the second half-mile in 121.1 seconds.

● How many seconds did it take
  him to run the mile?

Think To find how many seconds in all,
add.

$$118.2 + 121.1 = ?$$

Step 1
Line up the
decimal points.

$$
\begin{array}{r}
118.2 \\
+121.1 \\
\end{array}
$$

Step 2
Add as with whole numbers.
Write the decimal point
in the answer.

$$
\begin{array}{r}
118.2 \\
+121.1 \\
\hline
239.3 \\
\end{array}
$$

Roger Bannister ran a mile in **239.3 seconds.**

Sometimes you need to regroup tenths and hundredths.

● $2.67 + 3.75 = ?$

Step 1
Line up the decimal points.
Add the hundredths.
Regroup.

$$
\begin{array}{r}
1 \\
2.6\,7 \\
+3.7\,5 \\
\hline
2 \\
\end{array}
$$

Step 2
Add the tenths.
Regroup.

$$
\begin{array}{r}
1\ 1 \\
2.6\,7 \\
+3.7\,5 \\
\hline
4\,2 \\
\end{array}
$$

Step 3
Add the ones.
Write the decimal
point in the answer.

$$
\begin{array}{r}
1 \\
2.6\,7 \\
+3.7\,5 \\
\hline
6.4\,2 \\
\end{array}
$$

PRACTICE ● Add.

1. $\begin{array}{r}3.6\\+4.2\end{array}$	**2.** $\begin{array}{r}0.7\\+0.8\end{array}$	**3.** $\begin{array}{r}7.3\\+7.1\end{array}$	**4.** $\begin{array}{r}6.2\\+4.9\end{array}$	**5.** $\begin{array}{r}8.3\\+4.2\end{array}$
6. $\begin{array}{r}7.09\\+7.07\end{array}$	**7.** $\begin{array}{r}8.41\\+6.99\end{array}$	**8.** $\begin{array}{r}3.67\\+4.84\end{array}$	**9.** $\begin{array}{r}10.35\\+20.35\end{array}$	**10.** $\begin{array}{r}20.20\\+19.58\end{array}$

EXERCISES • Add.

11. 4.8
  +7.6

12. 2.3
  +9.7

13. 5.6
  +8.1

14. 6.2
  +8.6

15. 5.5
  +6.2

16. 8.29
  +4.36

17. 8.08
  +4.06

18. 0.05
  +0.39

19. 10.78
  +23.17

20. 34.98
  +43.06

21. 52.93
  +35.97

22. 87.40
  +52.73

23. 61.47
  + 8.00

24.   9.48
  +20.10

25. 35.63
  +10.24

26. 45.00
  +34.28

27. 20.47
  + 7.25

28. 12.06
  +27.14

29. 24.39
  + 3.60

30.   5.00
  +48.79

31. $7.9 + 5.6 = \underline{}$

32. $5.04 + 7.02 = \underline{}$

33. $4.36 + 8.20 = \underline{}$

34. $9.4 + 1.8 = \underline{}$

35. $46.76 + 29.36 = \underline{}$

36. $10.29 + 16.90 = \underline{}$

37. $7.00 + 1.39 = \underline{}$

38. $5.36 + 4.51 + 7.87 = \underline{}$

★ **39.** $17.85 + 2 + 3.9 = \underline{}$

PROBLEM SOLVING • APPLICATIONS

40. Tanya ran around the school track twice. The first lap took her 23.57 seconds. The second lap took her 25.83 seconds. What was her total time for the two laps?

41. Peter runs each day to practice for a race. On Friday, he ran 2.7 kilometers. On Saturday, he ran 3.5 kilometers. How far did he run in the two days?

42. Samantha is practicing the 50-yard dash. Her times are 8.7 seconds, 9.2 seconds, and 9.1 seconds. What is her average time?

THINKER'S CORNER

This is a **magic square.**
The sum of the numbers in each row, column, and diagonal is the same.
The **magic sum** is 10.5.

$4.2 + 3.5 + 2.8 = \mathbf{10.5}$

Complete the magic square.

row ⟶

diagonal

?	?	4.2
?	3.5	?
2.8	?	?

⟵ column

Decimals • **381**

Subtracting Decimals

John Weissmuller swam the 100-meter freestyle swimming race in 58.6 seconds. Rowdy Gaines set an Olympic record when he swam the same distance in 49.8 seconds.

● How many fewer seconds did Rowdy Gaines swim than John Weissmuller?

Think You need to know how many fewer seconds. So subtract.

$$58.6 - 49.8 = ?$$

Step 1
Line up the decimal points.

```
  58.6
- 49.8
```

Step 2
Regroup.
Subtract the tenths.

```
   7 16
  5 8̷.6̷
- 4 9.8
       8
```

Step 3
Regroup.
Subtract the ones.

```
    17
  4 7̷ 16
  5̷ 8̷.6̷
- 4 9.8
     8 8
```

Step 4
Write the decimal point in the answer.

```
    17
  4 7̷ 16
  5̷ 8̷.6̷
- 4 9.8
     8.8
```

Rowdy Gaines swam **8.8 seconds fewer** than John Weissmuller.

More Examples

● $8.42 - 2.67 = ?$

Step 1
Regroup.
Subtract the hundredths.

```
    3 12
  8.4̷ 2̷
- 2.6 7
       5
```

Step 2
Regroup.
Subtract the tenths.

```
      13
    7 3̷ 12
  8.4̷ 2̷
- 2.6 7
     7 5
```

Step 3
Subtract the ones.
Write the decimal point in the answer.

```
      13
    7 3̷ 12
  8̷.4̷ 2̷
- 2.6 7
   5.7 5
```

PRACTICE • Subtract.

1. 8.9 −3.6	**2.** 7.5 −4.1	**3.** 6.3 −2.5	**4.** 9.8 −7.9	**5.** 7.6 −2.7
6. 6.45 −3.31	**7.** 8.94 −4.22	**8.** 4.83 −3.18	**9.** 7.51 −6.47	**10.** 8.78 −8.66

EXERCISES • Subtract.

11. 4.5 −1.3	**12.** 6.3 −3.8	**13.** 8.8 −6.9	**14.** 7.2 −1.5	**15.** 7.3 −5.2
16. 6.93 −5.27	**17.** 8.35 −6.87	**18.** 4.82 −2.76	**19.** 6.22 −4.38	**20.** 81.42 −43.75
21. 5.64 −4.93	**22.** 25.32 −19.15	**23.** 40.43 − 9.28	**24.** 19.38 −17.54	**25.** 67.24 −15.96
26. 92.36 − 4.72	**27.** 6.18 −0.39	**28.** 77.3 −47.5	**29.** 34.43 −12.87	**30.** 95.72 − 1.36

31. $9.5 - 8.7 = \underline{?}$ **32.** $17.63 - 13.59 = \underline{?}$ **33.** $69.48 - 43.98 = \underline{?}$

34. $6.5 - 2.7 = \underline{?}$ **35.** $5.23 - 0.64 = \underline{?}$ **36.** $52.64 - 13.83 = \underline{?}$

37. $13.17 - 1.48 = \underline{?}$ **38.** $24.82 - 3.92 = \underline{?}$ **39.** $91.46 - 15.07 = \underline{?}$

★**40.** $25.374 - 25.121 = \underline{?}$ ★**41.** $16.892 - 7.784 = \underline{?}$ ★**42.** $78.431 - 52.695 = \underline{?}$

PROBLEM SOLVING • APPLICATIONS

43. The 1980 Olympic record for the women's 100-meter freestyle swim was 54.79 seconds. In 1984, this race was won in 55.92 seconds. How much faster was the 1980 record time?

44. In 1972, Mark Spitz won the men's 100-meter freestyle swim in 51.22 seconds and the 100-meter butterfly in 54.27 seconds. How much longer was his time for the 100-meter butterfly?

45. In the history of Olympic games, the highest and lowest scores for women's springboard diving were 539.9 and 78.62. The height of the springboard was 3 meters. How many more points was the highest score?

46. In 1984, Rowdy Gaines won the men's 100-meter freestyle with a time of 49.8 seconds. What information do you need to know how much faster he swam than Jorg Woithe in 1980?

Zeros in Addition and Subtraction

James is practicing for a ski race. His total time for the first try of the day is 52.1 seconds. The time for his second try is 54.76 seconds.

● What is his total time for the two races?

Think To find the total time for the two races, add.

$$52.1 + 54.76 = ?$$

Step 1
Write 52.1 as 52.10.

```
 52.10
+54.76
```

Step 2
Add.

```
 52.10
+54.76
106.86
```

James's total time is **106.86 seconds**.

Sometimes you need to write more than one zero before you subtract.

● 7 − 3.48 = ?

Think Another name for 7 is 7.00.

Step 1
Write 7 as 7.00.

```
 7.00
-3.48
```

Step 2
Regroup and subtract.

```
      9
  6 10 10
 7.0 0
- 3.4 8
  3.5 2
```

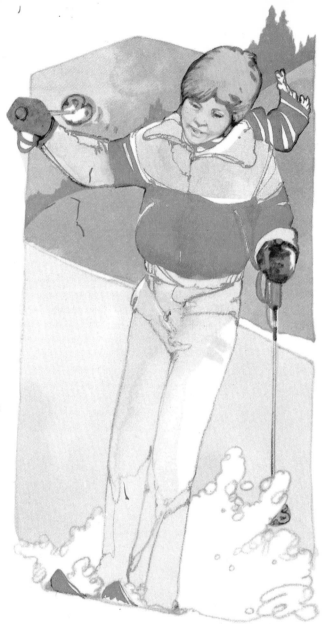

PRACTICE • Add.

1. 7.31
   +4.5

2. 6.42
   +2.5

3. 8.7
   +4.98

4. 39.65
   + 7.3

5. 18.2
   +14.95

Subtract.

6. 9
   −4.63

7. 6.8
   −2.15

8. 17
   − 8.39

9. 23.4
   − 6.13

10. 47
    − 3.58

EXERCISES • Add.

11. 5.42
    +6.3

12. 8.7
    +4.51

13. 6.95
    +4.3

14. 18.4
    + 3.72

15. 15.95
    +23.28

16. 4.93
    +14.8

17. 17.89
    +32.6

18. 20
    + 6.25

19. 67.3
    +14.8

20. 26.43
    +18

21. 6.29 + 4.1 = ___?___

22. 9.6 + 4.87 = ___?___

23. 17.6 + 39.8 = ___?___

24. 52.6 + 7.63 = ___?___

25. 9.18 + 73 = ___?___

26. 45.8 + 63.09 = ___?___

Subtract.

27. 9
    −6.18

28. 8.6
    −7.32

29. 17.6
    −13.91

30. 43.8
    − 9.9

31. 83
    −41.26

32. 63.4
    − 9.87

33. 16.4
    − 4.9

34. 35.6
    − 9.04

35. 23
    − 8.26

36. 65
    −17.48

37. 8 − 6.92 = ___?___

38. 9 − 4.32 = ___?___

39. 6.4 − 2.97 = ___?___

40. 18.4 − 6.82 = ___?___

41. 46.1 − 16.89 = ___?___

42. 93.7 − 42.9 = ___?___

★ 43. 19.7 − 8.592 = ___?___

★ 44. 82.4 − 16.307 = ___?___

★ 45. 87 − 14.376 = ___?___

PROBLEM SOLVING • APPLICATIONS CHOOSE • mental math • pencil and paper • calculator SOLVE

46. Serge skated 500 meters in 51.8 seconds. The world record for speed skating is 36.91 seconds. How many seconds more is Serge's time than the world record?

47. Joseph swam 200 meters in 24.9 seconds. Marta swam 200 meters in 31.5 seconds. How much faster did Joseph swim the 200 meters than Marta?

48. Ingrid buys a pair of ice skates for $26.99. She gives the clerk 3 ten-dollar bills. How much change does she receive?

Write Your Own Problem

Write a story problem about a ski race or a skating race. Write the problem so that you will have to add or subtract two decimals.

PROBLEM SOLVING • STRATEGIES

Using Estimation with Decimals

It is not always necessary to find the exact answer to a problem. Sometimes the estimate is good enough.

In a Special Olympics race, the first lap took Sharon 29.3 seconds.

● What is 29.3 rounded to the nearest whole number?

> **If the tenths place in a decimal is less than 5, round down.**

Think   0.3 is less than 0.5.

So 29.3 rounded to the nearest whole number is **29**.

The second lap around the track took Sharon 25.97 seconds.

● What is 25.97 rounded to the nearest whole number?

> **If the tenths place in a decimal is 5 or more, round up.**

Think   0.97 is more than 0.50.

So 25.97 rounded to the nearest whole number is **26**.

 PROBLEMS • Round to the nearest whole number.

1. 3.2   **2.** 5.84   **3.** 76.6   **4.** 8.26   **5.** 87.30

Choose the best estimate. Choose **a, b,** or **c.**

6. 6.5 + 5.4   **a.** 7 + 5   **b.** 6 + 5   **c.** 6 + 6

7. 87.5 − 85.0   **a.** 87 − 85   **b.** 87 − 86   **c.** 88 − 85

8. 34.6 × 7.8   **a.** 34 × 8   **b.** 35 × 8   **c.** 35 × 7

9. Jane runs the 100-meter race in 17.3 seconds. Charles takes 0.8 seconds more. How long does Charles take to run the 100-meter race?

   a. 17 + 1   **b.** 17 + 0   **c.** 18 + 1

10. Donald swims 200 meters in 3.4 minutes. Donald's younger sister, Susan, takes twice as long to swim the 200 meters. How long does Susan take to swim the 200 meters?

    a. 4 × 2   **b.** 3 × 2   **c.** 3 × 3

11. Joan, Maggie and Gerald swam on a swim team. They earned 33.57 points for diving. They each earned the same amount of points. How many points did each team member earn?

    a. 33 ÷ 3   **b.** 34 ÷ 3   **c.** 33 ÷ 4

12. Yvonne is trying to improve her time in the 500-meter speed skating race. Her fastest time is 1.65 minutes. Her slowest time is 3.3 minutes. How much longer is her slowest time than her fastest time?

    a. 3 − 2   **b.** 3 − 1   **c.** 4 − 2

13. In the 1,500-meter skating race, Carmela's time is 3.1 minutes. Jill's time is 0.8 minutes longer. What is Jill's time?

    a. 5   **b.** 3   **c.** 4

14. Raoul swims 198 meters in 4.7 minutes. Michelle swims the race in 0.8 minutes less. What is Michelle's time for the 198-meter race?

    a. 3   **b.** 4   **c.** 5

15. Bobby earned 5.3 points for diving. Lisa earned twice as many points for her diving. How many points did Lisa earn in the diving competition?

    a. 10   **b.** 9   **c.** 11

16. Jerry and Tim entered the bobsled race. Their team won 5 races. They earned a total of 45.58 points. Jerry and Tim divided the points evenly. How many points did each boy earn?

    a. 22   **b.** 23   **c.** 24

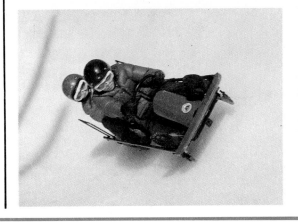

CHAPTER REVIEW

Part 1: VOCABULARY

For Exercises 1–9, choose from the box at the right the word(s) that best completes each statement.

1. The number 0.24 is called a __?__ . (Page 370)

2. To find which decimal is greater, you __?__ . (Page 374)

3. The __?__ 4 is the same as 4.00. (Page 384)

4. In the number 6.28, the 8 is in the __?__ (s) place. (Page 372)

5. The number $6\frac{3}{10}$ is called a __?__ . (Page 370)

6. The decimal 0.2 is __?__ to the fraction $\frac{2}{10}$. (Page 370)

7. In the number 34.62, the 6 is in the __?__ place. (Page 372)

8. The decimal 0.50 is __?__ to 0.5. (Page 374)

9. To add or subtract decimals, first line up the __?__ . (Page 380)

> compare
> decimal
> decimal points
> equal
> hundredth
> mixed number
> tenths
> whole number

Part 2: SKILLS

Write the decimal that tells how much is blue. (Pages 370–373)

10.  11. 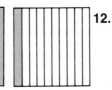 12.

Write each decimal. (Pages 370–373)

13.

hundreds	tens	ones	tenths
3	4	2	6

14.

tens	ones	tenths	hundredths
5	8	7	1

15. $2\frac{1}{10}$ **16.** $11\frac{4}{10}$ **17.** $35\frac{1}{10}$ **18.** $7\frac{57}{100}$ **19.** $\frac{9}{100}$

20. eight and five tenths

21. seven tenths

22. twelve and twenty-six hundredths

23. one hundred four and nine hundredths

Write $>$, $<$, or $=$. (Pages 374–375)

24. 3.2 ⬤ 3.5   **25.** 13.42 ⬤ 13.24   **26.** 6.20 ⬤ 6.2

Add or subtract. (Pages 380–385)

27. 2.4
$+3.5$

28. 5.3
$+7.9$

29. 31.40
$+16.58$

30. 48
$+29.15$

31. 24.37
$+\ 7.53$

32. 7.8
-4.3

33. 6.2
-1.7

34. 5.14
-0.39

35. 23.56
$-\ 7.48$

36. 34.91
-12.78

37. 8.23
$+6.4$

38. 13.7
$-\ 9.18$

39. 42
$-\ 3.27$

40. 25.4
$+\ 0.67$

41. 6
-5.98

Part 3: *PROBLEM SOLVING • APPLICATIONS*

Work backwards to solve. Use opposite operations. (Pages 376–337)

42. Beth entered the downhill ski race. If you take her time in minutes, add 50, and multiply by 34, the result is 1,768. How many minutes did Beth take to complete the downhill ski race?

43. In the high jump, Allen won the event. If you take the number of centimeters that Allen jumped, subtract 55, and divide by 2, the result is 51. How many centimeters did Allen jump in the high jump?

Choose the best estimate. Choose **a**, **b**, or **c**. (Pages 386–387)

44. Shana runs the 100-meter race in 18.2 seconds. John takes 1.6 seconds longer. How long does John take to run the 100-meter race?

a. $18 + 1$ **b.** $18 + 2$ **c.** $19 + 1$

45. Mary earns 6.89 points for diving. Jeff earns 13.6 points. How many points did they earn together?

a. 19   **b.** 20   **c.** 21

CHAPTER TEST

Write a decimal that tells how much is blue.

1.   **2.**   **3.**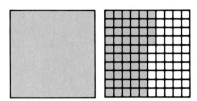

Write each decimal.

4.

tens	ones	tenths
5	0	6

5.

hundreds	tens	ones	tenths	hundredths
3	1	7	0	8

6. $9\frac{9}{10}$

7. $\frac{61}{100}$

8. $239\frac{5}{100}$

9. eight and one tenth

10. sixteen and twenty-four hundredths

Write $>$, $<$, or $=$.

11. 11.6 ⬤ 1.6

12. 9.74 ⬤ 9.50

13. 52.9 ⬤ 52.90

Add or subtract.

14. 4.2
$+1.8$

15. 15.6
$+\ 6.7$

16. 8.3
$+0.89$

17. 24
$+78.78$

18. 6.3
-0.9

19. 14.5
$-\ 7.8$

20. 30.4
-17.98

21. 62
-14.73

Work backwards to solve. Use opposite operations.

22. Yolanda won the long jump event. If you take the number of meters she jumped, add 34, and multiply by 87, the result is 3,480. How many meters did Yolanda jump?

23. Bill entered the diving events. If you take the number of points he earned, divide by 5, and add 87, the result is 89. How many points did Bill earn?

Choose the best estimate. Choose **a, b,** or **c.**

24. In the long jump, Karen jumps 6.4 meters, and Josh jumps 7.5 meters. How much farther does Josh jump than Karen?

   a. $7 - 6$ **b.** $8 - 6$ **c.** $8 - 7$

25. In the slalom race, Mary's time was 4.7 minutes. Sue's time was 5.0 minutes. What was their time all together?

   a. 9   **b.** 10   **c.** 11

ENRICHMENT

Decimal Measures

Sarah is getting the gym ready for track events. She is placing strips of colored tape on the floor to show where each event takes place. The first piece of tape is 7 meters 45 centimeters long.

● How many meters is this?

Think $1 \text{ m} = 100 \text{ cm}$
$1 \text{ cm} = \frac{1}{100} \text{ m}$

$7 \text{ m } 45 \text{ cm} = 7 \text{ m} + 45 \text{ cm}$
$= 7 \text{ m} + \frac{45}{100} \text{ m}$
$= 7 \text{ m} + 0.45 \text{ m}$
$= 7.45 \text{ m}$

● How many meters is 250 centimeters?

Think $100 \text{ cm} = 1 \text{ m}$
$1 \text{ cm} = \frac{1}{100} \text{ m}$

$250 \text{ cm} = 200 \text{ cm} + 50 \text{ cm}$
$= 2 \text{ m} + 50 \text{ cm}$
$= 2 \text{ m} + \frac{50}{100} \text{ m}$
$= 2 \text{ m} + 0.50 \text{ m}$
$= 2.50 \text{ m}$

EXERCISES • Write each measure as a number of meters. Use a decimal.

1. 2 m 30 cm
2. 5 m 85 cm
3. 490 cm
4. 615 cm

5. 327 cm
6. 3 m 63 cm
7. 208 cm
8. 4 m 55 cm

9. 6 m 42 cm
10. 424 cm
11. 1 m 70 cm
12. 560 cm

13. 4 m 6 cm
14. 93 cm
15. 306 cm
16. 2 m 9 cm

ADDITIONAL PRACTICE

SKILLS

Write as a decimal. (Pages 370–373)

1. $\frac{69}{100}$ **2.** $\frac{7}{10}$ **3.** $5\frac{1}{10}$ **4.** $8\frac{53}{100}$ **5.** $17\frac{9}{100}$ **6.** $13\frac{2}{10}$

7. three and four tenths   **8.** nine and twenty-one hundredths

9. twelve and three tenths   **10.** forty and eleven hundredths

Write $>$, $<$, or $=$. (Pages 374–375)

11. 274 ⬤ 2.7   **12.** 6.87 ⬤ 7.86   **13.** 3.80 ⬤ 3.08

Add or subtract. (Pages 380–385)

14. 2.7	**15.** 1.6	**16.** 0.85	**17.** 15.94	**18.** 23.72
+9.2	+7.9	+3.78	+ 5.57	+48.68

19. 6.49	**20.** 8.5	**21.** 13	**22.** 76.51	**23.** 18.63
+7.6	+4.91	+ 9.82	+ 5.8	+31.4

24. 7.4	**25.** 9.6	**26.** 3.7	**27.** 4.17	**28.** 15.92
−5.1	−2.5	−1.9	−1.74	− 8.83

29. 13.36	**30.** 8	**31.** 34	**32.** 92.4	**33.** 69.0
−12.99	−2.56	−16.71	−33.41	− 0.98

PROBLEM SOLVING • APPLICATIONS

Work backwards to solve. Use opposite operations. (Pages 376–377)

34. Paul won the 200-meter butterfly. If you take his time, subtract 2, and multiply by 10, the result is 20. How many minutes did it take Paul to swim the 200-meter butterfly?

35. Matt won the most ribbons at the swim event. If you take the number of ribbons that he won, add 578, and divide by 45, the result is 14. How many ribbons did Matt win at the swim event?

Choose the best estimate. Choose **a**, **b**, or **c**. (Pages 386–387)

36. Shana swims the 100-meter butterfly in 1.3 minutes less that her old record of 3.4 minutes. What is her new record?

   a. 3 − 2   **b.** 4 − 1   **c.** 3 − 1

37. David earned 23.5 points in the diving competition. His brother, Jason, won 19.2 points. How many points did the two brothers earn in all?

   a. 42   **b.** 43   **c.** 44

PROBLEM SOLVING MAINTENANCE

Solve.

1. Chris spent $0.69 for shoelaces for his running shoes. He gave the clerk $1.00. He received 1 penny and some nickels in change. How many nickels did he receive? (Page 46)

2. There were 378 reporters at the Olympics. There were also 189 television cameramen. How many more reporters than cameramen were there? (Page 74)

3. The Olympic athletes were staying in 4 buildings. The cafeteria in each building served 138 meals per day. How many meals were served in one day? (Page 126)

4. There are 47 track events scheduled in the Olympics. There will be 5 events each day. There are 4 athletes entered in each event. How many athletes will be in the track events? (Page 174)

5. Each athlete drinks 32 ounces of milk everyday. They drink 8 ounces at breakfast and 10 ounces at lunch. How many ounces do they drink at supper? (Page 260)

6. One runner practiced 5 hours on Monday. He practiced 1 more hour in the morning than in the afternoon. How long did he practice in the morning and in the afternoon? (Page 322)

7. Diane is packing 112 Olympic medals in boxes. Each box holds 6 medals. How many medals will be left over? (Page 346)

8. Dean was unloading 18 boxes of apples and bananas needed for snacks for the runners. Each box weighed 28 pounds. How many pounds of fruit did he unload? Write the number sentence and then solve. (Page 358)

9. The first Summer Games were held in Athens, Greece. If you take the year these games were played, add 506, and subtract 30, the result is 2,372. In what year were the first Summer Games held in Greece? (Page 376)

10. Roberto earned a score of 7.6 points for diving. Ron earned a score of 8.2, and David earned 9.1. About how many points did they earn altogether? Estimate your answer. (Page 386)

Mixed Practice • Choose the correct answers.

1. What is the name of the figure?

   A. triangle
   B. pentagon
   C. rectangle
   D. not here

2. What is the name of the figure?

   A. cube
   B. cone
   C. square
   D. not here

3. What is the name of the figure?

   A. circle
   B. cone
   C. cylinder
   D. not here

4. What is the perimeter of the square?

   3 cm

   A. 9 cm   B. 12 cm
   C. 6 cm   D. not here

5. What is the perimeter of the rectangle?

   6 cm

   4 cm

   A. 10 cm   B. 18 cm
   C. 16 cm   D. not here

6. What is the area of the rectangle in square centimeters?

   A. 9   B. 10
   C. 12   D. not here

7. What is the area of the rectangle in square inches?

   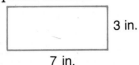
   3 in.
   7 in.

   A. 21   B. 20
   C. 10   D. not here

8. What is the volume of the box in cubic centimeters?

   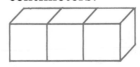

   A. 6   B. 3
   C. 5   D. not here

9. What is the volume of the box in cubic centimeters?

   6 cm
   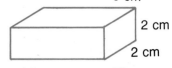
   2 cm
   2 cm

   A. 10   B. 12
   C. 24   D. not here

10. A pentagon has 5 sides. Each side is 14 centimeters. What is the perimeter of the pentagon?

    A. 19 cm   B. 59 cm
    C. 60 cm   D. not here

11. Daniel measured the den for new carpet. The room was 8 feet wide and 12 feet long. How many square feet of carpet should Daniel buy?

    A. 20 sq ft   B. 96 sq ft
    B. 40 sq ft   D. not here

Geometry

At the World's Fair held in Montreal, Canada in 1967, the United States pavilion had the shape of a *geodesic dome*. The dome contained hundreds of *hexagons*. The hexagons were **congruent** to each other.

- When are two polygons congruent?

The Leaning Tower of Pisa is not **perpendicular** to the ground.

- How many **right angles** are formed by two perpendicular lines?

Points, Lines, and Line Segments

Below is a drawing of the iron grid pattern of the Eiffel Tower. Each support arm is a line segment.

A line segment *is straight.*
It has two endpoints.

A •————————• B

Read: **line segment *AB*** or **line segment *BA***

Write: $\overline{AB}$ or $\overline{BA}$

A line *has no endpoints.*
It goes on forever in both directions.

Eiffel Tower in Paris, France

● A line is named by any two points on it.

Read: **line *CD*** or **line *DC***

Write: $\overleftrightarrow{CD}$ or $\overleftrightarrow{DC}$

● Line *AB* and line *CD* cross. Lines that cross are **intersecting lines**.

● Line *PQ* and line *RS* can never cross. They are always the same distance apart. Line *PQ* and line *RS* are **parallel lines**.

PRACTICE • Is each a segment? Write YES or NO.

1.

M •〰〰• Y

2.

P •————————• B

3.

J •〰〰〰• H

Name each segment.

4.

M •————————• N

5.

E •
     \
      • F

6.

V •
      \
       • W

EXERCISES • Name each segment.

7.

8.

9.

Name each line.

10.

11.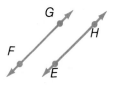

12.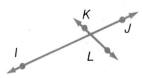

Write INTERSECTING or PARALLEL for each.

13.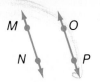

14.
G
H
F
E

15.
K
J
I
L

16.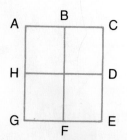

17.
S
Q
T
R

★**18.**
U
X
W
Y

Draw a picture for each.

19. line *PW*

20. segment *RU*

21. line *MJ* intersecting line *NS*

PROBLEM SOLVING • APPLICATIONS

22. Name the parallel line segments in this window.

A   B   C

H   D

G   E
     F

★ **23.** Name the 10 line segments that are in this gate.

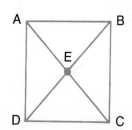

THINKER'S CORNER

This is a close-up picture of a section of the iron grid pattern of the Eiffel Tower. How many line segments can you find? Name them.

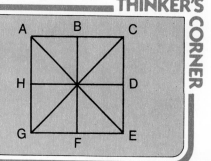

Rays and Angles

Remember that a line has no endpoints.
It goes on forever in both directions.

> **A ray has one endpoint.**
> **It goes on forever in one direction.**

Leaning Tower of Pisa

● You use two letters to name a ray.
The endpoint is always the first letter.

Read: **ray *KL***   Write: $\overrightarrow{KL}$

> **Two rays that have the same endpoint**
> **form an angle. The endpoint is called**
> **the vertex of the angle.**

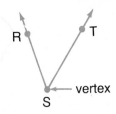

● You can use three letters to name an
angle. The vertex is always the
middle letter.

Read: **angle *RST* or angle *TSR***
Write: ∠ *RST* or ∠ *TSR*

● A **right angle** forms a square corner. Perpendicular lines
form four right angles.

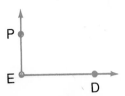

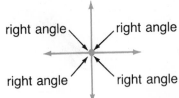

● Two intersecting lines that form right angles are **perpendicular**.

The Leaning Tower of Pisa in Italy is <u>not</u> perpendicular to the ground.

PRACTICE • Name each ray.

1.

2.

3.

Name each angle.

4.

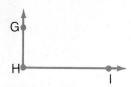

5.

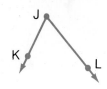

6.

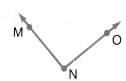

EXERCISES • Name the angles. Is the angle a right angle? Write YES or NO.

7.

8.

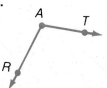

9.

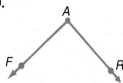

How many right angles does each figure have?

10.

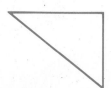

11.

12.

PROBLEM SOLVING • **APPLICATIONS**

Use the drawing of the castle to answer these questions.

13. Name twelve right angles.

14. Name 8 angles that are <u>not</u> right angles.

15. Name two rays for ∠*CAB*.

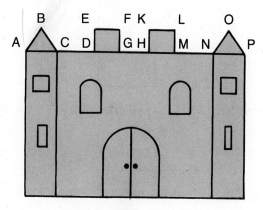

Use the drawing at the right.

★ **16.** Name five different rays.

★ **17.** Name nine different angles.

★ **18.** Name three right angles.

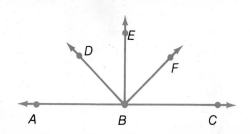

Polygons

The largest office building in the world is the Pentagon. Each of its five walls is 921 feet long! Each wall is an example of a plane. A **plane** is a flat surface like your desk. The faces of all solid figures are **plane figures**.

Here are examples of some plane figures.

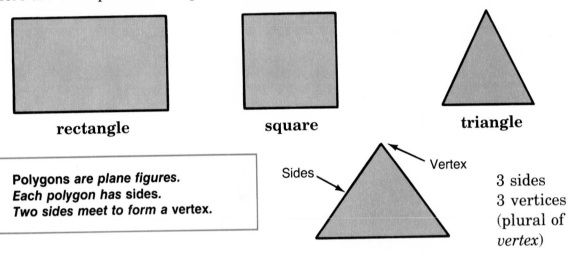

rectangle   square   triangle

Polygons *are plane figures.*
Each polygon has sides.
Two sides meet to form a vertex.

Sides

Vertex

3 sides
3 vertices
(plural of *vertex*)

Some polygons have special names.

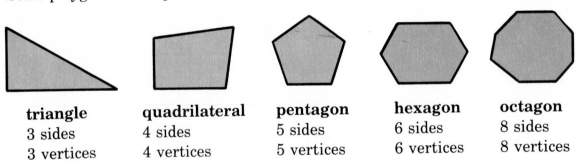

triangle
3 sides
3 vertices

quadrilateral
4 sides
4 vertices

pentagon
5 sides
5 vertices

hexagon
6 sides
6 vertices

octagon
8 sides
8 vertices

PRACTICE • Is it a polygon? Write YES or NO.

1.
2.
3.
4.

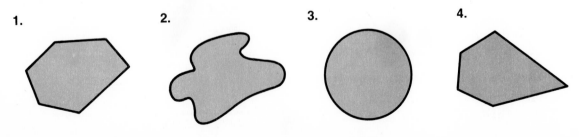

EXERCISES • Tell how many sides and vertices. Name each polygon.

5.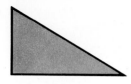

_?_ sides

_?_ vertices

6.

_?_ sides

_?_ vertices

7.

_?_ sides

_?_ vertices

8.

_?_ sides

_?_ vertices

9.

_?_ sides

_?_ vertices

10.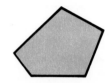

_?_ sides

_?_ vertices

11.

_?_ sides

_?_ vertices

12.

_?_ sides

_?_ vertices

13.

_?_ sides

_?_ vertices

Match.

14.

15.

16.

17.

18.

a. pentagon

b. quadrilateral

c. hexagon

d. triangle

e. octagon

PROBLEM SOLVING • APPLICATIONS

19. I have 8 sides and 8 vertices. What plane figure am I?

★ **20.** A **decagon** is a polygon that has 10 sides. How many vertices does it have?

Congruent Line Segments and Polygons

At Expo '67, the World's Fair held in
Canada, the United States pavilion
was in the shape of a **geodesic dome**.
Notice the hexagonal pattern of each
section of the dome. The hexagonal
shapes are *congruent* to each other.

> **Congruent polygons** *are the same size and shape.*

Here is a close-up picture of a
section of the geodesic dome.
Each line segment that makes up the
sides of each hexagon are congruent.

> **Congruent line segments** *are the same length.*

● Are these two polygons congruent?

Think Trace one polygon and place it on
top of the other. If they match
exactly, then they are congruent.

These polygons **are congruent**.

PRACTICE • Are the polygons congruent? Write YES or NO.

1.

2.

3. 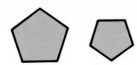   **4.**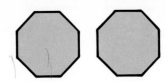

EXERCISES • Tell which polygon is congruent to the first polygon in each row.

5.   **a.**   **b.**   **c.**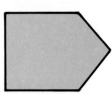

6.   **a.**    **b.**   **c.**

7.    **a.** 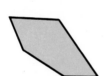   **b.** 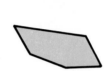   **c.**

PROBLEM SOLVING • APPLICATIONS

8. A rectangle is a special kind of quadrilateral. Which sides are congruent?

9. A square is a special kind of rectangle. Which sides are congruent?

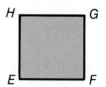

10. The playground is in the shape of a square. Each side is 78 meters long. Find the perimeter. You can draw a picture to help you.

11. How many pairs of congruent triangles can you find in the cat?

PROBLEM SOLVING • STRATEGIES

Using Geometric Patterns

Sometimes you must find a pattern to solve a problem.
You have seen patterns that are made up of numbers.
Other patterns are made up of geometric figures.

● What are the next two figures in this pattern?

Think What is the **order** of the figures?

Two triangles and then two circles.

The next two figures are circles.

● What are the next two figures in this pattern?

Think What is the **size** and **position** of the figures?

A large triangle and then a smaller triangle that is upside down.

These are the next two figures.

PROBLEMS • Draw the next four figures for each pattern.

1.

Some problems depend on
what you see. Look for a
geometric pattern.

3.

4.

2.

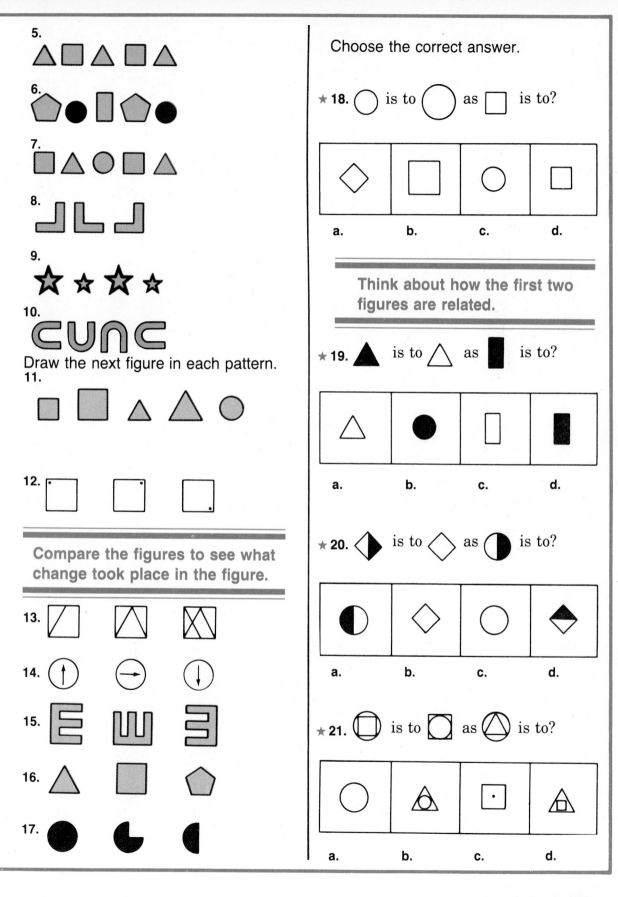

5.

6.

7.

8.

9.

10.

Draw the next figure in each pattern.

11.

12.

Compare the figures to see what change took place in the figure.

13.

14.

15.

16.

17.

Choose the correct answer.

★ **18.** ◯ is to ◯ as ☐ is to?

a.　　　b.　　　c.　　　d.

Think about how the first two figures are related.

★ **19.** ▲ is to △ as ▮ is to?

a.　　　b.　　　c.　　　d.

★ **20.** ◀ is to ◇ as ◖ is to?

a.　　　b.　　　c.　　　d.

★ **21.** ⬜ is to ⬜ as △ is to?

a.　　　b.　　　c.　　　d.

MID-CHAPTER REVIEW

Name the line segment. (Page 396)

1.

D _____ E

Name the line. (Page 396)

2.

Name the angle. (Page 398)

3.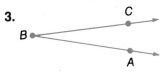

Name two rays. (Page 398)

4.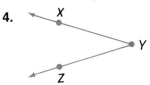

Name each polygon. Tell how many sides and vertices. (Pages 400–401)

5.   __?__ sides __?__ vertices

6.   __?__ sides __?__ vertices

7.   __?__ sides __?__ vertices

Are the polygons congruent? Write YES or NO. (Pages 402–403)

8.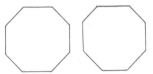

9.

Draw the next figure in each pattern. (Pages 404–405)

10.

11.

MAINTENANCE • MIXED PRACTICE

Write each decimal.

1. $\frac{5}{10}$

2. $6\frac{2}{10}$

3. $12\frac{24}{100}$

4. $5\frac{7}{100}$

5. __?__ g = 5 kg

6. __?__ oz = 3 lbs.

7. __?__ cm = 1 meter

8. 7 km = __?__ m

9. Write the standard number for four million, two hundred six thousand, forty-eight.

10. Write 4,528 in expanded form.

11. Sally skis 10.6 kilometers on Monday. She skis 3.2 kilometers in the morning. How many kilometers does she ski in the afternoon?

12. Andy pays $2.05 for lunch at the lodge. He pays $5.72 for dinner. How much more does Andy pay for dinner than for lunch?

Landscape Architect

Landscape architects help plan and design the arrangement of trees, walks, and gardens for parks and playgrounds.

Instead of drawing a plan for the garden, John used straws of different lengths. He made these two plans.

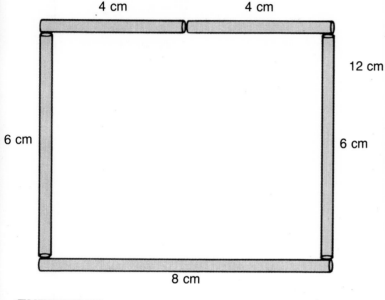

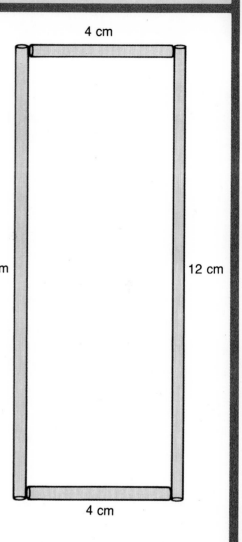

EXERCISES

1. What is the perimeter of each rectangle?

2. Get 7 straws and a centimeter ruler.
   Measure and cut the straws so that you have:

   2 straws that are each 12 centimeters long,
   1 straw that is 8 centimeters long,
   2 straws that are each 6 centimeters long, and
   2 straws that are each 4 centimeters long.

   Use the straws to make as many different rectangles as you can. Find the perimeter of each rectangle.

3. Now use the straws to make as many different triangles as you can. Find the perimeter of each triangle.

Circles

The Superdome in New Orleans is the largest indoor stadium in the world. It can seat almost 98,000 people. Its circular roof measures 680 feet in *diameter*.

- Look at the circle below. Notice that points P, T, and R are points on the circle.

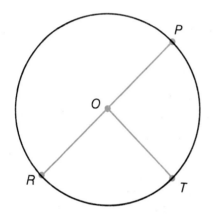

Point O is the **center** of the circle.

Line segment *OT* is a **radius**. A **radius** is a line segment from the center to any point on the circle.

Line segment *RP* is a **diameter**. A **diameter** is a line segment that passes through the center and has its endpoints on the circle.

- You can use a **compass** to draw a circle. Draw a line segment that is the length of the radius. Open the compass to this length.
Then draw the circle.

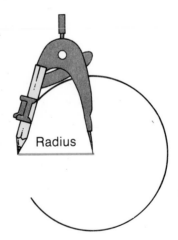

Radius

PRACTICE • Use the circle to answer Exercises 1–3.

1. Name the center of the circle.

2. Line segment *AB* is a diameter. Name another diameter.

3. Line segment *PC* is a radius. Name three more.

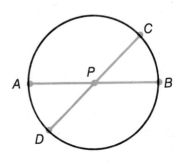

EXERCISES • Use the circle to answer Exercises 4–6.

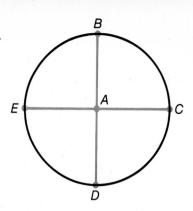

4. Name the center of the circle.

5. Name two diameters.

6. Name one radius.

What part of the circle is

7. line segment *KL*?

8. point *K*?

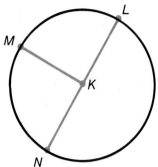

9. line segment *NL*?

10. line segment *KM*?

Draw a circle with a

11. radius of 2 cm.   12. radius of 4 cm.   13. diameter of 6 cm.

PROBLEM SOLVING • **APPLICATIONS**

14. The length of radius *BO* is ___?___ cm.

15. The length of diameter *BA* is ___?___ cm.

16. The diameter of the circle is ___?___ times as long as the radius.

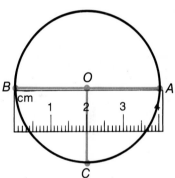

CALCULATOR • **Distance around ÷ diameter.**

Copy this table. Find some objects that are in the shape of a circle. Use a string to measure the distance around the circle to the nearest centimeter. Measure the diameter to the nearest centimeter. Use a calculator to complete the last column of the table. What do you notice about the numbers in the last column?

Object	Distance Around	Diameter	Distance Around Divided by Diameter

Lines of Symmetry

The Taj Mahal of India was built nearly 300 years ago. The blue line is drawn down the middle of the building.

● Does the left half of the building match the right half?

Think Trace and cut out the Taj Mahal. Fold it along the blue line. Do the halves match?

The building is **symmetric** because the two halves match. The line along the fold is a **line of symmetry**.

● Does a rectangle have more than one line of symmetry?

Think Trace and cut out this rectangle. Fold it along line **AB**. Do the halves match?

Unfold it. Now fold it along line **CD**. Do the halves match?

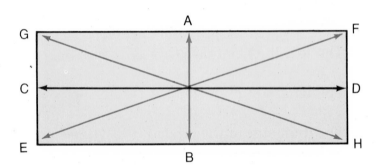

● Are lines **GH** and **FE** lines of symmetry?

A rectangle has two **lines of symmetry**.

PRACTICE • Is the blue line a line of symmetry? Write YES or NO.

1.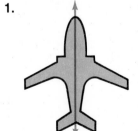

2.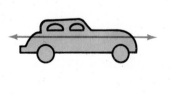

3.

4.

EXERCISES • Trace each figure and cut it out. Fold the figure to find a line of symmetry. Draw a line of symmetry.

5.

6.

7.

8.

9.

10.

11.

12.

Trace each figure and cut it out. Fold the figure to find lines of symmetry. How many lines of symmetry can you draw?

13.

14.

15.

16.

17.

18.

19.

20.

PROBLEM SOLVING • APPLICATIONS

Below are sketches of famous buildings.
Trace and cut out each sketch. How many lines of symmetry can you draw for each picture?

21.

Parthenon
Athens, Greece

22.

Arc de Triomphe
Paris, France

23.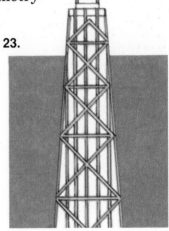

John Hancock Center
Chicago, Illinois

Solid Geometric Figures

The Great Pyramid in Egypt is one of the Seven Wonders of the World. *Pyramids* are one of the basic solid geometric figures.

● Many common objects are shaped like solid figures.

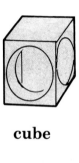

cube

rectangular prism

cylinder

cone

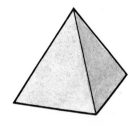

pyramid

sphere

● Each flat surface of this **rectangular prism** is called a **face**.
Two faces meet at an **edge**.
The edges meet at a **corner**.

A **rectangular prism** has 6 faces, 12 edges, and 8 corners.

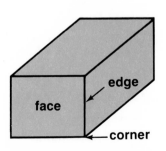

PRACTICE • Name the figures.

1.

2.

3.

EXERCISES • Name the figures.

4.

5.

6.

7.

8.

9.

Tell how many.

10.
___?___ faces
___?___ edges
___?___ corners

11.
___?___ faces
___?___ edges
___?___ corners

12.
___?___ faces
___?___ edges
___?___ corners

13.
___?___ faces
___?___ edges
___?___ corners

PROBLEM SOLVING • APPLICATIONS

This figure is a pentagonal prism.

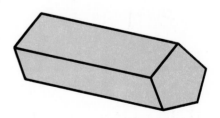

14. This solid figure has two kinds of plane figures as its faces. Name them.

15. How many faces, edges, and corners does it have?

★ 16. Find the area of each face of this rectangular prism. Add the areas to find the total **surface area**.

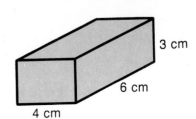

3 cm

6 cm

4 cm

Geometry • **413**

NON-ROUTINE PROBLEM SOLVING

Anthony is making posters for his classroom bulletin board. He needs more crayons to finish the posters.

Anthony saw this coupon in a newspaper. On double-coupon days at Fieldings, he can save twice the amount printed on the coupon.

This ad was also in the newspaper. Anthony wrote these statements to help him decide where to buy the crayons.

a. If I buy 1 box at Fieldings, I can save $0.25.

b. If I buy 1 box at Fieldings on double coupon days, I can save $0.50.

c. If I buy 2 boxes at the Color Wheel, I will get 1 box free.

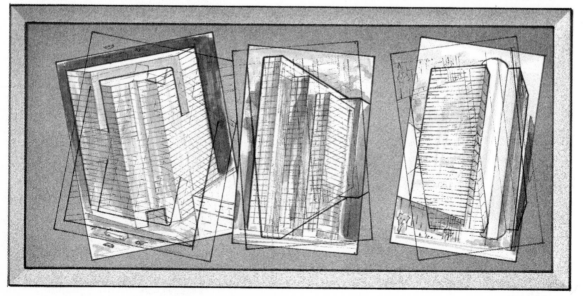

FINDING THE COST

Complete. Use the coupon for Fieldings.

1. If one box costs $2.60, then Anthony will pay __?__ for 1 box.

2. If one box costs $2.60 and he has only one coupon, Anthony will pay __?__ for 2 boxes.

3. If one box costs $2.60 and it is double-coupon day, then Anthony will pay __?__ for 1 box.

4. If one box costs $2.60, it is double-coupon day, and Anthony has only one coupon, then Anthony will pay __?__ for 2 boxes.

Complete. Use the ad for the Color Wheel Store.

5. If one box costs $2.55, then Anthony will pay __?__ for 1 box.

6. If one box costs $2.55, then Anthony will pay __?__ for 2 boxes.

7. If Anthony buys 2 boxes for __?__, then he will get __?__ boxes.

8. If Anthony gets 3 boxes for $5.10, then he really paid __?__ for each box.

MAKING A CHOICE

9. Suppose you were Anthony. You need 2 boxes of crayons. At which store would you buy them?

   Give a reason for your answer.

CHAPTER REVIEW

Part 1: VOCABULARY

For Exercises 1–12, choose from the box at the right
the word that best completes each statement.

1. A straight line with two endpoints is a __?__ __?__. (Page 396)

2. A __?__ has no endpoints. It goes on forever
   in both directions. (Page 396)

3. A line is named by any two __?__ on it. (Page 396)

4. Lines that cross are __?__ lines. (Page 396)

5. Lines that never cross are __?__ lines. (Page 396)

6. A __?__ has one endpoint. It goes on forever
   in one direction. (Page 398)

angle
congruent
diameter
intersecting
line
line segment
parallel
perpendicular
points
radius
ray
symmetry

7. Two rays that have the same endpoint form an __?__. (Page 398)

8. Two intersecting lines that form right angles are __?__. (Page 398)

9. Figures that are the same size and shape are __?__. (Page 402)

10. A line segment from the center of the circle to any point
    on the circle is the __?__. (Page 408)

11. A line that passes through the center of the circle and has
    its endpoints on the circle is the __?__. (Page 408)

12. A line drawn through the center of an object that divides the
    object into two equal parts is called a line of __?__. (Page 410)

Part 2: SKILLS

Write the letter for each figure. (Pages 396–399)

13. a segment   **14.** a line

15. intersecting lines

16. parallel lines

17. a ray   **18.** a right angle

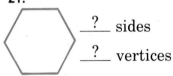

Tell how many sides and vertices. Name each polygon. (Pages 400–401)

19.

___?___ sides

___?___ vertices

20.

___?___ sides

___?___ vertices

21.

___?___ sides

___?___ vertices

22. Name the center of the circle, two diameters, and one radius. (Pages 408–409)

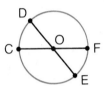

Is the blue line a line of symmetry? Write YES or NO. (Pages 410–411)

23.

24.

25.

Name the shapes. Then tell how many. (Pages 412–413)

26.

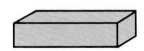

___?___ faces

___?___ edges

___?___ corners

27.

___?___ faces

___?___ edges

___?___ corners

Part 3: PROBLEM SOLVING • APPLICATIONS

Draw the next figure in each pattern. (Pages 404–405)

28.

29.

CHAPTER TEST

Write the letter for each figure.

1. a segment

2. a line

3. intersecting lines

4. parallel lines

5. a ray

6. a right angle

Name each polygon. Tell how many sides and vertices.

7. ___?___

8. ___?___ sides

___?___ vertices

9. ___?___

10. ___?___ sides

___?___ vertices

11. ___?___

12. ___?___ sides

___?___ vertices

Are the polygons congruent? Write YES or NO.

13.

14.

Name the

15. center of the circle ___?___

16. two diameters ___?___

17. one radius ___?___

Is the blue line a line of symmetry? Write YES or NO.

18.

19.

Name each shape. Then tell how many.

20. ___?___

21. ___?___ faces

___?___ edges

___?___ corners

22. ___?___

23. ___?___ faces

___?___ edges

___?___ corners

Draw the next figure in each pattern.

24.

25.

ENRICHMENT

Drawing Similar Figures

Figures that have the same shape are **similar figures**. Similar figures are not congruent. They may differ in size.

For example, if side **DE** is twice as long as side **AB**, then $\overline{DF}$ is twice as long as $\overline{AC}$. Also, side **FE** is __?__ as long as side **CB**.

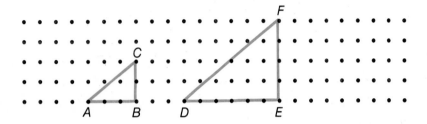

EXERCISES • Trace each figure. Then draw a similar figure with sides twice as long.

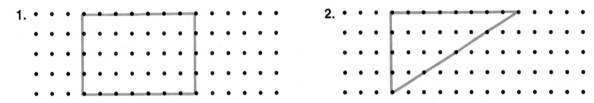

In each exercise, trace each figure. Then draw a similar figure with sides three times as long.

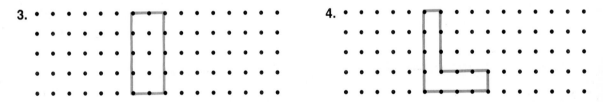

In each exercise, trace each figure. Then draw a similar figure with sides half as long.

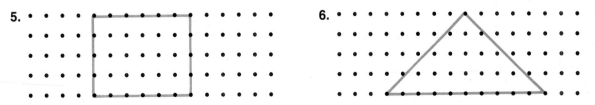

ADDITIONAL PRACTICE

SKILLS

Write the letter for each. (Pages 396–399)

1. a line

2. a right angle

3. parallel lines

4. a segment

5. intersecting lines

6. a ray

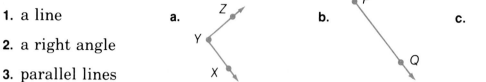

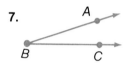

Name each angle. Is it a right angle? (Pages 398–399) Write YES or NO.

7.

8.

Are the polygons congruent? (Pages 402–403) Write YES or NO.

9.

10.

Use the circle. Name the center of the circle. one diameter, and one radius. (Pages 408–409)

11.

How many lines of symmetry can you draw? (Pages 410–411)

12.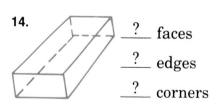

13.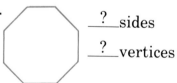

Name each figure. (Pages 400–401, 412–413)

14.
  _?_ faces
  _?_ edges
  _?_ corners

15.
  _?_ sides
  _?_ vertices

PROBLEM SOLVING • APPLICATIONS

Draw the next figure in each pattern. (Pages 404–405)

16.

17.

18.

420 • Chapter 13

Each of these problems contains a common error.

a. Find the correct answer.

b. Find the error.

1.
$$\begin{array}{r} 15.25 \\ +26.98 \\ \hline \mathbf{4,223} \end{array}$$

2.
$$\begin{array}{r} 6.72 \\ -3.65 \\ \hline \mathbf{3.7} \end{array}$$

3.
$$\begin{array}{r} 92.64 \\ +54.73 \\ \hline \mathbf{146.137} \end{array}$$

4. $9.45 + 3.6 = \underline{\ ?\ }$

$$\begin{array}{r} 9.45 \\ +\ 3.6 \\ \hline \mathbf{98.1} \end{array}$$

5. $7 - 2.67 = \underline{\ ?\ }$

$$\begin{array}{r} 7 \\ -2.67 \\ \hline \mathbf{5.67} \end{array}$$

6. Write a decimal for $\frac{8}{100}$.

$\frac{8}{100} = \mathbf{0.80}$

7. Write $>$, $<$, or $=$.

5.6 ● 5.60

$5.6 < 5.60$

8. Name the figure.

It is a **cylinder.**

9. Name the polygon.

It is an **octagon.**

10. Name the angle.

$\angle AMP$

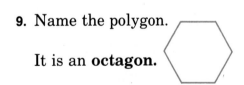

11. Name the ray.

$\overrightarrow{RS}$

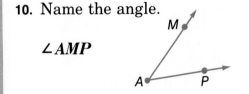

12. Copy this rectangle.
Draw a line of symmetry.

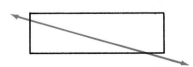

13. What part of the circle is line segment OR?

Line segment OR is a **diameter.**

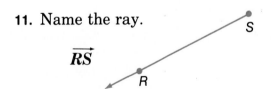

CUMULATIVE REVIEW
Chapters 1 through 13

Choose the correct answers.

1. Round 6,485 to the nearest ten.

A. 6,500   **B.** 6,480
C. 6,490   **D.** not here

2.
$$\begin{array}{r} 4,800 \\ -2,976 \\ \hline \end{array}$$

A. 1,926   **B.** 1,914
C. 1,814   **D.** not here

3.
$$\begin{array}{r} 947 \\ \times\ 60 \\ \hline \end{array}$$

A. 54,820   **B.** 56,820
C. 56,920   **D.** not here

4. $7\overline{)9,864}$

A. 1,409 r8   **B.** 1,309 r1
C. 1,409 r1   **D.** not here

5. $\frac{5}{8} = \frac{?}{16}$

A. 5   **B.** 21
C. 10   **D.** not here

6. $\frac{4}{10} + \frac{3}{10} = \underline{\ ?\ }$

A. $\frac{7}{20}$ **B.** $\frac{7}{10}$
C. $\frac{12}{10}$ **D.** not here

7.
$$\begin{array}{r} 428 \\ \times\ 67 \\ \hline \end{array}$$

A. 28,576   **B.** 28,676
C. 28,567   **D.** not here

8. $76\overline{)497}$

A. 6 r41   **B.** 6 r43
C. 6 r42   **D.** not here

9. Which number is equal to fourteen and nine hundredths?

A. 14.09   **B.** 14.12
C. 14.90   **D.** not here

10. Peter won the 300-meter race. If you take his time, subtract 2, and multiply by 10, the result is 50. How many minutes did it take Peter to run the 300-meters?

A. 7   **B.** 20
C. 12   **D.** 62

11. It took Shannon 24.37 seconds to run her first lap around the track. It took her 29.75 seconds to run the second lap. Choose the estimate that shows how much longer it took her to run the second lap.

A. $24 + 30 = \underline{\ ?\ }$ **B.** $30 - 24 = \underline{\ ?\ }$
C. $29 - 25 = \underline{\ ?\ }$ **D.** $25 + 30 = \underline{\ ?\ }$

12. Choose the decimal for

tens	ones	tenths
2	8	6

A. 286   **B.** 28.6

C. 2.86   **D.** not here

13. Choose the correct sign.

14.09 14.9

A. =   **B.** <

C. >   **D.** not here

14. 7.32 + 6.8 = ___?___

A. 8.00   **B.** 14.12

C. 13.12   **D.** not here

---

15.   37.6
     −18.79

A. 18.81

B. 18.99

C. 19.81

D. not here

16. Choose the name for the figure.

A. intersecting lines

B. a ray

C. right angle

D. not here

17. Choose the name for the figure.

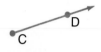

A. a line

B. a ray

C. a segment

D. not here

---

18. Choose how many sides and vertices.

A. 5 sides, 5 vertices

B. 6 sides, 12 vertices

C. 6 sides, 6 vertices

D. not here

19. Choose a name for the diameter of the circle.

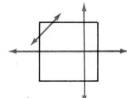

A. $\overline{OD}$

B. $\overline{CD}$

C. $\overline{OF}$

D. not here

20. Which line is the line of symmetry?

A. red

B. blue

C. green

D. not here

---

21. Tara measured the hem and the collar of her dress so that she could buy ribbon for trim. The hem measured 36.6 centimeters, and the collar measured 11.9 centimeters. About how many centimeters of ribbon should she buy?

A. 48   **B.** 47

C. 50   **D.** 49

22. Choose the next four figures for the pattern.

A. ☐△○☐   **B.** △○☐△

C. ☐○△☐   **D.** ○☐△○

TABLE OF MEASURES

Metric

United States Customary

Length

10 millimeters (mm) = 1 centimeter (cm)
100 centimeters = 1 meter (m)
1,000 meters = 1 kilometer (km)

12 inches (in.) = 1 foot (ft)
36 inches ⎫
3 feet ⎭ = 1 yard (yd)
5,280 feet ⎫
1,760 yards ⎭ = 1 mile (mi)

Area

100 square millimeters (sq mm) = 1 square
centimeter (sq cm)
10,000 square centimeters = 1 square
meter (sq m)

144 square inches (sq in.) = 1 square
foot (sq ft)
9 square feet = 1 square
yard (sq yd)

Volume

1,000 cubic millimeters (cu mm) = 1 cubic
centimeter (cu cm)
1,000,000 cubic centimeters = 1 cubic
meter (cu m)

1,728 cubic inches (cu in.) = 1 cubic
foot (cu ft)
27 cubic feet = 1 cubic
yard (cu yd)

Capacity

1,000 milliliters (mL) = 1 liter (L)

2 cups = 1 pint (pt)
2 pints = 1 quart (qt)
4 quarts = 1 gallon (gal)

Mass/Weight

1,000 milligrams (mg) = 1 gram (g)
1,000 grams = 1 kilogram (kg)

16 ounces (oz) = 1 pound (lb)
2,000 pounds = 1 ton (T)

Time

60 seconds (s) = 1 minute (min)
60 minutes = 1 hour (h)
24 hours = 1 day (d)
7 days = 1 week (wk)
28 to 31 days = 1 month (mo)
12 months ⎫
52 weeks ⎭ = 1 year (yr)
100 years = 1 century (cen)

TABLE OF SYMBOLS

+	plus
−	minus
×	times
÷	divided by
=	equals or is equal to
≠	is not equal to
>	is greater than
<	is less than
≅	is congruent to
…	pattern continues without end
( )	parentheses: do the operation inside the ( ) first.
3 r2	three remainder two
7.3	decimal point: seven and three-tenths
$\frac{3}{4}$	fraction: three-fourths
∟	right angle
∠ ABC	angle ABC
°	degree (angle or measurement)
°C	degree Celsius
°F	degree Fahrenheit
. A	point A
$\overline{AB}$	line segment with endpoints A and B
$\overrightarrow{AB}$	ray AB with endpoint A
$\overleftrightarrow{AB}$	line through points A and B
25¢ or $0.25	money: twenty-five cents
$3.50	money: three dollars and fifty cents
2:15	time: two fifteen

GLOSSARY

Addend   A number that is added. (p. 2)

> *Example:* 6 + 8 = 14.   The addends are 6 and 8.

Addition (+)   An operation on two numbers to find out how many in all or how much in total. (p. 2)

> *Example:* 7 + 9 = 16. 7 and 9 are addends. 16 is the sum.

Angle   Two rays with the same endpoint. The endpoint is the vertex of the angle. (p. 398)

> *Example:*

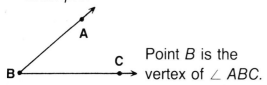

Point *B* is the vertex of ∠ *ABC*.

Area   The number of square units needed to cover a surface. (p. 222)

> *Example:* The area of this rectangle is 6 square units.

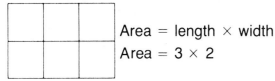

Area = length × width
Area = 3 × 2

Average (mean)   The quotient found by dividing a sum by the number of addends. (p. 192)

> *Example:* The average of 1, 2, and 6 is 3 because 1 + 2 + 6 = 9 and 9 ÷ 3 = 3.

Bar graph   A graph with bars (rectangles) of different heights to show and compare information. (p. 138)

Circle   A closed curve with all points an equal distance from a center point. (p. 408)

> *Example:*

Common denominator   A number used as a denominator to make two or more equal fractions. (p. 300)

> *Example:* 12 is a common denominator of $\frac{1}{3}$ and $\frac{5}{6}$.

Cone   A solid with one circular face. (p. 412)

> *Example:*

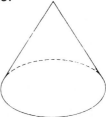

Congruent Having the same size and shape. (p. 402)

Congruent line segments Line segments that have the same length. (p. 402)

Congruent polygons Polygons that have the same size and shape. (p. 402)

Coordinate graph A drawing of numbered lines that cross at right angles and are used to name the positions of points. (p. 146)

Corner The point where edges of a solid meet. (p. 412)

Cube A rectangular prism with six congruent square faces. (p. 412)
Example:

Customary measurement system A measurement system that uses inches, feet, yards, and miles as units of length; cups, pints, quarts, and gallons for liquid capacity; ounces, pounds, and tons as units of weight; and degrees Fahrenheit as units of temperature. (p. 246)

Cylinder A solid with two bases that are congruent circles. (p. 412)

Decimal A number that uses place value and a decimal point to show tenths, hundredths, and so on. (p. 370)
Example: 2.78 Read two and seventy-eight hundredths.

Degree Celsius (°C) A standard unit for measuring temperature in the metric system. (p. 238)
Example: Water freezes at 0°C and boils at 100°C.

Degree Fahrenheit (°F) A standard unit for measuring temperature in the customary measurement system. (p. 258)
Example: Water freezes at 32°F and boils at 212°F.

Denominator The number below the bar in a fraction. (p. 270)
Example: $\frac{3}{5}$ The denominator is 5.

Diameter A line segment through the center of a circle with endpoints on the circle. (p. 408)

Difference The answer to a subtraction problem. (p. 8)
Example: $14 - 9 = 5$ The difference is 5.

Digit Any one of the ten symbols 0, 1, 2, 3, 4, 5, 6, 7, 8, or 9. (p. 26)

Dividend The number that is divided in a division problem. (p. 112)
Example: $12 \div 4$ 12 is the dividend.

Divisible   A number is divisible by another number if the quotient is a whole number and the remainder is 0. (p. 209)
Example: 18 is divisible by 3.

Division ($\overline{)}$ or $\div$)   An operation on two numbers that results in a quotient and a remainder. (p. 112)

Divisor   The number by which the dividend is divided. (p. 112)
Example: 6 r2
5$\overline{)32}$ The divisor is 5.

Edge   The line segment where two faces of a solid meet. (p. 412)
Example:

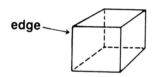

Endpoint   A point at the end of a line segment or ray. (p. 396)

Equals (=)   Has the same value.
Example: 6 + 8 = 14 (p. 2)

Equation   A number sentence with an equals sign (=). (p. 2)
Examples: 5 + 8 = 13; 17 − 9 = 8.

Equivalent fractions   Fractions that name the same number. (p. 276)
Example: $\frac{1}{2}$ and $\frac{2}{4}$ are equivalent fractions.

Estimate   To guess a reasonable answer. One way to estimate is to round the numbers before doing the problem. (p. 62)

Even number   A whole number with 0, 2, 4, 6, or 8 in the ones place. (p. 179)
Examples: 2, 16, 78, and 340 are even numbers.

Expanded form   A way to show a number as a sum of multiples of ten. (p. 26)
Example: 635 = 600 + 30 + 5

Face   A flat surface of a solid. (p. 412)
Example:

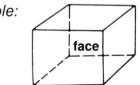

Factor   A number that is multiplied. (p. 96)
Example: 8 × 7 = 56   The factors are 8 and 7.

Fraction   A number that names part of a whole or group. (p. 270)
Example: $\frac{2}{3}$ 2 is the numerator. 3 is the denominator.

Grouping property of addition   The way in which addends are grouped does not change the sum. (p. 6)
Example: (3 + 2) + 4 = 3 + (2 + 4).

Grouping property of multiplication   The way in which factors are grouped does not change the product. (p. 104)
Example: (2 × 3) × 4 = 2 × (3 × 4)

Hexagon   A polygon with six sides. (p. 400)

Intersecting lines   Lines that meet or cross. Intersecting lines have only one point in common. (p. 396)
Example:

Length   The measurement of an object from end to end. (p. 216)

Like fractions   Fractions with the same denominator. (p. 292)
Example: $\frac{2}{5}$ and $\frac{3}{5}$ are like fractions.

Line   A straight path extending in both directions with no endpoints. (p. 396)

Line graph   A graph in which a line is used to show a change. (p. 144)

Line of symmetry   A line that divides a figure into two congruent parts. (p. 410)
Example:

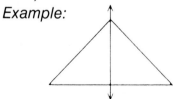

Line segment   Part of a line with two endpoints. (p. 396)

Magic square   The sum of the numbers in each row, column, and diagonal is the same. (p. 381)

Example:

4	3	8
9	5	1
2	7	6

Metric system   A measurement system that uses centimeters, meters, and kilometers as units of length; milliliters and liters as units of capacity; grams and kilograms as units of mass; and degrees Celsius as units of temperature. (p. 216)

Minus $(-)$ A symbol that shows subtraction. (p. 8)
Example: $15 - 6 = 9$ Read fifteen minus six equals nine.

Mixed number   The sum of a whole number and a fraction. (p. 284)
Example: $3\frac{1}{2} = 3 + \frac{1}{2}$

Multiplication $(\times)$ An operation on two numbers, called factors, which results in a product. (p. 96)
Example: $8 \times 9 = 72$ 8 and 9 are factors and 72 is the product.

Numerator   The number above the bar in a fraction. (p. 270)
Example: $\frac{2}{3}$ The numerator is 2.

Octagon   A polygon with eight sides. (p. 400)
Example:

Odd number   A whole number that is not a multiple of 2. An odd number ends in 1, 3, 5, 7, or 9. (p. 179)
   Examples: 7, 19, 53, 235 are odd numbers.

Order property of addition   The order in which addends are added does not change the sum. (p. 2)
   Example: 6 + 4 = 4 + 6

Order property of multiplication The order in which factors are multiplied does not change the product. (p. 104)
   Example: 5 × 7 = 7 × 5

Ordered pair   A pair of numbers used to locate points on a grid. (p. 146)

Palindrome   A number that reads the same forward or backward. (p. 91)
   Examples: 141; 5,665; 22,022 are palindromes.

Parallel lines   Lines that do not intersect. Parallel lines are always the same distance apart. (p. 396)
   Example:

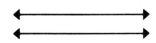

Parentheses ( )   A grouping symbol. Parentheses tell which part or parts of a problem to do first. (p. 6)
   Example: (8 + 7) − 9 Do (8 + 7) first.

Pentagon   A polygon with five sides. (p. 400)

Perimeter   The distance around a shape. The perimeter of a shape is the sum of the lengths of the sides. (p. 220)
   Example:

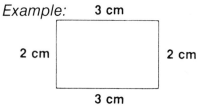

   Perimeter = 3 + 2 + 3 + 2 = 10 cm

Period   Each group of 3 digits in a large number. (p. 40)
Example: 54,371
The ones period is 371.

Perpendicular lines   Two intersecting lines that form four right angles. (p. 398)

Pictograph   A way to show comparisons. A key always appears on a pictograph showing how many each object represents. (p. 140)

Place value   The value given to the place in which a digit appears in a number. (p. 26)
   Example: 5,347   The place value of 3 is hundreds. The place value of 7 is ones.

Plus (+)   A symbol that shows addition. (p. 2)
   Example: 5 + 8 = 13   Read five plus eight equals thirteen.

Polygon   A closed plane figure formed by three or more line segments joined at the endpoints. (p. 400)

Prime number   A whole number greater than one that has only two factors: 1 and itself. (p. 131)
>   *Examples:* 2, 3, 5, 7, 11, 13, 17, 19 are all prime numbers.

Prism   A solid with two parallel faces that are congruent figures. (p. 412)

Probability   The chance of an event occurring, written as a fraction between 0 (the event is impossible) and 1 (the event is certain). (p. 21)
>   *Example:* The probability of a coin landing heads is equal to $\frac{1}{2}$.

Product   The answer to a multiplication problem. (p. 96)
>   *Example:* $7 \times 12 = 84$ The product is 84.

Property of one for multiplication   When one of the two factors is 1, the product equals the other factor. (p. 104)
>   *Examples:* $5 \times 1 = 5$; $16 \times 1 = 16$.

Pyramid   A solid figure. One face is a triangle, rectangle, or other shape with angles. The other faces are triangles. (p. 412)
>   *Example:*

Quadrilateral   A polygon with four sides. (p. 400)

Quotient   The answer to a division problem. (p. 112)
>   *Example:* $12 \div 3 = 4$ The quotient is 4.

Radius (pl. radii)   A line segment with one endpoint at the center of a circle and the other endpoint on the circle. (p. 408)
>   *Example:*

Ray   A part of a line that has one endpoint and extends on and on in only one direction. (p. 398)
>   *Example:*

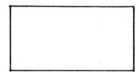

Rectangle   A shape with four sides and four right angles. (p. 400)
>   *Example:*

Rectangular prism   A solid with six faces that are rectangles. (p. 412)
>   *Example:*

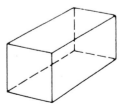

Remainder The number left over in a division problem. The remainder must be less than the divisor. (p. 124)

Example: 3r4
          5) 19   The remainder is 4.

Right angle An angle with the same shape as the corner of a square. (p. 398)

Example:

Roman numerals Symbols used by the Romans to name numbers. Roman numeration does not use place value. (p. 51)

Examples:

I	V	X	L	C	D	M
1	5	10	50	100	500	1,000

Rounding Expressing a number to the nearest thousandth, hundredth, tenth, one, ten, hundred, thousand. (p. 30)

Example: 37.85 rounded to the nearest tenth is 37.9.

Sphere A solid with all points the same distance from a center point. (p. 412)

Example:

Square A shape with four equal sides and four right angles. (p. 400)

Example:

Standard form The usual way of writing a number. (p. 26)

Example: The number seventy-eight is written 78 in standard form.

Subtraction (−) An operation on two numbers to find how many are left or how much greater one number is than the other. (p. 8)

Example: 15 − 6 = 9   9 is the difference.

Sum The answer to an addition problem. (p. 2)

Example: 12 + 7 = 19   The sum is 19.

Thermometer An instrument for measuring temperature. (p. 238)

Times (×) A symbol that shows multiplication. (p. 96)

Example: 5 × 9 = 45   Read five times nine equals forty-five.

Triangle A polygon with three sides. (p. 400)

Unlike fractions Fractions with different denominators. (p. 300)
Example: $\frac{3}{4}$ and $\frac{2}{3}$ are unlike fractions.

Vertex (pl. vertices) The point at which two rays of an angle, two sides of a polygon, or three or more edges of a solid meet. (p. 398)

Volume The number of cubic units needed to fill a solid. (p. 226)
Example: The volume of this cube is 8 cubic units.

Volume = length $\times$ width $\times$ height

Zero property for addition When 0 is added to any addend, the sum equals the addend. (p. 2)
Examples: $9 + 0 = 9; 0 + 12 = 12.$

Zero property for multiplication If 0 is a factor, the product is always 0. (p. 104)
Examples: $13 \times 0 = 0; 0 \times 7 = 0.$

INDEX

Addend(s), 2, 426
    grouping, 6–7
    more than two, 66–67
Addition, 426
    with calculator, 39, 63
    with computer, 53, 153
    of decimals, 380–381
    estimating sums, 62–63
    facts, 2–3
    facts drill, 4–5
    families of facts, 14–15
    of fractions, 292–293
    of fractions with unlike
        denominators, 300–
        301
    of greater numbers, 64–
        65
    of mixed numbers, 298–
        ·299
    of money, 84–85
    of more than two
        addends, 66–67
    properties of, 2, 6, 428,
        430, 433
    regrouping ones, tens,
        and hundreds, 60–61
    regrouping tens and
        ones, 56–59
    or subtraction, 74–75
    of three-digit numbers,
        58–59
    of two-digit numbers,
        56–57
Additional practice, 22, 52,
    92, 132, 152, 180, 210,
    266, 310, 336, 364,
    392, 420
A.M., 240–241
Angles, 398–399, 426
    right, 398–399, 432
    vertex of, 398, 433
Area, 426

customary units of,
    250–251
fractional, 265
metric units of, 222–223
multiplying to find, 224–
    225
Averages, 192–193, 426

Bar graphs, 138–139,
    426
    making, 143
BASIC, 53, 153
Buy, choosing the better,
    379
Buying, mail-order, 325

Calculator
    addition with, 11, 39,
        63, 107
    changing fractions to
        decimals, 375
    dividing with, 189, 275,
        353, 375, 409
    multiplying with, 165,
        321
    subtracting with, 11, 77,
        115
    using a formula, 189,
        353
    when to use, 45, 61, 83,
        103, 125, 157, 173, 201,
        257, 317, 345, 385
Career applications
    Carpet installer, 349
    Chefs, 169
    Food services, 197
    Landscape architect,
        407
    Poll taker, 37
    Store clerk, 69
Celsius
    degrees, 238–239, 427

thermometer, 238–239,
    432
Center, of circle, 408–409
Centimeter, 216–217
    cubic, 226–227
    square, 222–223, 265
Cents point, 84
Change, making, 46–47
Choosing a problem solving
    strategy, 93, 181, 337,
    393
Circles, 408–409, 426
    center of, 408–409
    diameter of, 408, 427
    drawing, 408
    radius of, 408–409, 431
Common Errors, 133, 211,
    311, 365, 421
Comparing
    decimals, 374–375
    fractions, 280–281
    numbers, 38–41
Compass, 408
Compatible numbers, 342
Computation,
    method of, 45, 61,
        83, 103, 125, 157,
        173, 201, 257,
        317, 345, 385
Computer Applications
    BASIC, 23, 53, 153
    central processing unit
        (CPU), 23
    chip, 23
    ENTER, 53, 153
    flowcharts, 267
        and problem solving,
        267
    input, 23, 53, 153
    keyboard, 23
    output, 23, 53, 153

PRINT command,
+ and −, 53
* and /, 153
processing, 23
RETURN, 53, 153
SHIFT. 53
space bar, 53, 153
storage, 23
Cone, 412–413, 426
Congruent line segments, 402–403, 427
Congruent polygons, 402–403, 427
Consumer applications,
Changing units of measure, 289
Choosing the better buy, 379
Mail order buying, 325
Reading maps, 237
Telephone, 109
Corner, 412–413, 427
Cube(s), 412–413, 427
Cubic centimeter, 226
Cubic foot, 252–253
Cubic inch, 252–253
Cubic meter, 228–229
Cubic yard, 252–253
Cumulative Review, 134–135, 212–213, 312–313, 366–367, 422–423
Cup, 254–255
Customary units, 246–259, 427
Cylinder, 412–413, 427

Days, 240
Decimals, 427
adding, 380–381
decimals, 386–387
hundredths, 372–373
measures, 391
subtracting, 382–383
tenths, 370–371
writing zeros before adding and subtracting, 384–385
Degrees
Celsius, 238–239, 427

Fahrenheit, 258–259, 427
Denominators, 270, 427
adding fractions with unlike, 300–301
subtracting fractions with unlike, 302–303
Diameter, 408–409, 427
Difference, 8, 427
estimating the, 76–77
using a calculator, 77
Digits, 26–27, 427
Dividend, 184, 427
Dividing by one-digit numbers
averages, 192–193, 426
four-digit quotients, 200–201
money, 202–203
placing the first digit, 190–191
three-digit quotients, 188–189
two-digit quotients, 184–187
zero in quotient, 198–199
Dividing by two-digit numbers
correcting over-estimates, 344–345
correcting under-estimates, 352–353
money, 356–357
rounding divisors down, 342–343
rounding divisors up, 350–351
by tens, 340–341
two-digit quotients, 354–355
Divisibility rules for two, three, and five, 209, 428
Division, 428
with calculator, 189
with computer, 153
dividend, 184, 427
divisor, 184, 342–343, 350–351, 428

by 8 and 9, 120–121
facts (drill), 123
finding equivalent fractions with, 282–283
by four and five, 114–115
or multiplication, 126–127
properties of, 122–123
quotients, 112, 124–125, 431
remainders, 124–125, 432
by six and seven, 118–119
by two and three, 112–113
two uses of, 116–117
Divisors, 184, 342–343, 350–351, 428
rounding down, 342
rounding up, 350–351
Dollar sign, 84
Drawing
a circle, 408
a picture, 34–35
similar figures, 419

Edge, 412–413, 428
Eight
dividing by, 120–121
as factor, 102–103
Endpoints, 396, 398, 428
Enrichment, 21, 51, 91, 131, 151, 179, 209, 265, 309, 335, 363, 391, 419
Equivalent fractions, 276–277, 428
finding by dividing, 282–283
finding by multiplying, 278–279
Estimating, 62–63, 64, 66, 76–77, 78–79, 80, 82, 84, 173, 320–321, 428
compatible numbers, 342

correcting overestimates, 344–345

correcting under-estimates, 352–353

decimals, 386–387

differences, 76–77, 78–79, 80, 82

measurement,
  lengths to the nearest centimeter, 217
  lengths to the nearest inch, 247

mixed numbers, 304–305

problem solving strategies,
  using estimation, 204–205
  using estimation with decimals, 386–387
  using estimation with mixed numbers, 304–305

products, 173, 320–321

quotients, 342

range of answers, 304

reasonableness in context, 218–219, 230–231, 232–233, 239, 248–249, 255, 256, 259

rounding fractions, 304–305

sums, 62–63, 64, 66

using a calculator, 63, 77, 165

using estimation, 204–205

when to use, 83, 173

with money, 84, 173

Even products, 179

Expanded form, 26–29, 428

Face, 412–413, 428

Factors, 428
  eight and nine as, 102–103, 428
  four and five as, 98–99
  missing, 110–111
  six and seven as, 100–101
  two and three as, 96–97

Fahrenheit
  degrees, 258–259, 427
  thermometer, 258–259, 432

Families of facts, 14–15

Figures
  plane, 400–401
  solid geometric, 412–413
  symmetric, 410–411

Five
  dividing by, 114–115
  divisibility rules for, 209
  as factor, 98–99

Foot, 248–249
  cubic, 252–253
  square, 250–251

Formulating Problems, 13, 117, 127, 175, 245, 329, 331, 347, 359, 385

Four
  dividing by, 114–115
  as factor, 98–99

Four-digit quotients
  dividing by one-digit numbers, 200–201
  multiplying one-digit numbers by, 170–171

Fractional areas, 265

Fractions, 428
  adding, 292, 293
  adding mixed numbers, 298–297
  adding with unlike denominators, 300–301, 433
  with calculator, 375
  comparing, 280–281
  denominator, 270, 427
  equivalent fractions, 276–279, 282–283, 428
  estimation with mixed numbers, 304–305
  finding part of a group, 274–275
  and groups, 272–273
  like fractions, 292, 429
  in lowest terms, 282–283, 429
  and mixed numbers, 284–285, 290–291, 429
  numerator, 270, 429
  probability as, 309
  subtracting, 296–297
  subtracting mixed numbers, 298–299
  subtracting with unlike denominators, 302
  sums of one and greater than one, 294–295
  using a calculator, 275

Gallon, 254–255

Geometry
  angles, 398–399, 426
  circles, 408–409, 426
  intersecting lines, 396–397, 429
  line segments, 396–397, 429
  lines, 396–397, 429
  lines of symmetry, 410–411, 429
  parallel lines, 396–397, 430
  points, 396–397
  polygons, 400–401, 402–403, 430
  rays, 398–399, 431
  solid geometric figures, 412–413

Gram, 232–233

Graphs
  bar, 138–139, 426
  collecting data, to make, 142–143
  line, 144–145, 429
  locating points on a grid, 146–147
  ordered pairs, 146–147, 151, 430
  pictographs, 140–141, 430

Greater numbers
  adding, 64–65
  subtracting, 82–83

Greater products,
multiplying one-digit
numbers by, 164–165
Greater than, 38–39
Grid
locating points on a,
146–147
Group(s)
finding part of a, 274–
275
and fractions, 272–273
Grouping addends, 6–7

Hexagon, 400–401, 429
Hours, 240–241
Hundred, rounding to
nearest, 30–31
Hundreds, 26–27
regrouping ones, tens,
and, 60–61
Hundred thousand, 40–41
Hundredths, 372–373

Inch, 246–247
cubic, 252–253
square, 250–251
Information
missing, 234–235
too much, 174–175
Intersecting lines, 396–
397, 429

Kilogram, 232–233
Kilometer, 218–219
square, 222–223

Length, 429
customary units of,
246–249
metric units of, 216–219
Less than, 38–39
Line graphs, 144–145, 429
Line segment, 396–397,
429
congruent, 402, 427
Lines, 396–397, 429
intersecting, 396, 429
parallel, 396–397, 430
Lines of symmetry, 410–
411, 429

Liquids
customary units of,
254–255
metric units of, 230–231
Liter, 230–231
Logical reasoning (See
Thinker's Corner)
(See also Non-Routine
Problem Solving)
Lowest terms, fractions in,
282–283, 429

Mail-order buying, 325
Maps, reading, 237
Measure, changing units
of, 289
Measures, decimal, 391
Measurement
area, 222–225, 250–
251, 426
changing units of, 289
customary units, 246–
259, 427
length, 216–219, 246–
249
liquids, 230–231, 254–
255
metric units, 216–233,
238–239, 429
perimeter, 220–221,
250–251, 430
temperature, 238–239,
258–259
time, 240–241
time intervals, 242–243
volume, 226–227, 252–
253, 433
weight, 232–233, 256–
257
Mental Math
addition, 3, 7, 27, 29, 43,
58–59, 373
decimals, 373
division, 185, 189, 282
fractions, 282
money, 173
multiplication, 103, 157,
158–159, 165, 171,
173, 316–317, 319

strategies,
changing numbers and
operations, 27, 29,
43, 173, 282,
373
compensation, 70
computing left to right,
58–59
using facts, 3, 7, 103,
157, 165, 171, 185, 282
using patterns, 165,
171, 316–317, 319
using properties, 3
using the distributive
property, 158–159
subtraction, 70
when to use, 45, 61, 83,
103, 125, 157, 173, 201,
257, 317, 345, 385
Meter, 218–219
cubic, 228–229
square, 222–223
Method of computation,
45, 61, 83, 103, 125, 157,
173, 201, 257, 317, 345,
385
Metric units, 216–233,
238–239, 429
Mid-Chapter Review, 36,
68, 108, 168, 196, 236,
288, 324, 348, 378, 406
Mile, 248–249
Milliliter, 230–231
Millions, 42–43
Minutes, 240–241, 242–
243
Mixed numbers, 284–285,
429
adding, 298–299
and fractions, 290–291
subtracting, 298–299
Money, 44–45
adding and subtracting,
84–85
cents point, 84
dividing by one-digit
numbers, 202–203
dividing by two-digit
numbers, 356–357

dollar sign, 84
making change, 46–47
multiplying by one-digit
numbers, 172–173
multiplying by two-digit
numbers, 328–329
Multiplication, 429
with calculator, 107, 321
with computer, 153
or division, 126–127
eight and nine as
factors, 102–103
estimating products,
173, 320
even and odd products,179
facts drill, 106
lattice method, 335
to find area, 224–225
to find volume, 228–229
finding equivalent
fractions by, 278–279
four and five as factors,
98–99
missing factors, 110–111
of money, 172–173,
328–329
properties of, 104–105,
428, 430, 431, 433
six and seven as
factors, 100–101
by ten, 316–317
by tens, 318–319
two and three as
factors, 96–97
Multiplying by one-digit
numbers
four-digit numbers, 170
greater products, 164
money, 172–173
regrouping ones, 158–
159
regrouping ones and
tens, 160–161
three-digit numbers,
162–163
two-digit numbers, 156–
157
Multiplying by two-digit
numbers

money, 328–329
by ten, 316–317
by tens, 318–319
three-digit numbers,
326–327
two-digit numbers, 320–
321

Nine
dividing by, 120–121
as factor, 102–103
Non-Routine Problem
Solving, 86–87, 194–
195, 286–287, 414–415
Number(s)
adding three-digit, 58
adding two-digit, 56–57
comparing and ordering,
38–39
even, 179, 428
greater, 64–65
mixed, 284–285, 429
odd, 179, 430
palindrome, 91, 430
prime, 131, 363, 431
sentences, 14–15, 358–
359, 428
subtracting three-digit,
72–73
subtracting two-digit,
70–71
Numerals, Roman, 51, 432
Numeration
comparing and ordering
numbers, 38–39
digits, 26–27, 427
expanded form, 26–29
428
hundreds, tens, and
ones, 26–27
millions, 42–43
money, 44–45
rounding to nearest ten
and hundred, 30–31,
432
rounding to nearest
thousand, 32–33, 432
standard form, 26–29
42–43

ten and hundred
thousands, 40–41
thousands, 28–29
using a calculator, 39
Numerator, 270, 429

Octagon, 400–401, 429
Odd products, 179
One, sums of, and greater
than, in adding
fractions, 294–295
One-digit numbers. See
Dividing by one-digit
numbers; Multiplying by
one-digit numbers
Ones, 26–27
regrouping, in
multiplication, 158
regrouping tens and,
56–59
regrouping tens,
hundreds, and, 60–61
and tens, in
multiplication, 160
Ordered pairs, 430
graphing, 151
to locate points on a
grid, 146–147
Ordering numbers, 38
Ounce, 256–257
Overestimates, correcting,
344–355

Palindromes, 91, 430
Parallel lines, 396–397,
430
Parentheses, 6, 430
Patterns, 404–405
Pentagon, 400–401, 430
Pentagonal prism, 413
Perimeter, 220–221, 250–
251, 430
customary units of,
250–251
metric units of, 220–221
Pictograph, 140–141, 430
Pictures
drawing, 34–35
Pint, 254–255

Place value, 26–27, 28–29, 40–43, 430
Plane, 400
    figures, 400–401
P.M., 240–241
Polygons, 400–401, 430
    congruent, 402–403
Pound, 256–257
Prime numbers, 131, 363, 431
Prisms, 431
    pentagonal, 413
    rectangular, 412–413, 431
Probability, 21, 431
    as a fraction, 309
Problem Formulation, 13, 117, 127, 163, 175, 245, 329, 331, 347, 359, 385
Problem solving applications
    addition and subtraction, 57, 59, 61, 63, 65, 67, 71, 73, 77, 79, 81, 83, 85, 89, 92
        89, 92
    addition and subtraction facts, 3, 5, 7, 9, 15, 19, 22
    with a computer, 267
    decimals, 371, 373, 375, 381, 383, 385, 389, 392
    dividing by one-digit numbers, 185, 187, 189, 191, 193, 199, 201, 203, 207, 210
    dividing by two-digit numbers, 341, 343, 345, 351, 353, 355, 357, 361, 364
    fractions and mixed numbers, 271, 273, 275, 277, 279, 281, 283, 285, 291, 293, 295, 297, 299, 301, 303, 307, 310
    geometry, 397, 399, 401, 403, 409, 411, 413, 417, 420

graphing, 139, 141, 145, 147, 149
    measurement, 217, 219, 221, 223, 225, 227, 229, 231, 233, 239, 241, 243, 249, 251, 253, 257, 259, 263, 266
    multiplication and division facts, 97, 99, 101, 103, 105, 111, 113, 115, 119, 121, 125, 129, 132
    multiplying by one-digit numbers, 157, 159, 161, 163, 165, 171, 173, 177, 180
    multiplying by two-digit numbers, 317, 319, 321, 327, 329, 333, 336
    numeration, 27, 29, 31, 33, 39, 41, 43, 45, 49, 52
Problem solving strategies
    add or subtract, 12–13, 74–75
    choosing a strategy, 93, 181, 337, 393
    collecting data to make graphs, 142–143
    drawing a picture, 34–35
    finding geometric patterns, 404–405
    guess and check, 323–324
    interpreting the remainder, 346–347
    maintenance, 93, 181, 337, 393
    missing information, 234–235
    more than one step, 260–261, 330–331
    multiply or divide, 126–127
    non-routine, 86–87, 194–195, 286–287, 414–415

one and two step problems, 16–17
    too much information, 174–175
    two uses of division, 116–117
    using estimation, 204–205
    with decimals, 386–387
    with mixed numbers, 304–305
    using number sentences, 358–359
    using a schedule, 245–246
    using tables, 166–167
    working backward, 377–378
    to count change, 46–47
Products, 96, 431
    even and odd, 179
    greater, 164–165
Projects, 37, 69, 143, 169, 193, 217, 237, 241, 247, 271, 289, 325, 349, 379
Properties
    of addition, 2, 6, 428, 430, 433
    of division, 122
    of multiplication, 104–105, 325, 349, 379, 428, 430, 431, 433
Pyramid, 412–413, 431

Quadrilateral, 400, 431
Quart, 254–255
Quotient(s), 112, 431
    correcting overestimates of, 344–345
    correcting underestimates of, 352–353
    four-digit, in dividing one-digit numbers, 200–201
    and remainders, 124

three-digit, in dividing one-digit numbers, 188–189

two-digit, in dividing one-digit numbers, 184–187

two-digit, in dividing two-digit numbers, 354–355

zero in, in dividing one-digit numbers, 198–199

Radius, 408–409, 431

Range of answer, 304

Rays, 398–399, 431

Rectangle, 400–401, 431

Rectangular prism, 412–413, 431

Regrouping

more than once, 78–79

ones, in multiplication, 158–159

ones, tens, and hundreds, 60–61

ones and tens, in multiplication, 160

tens and ones, 56–59

Remainder(s), 124–125, 432

interpreting, 346–347

Reviews, 18–19, 48–49, 88–89, 128–129, 148–149, 176–177, 206–207, 262–263, 306–307, 332–333, 360–361, 388–389, 416–417

Right angle, 398–399, 432

Roman numerals, 51, 432

Rounding, 432

decimals, 386–387

divisors down, 342–343

divisors up, 350–351

to tens, hundreds, 30

to thousands, 32–33

Schedule, using, 244– 245

Sentences, number, 14– 15, 358–359

Seven

dividing by, 118–119

as factor, 100–101

Sides, of polygon, 400–401

Six

dividing by, 118–119

as factor, 100–101

Skills Maintenance, (cumulative), 134–135, 212–213, 312–313, 366–367, 422–423

Skills Maintenance (periodic), 24, 36, 54, 68, 94, 108, 136, 154, 168, 182, 196, 214, 236, 268, 288, 314, 324, 338, 348, 368, 378, 394, 406

Solid geometric figures, 412–413

Sphere, 412–413, 432

Square(s), 400–401, 432

Square centimeter, 222–223, 265

Square foot, 250–251

Square inch, 250–251

Square kilometer, 222–223

Square meter, 222–223

Square yard, 250–251

Steps in problem solving, more than one, 260–261, 330–331

Subtraction, 432

or addition, 74–75

with calculator, 77, 115

with computer, 53

checking, 8

of decimals, 382–383

estimating, 76–80, 82

facts, 8–9

facts drill, 10–11

families of facts, 14–15

of fractions, 296–297

of fractions with unlike denominators, 302–303

of greater numbers, 82–83

of mixed numbers, 298–299

of money, 84–85

regrouping more than once, 78–79

of three-digit numbers, 72–73

of two-digit numbers, 70–71

zeros in, 80–81

Sum, 2, 432

Symmetry, lines of, 410–411, 429

Tables, using, 166–167

Temperature

customary units of, 258–259

metric units of, 238–239

Ten, multiplying by, 316–317

Tens, 26–27

dividing two-digit numbers by, 340–341

multiplying two-digit numbers by, 318–319

regrouping ones and, 56–59

regrouping ones and, in multiplication, 160–161

regrouping ones, hundreds, and, 60–61

Tenths, 370–371

Tests, 20, 50, 90, 130, 150, 178, 208, 264, 308, 334, 362, 390, 418

Thinker's Corner, 7, 15, 27, 29, 31, 43, 45, 57, 59, 61, 67, 71, 97, 101, 111, 159, 163, 171, 191, 199, 201, 203, 221, 225, 273, 281, 283, 299, 319, 327, 343, 345, 355, 373, 381, 397

Thousand, rounding to nearest, 32–33

Thousands, 28–29

Three
  dividing by, 112–113
  divisibility rules for, 209
  as factor, 96–97
Three-digit numbers
  adding, 58–59
  dividing by one-digit
    numbers, 188–191
  multiplying by one-digit
    numbers, 162–163
  multiplying by two-digit
    numbers, 326–327
  subtracting, 72–73
Time, 240–241
  intervals, 242–243
  using a schedule, 244–
    245
Ton, 256–257
Triangle, 400–401, 432
Two
  dividing by, 112–113
  divisibility rules for, 209
  as factor, 96–97
Two-digit numbers. *See
  also* Dividing by

two-digit numbers;
  Multiplying by two-digit
  numbers
  adding, 56–57
  multiplying by one-digit
    numbers, 156–157
  subtracting, 70–71
Two-digit quotients
  in dividing by one-digit
    numbers, 184–187
  in dividing by two-digit
    numbers, 354–355

Underestimates,
  correcting, 352–353
Unlike fractions, 300, 433

Vertex, 433
  of angle, 398
  of polygon, 400–401

Volume, 433
  customary units of,
    252–253

metric units of, 226–
    227, 433
  multiplying to find, 228–
    229, 252–253

Weight
  customary units of,
    256–257
  metric units of, 232–233

Yard, 248–249
  cubic, 252–253
  square, 250–251

Zeros
  in adding and
    subtracting decimals,
    384–385
  in quotient, in dividing
    one-digit numbers,
    198–199
  in subtraction, 80–81